Readings in

EARLY CHILDHOOD EDUCATION

LeRoy G. Baruth, Ph.D, Associate Professor, Department of Special Education, University of South Carolina.

Eleanor Duff, Ph.D., Associate Professor and Coordinator of Early Childhood Education, Department of Education, University of South Carolina, Columbia, South Carolina.

Special Learning Corporation

42 Boston Post Rd. Guilford, Connecticut 06437

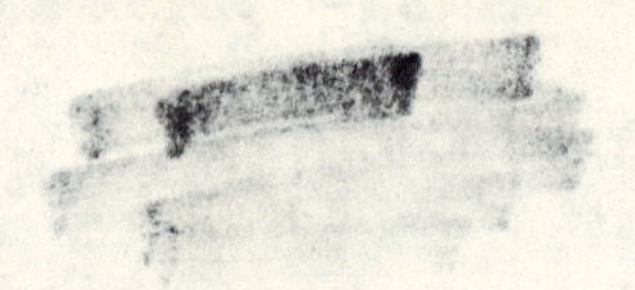

Special Learning Corporation

Publisher's Message:

The Special Education Series is the first comprehensive series designed for special education courses of study. It is also the first series to offer such a wide variety of high quality books. In addition, the series will be expanded and up-dated each year. No other publications in the area of special education can equal this. We stress high quality content, a superb advisory and consulting group, and special features that help in understanding the course of study. In addition we believe we must also publish in very small enrollment areas in order to establish the credibility and strength of our series. We realize the enrollments in courses of study such as Autism, Visually Handicapped Education, or Diagnosis and Placement are not large. Nevertheless, we believe there is a need for course books in these areas and books that are kept up-to-date on an annual basis! Special Learning Corporation's goal is to publish the highest quality materials for the college and university courses of study. With your comments and support we will continue to do so.

John P. Quirk

First Edition

2 3 4 5

ISBN 0-89568-100-5

SPECIAL EDUCATION SERIES

* ● Abnormal Psychology: The Problems of
        Disordered Emotional and Behavioral
        Development
  ● Administration of Special Education
  ● Autism
* ● Behavior Modification
        Biological Bases of Learning Disabilities
        Brain Impairments
  ● Career and Vocational Education for the
        Handicapped
  ● Child Abuse
* ● Child Psychology
  ● Classroom Teacher and the Special Child
* ● Counseling Parents of Exceptional Children
        Creative Arts
  ● Curriculum Development for the Gifted
        Curriculum and Materials
* ● Deaf Education
        Developmental Disabilities
* ● Developmental Psychology: The Problems of
        Disordered Mental Development
* ● Diagnosis and Placement
  ● Down's Syndrome
  ● Dyslexia
* ● Early Childhood Education
  ● Educable Mentally Handicapped
* ● Emotional and Behavioral Disorders
        Exceptional Parents
  ● Foundations of Gifted Education
* ● Gifted Education
* ● Human Growth and Development of the
        Exceptional Individual

  ● Hyperactivity
* ● Individualized Education Programs
  ● Instructional Media and Special Education
  ● Language and Writing Disorders
  ● Law and the Exceptional Child: Due Process
* ● Learning Disabilities
  ● Learning Theory
* ● Mainstreaming
* ● Mental Retardation
  ● Motor Disorders
        Multiple Handicapped Education
        Occupational Therapy
  ● Perception and Memory Disorders
* ● Physically Handicapped Education
* ● Pre-School Education for the Handicapped
* ● Psychology of Exceptional Children
  ● Reading Disorders
        Reading Skill Development
        Research and Development
* ● Severely and Profoundly Handicapped
        Social Learning
* ● Special Education
  ● Special Olympics
* ● Speech and Hearing
        Testing and Diagnosis
  ● Three Models of Learning Disabilities
  ● Trainable Mentally Handicapped
  ● Visually Handicapped Education
  ● Vocational Training for the Mentally Retarded

●   Published Titles   *Major Course Areas

TOPIC MATRIX

Readings in Early Childhood Education provides the college student with a comprehensive overview of the subject. This book is designed to follow the basic college course of study in Early Childhood Education.

COURSE OUTLINE:

Introduction to Early Childhood Education

I. Overview of Early Childhood Education
   A. Historical Influences
   B. Future Trends

II. Childhood Needs As Met By:
   A. Parents
   B. The Family
   C. The School

III. Communication Skills
   A. Language Development
   B. Reading

IV. Behavior
   A. Aggressive
   B. Meeting Society's Norm

V. Child Development
   A. Pre-Piaget
   B. Piagetian Influences
      1. Classroom
      2. Reading
      3. Comprehension

VI. Current Issues
   A. Public Attitude Toward Children
   B. Day Care - In the Schools? By the State?
   C. Television's Influence
   D. Child Abuse
   E. General Issues of Concern

Readings in Early Childhood Education

I. Historical Influences
   A. Overview of Early Childhood Education Today
   B. Implications for the Future

II. Parenting, the Family and the School

III. Language Development
   A. Influences
   B. Reading and Communication

IV. Behavior Management
   A. Parent/Teacher Input on Aggressive Behavior
   B. Parent/Teacher Influence on Character Development

V. Piagetian Influences
   A. Overview-Pre-Piaget
   B. Teacher's Role
   C. Reading and Comprehension

VI. Issues in Early Childhood Education
   A. Societal Discrimination
   B. Myths and Realities of Early Learning
   C. The Day Care Question
   D. Television
   E. Child Abuse
   F. State Leadership

Related Special Learning Corporation Titles

I. Readings in Child Abuse
II. Readings in Child Psychology
III. Readings in Individualized Educational Programs
IV. Readings in Mainstreaming

CONTENTS

1. Historical Influences

2. Parenting, the Family and the School

6. Issues in Early Childhood Education

GLOSSARY OF TERMS

accreditation Recognition given to an educational institution issued by some organization which sets up standards that must be compiled with in order to secure approval.

achievement Proficiency of performance in a given skill or body of knowledge.

achievement test An instrument designed to measure a person's knowledge, skills, and comprehension in a given field taught in school (i.e.: spelling, science, arithmetic)

affect development The progressive growth of feelings and emotions.

adolescence A period of development occurring between puberty and and maturity, generally from 13 or 14 years of age into the early 20's.

adoption The voluntarily acceptance of a child of other parents for one's own.

aggressiveness A tendency toward forceful outgoing action, characterized by taking the initiative.

apathy A lack of feeling characterized by indifference.

behavior Anything that an individual does, including both physical and mental activity.

behavior modification Technique for dealing with maladaptive behavior by reinforcing the desired behaviors and eliminating the undesired behaviors.

behavior problem Action that is disapproved of by dominant social groups.

bilingual Having equal ability in the use of two languages.

child abuse Severe injury to a child inflicted by a parent or other adult.

child development Interdisciplinary approach to the study of children placing emphasis on the importance of understanding children by learning about their mental, emotional, social, and physical growth.

cognitive development Maturation in the child's thought process through adoption to the environment and assimilation of information.

culturally deprived child A child from a social background which tends to be identified as inferior to the rest of the community.

curriculum A general overall plan of the content or specific materials of instruction that a school should offer to the student.

day care center An educational or custodial facility where children may be enrolled for half-day or full-day basis, with the main function being to supplement parental care for children.

early childhood education Usually refers to the program and curriculum for children in nursery school, kindergarten, and/or the primary grades 1 through 3.

emotionally disturbed child A child with a deep-rooted problem who frequently expresses feelings in a manner to hurt self or others.

family A group of two or more persons related by blood, marriage, or adoption and residing together.

family education Formal preparation included in the school curriculum for the purpose of effecting better parent-child, child-child, and parent-parent relationships.

fear An emotional upset characterized by a desire to flea or escape from the cause.

field trip A visit arranged by the school and undertaken for educational purposes where students can observe materials or activities related to in class subject matter.

Head Start Project A preschool child development program which provides education, medical care, social services and nutritional help for children from disadvantaged backgrounds.

imitation The conscious or unconscious patterning of acts, feelings, attitudes, achievements, or possessions after some model.

immunization The development of protection against a disease by inoculation, vaccination, or other means.

intelligence test An instrument used for measuring the ability to learn or the ability to deal with new situations.

kindergarten A school devoted to the education of small children, usually from 4 to 6 years of age, having organized activities with educational and social goals.

language development The learning of communication by means of vocal or written symbols.

learning change in response or behavior caused partly or wholly by conscious or unconscious experiences.

learning disability A significant discrepancy between a child's apparent capacity to learn and the actual level of functioning.

moral development The process by which the capacity to distinguish between right and wrong is achieved and influences the individual's social behavior.

motivation The practical art of applying incentives and arousing interest for the purpose of stimulating a student to perform in a desired way.

personality development The changes in structure and form of the personality that develops as the individual adjusts to inner demands and social impacts.

prenatal behavior The reactions and movements of the fetus within the uterus.

preprimary education An early childhood education program emphasizing the training, education, and total development of the child.

readiness test An instrument designed to measure the ability to engage in a new type of specific learning.

self-concept The individual's perception of himself/herself which includes abilities, appearance, and phases of daily living.

sibling One of two or more children defined as brother or sister within a family.

socialization The process of bringing the child to understand and accept the customs, standards, traditions, and culture of the group and to cooperate actively with that group.

socioeconomic background The environment indicative of both the social and economic status of an individual or group.

teacher aide A paraprofessional addition to the school staff performing a variety of noninstructional duties and sometimes even tutoring small groups or individuals.

test A group of questions or tasks to which a student is to respond, the purpose being to quantify a student trait that it is designed to measure.

theory A set of assumptions supported by related principles and serving as a basis for determining a course of action.

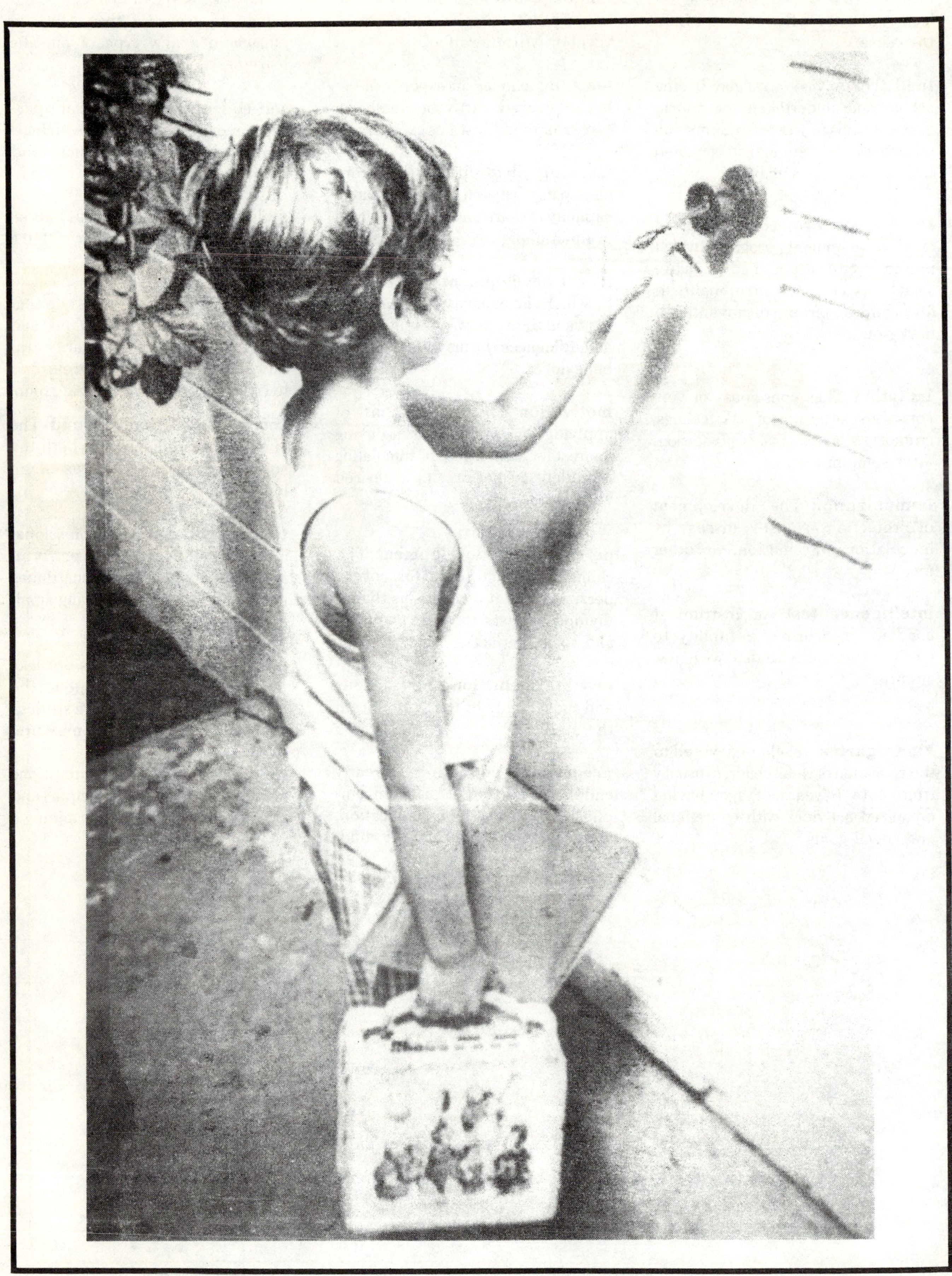

Office of Human Development Services, Department of Health, Education and Welfare.

PREFACE

Society is very interested in early childhood. Articles on child rearing and other related topics are included in many popular magazines. Manufacturers of children's toys attempt to convince parents that by using the toys their children will increase their intelligence or certainly their readiness for school. Television networks are currently under fire from consumer groups concerned about the quality of children's programs and also the effect of commercials. Federal and state governments have created and supported early childhood programs for the poor and oppressed. Because of this high level of interest by society, early childhood education has become one of the most exciting and significant disciplines in the field of education.

The purpose of this book is to address the most significant components in the early childhood field. The section on "Historical Influences" traces the development of the early childhood movement. In the next section, "Parenting, the Family and School," the roles of the school and family are delineated. "Language Development" stresses the importance of language acquisition at an early age. Suggestions are made in the "Behavior Management" section that will aid adults as they shape the behavior of children. "Piagetian Influences" offers applications and interpretations of developmental psychology in the elementary classroom. The concluding chapter, "Issues in Early Childhood Education," is a discussion of many of the current concerns in the field.

The field of early childhood education is vibrant and alive. *Readings In Early Childhood Education* will provide the reader with a better understanding of the components and issues involved.

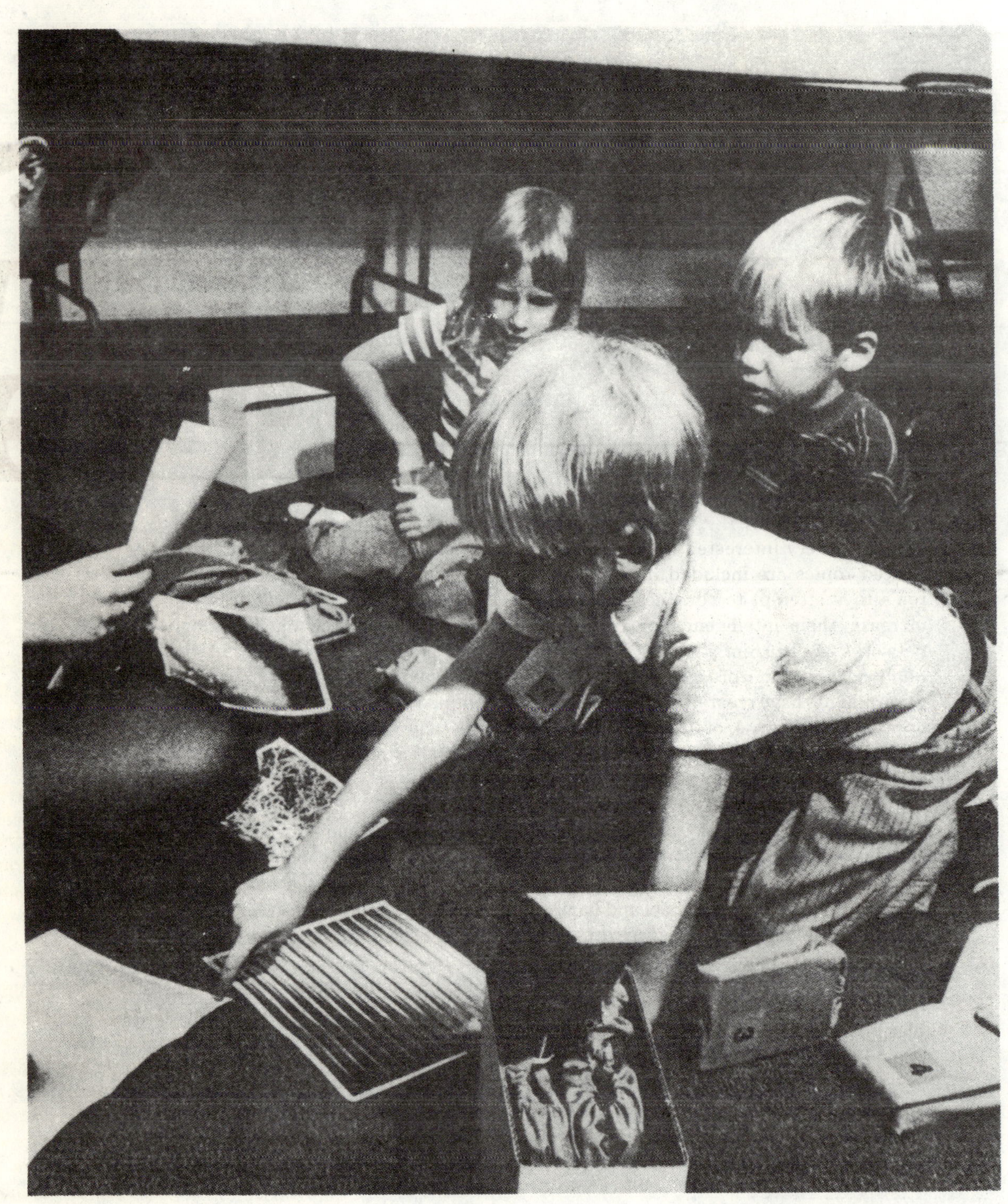

HISTORICAL INFLUENCES

Early Childhood Education as a field of professional study has been viewed by numerous individuals as holding answers to many of our nations social problems. Early Childhood Education programs have flourished nationwide over the last decade. In retrospect, Levenson explores the question "Whatever Happened to Early Childhood Education?" as she examines the happenings which have occurred since the mid sixties.

"Who Says We're a Child Centered Society," by Albert Rosenfield, calls attention to those conditions which continue to exist in society that permit the devastating waste of our most vital human resource---our very young.

For many children the first "formal group experience outside the home" continues to be kindergarten. In "Kindergarten: A Beginning," Milly Cowles describes the various parameters of this experience in light of its integral relationship to the total "school" curriculum. Throughout, she emphasizes the child and his developmental status as the basis upon which all effective instructional planning must rest.

It is obvious as we look historically at those influences affecting children's lives, that while technological developments have brought about vast changes in society, those changes have not brought with them a guarantee of an improved quality of life for all young children. In "Childhood 1776-1976: What Now?" Frost reviews a number of major influences which have impacted heavily upon children through the past two centuries. He further attempts to point out areas in need of attention if we are to accomplish opportunities for better lives in the future.

Legislative thrusts of the 60's provided the impetus for rapid growth in the development of programs for young children from socio-economically disadvantaged families. The Economic Opportunity Act of 1964 authorized the establishment of Head Start, a nationwide system of preschool programs designed to assist young disadvantaged children in preparing for the public school experience. In addition to the educational component, Head Start attempted to provide comprehensive services to children and families in a number of areas. With respect to the future of Head Start, Ziegler's paper, "America's Head Start Program: An Agenda for its Second Decade," suggests re-examination of goals and makes recommendations for program modifications for the future.

In the final paper in this section, "Today's Child - Tomorrow's World," Butler requires early childhood educators to make a critical decision as to the direction their actions should take in planning programs for children. To what degree should early childhood education focus on the future? What kinds of experiences will best meet the needs of children in preparing them to live in tomorrow's world? These and similar questions force educators to face new issues as they go about the task of planning programs for young children who will be living far into a future which will require skills and abilities unknown to us at this time.

Whatever
happened to
early childhood
education?

Dorothy Levenson

IN THE *1960s it was a common belief that education, nay early childhood education, would be the panacea to all our social problems. Today there are more graduates of kindergarten and nursery school than ever before. But what impact has it had? What has happened since the beginning of Head Start in the sixties? What is the nature of early childhood programs today?* INSTRUCTOR *asked education writer Dorothy Levenson. Here's her report:*

In the summer of 1965 an explosion rocked the sandboxes of the nation as children of poverty streamed into Head Start centers set up by the federal government under Lyndon Johnson's "Great Society" program. Education, it was felt, would cure all the ills of society and early childhood programs received the biggest shot of money and publicity they had ever known. The programs took off on a period of expansion. By 1966 some 25 percent of the three- to five-year-olds were in nursery schools or day care centers and by 1971 the figure had jumped to 40 percent.

Today most first-grade students are graduates of kindergarten. Many are also veterans of private nursery schools or publicly funded programs. In addition, it is believed that 97.5 percent of the children now arrive at school familiar with the electronic preschool, "Sesame Street."

This fall over 5.5 million children will have passed through Head Start classrooms and another million through day care funded basically by Social Security money. Across the country states have set up preschool programs since the sixties. In New York State, for example, the State Education Department has funded an experimental prekindergarted program in about 40 school districts since 1966. California, which had already provided day care for some children in public schools since World War II, began a massive Early Childhood Education program in 1974, designed to change the schools from kindergarten through third grade. Minnesota recently enacted its Early Childhood and Family Education program to cover prenatal care through five years of age.

"The experience that began in the 1960s has affected the lives of millions of children," according to Nancy Bogin, director of a prekindergarten program in New York. "They come into school from a different context. Their parents are different too. Most of the programs stressed parent involvement. The parents learned as well as the children. They now come to school with new expectations."

How preschool children learn has also become a well-funded concern for academic research since the sixties. Jean Piaget, the Swiss student of child behavior, has become if not exactly a household word an educational cliché. The idea of early childhood has expanded to include babies in diapers and even prenatal care. Small children have become big politics.

Political friends 'n' foes

Early childhood education *has* made friends in Washington. Rosalynn Carter and Joan Mondale have spoken out for day care. As a senator, Vice President Mondale fought hard along with Democratic Representative John Brademas, Indiana, to enact a major child care program. Senator Charles Mathias, a Maryland Republican, has written a bill, *The Early Childhood Assistance Act,* which would extend public education to four-year-olds, make use of empty classrooms, and provide jobs for teachers.

The American Federation of Teachers (AFT) has organized to push for an expenditure of 20 to 40 billion dollars to provide free and voluntary care for all children in the three- to five-year-old age group. The aim, according to AFT President Albert Shanker, is to "combine the job needs of its members with the day care needs of the nation."

But not everybody is in favor of putting young children in school. Raymond S. Moore and Dennis R. Moore of the Hewitt Research Center headquartered in Berrien Springs, Michigan, believe that education "wherever possible should be in the hands of parents until seven or eight." They think that separation from a mother is harmful below that age and that, in any case, children are not ready for

abstract thinking or learning to read until they are at least seven years of age.

Some politicians agree and others at all levels are wary of spending money for "blocks" and "paintbrushes." Even with the push in early childhood education during the last ten years, 25 percent of the nation's five-year-olds are still not enrolled in kindergarten. And just one-third of the states insist that kindergarten be part of the public school system.

Still other states are conservative in their financial support. New York state, for instance, provides only half the state aid money for kindergarten that it provides for other grades. That means, in most towns, that five-year-olds have only half a day of school. Their teachers have a full day and twice as many students as other grade teachers.

Licensed day care centers place only about one-sixth of the small children who need supervision. However, in many states state aid has decreased. In New York City a $75 million cut meant the closing of 100 centers. This is while the need for government aid increased with 37 percent of the nation's 1976 preschoolers having mothers who worked outside the home— an increase of eight percent in just six years.

Efforts to expand early childhood programs for young children have met some fierce opposition in Washington. Presidents Nixon and Ford vetoed bills to create more day care facilities. The latest version of the Mondale/ Brademas, efforts—*The Child and Family Service Act*—seems doomed to delay because of President Carter's commitment to balance the federal budget, and a squabble about who should run the centers. The AFT would like to see day care controlled by the public schools. Community groups running nonprofit day care centers fear that schools are too rigid to provide for the needs of very young children.

A variety of programs

There's tremendous variety in the existing early childhood programs. Head Start classrooms are found in public schools, church basements, big-city ghettos, Indian reservations. They are run by boards of education, community action agencies, tribal authorities. Day care centers have been set up by groups of college students, hospitals, charitable groups, or drug programs. Some private nursery schools charge stiff fees. Others are funded as parent cooperatives, with the parents doing much of the work to save on expenses. Still others are run as profit-making franchises for corporations as Howard Johnson's or McDonalds.

Then there's the *Play Group* movement which helps informal gatherings of parents eager to provide a "together" experience for themselves and their children. There's *Home Start* which works with three- to-six-year-old children who are not in Head Start. Teachers visit the children's homes bringing educational materials, and showing the parents how to use them with the children while also offering health and welfare services. *Follow Through*, a classroom program for Head Start graduates, is designed to help children retain the gains made.

Classroom methods are as different as the programs themselves. Head Start was initially designed with 12 different "planned variations." In one classroom with a "structured academic style" children chant reading and math drills in unison. In another with a "developmental approach" children are free to explore blocks and sand and water under the sensitive guidance of an adult.

Unfortunately, the differences among programs also extend to standards. There are only a few areas of the country which enforce strict guidelines for day care. Some centers keep children in crowded rooms watching television all day. Others have staff with few qualifications.

There is little diversity, however, in the sex of teachers. Women predominate. Less than one percent of New York state's 7,667 kindergarten teachers are men—although the figure has tripled in eight years.

Salaries paid to the teachers *do* vary. Programs run by public schools pay certified teachers the same scale as other teachers in the district. But with the shortage of public school jobs, some unemployed teachers have applied for jobs in private day care centers or nursery schools and have been shocked at the salaries offered. If early childhood education became part of the public schools, as the AFT proposes, salaries would go up and so would costs. Philadelphia has a program of quality day care, called *Get Set*, staffed by well-paid members of the Philadelphia Federation of Teachers.

When asked about the changes she would like to see in Head Start, Carrie Cheek, who provides technical assistance and training to a large number of programs in the northeast and is a vice president of the National Association for the Education of Young Children (NAEYC) said: "I would like to see all salaries leveled upward to the public

school rate. I would like to see all programs close for part of the year—like the public schools. Some Head Starts are open 12 months a year. Staggering vacations is too difficult. And I believe that no teacher—in Head Start or anywhere else—should have to teach two groups, one in the morning and one in the afternoon."

What will you find in model early childhood programs already in existence? A staff that realizes children learn from many people and that parents play a more important role in a child's life than any teacher. Children who learn in many ways, in classrooms full of materials like wooden blocks, sand, water, paints, animals, plants, books, pictures, music, trucks, dolls, and dress-up clothes. Children who learn outdoors as well as indoors and ride bikes, dig in the dirt, and climb rocks and ramps. They learn on the bus coming to school, walking to a local supermarket, taking a trip to the library. Good early education programs recognize that education is not just a matter for the schools. The whole community is involved.

In model programs young children receive individualized attention. The teachers who work with them need time to listen and time to help with tasks. In some early childhood classrooms many adults are used: certified teachers, paraprofessionals, high school students, and older people who serve as "foster grandparents."

In addition there are services built around the early childhood classrooms to provide support. Often social and health services are provided for families. There are training programs and career ladders for staff. Ten thousand Head Start parents have become certified teachers. The office of Child Development of the Department of Health, Education and Welfare (HEW), has a nationwide program to train certified child development associates to work in child care programs. Many day care centers are funded for the express purpose of helping parents leave the welfare rolls by allowing them to work or attend training courses.

Languages and ethnic groups formerly excluded from most educational planning are also included. (Go to the annual convention of NAEYC if you want to see what is probably the widest ethnic representation of any education group.)

Bilingual programs too have been set up in early childhood programs where there are concentrations of children speaking a language other than English. Many programs use adults who speak the same language or come from the children's same ethnic background as paid aides or volunteers. They create a "homey" atmosphere for the children and a sensitivity to their way of life. They also interpret language and customs for the teacher.

Parents play a part

Most publicly funded programs mandate "parent involvement" which can range from hiring and firing staff to raffling turkeys. Some parents act as the governing body in a cooperative, volunteers in the classroom, or drivers in the carpool. Whatever the formal activities, the most important result has been to help parents become more aware of their children's needs. For example,

Elise Carnegie, a teacher in New Rochelle, New York, assigns homework that will involve the parents— a drawing activity for example, or a story that needs to be read.

Head Start workers visit parents on the Hopi Reservation in Arizona. They find that one of their most important jobs is to convince parents that children learn in the Hopi language. English was the official language in the schools for so long that parents felt all education should take place in that tongue. The Head Start workers believe that a child should learn in his ancestral language—and that concepts, such as numbers and colors, are transferable from one to the other language.

In Redford Township, Michigan, mothers and children come to school together one morning each week to take part in the Parent Readiness Education Project (PREP). At the beginning of each school year, the children who will enter kindergarten the next year are tested. Those who show developmental lags or language problems are asked to attend PREP. In school, mothers are trained to work with their children at home.

Into the mainstream

Early childhood education programs pioneered mainstreaming of the handicapped into schools. New laws have further mandated that Head Start take 10 percent handicapped students for the next several years.

The town of Cheshire, Connecticut, for example, has a preschool program available to all handicapped children. Half the children in the classes are severely physically disabled. The other 50 percent have emotional or behavioral problems.

Each day the parents come to school with their children. They spend half their time working with the children on specific skills. Then the parents meet together to share problems and discuss solutions with a member of the staff.

What about the children?

What does research say about all these early childhood programs? What does early childhood education mean in terms of the child? Politicians, concerned that tax money not be wasted, have built evaluation into most publicly funded early education programs over the years. Children are tested . . . and tested . . . and tested . . . .

When Head Start was part of the "War on Poverty" many people felt that if children learned their numbers and colors and shapes they would "catch up" to the more affluent students they met later in school.

In 1969 the *Westinghouse Study* decided that Head Start children lost almost all they had learned once they started elementary school. Now, though, graduates have been around long enough to show something different. In February of this year Bernard Brown of HEW's Office of Child Development reported that children who attended Head Start eight years ago are seven or nine points ahead of where they would have been had they not attended.

Victoria Seitz, a psychologist with Yale University, followed a group of disadvantaged students for 10 years. Half the group were in Head Start and Follow Through Programs and half had no special help. The Head Start children performed better in school than the control group.

But other researchers have decided that the major problem is that we don't know enough about how children learn, or how their emotions and intellect affect their learning.

As programs and skill levels of children have changed over the years so have the children themselves, according to teachers who have worked with young children for a long time.

"At first it was all triangles and colors," said one preschool teacher. "If the children were having a snack we gave them triangular crackers and told them they were triangles. I never met a child who didn't know what color shirt he or she had on, but we taught them their colors just the same."

Today, there's a difference not just in the assessment of the needs of the youngsters but in the children's behavior. "I see a lot of violent children," says another teacher. "And I see kids who have no idea of the consequences of violence. They don't seem to know that someone can get hurt if you hit him. Maybe it's the result of watching television. They see a man get shot, or beat up and then next day he's on again at the same time, same channel, no damage done."

"It's been a long cold winter," notes a third teacher. "A lot of kids spent all their time in front of the TV—until eleven o'clock at night . . . . They eat in front of the TV set. Values are set by TV. We're dealing with a bunch of kids who spend most of their time relating to an inanimate object."

But children come into preschool knowing more, claim the less pessimistic teachers. "When I first started teaching, children only knew their nicknames," observes one early childhood educator. "Now they watch 'Sesame Street.' They arrive knowing their whole names and addresses. They often know their mother's name. They know the alphabet. They can count. They are more verbal."

So, whatever happened to early childhood education?

As you can see it's still here, undoubtedly to stay. But the form it takes will depend on what happens in Washington during the next few years. It will continue to have an impact on the elementary teacher who in turn can find ways to use the experiences children have had in early childhood programs. What can the elementary teacher do to better understand students' backgrounds when they enter first grade?

Ask parents about a child's preschool background. Has the child attended nursery school or a day-care center?

Visit centers children have attended locally and talk to the teachers. If the program is part of the school system, teachers can set up con-

tinuous records for each child.

Incorporate the rich array of early childhood materials into classrooms. Wooden unit blocks are great for hands-on math experiences in all grades. Dress-up clothes and hats provide for spontaneous dramatic efforts. Real gerbils and living plants can add to a science program.

Learn to use other people in the classroom, pioneered by many early childhood programs which used volunteer parents, paid professionals, high school students, or senior citizens.

Dorothy Levenson is a free-lance writer specializing in education.

Who Says We're a Child-Centered Society?

Our deformed, battered, undernourished, miseducated children give the lie to the claim we are a child-oriented culture

by Albert Rosenfeld

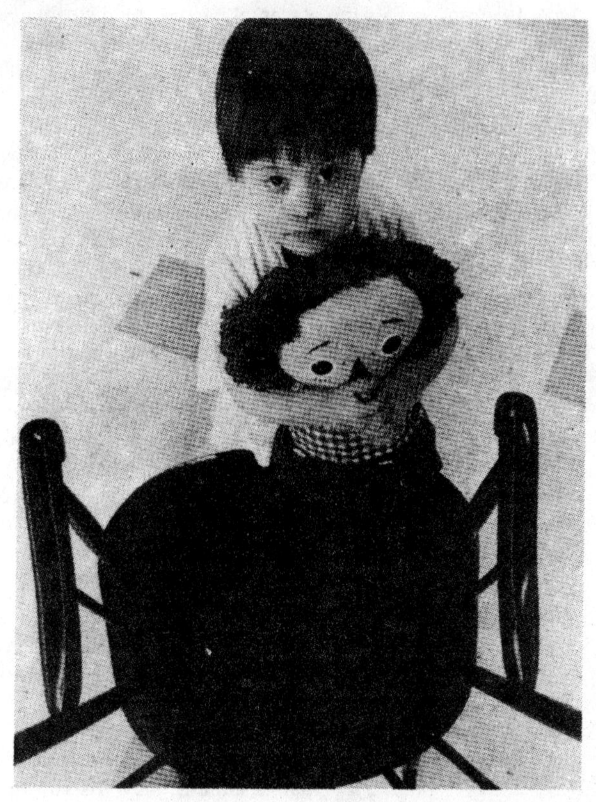

THE waste of human resources begins most extravagantly at the very beginning of life. In the United States each year, 50,000 babies die before they are a month old. Some 200,000 infants are born with birth defects—and birth defects, as the posters remind us, are for life. Another 245,000 are at risk because of their dangerously low weight at birth. The teenage pregnancy rate continues its steady rise—especially among girls under fifteen, who are both physically immature and emotionally unprepared for motherhood. At the same time, among maturer people who might be better equipped to raise healthier, happier children, parenthood has lately been rendered unfashionable. Columnist Ann Landers recently conducted a poll of her readers on "Parenthood—if you had a choice, would you do it again?" Some 70 percent of her respondents said they wouldn't!

According to a recent report of Health, Education, and Welfare's National Center on Child Abuse and Neglect, 1 million cases of child abuse are reported each year—and the real figure is estimated to be closer to 2 million.

We have often been called a "child-centered society." But do we really give a damn about children at all in this society? Do we begin to understand the extent to which our human resources are squandered so early in life? Take, for instance, the distressing results of malnutrition. (See "Starve the Child, Famish the Future," *SR/World*, March 23, 1974.) If the requisite proteins are not at hand during especially critical periods of development—such as the second trimester of pregnancy or the first six months of infancy—as much as 30 percent of the brain's neurons may never be formed, which means a lifetime shortage of 3 billion brain cells!

So it is clear that the waste begins even before the beginning of life—at least before the child's official birthday.

The limits to what a human being may become are largely dictated by the genetic information in the nucleus of the original fertilized egg from which that person derives. Few of us, if any, ever attain anything like 100 percent of our genetic potential. How close we come depends on each individual's personal history in the world. That world at the outset is the mother's womb—a protected place, but not quite so safe and cozy a hideout as we once believed. The incipient organism must get enough of all the right things, and it must get them when it needs them. Without sufficient nutrients to serve as building materials for new cells and organs at the precise time they are scheduled to be formed, the genetic instructions simply cannot be carried out properly.

Nor can that inchoate life withstand too many of the *wrong* things, especially at its most vulnerable stages. Blasts of radiation can damage it, viruses can invade it, a variety of drugs (including alcohol) can harm it. Its biochemistry can be upset, across the placental barrier, by disturbances in the mother's own biochemistry—which may have been caused initially just as readily by external as by internal factors: bad food, bad habits (such as excessive smoking), or bad news (say, an argument with the expectant father). "It is essential to bear in mind," as Dr. Sydney S. Gellis, of Tufts University Medical Center, reminds us in the journal *Hospital Practice*, "that the emotional state of the woman during pregnancy may also have an important impact on her developing fetus."

The future person, if he is unhappy with the deal dealt out to him, may well wish retrospectively that things had gone better in those helpless prenatal days when he or she was a mere "it" being acted upon by the interplay of genetics and environment. And while those intimate, personal— if unconscious—transactions were taking place in his immediate neighborhood, were his prospective father and mother preparing themselves for the tasks of parenthood? Would they be too poor or too uneducated or too unfortunate in their overall circumstances to see that he was properly fed, loved, brought along at the right pace at the right time?

Was he doomed in advance to poor schooling, low self-esteem, low economic status, lifelong handicaps of every variety? Ah, how much is decided for us, irrevocably and forever, before we are on hand to be consulted!

A BABY ant is much less vulnerable than a human baby. Its future behavior is written into its genetic manual of instructions. It is born knowing what it is supposed to do and how. But a human infant must *learn* all that over a long period of helplessness and dependence on other human beings to guide him toward some attainment of a fraction of his human potential. How many are cheated along the way—more by inadvertence than by villainy.

Nor are physical deprivations the only factors involved in the appalling early waste of potential. The growing brain and nervous system of an infant require not only food but "stimulus nutrition" as well; and if it is not supplied, especially at certain crucial phases of development, the whole organism suffers. We have learned much along these lines from animal experiments. A cat's eyes will be blind to specific kinds of images if deprived of seeing them at the times scheduled for programming the proper cells. (See "Observing the Brain Through a Cat's Eyes," by Roger Lewin, *SR/World*, October 5, 1974.) In order to sing its inherited songs, a bird must first hear other birds, and then *itself*, perform them. "Heredity is not enough," says Dr. David Krech, of the University of California at Berkeley. "All of the advantages of inheriting a good brain can be lost if you don't have the right psychological environment in which to develop it." Krech and his associates did a now-classic series of experiments, raising baby rats in "nursery schools" full of things to keep them interested, amused, and challenged. Rats thus raised not only had a measurably

greater *number* of neurons than other rats, but their brain cells were richer in their biochemical content.

Obviously, no such brain-cell counts have been done on human infants. But contemporary researchers in child psychology have demonstrated beyond doubt that infants cannot thrive without proper love, attention, and stimulation, no matter how well they are fed.

In the case of rats, stimulus nutrition can correct, in part, the handicaps caused by malnutrition. After brain-cell division has stopped, there can never again (so we now believe) be an increase in the number of neurons. But in a stimulating environment, the neurons that already exist can grow larger by some 15 percent and form myriad new connections, thus enabling the deprived rat to catch up considerably in its intellectual capacities. The same appears to be true of humans, Dr. Myron Winick, of Columbia University's Institute of Human Nutrition, has decided after a careful study of starved Korean orphans adopted by American parents. In a new, loving environment, they improved beyond what had previously been thought possible. "The permanent effects of early malnutrition," Winick believes, "are really a combination of poor nutrition and long-term environmental deprivation." The trouble is that the two all too often go hand in hand.

Meanwhile, our ideas about childbirth itself are changing—in some places drastically. The trend back to natural childbirth, breast-feeding, and the training of midwives was already under way when *Birth Without Violence*, written by the controversial French obstetrician Frederick Leboyer, appeared in this country, followed by a personal tour. It caught the public's fancy, said Harvard's Dr. T. Berry Brazelton in *Medical World News*, "because everybody feels we have been treating childbirth as if it were a disease. It should be a happy, normal event, but it isn't." The results, some believe, have been damaging to many newborns and to mother-infant relations; and the whole childbirth enterprise is being critically re-examined.

In fact, childbirth is being increasingly subsumed under the rubric "perinatology"—which has as much the flavor of an evangelical movement (and so it should) as a broad new medical specialty (see "Perinatology: New Science of Childbirth," by Saul Kent, *SR/World*, July 13, 1974). The perinatologist views the moment of birth as merely one point on a continuum that begins with the nutritional health of the mother-to-be *prior* to pregnancy and the preparation of teenagers for their future parenthood; then goes through the entire period of pregnancy and birth; and continues into an indefinite postnatal period. To provide proper perinatal care requires an unprecedented combination of medical specialties working together *without interruption* during this whole period; and it includes the training of new personnel, the invention of new techniques and equipment, the establishment of perinatal-care centers, and the education of prospective parents and their doctors.

The perinatal movement is being spearheaded in the public sector by the National Institutes of Health's National Institute for Child Health and Human Development (NICHD) and in the private sector by such organizations as the National Foundation–March of Dimes—which is coordinating the efforts of several medical organizations, including the AMA. In an article in *Contemporary Ob/Gyn*, the National Foundation's Gabriel Stickle and Paul Ma make the claim that, merely by applying the knowledge we already possess, this nation's infant-mortality statistics could be lifted quickly from fifteenth (the dismal position we now occupy) to seventh place among the world's nations. And with the necessary research support, says NICHD's director, Dr. Norman Kretchmer, we could not merely rise to No. 1—and help other nations rise with us—but could save untold lifetimes of misery and ineptitude.

Meanwhile, those tens of thousands of babies do continue to die early, and those hundreds of thousands continue to be born with birth defects—and those millions to be abused by their parents. There is no way to count up the dreadful cost: stunted bodies and minds. More accidents, more early suicides. More crime and violence. A society full of time bombs walking the streets. "My future was small," wrote Arthur Bremer, would-be assassin of Governor George Wallace, in his diary, "my past an insult to any human being." Despite the screaming need, few communities have resources to deal with the emotional problems of preschool children and their troubled young parents. (See "And Now—Preventive Psychiatry," *SR*, February 21, 1976.)

Nobody had a perfect childhood, nor do we know what that would be. But we know enough—and, if we cared enough, would mount a crash program to learn much more and to apply what we now know—to salvage a good measure of this appalling human wastage, to head off all those premature partial deaths that take place way back there in the very beginning.

Kindergarten: A Beginning

Milly Cowles
Professor of Early Childhood Education
University of Alabama in Birmingham

Where did kindergarten begin?

The story of the little boy who becomes famous as a man due to a warm, supportive environment that was provided by teachers, parents, or others is often told, and many of us are not immune from getting "lumps" everytime we hear it. Since their beginning, public schools in the United States have had always as their constituents the little boys and girls who have the potential to become "somebodies," and more importantly, the potential for becoming and being worthy in the eyes of themselves. The extreme **potency** of the earliest school years will some day be recognized for what **it is.** Undoubtedly, it is in the foundation period of any human endeavor that roots are laid as a basis for what is to come later. That is, the first "formal" out-of-the-home experience for the child is the most crucial for all later school experiences. For most children in the South, kindergarten is that period; therefore, that first year's curriculum must be established on the most knowledgeable and reasonable bases in order to guarantee each child the most solid and dynamic introduction to the wonders that can be and ought to be associated with all educational endeavors.

In reviewing the history of the development of kindergarten in our country, one finds that kindergartens began as private programs around 1855 in homes. Paralleling the kindergarten movement, in Massachusetts, as early as 1647, every town with at least fifty houses **had** to select a teacher who was to instruct reading and writing. By 1823, primary schools were the only free ones available to all potential pupils, but it is important to note that it was not until 1890 that the first state **required** school attendance. That was less than 100 years ago. The private kindergartens, then, were not the only level of education suffering from a lack of support. Interestingly, the first publicly supported kindergarten began in St. Louis, Missouri, during the superintendency of Dr. William T. Harris, a man ahead of his time. He was champion both for kindergartens **and** public education in the 1870's, long before either had gained much popular support. At the same time, Mrs. Elizabeth Peabody, a Massachusetts philanthropist, was pushing for the recognition of the value of kindergartens in the Boston area. After 1900, kindergartens were a regular part of the elementary school in the Northeast and Midwest, and Dr. Harris', Mrs. Peabody's and others' dreams were realized—but it took more than fifty years. Strangely, and not easily explained, the South lagged far behind in recognizing the value of programs for five-year-olds, and it was not until 1967 that Virginia became the first southern state to provide public monies for kindergarten programs. North and South Carolina both began "pilot" programs in 1969, and since then, other states have gradually phased in some publicly supported units.

Why have kindergartens?

In contemporary times, the rationale for support of programs for young children comes from various diverse sources. Benjamin Bloom[1] critiqued and reviewed all research studies of merit

---

[1]Benjamin Bloom, *Stability and Change in Human Characteristics* (New York: John Wiley and Sons, 1964), pp. 100-175.

conducted over more than a 30-year period that dealt with intelligence and school achievement. His analysis led him to conclude that "approximately 50 percent of general achievement at Grade 12 has been reached by the end of Grade 3." Likewise, in the area of intelligence, he found that approximately 50 percent of the variance associated with intelligence could be accounted for by the time children reach age four. Even more startling, he reported that 80 percent could be accounted for by the time the child reaches age eight. Bloom's work alone would be hard to ignore in pleading the case for sound kindergarten programs, but there is other evidence to add here. Research studies,[2] in which children who attended kindergarten have been compared to those who did not attend, have revealed the following:

Kindergarten attenders showed more interest in words, letters of the alphabet, numbers, being read to, and looking at books and magazines.

Kindergarten attenders are superior in number understanding, language usage, and copying in first grade.

Kindergarten attenders scored higher on reading tests at the end of first grade.

Kindergarten attenders showed better auditory discrimination, had faster rates of learning and superior motor coordination in first grade.

Kindergarten attenders had more satisfactory social adjustment in relation to peers and more satisfactory adjustment to school in the first three grades.

Kindergarten attenders showed better social attitudes, health habits, play behavior, and game participation in the first grade. They also performed better in reading, music, social science, language, and arithmetic.

Kindergarten attenders were superior at the beginning of first grade in reading achievement.

Kindergarten attenders' parents reflected a higher quality of "parent-school relationships."

There is, then, a realistic basis for the support of early education, and the same general curriculum principles guide the development of high quality programs in early childhood programs as in elementary or secondary ones.

The three basic considerations at all levels of schooling are the child, the society, and organized knowledge and skills. The society supports the school; therefore, its values and goals are upheld in most formal school curriculum plans, and the implementation of such plans attempts to reflect the best side of the social order. Obviously, children go to school to gain the knowledge and skills necessary to make them fully functioning self-realizers who will contribute to the betterment of the general culture. And that is the primary objective of all schooling. Since it is the child who goes to school and is the learner, his developmental patterns, in totality, have to be considered as the major source for curriculum planning.

Usually there is not much argument among educators that the three components—the child, the society, and organized knowledge and skills—are the primary factors in curriculum building considerations. Rather, the disagreements arise when the theoretical considerations have to be translated into day-to-day practice.

What is taught in kindergarten?

Kindergarten ought not be a year in which the first-grade program is extended downward. Instead, a quality package should be provided for the developmental level of the five-year-old child. The environment both indoors and out-of-doors should be designed to enhance the development of the child. A constant vigil must be maintained to ensure that the activities "match" the child, that they are neither too "easy" nor too "hard." Only through a feeling of mastery, or "I can do," does the child grow in his inner feelings of competency. For example, when formalized-standardized

---

[2]Southern Association of Colleges and Schools, "Research Findings," in *Early Childhood Education: A Case for the Kindergarten* (Atlanta: 1969), pp. 4-5.

reading and writing programs are introduced across the board to all kindergarten children, we may be introducing undue frustration and a grand opportunity for the child to see school as a place in which he does not fit. As those feelings grow, only more frustration and failure experiences follow.[3]

Kindergarten programs that follow research findings and expert opinion generally have learning environments planned from which varied activities facilitate the following vital areas in the child's development:

Gross Motor Development:

Activities such as balancing on one foot, hopping, skipping, throwing large and small balls, and catching objects are examples here. This area is vital to achieving an internal balance that facilitates fine motor development which is essential to reading, writing, and arithmetic.

Fine Motor Development:

This area follows the child's being skilled in large muscle development. Activities, in which children copy simple designs such as circles, rectangles, and squares and learn to differentiate them, and in which they can draw a person with at least six or more body parts, are vital to readiness for the eye-hand coordination needed for writing, reading, and arithmetic.

Personal-Social Development:

Activities that help the child develop a sense of exerting control over and being a part of his environment are vital to his having the psychological energy to learn. Although simple to adults, such exercises as washing and drying hands, helping with housekeeping, using eating utensils, buttoning, using the toilet independently, separating from the mother or primary caretaker, playing interactively with others, caring for personal things, and talking with other children and adults are important to being able to settle into school life.

Language Development:

Activities that develop the ability to describe past and present events in complete sentences are the building blocks for all later school work and are absolutely essential. Such items as pointing to and naming body parts, following simple one-step directions, knowing first and last name, recognizing and describing the environment in terms of color, shape, and size, and conversing in sentences are examples of language skills that can be developed in kindergarten.

Auditory-Perceptual Development:

This area of development is crucial before any formal study of sounds can be introduced to the child. Activities that facilitate this development are identifying gross sounds such as school bells, clapping and stomping, and less gross sounds such as cutting, tapping and loud whispers, and telling the location of sounds. Identifying rhyming words in familiar and then unfamiliar contexts, making up rhyming words, recognizing the same word repeated in a series, drawing sounds, and picking out spoken words that begin or end alike are other examples.

---

[3]Some few children are developmentally (socially, emotionally, physically, and intellectually) ready to read and write in kindergarten. Likewise, some first-grade children are ready to read and write, but even many first-grade children are not adept enough to handle what we place before them. It seems too bad that we use age to determine exactly when all children should do the same "things." Adults would probably not allow that kind of expectation to be placed on them. Unfortunately, children have to abide by our decisions. Chronological age assumes the greatest importance only at the beginning of schooling and in old age (e.g., mandatory retirement). Many experts in human development have stated that age by itself is the poorest criterion to use as a guide to development.

Auditory-Memory Development: This aspect of development is essential for many reading and writing skills and for just plain living skills. Examples of activities are imitating sounds (i.e., clock, train), reproducing sounds in various rhythmic patterns, following oral directions as in such games as *Simon Says*, retelling, in sequence, a story or an event, doing choral reading, and singing.

Visual-Perceptual Development: Without adequate development here, it is impossible to observe, classify, and make sense of the world, much less ever learn the basic skills. Activities such as observing and discussing differences in environmental objects, finding differences and likenesses in pictures, arranging forms in matched or directed sequences, connecting label words with objects (such as the sign "chair" with a chair), and tracing, coloring, and cutting evenly facilitate growth in visual-perceptual development.

Visual-Memory Development: Here we find a skill that is also vital for all later school work. Activities that help with growth are naming familiar but out-of-sight objects looked at on another occasion, naming from recall a series of no more than three to five objects viewed and then covered, identifying missing objects from a series, reproducing a series of pictures viewed and then scrambled, and filling in parts of an incomplete picture.

Problem-Solving Development: The areas of development mentioned above are all components that are necessary for the development of problem-solving. Careful observation of children for forty years by Jean Piaget and others has guided our thinking in education to the startling conclusion that children learn more from **each other** than from adults, and that their social interactions with each other are crucial for social, emotional, and intellectual development. We know that children's ability to think is governed entirely by what they have seen, experienced, and produced. They **can not** and **do not** think as adults and should not be expected to do so. The child's reasoning must be accepted as it is. Their thinking and reasoning are perceptually bound. To develop problem-solving abilities, children need to be guided to observe and predict, and there must be a broad array of activities in which they actively and personally take things apart, put them back together, and see, for example, how wheels roll, what pulleys and levers do, and have the opportunity every day to dabble in making something that is **designed** and created by them. That is why unit blocks, "messing around learning centers," music, and art are so vital to intellectual growth.

As a result of research studies, we know that 10 to 40 percent of all kindergarten "graduates" need more developmental activities in first grade and beyond. In a good setting, kindergarten is valuable, but no one can force real human development. Actually, the child's developmental level ought to be assessed carefully by the teacher, and then his instructional program should be tailored to allow him to experience success and positive growth. This is not to say that it is ever wise to wait until any given child is ready for an activity. We might, in that case, wait forever. Rather, if a child needs to reach a higher plateau in any skill area, then specific activities (that are aimed toward developing those skills) should be planned for the child. The educational program should be carefully designed and monitored to match the functioning level of the child. Following that kind of curriculum implementation, the child receives instruction at a level that is commensurate with where he is not where someone wishes he were **or** where someone **thinks** he ought to be.

1. HISTORICAL

How is kindergarten an integral part of the total school curriculum?

If curriculum programs are planned for children, then the primary curriculum would be meshed with the kindergarten curriculum. The first year of the primary curriculum sequence should be planned to begin where the child is. The base fact is that, unless an activity for any human of any age is geared to the comprehension level of the learner, it is virtually worthless. We would like to make the following final recommendations[4] that could possibly improve both kindergarten and primary programs:

1. Strengthen public education through the extension of an early childhood organizational structure that includes pre-primary and primary education.

2. Prepare administrators specifically for early childhood education and have their activities coordinated.

3. Use all theoretical, foundational, and historical knowledge available rather than being bound to one particular theory.

4. Work to eliminate continuity and articulation problems as children progress from one organizational level to another.

5. Develop esthetically pleasing in- and out-of-door spaces that are designed to meet all developmental needs of children.

6. Develop curriculum sequences that range from simple to concrete to complex and that involve self-selection of activities by learners within the framework of individualization.

7. Provide differentiated staffing patterns that include men and women, professionals and paraprofessionals within the context of adequate numbers of such personnel.

8. Plan and implement continuous teacher training.

9. Involve parents in such a way that rights and responsibilities of both parents and professionals are protected and enhanced.

10. Develop reasonable, developmental goals for the early childhood years and then tailor them to **each** child.

11. Develop evaluation that is formative, summative, and longitudinal.

---

[4]Milly Cowles, "Education for the Young Child," in *School of the Future Now* (Washington: Association for Supervision and Curriculum Development, 1972), pp. 17-26.

Childhood 1776–1976: What Now?

The struggle for freedom and independence of this country during the Revolutionary War took an awesome toll in human misery and death. During the terrible winter of 1777 and 1778 General Washington suffered the loss of 3,000 of his 11,000 ragged and hungry troops. Perhaps the life these men experienced during childhood fortified them in some strange and cruel way for the inhuman conditions of that long winter, for they were conditioned from early childhood to expect the inevitability of short life — over half their siblings and age-mates had died before the tender age of 10 and average life expectancy was 32 years. Not even the most bizarre conditions of war matched the ferocity of common childrearing circumstance in crippling and snuffing out human life. Childhood during that period was a bad dream, but its earlier history was a nightmare, marked by centuries-long eras of infanticide, abandonment, and child slavery.

Upon this legacy childrearing during the early years of American independence was built, for childrearing in our new nation had its roots in the practices of the seventeenth century colonies and to earlier ties with the Old World. Cable (1972) described the dangers of the early years. At birth the colonial child's mouth was swabbed out with a dirty rag and he was swaddled tightly from neck to legs to prevent spinal curvature and head wobbling. Fortunately, most babies were breastfed, for the regular feeding of cow's milk from unsanitary containers was often lethal. Poor sanitation was an ever-present danger. Diapers were simply hung up to dry and then reused. Babies were rarely given baths for fear they would catch cold. And when a physician was brought in he would likely bleed, purge, dose and blister the sick individual, whether infant or adult.

If the infant survived to toddlerhood he was put to work learning household and barnyard tasks so that he could take on adult roles as early as possible. By the age of six to eight the boys were skillful at the father's job (farming, etc.) and the girls at homemaking. All this was done, of course, to keep the child from idleness and sin. Hard work, education and strict discipline were essential for salvation. This Puritan ethic, carried over from the Old World, dominated childrearing until the middle of the nineteenth century and retains carry-over effects to the present time.

The influence of religion was seen in every aspect of life. Play and idleness were prohibited by law in at least one colony. Even children or servants tending livestock were required to keep their hands busy with chores and their minds on religion. Boys and girls were not to engage in light conversation in order that modesty and honesty be preserved. The accepted alternative to working or studying was praying, attending church, and studying the bible or catechism.

Punishment was Severe

Punishment for disobedience was severe. A Connecticut law specified the penalty of death for disobedience by people over 14 years of age. In all the colonies, insubordination of children and servants was an offense calling for a public whipping or a public confession. The Biblical admonition, "Spare the Rod and Spoil the Child," was applied with gusto by fathers and schoolmasters alike. The history of childrearing in America is documented in great frequency with stories of brutality; locking children in cold, rat-infested basements, cruel beatings (sometimes fatal), rubbing salt in wounds, burning with hot water and stoves, etc., etc. But conscience, derived from a firm belief in hell-fire for the sinful and salvation for the pure, was perhaps a far greater deterrent to disobedience than all the sticks laid across bare backs. In matters of religion the usual reserved, emotionless character of the Puritan went out the window. The religious "experience" overtook him into a crescendo of crying, groaning, screaming, rolling on the floor and gnashing of the teeth (Cable, 1972). All work and study were engaged in with vigor for every idle moment was filled with guilt and anxiety.

There were no teenagers in the colonial period (the word didn't even exist). There was infancy, a brief period of childhood and adulthood. Children were seen as little adults, befitting the responsibilities placed upon them at an early age.

Hell-fire and Promenading

This portrait of Puritan childrearing, although dominant in the early colonies, was by no means the only pattern in existence. The settlers of the Northern colonies and the settlers of the Southern colonies held somewhat differing views on childrearing. Hell fire and damnation were indeed preached but children of the Northern colonies were allowed to celebrate certain holidays, take dancing lessons, go sleighing, ice skating and promenading, and engage in kissing games. Children in the South, like New England children, worked hard and suffered the same hazards to health and life. But education was not so closely tied to salvation and the emphasis upon education was not as strong.

The upper-class Southern young went to school and church. Out of school they visited with friends, took lessons on proper dress and talk, attended balls and barbeques, took dancing lessons, raced their horses, and went to cock-fights. Even in the New England towns moral standards were slackening during the latter 1700's. In the earlier days, the penalty for adultery was death but now adulterers were forgiven by public confession in the church and cohabitation of engaged couples was regarded as less sinful than cohabitation by couples not engaged. Adultery was implicitly encouraged by the custom of "bundling" young, unmarried couples in bed together on cold nights fully clothed, under the watchful eye of the girl's parents, often with a board inserted between them for additional security (Cable,

1. HISTORICAL

1872). Bundling came into rapid disfavor with the birth of an unusually large number of seven-month babies, partly attributable, it appears, to the relaxed views of boy-girl visiting, sleighing, kissing and all night dancing.

Toward A New Permissiveness

During our early years as a nation, children continued to be dressed like grownups. The overall level of education declined but class consciousness made it essential that upper class children be literate. The bright child was pushed toward greater levels of accomplishment and foreigners were amazed at the adult-like understanding of little American children. Public education was generally of low quality but many parents pushed their children at home into early learning and some could spell and recite the alphabet at age two. Toward the end of the century books for children made their appearance, stressing nobility and moral obedience, in sharp contrast to the tales of the deathbed so common in the early colonial period.

John Locke's *Some Thoughts Concerning Education*, published in 1689, might be considered the early equivalent to Dr. Spock's *Baby and Child Care*. For good or bad his advice influenced childrearing throughout the eighteenth century. The very young were to eat plain food, drink no strong drink, and get plenty of sleep ("early to bed and early to rise"). They were bathed in cold water and their bodies exposed to air. Taking Locke literally, many parents gave their children a naked dip in cold water each morning to prevent illness.

By the late 1800's, coinciding with America's first centennial celebration, urban middle-class childrearing had grown to be quite permissive by old standards. The more moderate churches were gaining members and the doctrine of original sin was being tempered by the view that children were neither good nor bad at birth but merely formless clay to be nurtured. Both the more moderate churches and the child care writers of the period warned against harshness, overprotectiveness and too much memory work. Scripture retained its position of importance but the application of the rod had become symbolic, meaning to "rule gently," a task that even mothers could now assume. Writers like John Abbott in *Mother at Home* tempered strict obedience with tenderness and religious sentiments but Dr. Spock himself would have been considered conservative by some of the child care writers. In *The Science of Motherhood*, Hannah Whitall advised parents to be polite to their children, to *win* them to goodness. If your child cuts holes in the curtains and hammers nails into the furniture, give him paper to cut and blocks to nail, and give him *reasons*. Don't nag, don't drive, don't punish, and don't use "don't." This model for childrearing lives on today in many homes and some schools. Of course, the conservative religious groups and the rural lower class would have none of this liberal, sinful nonsense and continued steadfast with their strict discipline.

Many Children Homeless

The orphans and the very poor, particularly in cities, were in a class by themselves. The heavy mortality rate left hundreds of children homeless (in Ohio alone there were 70 institutions for homeless children in 1893). Seaport cities were filled with homeless immigrants. On every hand were hungry, sick children, many choosing the streets over the almshouses where the insane and the dying, the young and the old were thrown together in overcrowded quarters. Large areas of cities were centers of crime and misery. Squatters' villages and refugee quarters were crowded with monkeys, dogs and children. Disease frequently swept these areas and adults trained children in the arts of begging, thievery, picking pockets, and prostitution (Committee on Child Saving Work, 1893).

There were no adoption laws. The more fortunate children were loaded into trains by the Children's Aid Society and shipped to frontier areas to live and work on farms. The less fortunate were put to work in factories, beginning as early as age three, to work from dawn to dusk for the piddling wages of 50 cents to two dollars a week.

The Biblical admonition, "Do unto thy neighbor," did not generally apply to homeless children whose delinquent behavior was linked to man's "primitive savagery." This social Darwinism view was the fuel for social snobbery of the upper-class whose claim to superiority was immaculate manners and affiliation with the "right" neighborhood, the "right" church, the "right" boarding school and the "right" circle of friends. This social class snobbery, less a measure of money than a right of blood, and the elitist social values and institutions it spawned, were to flourish and grow into lodges, sororities, fraternities, social clubs and jet set swinging of the 20th century.

By 1900 the diversity of present-day America was already established. The well-mannered, tutored, worldly young of the wealthy Southern plantation owner contrasted sharply on social dimensions to the poor, orphan, ragged child of the Boston street gangs who fought modern day versions of the deadly territorial "rumble." The obedient, prayerful, discreet, precocious child of the upper class Northern family lived social generations apart from the illiterate, laboring black slave child, and poor farmer's child of the South. This nightmare of the American dream, overindulgence for some and poverty for many, with all its national and universal consequences, was nourished on the souls of the poor, and remains to haunt us in this modern age of growing scarcity and economic upheaval.

Scientists and Sages

By the turn of the twentieth century the role of the mother in rearing her children was being circumvented by the childrearing expert. Friedrich Froebel, a student of the gentle schoolmaster Johann Pestallozi, established the first kindergarten in Germany in 1827. Setting a precedent that endures today, American scholars went abroad to visit Froebel's school and the first kindergarten was opened in Watertown, Wisconsin in 1855. By 1900 about 3,000 public and private kindergartens were operating in the United States, employing 5,000 teachers and enrolling 100,000 children.

Even during this primitive (by today's standards) educational period educators were torn between two camps, the idealistic, introspective school of Froebel and the progressive, scientific school of the great American educator-philosopher John Dewey. The resulting bitter debates at conferences of the International Kindergarten Union led to the formulation of position papers by staunch "conservative," "moderate," and "liberal" advocates (Weber, 1969). The liberals brought the new psychology of G. Stanley Hall and, consequently, the evolutionary views of Charles Darwin into play. *Science* entered the scene and "correct" childrearing became the focus of professional and scientific interest. While Hall was engaging in naive (by today's standards) but important scientific studies of humans, Edward L. Thorndike was engaged in pioneering work in animal psychology from which emerged his well-known laws of exercise, effect and readiness.

This early interest in child study swept the United States and Europe and exposed the genius of Montessori, Terman, Gesell, Freud, Watson, Pavlov, and Wertheimer. During the span of a few brief years, following the first scientific study of children by Wilheim Preyer in 1882, child study grew from a primitive beginning into the child development movement, an event marked by the opening of the Iowa Child Welfare Research Station in 1917.

Childhood was now the subject of major scientific interest and early childhood education was legitimized. A flurry of activity led to the establishment of the National Committee on Nursery Schools (1926) (which later became the National Association for Education of Young Children) and the Association for Childhood Education International (1930). These organizations, strengthened by the creation of the Southern Association for Children Under Six in 1950, continue among the influential voices for children.

The experts had their influence on parents. The Dr. Spock of his time, pediatrician L. Emmett Holt, shook off the permissive sages, admonishing mothers against rocking babies, picking them up when they cried, or allowing them to play with food. His book, *Care and Feeding of Children,* influenced generations of parents.

Holt's spartan rules of childrearing were further supported by the advice of the scientists. John Watson, for example, urged that children be trained by cold, scientific methods. Conditioned reflex training was as appropriate for children as it was for Pavlov's dogs. Training manuals for parents appeared and fathers were to participate in childrearing.

Politics and Panaceas

As awareness of conditions for children increased the scientists and sages were joined by social reformers who were outraged at the abuses suffered by children in rural and urban slums. The practice of Congress to appropriate huge sums to fight hog cholera and cotton-boll weevils and nothing for children came under sharp attack. Children, not hogs and boll weevils, were declared America's most precious resource. Under this pressure the first White House Conference on Children was held in 1909 to deal with political and practical concerns for children. Once every decade since that time the Conference has convened to reevaluate the nation's commitment to children and to establish priorities for the decade to come. Interestingly, the participants of each Conference in turn directed their attention inward to project personal priorities and backward to reflect upon dilemmas of the past decade (Beck, 1973). The problems of the future played second fiddle to the current national mood, tempered by social, political and economic circumstances and the opinions of experts. The Conference mood swung from outrage over child abuse in 1907 to the inherent "rights" of children and youth in 1970. In 1919 the Conference was dominated by physicians (experts) with hard data to support new program standards. The 1930 Conference fielded 3,000 participants, up from an initial 2C0. Again the proceedings were dominated by experts. The proper role of the parent in childrearing was a major theme. For the first and perhaps last time, the participants were generally optimistic about the survival of the traditional nuclear family structure. Perhaps the strange familial solidification of depression years created this fleeting promise — a promise that was to be broken by the very next assembly.

In 1940 the specter of war hung over the nation and the conference deliberations, true to national mood, extolled the virtues of freedom, democracy, patriotism and the American way of life. These were survival matters, of course, and not to be taken lightly. Americans still remembered the bitter lessons of the great war when in 1950 the White House Conferees, transfixed by the threat of the atomic bomb, invoked religion and involved common citizens, youth, and Dr. Spock in their quest for wisdom. And wisdom was needed, for the sovereignty of the family was under heavy duress from broken homes and divorce. A related problem, rapidly growing alienation of youth, was the subject of sufficient concern in 1960 that separate conferences, one for children (0-13) and one for youth (14-24) were held in 1970.

President Nixon addressed the 1970 Conference on Children, identifying the concern of the Conference as the well-being of the nation's children and called the present system of assistance, involving six million children, "an unfair and tragic system." The conferees met the President's challenge by developing a list of 16 major concerns, headed by "Comprehensive family-oriented child development programs including health services, day care, and early childhood education." But on December 9, 1971 President Nixon vetoed a $2 billion legislative measure designed to provide educational and health care for the children of low-income working mothers. Small wonder that Americans have more confidence in their garbage collectors than they have in their incumbent politicians. Seventy-six years into the twentieth century, two hundred years an independent nation and political priorities, hogs and boll weevils, space and Vietnam, sheiks and shahs still outrank our most precious resource — children.

Those prone to nostalgia long for the past, "the good old days when times were bad." Senior citizens speak of the bad times as good for character development and reminisce fondly of the good times — the closeness of the land, the warmth of family cohesiveness. Of course those who failed to survive or ended up in lunatic asylums are not around to share their versions. If history is of value, we can give up the wasted dream of an America returning to a previous way of life. A society does not heal its imperfections by rejecting its accomplishments. Even those few with racy visions and hippie souls who seek a more natural existence end up sorting out their experiences in a kind of modern day computer style. They keep up their immunizations, get their cavities filled, borrow from the nutritionist's laboratories, hitch rides in capitalists' automobiles, and borrow money from the Feds to attend the system's schools. An important difference with this growing number who march to a different drummer is that they have deep and interesting feelings about what they are doing.

They are not, as casual observers believe, seeking a return to the "good old days." For the most part they are not even aware, in their youth, of the idyllic, pastoral childhood setting of grandparents' memories. The amazing thing about our youth is that these ideas came out of their own heads. From their own experience they know that something is painfully wrong about a society comprising five to six percent of the world's population that consumes over 40 percent of the world's resources, a society whose garbage could meet the needs of another population of the same size. Vivid realism, not nostalgia, guides their visions.

Realism is that American society of 1976 is unlike any that ever existed. Children and youth of 1976 are as different from the children of 1776 as muskets are different from H bombs. They are different because of how they feel and what they know. Today's school age child knows more about murder, sex, violence, divorce, drugs, schools and technology than George Washington knew. He spends more time with television than he spends at school or with his parents. Fifty separate studies involving 10,000 children *all* show that TV violence increases aggressive behavior in children. It is estimated that over

300,000 (10 percent) of American school children are taking prescription drugs which stimulate the central nervous system. Almost 300 teachers in New York City schools alone were assaulted by pupils during the first three months of the present school year. Almost half of the four to six year old children in one study said they like TV better than their daddies. And it appears that the feeling is mutual. When Ann Landers asked her readers to respond to the question, "If you had it all to do over again would you have children?", 70 percent of the 10,000 responding said "no."

A Study in Contrast

Childhood in America today is a study in contrast. If you want to see life lived much as it was lived 200 years ago, the poverty-ridden mountain families, reservation Indians, Southwest Chicanos and inner city slum dwellers offer cases on every hand. Primitive circumstances of health, sanitation, nutrition and childbearing rival the most bizarre circumstances of 1776.

On the other hand *typical* middle class American children are overfed, overpampered, showered with material goods, clothing, toys, and gadgets. Their problem is not how to survive but how to make sense out of an unending explosion of stimuli. Yesterday's child could count on the security of an intact family structure, often broken by death but sufficiently large with older siblings, grandparents, aunts and uncles, to be secure. Today's child sees his security slipping away in a steady, accelerating stream of divorces and working mothers. Divorce rates increased over 700 percent in the past 100 years to reach a record 1,000,000 plus in 1975. For the first time in history the mothers of *most* children work outside the home. What is both bad and new is that liberated mothers are giving up mothering and no one, including fathers, is stepping in to assume it. (Fathers, incidentally, have never assumed their proper role.) The nobility once associated with homemaking has been eroded by an insatiable desire for academic, social and materialistic "success." The movement to liberate women, positive and sorely needed in many respects, does women, children and society no good when those

who seek only to be mothers and homemakers are made to look and feel like freaks. In the words of a well-known newscaster, "many mothers and homemakers don't seek to be liberated because they don't feel enslaved."

The present erosion of the traditional American family structure has its roots in history: the permissiveness of child rearing practices of the 19th century, refueled by Dr. Spock in the 20th century; the shift from moral and religious standards in childrearing and adult conduct to increasing reliance on the scientist-expert — the psychologist, the medical doctor, the psychiatrist and the space age engineer; the growth in sexual permissiveness that paralleled increasing sophistication of transportation and communication; the boredom of materialistic overabundance. In a curious way all of this came about from sincere efforts to make a better world for children. And in many respects that purpose was accomplished. For most American children, comfort, health, long life, education and a reasonable degree of emotional security are assured. For countless others poverty, disease, loneliness and ignorance are a way of life. In the present decade it has become clear that a strange paradox exists in the American way of life. The most "successful," those who succeed in securing the greatest comfort for self are in-sodoing contributing to the discomforts of others.

Science & Common Sense: 1776-1976

The lesson to be learned from history is that teaching children how to live with self, others and nature is a process of delicate balance between science and common sense, intellect and morality. Both the extremes and excesses of 1776 and those of 1976 are damaging to children.

The proper alternative to the poverty of 1776 is not the overindulged egocentered child of 1976. In the name of self-concept Americans have placed psychological blinders on children, tunnelling their vision away from the poverty and misery of ghettoes, and projecting their thoughts and concerns from others onto self. What the modern pampered, extravagant American has yet to learn and teach his children is that the source of enduring, healthy concept of self is one's concern for others. What today's child says to a hungry world in the 21st century will be survival matters — not *my* children's survival, not *their* children's survival, but *our* children's survival.

The proper alternative to the whipping stocks of 1776 is not the Dr. Spocks of 1946. In 1976 Dr. Spock admitted that he should have advocated more firmness in rearing children. But the damage was done as millions of American parents indulged their children as no other generation in history was ever indulged. Spock should have been spanked earlier. Children look to adults for mature guidance but stand confused in the presence of parents fearful to set expectations and teach common standards of decent behavior lest they injure tender personalities or spark disapproval in children.

The proper alternative to child slavery in factories is not several hours of daily zombie-like existence with the boob-tube. Children learn to be responsible for themselves and for others when they have meaningful, humane, roles of responsibility in the family, in the school, and in the community. Fortunately, modern conceptions of child responsibility have changed. Children's need to learn responsibility, to develop autonomy, has not changed.

The proper alternative to six-hour hell and damnation sermons and learning to read with the King James Bible is not the abolition of any reference to moral and spiritual matters in the home or in the school. It seems foolish to assume that the present state of agnostic education in American could have been the intent of our founding fathers who invoked the deity in every concern of family, school, and government. "In God We Trust" was emblazoned on their buildings, their money and their conscience. The scientists of the twentieth century enriched our children's physical comfort. The psychologists and educators stimulated their cognitive development, but they collectively ignored or debased children's

spiritual development. Now in 1976, Donald T. Campbell, President of the prestigious American Psychological Association, has finally come to believe that "religion and other moral traditions are not only useful but scientifically valid." It is scientifically wrong to assume that repressive or inhibiting moral traditions are of no value. There is "an underlying wisdom in the recipes for living that tradition has supplied us."

What fickle people Americans are. One generation of science prompts us to ignore centuries of history. One little old lady in Austin, Texas, acting virtually alone, compels the Supreme Court to take spiritual development out of the schools, and our powerful professional organizations — you and I — stand by in silence.

The proper alternative to the intact, extended family of 1776 is not the loneliness of latch key children whose parents work. It's time to admit that American families of 1976 are not like those · of 1776. While the intact family exists for most, broken and part-time families exist for many others. Most families don't do the job alone anymore. We may not like it, but it's time to realize that many parents are not around to take care of their children. Some parents don't know how to take care of their children, and a few parents are too sick to take care of their children. One of the most pressing needs in child care today is a rich array of child care and family help services, graduated in cost, completely voluntary and community controlled. What better gift, in this bicentennial year, could Americans give to children of fragmented families.

I wish to make it clear that this proposition of child care and family services is a necessary reaction to the imperfections of our society and the effects of natural circumstance. I do not advocate that patterns of institutional care for young children are right or proper substitutes for the family, and I do not know any educators who do. Rather they are patterns critically needed to ensure that those children, who for any reason are denied

positive family care, receive that care through an alternate arrangement, that any parent or potential parent who for any reason is unable or incapable of nourishing his/her young is assisted in doing so.

History says that this is a just and honorable task. Conscientious Americans through the generations have agonized over the plight of ragged, hungry and abandoned children wherever they exist in the world, and for whatever reason. But Americans have yet to learn what some other modern countries already know. Child care is a community as well as a family responsibility. The family will endure as the fundamental unit for childrearing as the community learns to assume its supporting role. The greatest rewards will come when communities of people join hands to sanctify, to uplift, to preserve and to strengthen our historical family structure. In 1776 and in 1976 the family was and is our most essential link to civilization — our most cherished exhibition of honor and dignity — our most precious gift to children.

Selected Bibliography

Anderson, J. E., "Child Development: An Historical Perspective," supplement to *Child Development*, 1956, 27(2):181-227.

Aries, P., *Centuries of Childhood*. New York: Alfred A. Knopf, Inc., 1962.

Beck, R., "The White House Conferences on Children: An Historical Perspective." *The Rights of Children*, Harvard Educational Review Reprint No. 9, 1973, 43(4):88-103.

Bremmer, R. H. (Ed.), *Children and Youth in America*, 3 vols. Cambridge, Mass.: Harvard University Press, 1970-74.

Cable, M., *The Little Darlings: A History of Child Rearing in America*. New York: Charles Scribners Sons, 1972.

Committee on the History of Child-Saving Work. *History of Child Saving in the United States*. Report to the National Conference of Charities and Correction, Chicago, June 1893. Reprinted by Patterson Smith Publishing Corporation, Montclair, New Jersey, 1971.

DeMause, L., *The History of Childhood*. New York: Psycho-History Press, 1974.

Frank, L. K., "The Beginnings of Child Development and Family Life Education in the Twentieth Century." *Merrill-Palmer Quarterly*, 1962, 8(4): 207-227.

Osborn, D. K., *Early Childhood Education in Historical Perspective*. Athens, Ga.: Education Associates, 1975.

Weber, E., *The Kindergarten: Its Encounter With Educational Thought in America*. New York: Teachers College Press, 1969.

America's Head Start Program:
An Agenda for Its Second Decade

Edward F. Zigler

Edward F. Zigler, Ph.D., is Sterling Professor of Psychology, Yale University, New Haven, Connecticut. From 1970-72, he was Director of the HEW Office of Child Development.

As most of you know, my life has been closely intertwined with the Head Start program. I am proud that I was a member of the original planning committee for Head Start. During the years I served as the first director of the Office of Child Development, I was also the public servant responsible for Head Start. And, finally, for the past twelve years of my life, I have studied and evaluated the effects of the Head Start program.

Given my involvement with Head Start, I am troubled by the misunderstanding and confusion that continue to surround this bellwether program. Both the Associated Press and the New York *Times* have erroneously reported in the last year that Head Start has ceased to exist. In response to the New York *Times*'s error, I wrote the following letter:

The New York *Times* erred in its assertion that Head Start is dead. Head Start, the most innovative program ever mounted on behalf of America's children, is alive and well. Your mistaken assertion is illustrative of the misunderstandings, controversy, and confusion that have surrounded the Head Start program since its inception over a decade ago. At a cost of over $400 million per year, the Head Start network continues to provide a preschool educational program enriched by a broad spectrum of social services to over 200,000 of America's economically disadvantaged children. Furthermore, over the years, the Head Start

program has proven to be a valuable national laboratory for the development and assessment of a whole array of intervention efforts, such as the Home Start program, efforts relevant to the outcome and development of all of our nation's children.

Your editorial was correct in indicating that Head Start is a vulnerable program that has suffered many trials and tribulations. The history of this program has been one of moving from crisis to crisis, with Head Start people at local levels never feeling very confident that they would receive the following year's funding. Particularly detrimental to the Head Start program has been that coterie of psychologists, early childhood educators, and social policy analysts who have regularly, albeit erroneously, proclaimed the failure of the Head Start program. However, those Americans closest to and therefore most knowledgeable about Head Start, namely those American families whose children utilize it, have never wavered in their praise and support of this program. Head Start has continued to be funded because a bipartisan group in Congress has refused to turn a deaf ear to that relatively powerless segment of society that has always been Head Start's most fervent champion.

What of Head Start's future? It remains problematic. For this reason, the Head Start program needs the active support of all those who feel that no national effort should take priority over the health and development of our nation's children.

Scholars continue to argue over whether Head Start has been a success or a failure. Anyone conducting an appropriate evaluation would have to conclude that Head Start has been a success. Why, then, is there an argument?

Let us now ask the central question: Do children who experience Head Start manifest greater gains on cognitive and personality measures than do comparison children who have not had the Head Start experience? The answer to this question is a resounding "Yes." Why then has it become fashionable to speak of the failure of Head Start? The assertion of Head Start's failure is based upon the reported finding that the advantage of Head Start children over non-Head Start children is not maintained once the children have spent two or three years in elementary school. But how is this finding to be interpreted? The raw data would appear to represent more an indictment of schools rather than of Head Start.

I would like to issue a serious warning against the popular "fade-out" notion. That is, the current conventional wisdom concerning the impact of Head Start is that the gains in performance obtained by Head Start children as compared to non-Head Start controls fade out a year or two into the elementary school grades. My own considered views concerning this bit of conventional wisdom are that it is more conventional than it is wise. From the Wolff and Stein report (1966), through the Westinghouse report (1969), to Bronfenbrenner's scholarly analysis conducted for OCD (1974), we have been informed that there are no striking long-term effects accruing from a one-year Head Start experience. This has been repeated so often that many now treat this conclusion as beyond question. I choose to question it. In flocking to this position, thinkers have ignored a relatively large and consistent body of evidence which indicates that the benefits of participating in a preschool intervention program have much greater staying power than currently popular views would have us believe. For those of you who are not prepared to accept that there are discernible effects accruing from Head Start attendance, I recommend that you read a recently prepared review of the evidence on this point by Frank Palmer (1975). I assert here today that besides being erroneous, the worst danger of the "fade-out" position is that it provides ammunition to those in America who feel that spending money in an effort to improve the lives of economically-disadvantaged children is a waste.

I ask decision makers not to set social policy on the basis of the conclusion that there are no long-term effects of Head Start attendance. I say to these decision makers that the evidence on this point is not as unidirectional as many currently believe. Bad science makes for bad social policy. I ask my colleagues in the research community to forego the temptation of delivering definitive pronouncements concerning the "fade-out" issue and await instead the collection and analyses of more data. Such a stance strikes me as currently being the only reasonable one if thinkers are to combine social responsiblity with the researchers' deeply-ingrained attitudes of skepticism and objectivity. (Zigler 1976, pp. 5-6)

This position, which I advanced about three years ago, not only remains valid but has been strengthened by several recent papers that have come out of the Longitudinal Research Consortium headed by Professor Irving Lazar at Cornell (see Moore 1978). The evidence is now clear that Head Start does indeed have long and important lasting effects.

I think the long-term effects of Head Start depend on two factors:

- Getting parents involved in the training of their own children, and

- Guaranteeing that schools follow the Head Start program with further intervention efforts.

These factors illustrate two types of continuity. First, there should be continuity between the Head Start program and the child's home. The parent is that wonderful lever that makes the efforts of the Head Start program mount in importance. If the parent will continue the Head Start center work at home, the effect will be greatly enhanced. Secondly, there should be continuity between the Head Start program and subsequent kindergarten and elementary schooling. We can never inoculate children in one year against the ravages of deprivation; there must be continuity. It is crucial that the schools follow the Head Start effort with a dovetailed second intervention that builds upon the gains of Head Start.

. . . the research issue of the next five years will not be whether Head Start is effective, but rather how to determine which children benefit maximally from the Head Start program.

In regard to whether Head Start is a success or a failure, I think the issue is beyond debate. I think the research issue of the next five years will not be whether Head Start is effective, but rather how to determine which children benefit maximally from the Head Start program.

Warnings: What Head Start Must *Not* Become

This basically positive view does not mean that we should rest on our laurels. I prefer to think of Head Start not as a static program but as an evolving concept, an effort that must continue to grow and develop. What, then, should be the future of Head Start? Head Start is essentially America's national laboratory for testing and refining our nation's efforts to improve the quality of life for our country's children. Let me begin by clearly enunciating what Head Start should *not* become.

First, I think **we must repudiate forever the view that higher IQ scores and their close correlate, elementary school grades, are the ultimate goals of the Head Start effort.** The back-to-basics movement represents a new threat to what is best about the Head Start effort. The issue here is whether we shall commit ourselves to a narrow cognitive development approach or to a wider whole-child approach. The back-to-basics and cognitive development emphasis is based on a fallacy: the now-discredited deficit hypothesis that the central problem for economically disadvantaged children is their intellectual inadequacy. The children of the poor have as much intellectual potential as the children of the affluent. When we began Head Start, scholars were publicly saying that poor children did not have the intellectual capacity to be able to store cognitively and retrieve their own names. Some of you perhaps remember that sad epoch when we were putting children's names over a mirror so they would be able to learn their own names. This is where the cognitive emphasis ultimately leads.

. . . the primary goal of Head Start is to promote socially competent human beings.

Let us proclaim instead that the primary goal of Head Start is to promote socially competent human beings. What do we mean by a socially competent human being? What would be the measurable indicators that we had succeeded with Head Start? The measure of social competence includes the physical and mental health and well-being of the children we serve. That is why it is so fitting for the Head Start

program to serve handicapped children. Only five or six years ago, handicapped children were *not* included in the Head Start program. Today, 10 to 12 percent of the Head Start children are handicapped, and the job that Head Start people have done stands as a model to the school system of what mainstreaming is really all about. Head Start has shown that mainstreaming requires training and preparation, not just the willy-nilly placement of children together. Since the incidence of handicap is much greater among the poor than among the nonpoor, Head Start was a little slow to reach out to this segment of the population. I can only say that I take my share of the blame. But I am proud to have all of you as colleagues who at least acted better late than never.

In addition to the physical health and well-being of children, we should look at formal cognitive ability, including language and closely-related intellectual skills, in its proper place. That is the second aspect of social competence. The third aspect, which I have been talking about as long as Head Start has been in business, is to work on the emotional, motivational development of children. I am convinced that where we made our error was in ever thinking that poor children suffered from lack of intelligence. The real problem is that they frequently do not use optimally the intelligence they have. And the job of Head Start is to develop the emotional and motivational skills that are the heart of school performance and mind performance.

Three factors are particularly important in producing a socially competent human being. One is the locus of control variable: Does the child really feel in charge, that things happen because he or she makes them happen, or is the child just a passive victim of outside forces? The children who feel they can possess the necessary competence to accomplish a task will become the competent adults. I also ask you to work very closely with children to see that they develop a healthy and appropriate responsivity to adults. And finally I ask you to continue the work that has been basic to Head Start since its inception, that we do everything we can to respect the child's culture, the child's sense of home and worth. In short, we should do everything possible to develop a positive self-image among children in Head Start centers.

Those emotional and motivational variables are part of the social competence we are talking about.

Now, another warning. As Head Start ages, **we must guard against becoming an elitist group of self-proclaimed experts to whom parents turn over their children** so the children will be raised properly. Children are raised by parents in their homes and not by Head Start personnel in centers. All the good that Head Start can do can be wiped out if we do anything to disparage the parents of the children we serve. Head Start is the only institution on the national scene that represents a true partnership between families and professionals who serve these families. It is this viable partnership that represents what is unique and revolutionary about the Head Start effort. This partnership lies at the heart of our success, and we should rededicate ourselves to the basic principle that Head Start reflects the wisdom and competence of the parents who utilize its services.

In the future, **we should also not waste our energies seeking magic periods.** I have now witnessed fifteen years of this aimless search. We have one group of experts who say that the magic period is the nine months *in utero*, and that we should concentrate all our energies on this period. Then we have another group of experts who say the magic period is the first year of life, the only time period worth intervening in. Another group is still holding to the two years before school as the crucial period. Still another group of experts maintains that the first three elementary grades is the magic period. Now, believe it or not, another group of workers tells us that adolescence is the critical period in the life cycle.

This is a useless and nonsensical argument. These are all magic periods. Let us take seriously what developmental psychologists have to teach: There is a continuity to human life, one period built upon another, each period important, each period needing a special set of nutrients and programs for the child at that age. Certainly we must have good prenatal care; we also want infant programs; we need preschool and school-age programs; and we can still help children in adolescence. The problem with magic periods is the tendency to give up on children who have outgrown them. In my view, one should never give up on a child, regardless of age. There is always some kind of program that could be helpful, and it is our responsibility to deliver these programs to children, *whatever* their ages.

Analogously, in the future **we should stop viewing Head Start as a panacea required by every child whose family income falls below some arbitrary figure.** Head Start has already started to evolve from a single program into a center with a variety of programs serving the myriad needs of children and families residing in neighborhoods where the Head Start center is situated. Rather than expecting children to fit the requirements and characteristics of Head Start, Head Start should become a center containing many programs tailored to fit the needs of the childen and their families. This model of the Head Start program of the future already exists in the Administration for Children, Youth, and Families (ACYF) Child and Family Resource programs. In my opinion, this model is the wave of the future.

Recommendations: What Head Start Should Do

Now that I have briefly summarized what Head Start should *not* do, I would like to make a threefold set of recommendations for what it should do:

- We need a change in Head Start's basic stance;

- Head Start needs a substantive program agenda; and

- There should be a political agenda for those who support Head Start and those who feel that the healthy development of children should be our nation's top priority.

Perhaps some people will think me naive to try to move into the political arena. It is true that I probably know more about t-tests and multivariate analysis than I know about that land of Oz we call Washington, D.C. But, if I have learned one lesson in my twenty years of experience in this field, it is that accomplishments on the substantive program front rarely outdistance those on the political front. I'm asking you to care for children. I'm also asking you to be social activists. Let us remember our community action roots and not be bashful. Too often people who care about children think that because our cause is just we really don't have to fight for it. But other people have other agendas. We cannot compete as a lobby group with the National Rifle Association, but we *can* speak with one voice; we can be heard.

The basic stance of Head Start **must change from a defensive to an offensive posture.** After the first summer, Head Start was a smash hit; we were the "Sesame Street" of 1965. Then the Westinghouse report (1969) came along and we went from being viewed very positively to somewhat negatively. Finally, through our own efforts and the new programs in Head Start, we moved from a negative to a somewhat neutral position in people's attitudes toward us.

Why have we been so orphanlike, standing hat in hand, begging to please keep the program alive? Why have we never just sold what we had to sell?

Now I say to you, I have lived through some dark days in Head Start. Why have we been so orphanlike, standing hat in hand, begging to please keep the program alive? Why have we never just sold what we had to sell? Instead we have always pleaded for one more year, with the promise to show some "results" by then. Why did we take that stance? The nadir of the Head Start program in America probably took place about 1970 when I went to Washington to become the director of the Office of Child Development. One of the first tasks I was called upon to perform was to attend a meeting at the Office of Economic Opportunity. And what I was confronted with about one week into my Washington experience was a three-year phase-out plan for the Head Start program. The Nixon administration had decided that Head Start would go; in that period all the War on Poverty programs were being phased out and Head Start was just included in the group. Well, that frightened me, and we did what we had to do to keep Head Start alive. It wasn't a matter of more money; it was a matter of keeping the program alive. This is a story with nothing but

heroes. Head Start parents came to the rescue of the program; Department of Health, Education, and Welfare (HEW) Secretary Elliot Richardson took our case to the White House. I saw Republicans and Democrats combine to say, "This is the one program that we wanted for children; let's not spoil it now."

The evidence is increasingly clear that Head Start works and can work even better if we can expand Head Start into areas in which children and families need service.

That incident indicates to you why we were so passive in our approach to Head Start. We had to be passive because we were, frankly, scared to death. But the days when we must be scared to death are over. We no longer have to stand hat in hand. The evidence is increasingly clear that Head Start works and can work even better if we can expand Head Start into areas in which children and families need service. We are taking this evidence to the Hill, and we are taking it to our friends in the administration. Now this kind of expansion cannot be done with mirrors. It will require more money. Too often in the past we at the national level have passed new tasks down to the regions and local levels and said, "Hey, do this," without a dollar to do these new things. You have all worked for less than you are worth; you have received low salaries and low prestige. Your commitment is on record. But you can only ask people to work for nothing without adjustment for inflation for so long. And we must seize the moment now to make up for the inequities that you have suffered for many years. That is my political standpoint: Change it from passive to assertive, from negative and reserved to positive and demanding.

Head Start's Agenda

What is my substantive agenda? Here I feel more comfortable than when I make political pronouncements. I am a student of child development and of the family's importance in that development. What do I see then as being important items on our Head Start agenda over the second decade in the life of this program?

First, **we must do better in the Child Development Associate program.** We must produce a cadre of workers in this country who can care for children. At the risk of appearing a little inconsistent with my stance on magic, I do believe there is some magic somewhere in Head Start and in childhood intervention. The magic is not in ages or even in particular types of programs. It is in the relationship between the adult caregiver and the child being cared for. That's where the magic is. If we want Head Start to be a success, then we need to make sure that every adult caregiver in every Head Start center in this nation has the skills and abilities to be an optimizer of the development of the children in his or her charge.

Now I will make a somewhat revolutionary appeal, an appeal that has divided Head Start people in the past, but I will risk your wrath. I think that the day will soon come when **Head Start will be expanded to include nonpoor children.** I have never believed in the philosophy that poor children should go to one center and more affluent children to another. Now I am enough of a realist to see that we cannot do everything overnight; we have to have some priorities. I think that besides serving children of the poor, Head Start should give the following groups priority. I think we must continue our efforts and thrust toward handicapped children whatever their family income. I think we should make a special effort in regard to non-English-speaking children. Finally, I think we should make a special effort to give some priority to children of single-parent families in which that single parent works. Somebody must care for these children, and too many of them are not cared for today.

Beyond expanding Head Start to meet these new priorities, I also think **we should expand Head Start services.** I believe that Head Start should play a very simple role in the new inoculation effort. A tragedy is taking place in America. The Center for Disease Control in Atlanta indicates that the inoculation rate in America is down 50 percent; this declining curve means illness and death for children. I am pleased that HEW Secretary Joseph A. Califano has spoken out in favor of inoculating children. I cannot believe that a nation that can go to the moon cannot get children vaccinated against polio and measles and other childhood ailments. Head Start has a special role to play in an inoculation program. In the ghettos and slums of this country and in the Appalachian poverty areas, some 70 percent of the children are probably not inoculated. Why are they not inoculated? People sound very righteous when they say, "Look, poor people can take their children to a hospital and get them inoculated for nothing. Why don't they do it?" And I say to them, "Have you ever been to one of those hospitals and seen how poor people are treated there?" That's why Head Start could play a special role, because the one thing the Head Start has that the American health system does not have is credibility with parents. If we decide to inoculate the children in neighborhoods, they are more likely to come to Head Start than anywhere else.

Some other very quick ideas for this idealistic agenda: It's time for Head Start to move into doing something about the number one killer of America's children—accidents. **Head Start should develop a formidable accident prevention program.** (See Ross and Seefeldt 1978.) Another problem is teenage motherhood. While the birthrate in this nation declines, teenage births are soaring. These young children who are trying to raise children need our help. We can draw on our experience with the Parent and Child Centers and the Education for Parenthood Program to **provide services to teenage mothers in our Head Start centers,** if we decide to do so.

Head Start centers must also become active agencies to combat child abuse, which has now reached the epidemic figure of one million cases a year. I can't believe that the National Center on Child Abuse and Neglect in ACYF cannot be coordinated with the Head Start program for the benefit of children.

In conclusion, I want to give you a brief political agenda that must be accomplished if we are going to do any of these things. There are two basic requirements. One is that we have to have a vocal and effective lobby on behalf of children and families, and you are the nucleus of that lobby. We must also have a strong and effective ACYF that can be the focal point for developing and then implementing social policy. ACYF continues to be vulnerable. It was created by Executive Order, and any time the powers-that-be would like to, they can abolish it.

We must do everything we can to support ACYF and its Commissioner, Dr. Blandina Cardenas. We must see that ACYF is legislated by Congress. We must do everything possible to see that the prestige of the ACYF Commissioner is enhanced. Dr. Cardenas has my support; I will work with her as closely as I possibly can so that she can become the very best Commissioner of ACYF.

ACYF has already suffered a very serious reversal since my tenure. When the Commissioner of ACYF was made responsible to an Assistant Secretary, that was a different ballgame than when I dealt directly with the Secretary of HEW. We should insist that the Commissioner be a presidential appointee in the same way that the Assistant Secretary for the Office of Human Development Services is a presidential appointee so that we are talking about two people who at least have the same status in their interactions.

I ask HEW Secretary Califano to stop making a political football out of Head Start. We have important work to do. You are here doing the work that Head Start people should do, becoming knowledgeable about how to help children. The children need our undivided attention; they don't need all this "where's Head Start going to be next year?" I ask Secretary Califano and I ask the White House to step forward and state unequivocally and

clearly that Head Start has been a smashing success and will remain in ACYF.

I have thought about these matters and I find myself much more optimistic than I have been in a very long time. You have done a magnificent job. I am grateful to you and all I can say in conclusion is that I am very proud to be one of your colleagues.

References

Bronfenbrenner, U. *A Report on Longitudinal Evaluations of Preschool Programs.* Vol. 2. *Is Early Intervention Effective?* Washington, D.C.: Department of Health, Education, and Welfare, 1974. Publication No. (OHD) 74-25.

Moore, S. G. "The Persistence of Preschool Effects: A National Collaborative Study." *Young Children* 33, no. 3 (March 1978): 65-71.

Palmer, F. "Has Compensatory Education Failed? No, Not Yet." Unpublished manuscript, State University of New York, Stony Brook, 1975.

Ross, S. P., and Seefeldt, C. "Young Children in Traffic: How Can They Cope?" *Young Children* 33, no. 4 (May 1978): 68-73.

Westinghouse Learning Corporation. *The Impact of Head Start: An Evaluation of the Effects of Head Start on Children's Cognitive and Affective Development. Executive Summary.* Ohio University Report to OEO, Clearinghouse for Federal Scientific and Technical Information, June 1969.

Wolff, M., and Stein, A. *Factors Influencing the Recruitment of Children into the Head Start Program, Summer 1965: A Case Study of Six Centers in New York City (Study II).* New York: Yeshiva University, 1966. Office of Economic Opportunity Project No. 141-61.

Zigler, E. F. "Head Start: Not a Program but an Evolving Concept." In *Early Childhood Education: It's an Art? It's a Science?* edited by J. D. Andrews. Washington, D.C.: National Association for the Education of Young Children, 1976.

Annie L. Butler

Annie L. Butler, Ed.D, is Professor of Early Childhood Education in the School of Education, Indiana University Bloomington, and was formerly an Associate in Child Development for the New York State Education Department. Her areas of experience include teaching at the college level in New Jersey and New York, directing nursery schools, teaching three-to five-year-olds, and serving as a consultant in early childhood education.

Today's Child—

Tomorrow's World

Planning the education of today's child to live in tomorrow's world places us unquestionably in the midst of one of the most controversial issues in early childhood education. To what degree should early childhood education focus on the future?

As early childhood educators, we are generally more concerned about today's child in today's environment and in many respects rightly so. The young children we teach can generally be described as present oriented, having neither a very good understanding of the present nor the past, not to mention the future.

Thinking ahead to the future presents unique problems. Toffler and other futurists have been very strong in their criticism of today's education as built on the past model of industrial bureaucracy. These criticisms apply to early childhood education to the extent that regimentation, lack of individualization, rigid systems of seating, grouping, and grading, and the authoritarian role of the teacher are characteristic of programs. A more directly recognizable carry-over from this kind of education is the "downward push" which it exerts—the pressure on the kindergarten teacher to get the child ready for first grade, the elementary school to get the child ready for junior high, and so on up the ladder. Fortunately, not all programs for young children can be characterized in this way. Many early childhood educators do recognize that the task of helping today's child deal with tomorrow's world is to *provide a present which is relevant to the future but which is at the same time consistent with the developing abilities of young children.* In this context, it is important to review some of the realities of the present edu-

1. HISTORICAL

cational scene because only from this frame of reference can we look ahead to the future.

SOME CONSISTENT TRENDS

Period of Consolidation of Findings

Today's world of early childhood education is somewhat less in the limelight than it was ten years ago. We appear to be in a period of consolidation of findings. Kagan (1975) has disturbed a few people with his conclusions that the effects of deprivation on Guatemalan children are not necessarily permanent. Raymond Moore (1972) testified before Congress that formal schooling should not begin before age eight, and that Project Head Start did not make the dramatic changes hoped for in the intellectual abilities of young children. These events have made ripples, but have not generally changed the views of those knowledgeable about early childhood education. What seems to be developing is a deeper understanding of the complexity of human behavior and difficulty of changing its direction with short-term or stop-gap methods.

No evidence to date is strong enough to cause us to question the importance of the first six years of life. Considering the number of children who have a less than optimum environment during their earliest years, how fortunate it is if this environment is not an irreversible determinant of behavior.

There is some evidence that if a program is sufficiently intensive, it can make a difference in the child's performance. There is, however, a moral question involved in such intensive intervention—how much right does an outsider have to intervene in a family's rearing of its children? Of greater significance to us as teachers are findings that gains made by the children in so-called "compensatory" programs are related to program emphases, and that affective characteristics such as motivation and self-worth, which are strongly affected by environment, are more sus-ceptible to change than is readiness, which has a stronger heritable factor.

Growth of Programs Through Funding

The greatest boosts to early childhood education have come through state and federal funding. Currently 35 states provide some kind of aid to kindergartens. This does not mean that all five-year-old children are in kindergarten nor does this mean that there is stability or quality. Unfortunately, in some states every budget crunch means a renewed consideration of the appropriation of state funds for kindergarten. Kindergartens are subject to the same problems of overcrowding and underequipping as other local school programs, creating very serious questions regarding quality.

While federal funding of programs has been even less stable, the need for guidelines and standards has been recognized in planning, and a definite attempt has been made to influence programs toward consistency with the characteristics of children and, currently, to influence the continuity of the child's educational experience. Increases in funding, especially for day care, have in no way kept pace with need, but recent legislative attempts seem to have profited from some of the criticisms and controversy of several years ago.

Divergent Philosophies

One direct result of federal funding of early childhood programs and research has been the development of divergent program models. On the one hand, the effect on the field has been positive inasmuch as new programs have been created and rethinking of all programs has been stimulated; however, the lack of agreement among professionals has created a certain amount of divisiveness when unity of purpose might be a definite asset. Not only do we have programs which are supported by different philosophical and research bases, but we also have programs which employ a wide range of facilities and approaches. The Early Childhood Task Force of the Education Commission of the States questioned the usual classroom approach for the education of all children, recommending some combination of home- and school-based programs. Use of television and mobile facilities have been explored but possibilities have not been exhausted. This is an area in which consolidation of findings may work to our advantage. No doubt we do need certain kinds of diversity because of differences in children, families, and geographical locations, but we have not yet reached a point of rational decision making.

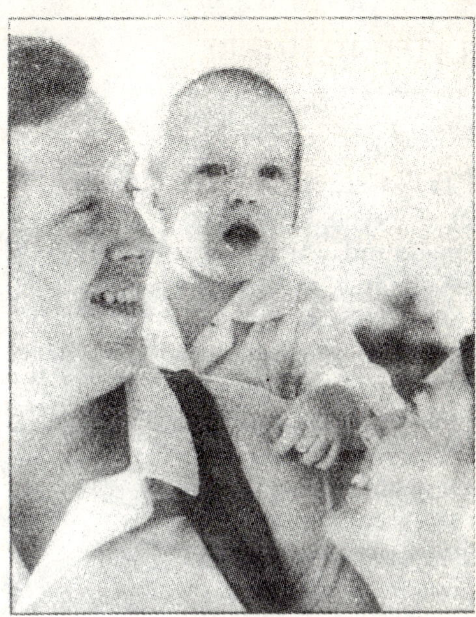

Increased Day Care Needs

The number of working mothers with children under the age of six increases each year, yet this has been an extremely difficult need for the country to respond to. The care of children, despite the figures on need, is still considered by many to be entirely a family responsibility, without regard to whether it is satisfactorily met, and thus the funding of programs is highly controversial.

One of the most controversial issues in day care is based on the fear of some that the school or center will replace the home in the role of inculcating the values of society. This is a particularly serious problem if children come from minority and low-income groups and staff come from different income and racial groups. Although awareness is growing, teachers do not like to be reminded that all sorts of values are transmitted to children through the curriculum, simple physical aspects of the classroom, authority of the teacher, and age or social class segregation. Seldom are teachers able to analyze their own values and those of the families they serve. Yet, family life styles of today are so vastly different for the children within any classroom that it is critical to accept ways of behaving that might have been rejected in the classroom of a few years ago.

The fact that many children in day care come from low-income and minority homes also increases the need for comprehensive programs. The provision of medical, nutritional, dental, and social services requires an interdisciplinary staff as well as many cooperative working relationships within the community.

Involvement of Parents

Along with an increased emphasis on day care needs has come an equally significant trend toward greater involvement of parents, not only in participation in centers but also in programs enabling them to become better educators of their own children. Parents of both low-income and ethnic groups have become much more articulate in expressing their desires for their children, with the result that programs for racial and cultural groups are beginning to reflect their distinctive qualities.

1. HISTORICAL

FACTORS RELATED TO FUTURE SUCCESS

Futurists from a wide range of disciplines agree on five assumptions: (1) today's schools and universities are too past- and present-bound; (2) technological and social change is outracing the educational system; (3) the concept of the future is closely bound up with the motivation of the learner; (4) the future is not merely a "subject" but a perspective as well, and calls for a new organization of knowledge; and (5) that a focus on the future is relevant to all learners, regardless of age (Toffler 1974, pp. xxiv-xxv).

Benjamin Singer (1974) indicates that the development of a "future-focused role-image" is essential early in life to provide both a motive and a means for achievement in the future. The sense of time, as expressed by the child, seems to commence between the ages of two and two-and-a-half, when words designating the future begin to appear in the child's speech. At that time, words dealing with the future are tied to activities and concrete events. By the end of the third year, the child begins to comprehend "future roles." According to Singer, it is at this time that differences begin to become apparent in the parents' behavior toward the child that seem to condition the development of different time perspectives, aspirations, and the necessary behavior to achieve them. The process begins with the idea that the parent generates concerning the child's future.

Research on Head Start children has led to the discovery that an important factor connected with the child's success during the program was the parents' occupational expectations for the child in the future. How young people see their future is directly connected with their academic performance and with their ability to live, cope, and grow in a high-change society. Future-conscious education is a key to adaptability. The authors of *Learning for Tomorrow* argue it is especially significant for

women and for the children of ethnic minorities which today can be regarded as "future deprived" (Toffler 1974, p. xxiv).

TODAY'S CHILD IN TOMORROW'S WORLD

One way of looking ahead at the future is to extract from today's early childhood educational philosophies those things which are at least worthy of further consideration. It is at once apparent that the problem is different for children of various income groups. The large majority of middle-income parents have a future-focused role-image for their children which is conveyed to the children at an early age. Sometimes it is conveyed too strongly at too early an age. To convey a future-focused role-image is much more difficult for parents who, themselves, are unemployed or employed at such meager wages that they must worry whether the family will be fed from one month to the next; parents who of necessity are so present-oriented can hardly convey a future-focused role-image to their children.

An examination of educational programs will also bring out differences in their ability to help children form future-focused role-images. These differences arise from the different things which are stressed in the program. The question that has to be answered is: *"What are the characteristics of young children which, if encouraged, will help them be better able to cope with the world of tomorrow?"* Some directions for early childhood education seem to rise clearly from the futurists' projections.

Focus on the Development of Coping Skills

This is only a new slant on an old emphasis. The young child's interest and involvement in the process of learning provides the basis for helping the child to identify multiple ways to

CANDICE LOGUE

find out about things and to solve problems. Instead of providing children with ready-made answers, it is important to provide them with varied real situations in which a variety of coping skills can be used, and to facilitate their use of such skills by asking questions such as: "How could you find out. . .? How many ways can you . . . ? What would happen if . . . ?" Try to create within the child's responses a kind of flexibility and power to adapt quickly, rather than seeking a response in terms of rules and carefully transmitted conduct codes. Real choices beginning with such simple things as whether to work a puzzle or read a book, or whether to use tempera or crayon for a painting can be made by quite young children. Older children can engage in practical problem-solving situations which involve selecting from among several alternatives. Children will thus learn to feel comfortable in situations where answers are not all known. They should develop the creative resources to find solutions when none currently exist.

Consideration of Affect in the Approach to Cognitive Skills

In the last decade, even those programs which resisted giving priority to cognitive goals found themselves giving consideration to how they provided for children's mental or intellectual development. We need to consider how we can encourage the child to *want* to learn more and more. The emphasis here is on both a desire to learn and the development of the skill of learning. Children will have even greater needs for reading, writing, and expressing themselves than in the past. Their world has already expanded so that understanding of society in our country is no longer enough, as children's lives are influenced by our interdependence with other nations. It is important that we create an atmosphere in which children have many opportunities to explore, touch, taste, listen, and experiment. Further, we must help them want to communicate the results of their exploration and to find answers to the questions that arise from it. As

1. HISTORICAL

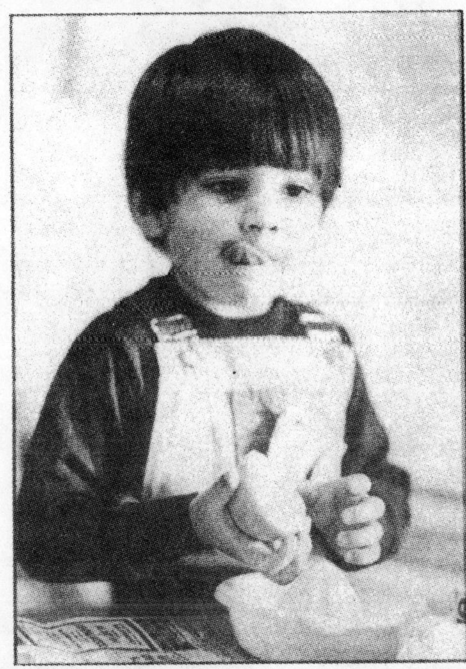

STEVE HERZOG

adults we can provide the setting, facilitate children's learning, and help them enjoy the satisfactions and successes that result. The responsibility extends beyond the actual facts or skills learned to the development of a joy of learning and the motivation to move on to new and more stimulating tasks.

Acquisition of a Future-Focused Role-Image

Cultivation of the future-focused role-image begins with the development of the self-image. School experiences should enable children to see themselves as competent and worthy people. In order to have these feelings, children must really be competent to do the things which are expected of them. The classroom, therefore, must provide for a variety of abilities and must aid children in selecting activities which are challenging but which at the same time allow them to be successful. Children must also like others and feel liked; their behavior must be reasonably acceptable to other children and adults.

Teachers can extend what they usually do to help children become aware of occupational options. In addition to taking the children into the neighborhood to learn about some occupations people engage in, teachers can greatly extend the kinds of materials they provide to help children role-play their observations of different occupations. A further step can be taken to introduce into children's discussions other occupational roles, those that might come into existence, and what the children might be when they grow up. Greater awareness of future roles can be created without violating the child's more prominent present orientation.

Emphasis on Humaneness

To live in the twenty-first century in sustained peace, it will be preferable for people to see themselves as relatively more cooperative than competitive. This means that the children's thoughts will need to depart from those of their twentieth century ancestors who placed greater stress on individually-oriented competition than on group-oriented collaboration. Fortunately, young children have not yet become competitive and small group projects can be provided to help them work together to achieve their purposes.

Children also need to become aware of their interpersonal interactions with other children and adults. Perhaps of all the things that a teacher of young children can appropriately do, it is most important to help children understand how other people respond to their behavior, and how they respond to the behavior of other people. At a time when children are first becoming interested in doing things with other children, they will learn the human relationships skills that form the basis for the way they will interact with people. In order to do this, children must be able to relate freely to other children and they must have adult guidance for meeting a variety of situations.

Significance of Working with Parents

To suggest at this point that the role of the parent must be given careful consideration hardly seems necessary. Most parents want the best for their children but often their knowledge of education is limited to their own experience as a child in a school which was past oriented. We must help parents look at their children's education from the perspective of the child's future world and the kind of skills needed to adapt to the many changes both in personal and occupational life. It seems clear that the school alone cannot accomplish all that is needed for successful coping with tomorrow's world— that this is a job for both the school and the parents. Our recent research, which shows greater success for preschool programs when parents are involved, provides the beginning support, but we need to extend this research to provide greater insight into ways that parents and schools can work together more successfully. Value conflicts must be resolved and consistent directions for programs must be developed.

CONCLUSION

Fortunately, those concerned with the planning of educational programs can usually see ways the programs need improvement. To the current concerns we need to add recognition of the need for planning ways to develop future-oriented skills. We need to focus more on the kinds of skills children will need to cope with tomorrow's world. This requires a different perspective from that commonly held. The degree to which success will be attained will be determined by the insight the adults have into the kinds of skills that will be needed and by their abilities to guide the children's learning. Since we are talking of the future, none of us knows for sure what will be needed, but creative adults who help children cope with situations in creative ways will do much to provide hope for the future.

References

Kagan, J. "The Resilient Child." In *One Child Indivisible,* edited by J. D. Andrews. Washington, D.C.: National Association for the Education of Young Children, 1975.

Moore, R. S., and Moore, D. R. "Early Schooling for All?" *Congressional Record* 118, no. 167 (1972): E8726-E8741.

Pierce, C. "The Preschooler and the Future." *The Futurist,* February 1972, pp. 13-15.

Shane, H. G. "Education for Tomorrow's World." *The Futurist,* June 1973, pp. 103-106.

Singer, B. "The Future-Focused Role-Image." In *Learning for Tomorrow,* edited by A. Toffler. New York: Vintage Books, 1974.

Toffler, A., ed. Introduction to *Learning for Tomorrow.* New York: Vintage Books, 1974.

Toffler, A. *Future Shock.* New York: Random House, 1970.

Office of Human Development Services, Department of Health, Education and Welfare.

PARENTING, THE FAMILY AND THE SCHOOL

A major issue in the field of Early Childhood Education is the family, the relationships, and it's influence on the young child's development and learning. Smith's "How Could Early Childhood Education Affect Families? relates educator's concern over effective collaboration of families, educators and helping professionals in providing the child with a quality developmental experience.

Burton White's paper "Reassessing Our Educational Priorities," and Sroufe's "Attachment and the Roots of Competence emphasize the importance of the role of the family as the child's first educational delivery system. The foundations of educational capacity: language development curiosity, social development and the roots of intelligence, occur during the first three years, when the primary attachment is to the parents. The mother role as the source for love, and a strong self-image is the subject of Jerome Kagen in "The Parental Love Trap."

Posing the question "Who Will Rear Our Children?" Hawkes suggests that child rearing, care and education should become a shared function between families and those institutions created to support the family.

Today parent's are encouraged to assume an active role in the decision making process affecting the education of their children. The parent-school relationship as a complex set of interactions dependent upon attention to a number of sensitive variables is described in "Parent-Teacher Interaction: A Developmental Process." "Could a Tutor Help Your Child?" extends the parent's responsibility outside the classroom in meeting the child's learning needs.

The importance of the family, and their relationships, upon the total development of children is becoming increasingly clear. With respect to cooperative educational decisions, it is imperative that teachers and parents each examine their own roles and responsibilities with respect to children and their learning. Through continuous growth and by taking the risks that close relationships require, today's adults can give the next generation a head start in realizing their full potential.

How Could Early Childhood Education Affect Families?

Marilyn M. Smith

Marilyn M. Smith, Ed.D., is Executive Director of the National Association for the Education of Young Children. She is a former nursery school teacher and college professor in early childhood development and education.

Much earlier in my professional career my statements were fraught with answers. But experience has taught me two important things. One, family and education issues are extremely complex, and I am no longer so sure about those definitive answers. Two, I have observed that people can be much more helpful by sharing with each other productive ways of thinking about an issue. Thus, this article will not attempt to offer specific answers to the question raised in the title; it will suggest different ways of thinking about families and their children.

I would like to begin by sharing a simple concept that I find extremely useful in my own thinking: The questions we ask are frequently much more important and deserve much more attention than the answers. If we are asking the wrong questions, what use is the answer?

A classic example of being misled by the wrong question is found during the initial years of Head Start when the continuation of funding for this innovative program was almost lost due to the question being asked. During those beginning years of Head Start, evaluators most frequently asked: "Will there be a significant increase in children's scores on standardized IQ tests?"

We were in the midst of a comprehensive, new preschool initiative whose purposes included—

- enlarging a child's repertoire of knowledge;

- increasing self-confidence;

- promoting curiosity and initiative;

- improving verbal skills;

- providing nutrition;

- providing health/dental assessment and treatment; and

- involving parents in the education of their children.

Yet decisions regarding the continuation of the program were to be based on the answers to one question—answers concerned with the results of standardized IQ tests (which are highly suspect as meaningful measures of cognitive development in preschoolage children).

This example highlights the importance of giving increased attention to formulating relevant questions about young children and their families. Irrelevant questions can control and direct our inquiry in fruitless pursuits.

Are We Asking the Wrong Question?

I propose that the wrong question is being asked in the assigned title "How Could Early Childhood Education Affect Families?" This title suggests some assumptions that I consider questionable.

This society has a history of rationalizing children's programs and services by presenting them as essential to some group other than children.

What about Children?

We might be closer to a more productive question if we substituted the word *children* for the word *families*. "How could early childhood education affect *children*?" This society has a history of rationalizing children's programs and services by presenting them as essential to some group other than children. Significant government initiatives in children's programs have come in response to economic crisis rather than concern about improving the quality of life for children:

The 1930s—the Great Depression. Children's programs were initiated and funded to provide jobs.

The 1940s—World War II. Children's programs were funded to allow women to join the work force in the war factories.

The 1960s—the War on Poverty. Head Start was initiated as one of the many approaches to improve economic opportunities.

It is interesting to ponder why we as a society are still unwilling to state straightforwardly that the developmental needs and rights of young children are the reasons for providing early childhood programs and services.

What about Society?

Another concern I have about the question posed in the title is that in the process of focusing on the family as the major reason for providing educational services for young children, we will be perpetuating this society's inclination to expect families to carry the entire responsibility for child development/nurturance without assistance from the community and society.

Numerous factors far outside the control of families are having an increasingly powerful influence on the capability of families to parent constructively and competently. I would like to focus on one of the most powerful factors—economic security. Effective parenting requires money and time:

Money for the essentials of shelter, food, medical services, and education.

Time for the adult/child interactions necessary for social, emotional, language, intellectual, and physical development of infants, toddlers, and children.

Yet for American families in the 1970s, efforts to acquire the necessary money frequently result in less time with children.

For most American families the motivation to provide well for their children is not the major problem.

In a high percentage of families with children—

- both parents are working,
- parents are carrying more than one job, and
- there are increasingly more single parent families.

All of these realities contribute to less time for parenting.

For most American families the *motivation* to provide well for their children is not the major problem. Rather, the *capability to provide* may be the more productive issue to pursue. In order to do this I suggest we examine "How could early childhood education affect children?" thus assisting families in providing what they want for their children.

Early Childhood Education Defined

To pursue the question of how early childhood education could affect children, we need to establish a working definition for "early childhood education." This term has come to be used rather loosely to stand for any form of group care of young children, but early childhood *education* may or may not be occurring in group care programs.

2. FAMILY

The Purpose of Early Childhood Education

The aim of education is to facilitate development. The aim of early childhood education is to facilitate the development of young children. Note what the goal of education is not. The goal of education is not maturation. It is not the goal of early childhood education to teach growing tall. It is not the goal of early childhood education to teach conservation.

The goal of early childhood education is to facilitate—

- cognitive development,
- emotional development,
- social development, and
- motor development.

Early childhood educators acknowledge the important role of maturation in these forms of development, but accompanying this is a high degree of respect for the importance of the quality of the experiences available to children in their early years.

The Strategy of Early Childhood Education

Early childhood education, as one strategy for facilitating the development of young children, sets about to increase the availability of—

- developmentally appropriate activities,
- adult/child interactions, and
- child/child interactions,

which will facilitate rather than inhibit the fulfillment of each child's potentiality.

The Setting for Early Childhood Education

There are many settings in which developmentally appropriate experiences for young children could occur. The setting itself is not a predictor of the quality and appropriateness of the activities and interactions for any or all of the children experiencing them. It is possible for appropriate early childhood education experiences to occur in—

- nursery schools;
- the family with parents, relatives, and friends;
- group day care centers for infants, toddlers, and preschoolers;
- home-based day care;
- Head Start programs;
- parent/child centers;
- front of the television; and
- home visitor parent training programs.

Great numbers of America's children will not receive appropriate developmental opportunities during their early years unless there is assistance available to their parents to help them achieve such experiences for their children.

How Could Early Childhood Education Affect CHILDREN?

Having established the purpose, strategy, and setting of early childhood education, let's return to the question, "How could early childhood education affect children?" One way to think about this question is to examine the chances for any American child born in the late 1970s to experience developmentally appropriate activities and interactions with people.

Environmental Statistics for America's Children of the 1970s

In order to contemplate the chances for a child to obtain a good orientation and foundation for a lifetime of successful learnings, consider this list of some environmental statistics that impact on America's children of the seventies. Try to predict the potential for developmentally appropriate opportunities to occur under these circumstances.

1. Contemplate the chances of a child's mother being employed outside the home:

   - During a child's infancy and toddlerhood, the chance is one in three (Women's Bureau 1977).

- Between the ages of three and five, there is close to one chance in two (Women's Bureau 1977). During 1948, there was only one chance in eight.

- For the schoolage child, there is more than one chance in two that mother will be employed (Women's Bureau 1977).

2. What chance is there that a child will be born to a family living in poverty? One chance in six.

3. The possibility of a child spending part of his or her childhood in a one-parent family is two chances in five (Keniston 1977).

4. What chance is there that a child's mother will be in her adolescent years? One chance in five (Children's Bureau 1978).

5. Who could project the number of children living in families experiencing high degrees of stress—people troubled by economic, social, and emotional burdens?

6. What chance is there that a young child will not be immunized against early childhood diseases? Two out of every five children are not immunized, thus making them vulnerable to contracting a lifelong disability (*America's Children 1976*).

7. About twelve percent of America's children suffer from handicapping conditions, and there is a very low probability that a child's problem will be identified before entering public school (*The Role of the Family in Child Development* 1975).

It is difficult to contemplate these statistics and not conclude that great numbers of America's children will not receive appropriate developmental opportunities during their early years unless there is assistance available to their parents to help them achieve such experiences for their children.

How could society assist and support, yet not control, families as they attempt to provide developmentally appropriate experiences for their children?

Elements of Developmentally Appropriate Experiences for Young Children

Let's examine the kinds of responses, experiences, and interactions that every new human being requires to obtain a good orientation and foundation for a lifetime of successful learning. The key question throughout this description is: How could society assist and support, yet not control, families as they attempt to provide these experiences for their children?

Predictability and Responsiveness. During the early days and weeks of infants' lives, they need many chances to learn that in a number of ways their unknown world is a predictable place. These new human beings must learn that some consistent adult will respond to their signals of the need for food, warmth, turning, and dryness. Only then can newborns begin to establish a comfortable expectation of being able to control to a certain extent, as opposed to that stressful feeling of helplessness.

- The infant cries—hopefully, someone responds with food, comfort, or dry diaper.

- The child smiles—hopefully, someone smiles back.

- The baby coos—hopefully, someone coos back.

- The infant stretches for a toy out of reach—hopefully, someone brings it closer so it can be grasped.

If these "hopefullies" become "certainties," these tiny human beings will begin to develop a firm knowledge of some predictability and control which in turn encourages them to explore new situations and new people—an extremely important factor for future development.

Stimulation and Opportunities for Varied Experiences. All forms of development—cognitive, language, motor, etc.—are directly related to opportunities to practice, experience, and receive feedback.

Not long ago, I was browsing in a bookstore and became intrigued by a toddler who was moving books stacked on a low shelf from one pile to another. There was an extreme variance in the size and weight of the books. At first the toddler used both hands to pick up each book. Then he began making judgments about when a book was light enough to carry with only one hand, thus being able to carry one in each hand. Then the toddler started to move a book that was the size and weight of a large encyclopedia. The book fell to the floor. He picked it up and continued to move other books. Later he came to another book the size of an encyclopedia and this time adjusted his body and exerted the necessary strength to move the book without it falling. Just imagine the inefficiency of trying to tell this child how to judge differences in weight and how to adjust his body and muscles to lift different weights and sizes. Look at the rapid, efficient learning that occurred when he simply had the opportunity to practice, experience, and receive feedback.

The point of this example is certainly not that every child needs to be taken to a bookstore to lift books, but that children cannot develop cognitive skills, concepts, and the ability to use symbols in a vacuum or a bland environment. Children need opportunities to *experience* a variety of materials, people, and places with adults or older children who can answer questions and stimulate further exploration. The young child who experiences a dull, repetitive environment, day after day, simply does not have the opportunity to exercise mind and body toward new skills and understandings. The young child who watches several hours of television every day is missing developmentally essential learning opportunities from interactions with peers, with materials, and with adults.

The unknown factor is how many thousands of children are subjected to the crippling experience of bland, nonstimulating,

nonresponsive environments. It cannot be predicted from obviously observable circumstances. Neither income level nor whether a child is in his or her own home or in out-of-home care predicts if a child is experiencing a rich, responsive environment.

Many believe that young children's major needs are for physical well-being and that intellectual development occurs only at those times when it has been planned for. Too often we view the minds of children like the light in our refrigerator. Just as the refrigerator light only functions when we open the door, we frequently act as though children's minds will stay turned off until we open the door with a planned intellectual experience. Children's minds, at least in the beginning, do not have an off and on button like the light in the refrigerator. Whatever children are experiencing, it influences the development of their foundation for intelligence, their attitudes, values, and aspirations.

Experiences with Symbolization. Competent use of symbol systems (language, gestures, numbers) forms the foundation for communication, logical thought, and manipulation of concepts. Children's development of symbol systems occurs by building bridges between direct experiences and verbal or nonverbal symbols for each experience. A crude form of symbolization at work is viewed when infants repeat the same sound to signal wanting mother or food, etc. However, in this example the infants have created their own symbol system and the adults do the translating. The challenge ahead for children is to decode the existing symbol systems of the world in which they live. Also, consider the many children who must face the challenge of learning to decode more than one language or dialect.

If anyone fails to appreciate the complexity and difficulties in gaining mastery of the world's symbol systems, just observe us as adult citizens of the United States currently trying to master the metric system. The symbol 98° Fahrenheit has real meaning to me—I can almost feel the meaning of that symbol. But 37° Celsius simply does not raise within me the same understanding. The difference, of course, is practice in attaching a specific symbol to an experience. Or recall traveling in a country where you did not know the language. Remember those feelings of uncertainty and vulnerability and empathize with the challenge that faces every infant and toddler. Appreciate the importance of assisting children in building essential bridges between experiences and symbols. The most natural way for this to occur is for adults to provide labels when the child is experiencing something.

- The child is climbing up and down stairs, and the adult talks about up and down.
- The child is playing with the water faucet in the bathtub, and the adult provides the symbols of hot and cold at the appropriate time.
- The child is tasting different foods, and the adult labels the sweet and sour.

The key question, of course, is how much assistance will each child have in mastering this skill of building bridges between experience and symbols? Children cannot master this skill without interaction with others.

The list of experiences that are essential to development could go on and on. While these are intended as samples rather than a comprehensive listing, two other experiences children need during their formative years must be briefly mentioned.

Guidance Toward Impulse Control. There is an extremely important balance between protecting oneself and asserting autonomy, and adapting to requirements for social functioning. Perhaps this is best stated as developing respect for self which assists greatly in learning respect for others and leads to one more of the most important experiences children need from their world.

Being Valued. Good, assured feelings about self are essential to being able to immerse all of one's attention and ability into successfully mastering the abilities discussed above.

What chance is there of a significant attitude change in our society to "think children"?

How Can Children Be Assured of Developmentally Appropriate Experiences?

This is another question for which there is no answer, but I do have four suggestions to guide our thinking.

Think Children

Let's not lose, if we ever had it, the ability to put ourselves in the shoes of children and consider how it would feel to be denied the basic opportunities essential for developing our fullest potential. Isn't this a basic right of every human being? A fair shake at exercising our potential toward developing competence.

What chance is there of a significant attitude change in our society to "think children"? After all, children are no longer an economic asset providing an extra set of hands to help support the family. In fact, each child is an added economic burden. And what chance is there for a "think children" movement when children do not vote and do not have money to contribute to campaigns and causes?

This society has recently experienced a significant change in attitude resulting from the environmental protection movement. Fifteen years ago how many people were consciously aware of protecting the environment? But in just a few years, a sophisticated campaign implanted a few simple concepts in the minds of Americans. The environment cannot vote, the environment cannot speak for itself, but the environment requires nurturance if it is to serve us well in the future. If this society's consciousness was pricked to "think environmental protection," is there not even more chance that it can be pricked to "think children"? Why not a Children's Nurturance Movement, so there will be competent individuals left on earth to use this protected environment?

Think Prevention

We are a society that tends to think treatment rather than prevention—to think short-term rather than long-term. Brazelton's work (see page 4 of this issue) with mothers and their newborn infants is a powerful example of how a small amount of preventive effort can make a great difference in the future. New mothers are helped to feel confidence and skill in observing and responding to their infants. Brazelton's work has documented significant differences in the absence of future problems of mothers and infants who experienced this preventive counseling as compared to mothers who were not in the program.

If our vision were long-term, we would immediately recognize the valid economic reasons for spending money on individuals during their early developmental years. There is really no comparison between the money it would take to enhance opportunities during the early years of life for healthy development as opposed to the money society spends supporting the millions of adults in prison, in mental institutions, those who cannot work for various reasons, etc. Critics of increased federal investment in services for families and their children contend that this will lead to a welfare state. But increased support of such programs does not have to result in loss of individual incentive—not if continued funding of these programs is dependent on successfully accomplishing the goal: that the majority of individuals become adults who are prepared to carry their own survival, are prepared for competition, are prepared to define life according to their own goals and not be limited by drastic deficiencies.

Another example of our short-term vision is that in feeling that our only responsibility is for our own children, we fail to recognize that the quality of life they will experience as adults is highly dependent on the peers they will interact with in their world. The interdependence of individuals in this society is great.

Think Community

In America today there appears to be some confusion and uncertainty about making a strong commitment to children. The Coalition of Labor Union Women Child Care Seminar compared child care services in three other countries with those in the United States (Jordan 1977). It concluded that in Israel, Sweden, and France "the national community assumed as much responsibility for the child's success as did the family. This was in marked contrast to the dominant view in the United States that the nation is a collection of individuals each of whom bears the major responsibility for his or her offspring and that furthermore the community must only intervene after a crisis develops" (Jordan 1977).

The American family is shouldering a terrific responsibility. At the same time many members of the community are searching for relevance in their lives, particularly the young and the elderly. Herein lies a wealth of resources to add to the cadre of early childhood professionals to assist in the provision of nurturance, stimulation, and care for America's young children.

Think Quality

No setting, including the family, assures children of the opportunities needed to facilitate rather than inhibit the fulfillment of their potential. The determining factor is the quality of the activities, the quality of adult/child interactions, the quality of child/child interactions. For those of us involved in the provision of developmental experiences for young children, herein lies our biggest challenge: to endeavor to achieve training, standards, ethics, and funds that will enable us to assure each child quality developmental experiences.

Conclusion

I would like to reemphasize the challenges that face us. The challenge to formulate questions that will lead us closer to finding ways to assure children of their birthright—their right to opportunities that will facilitate the development of their potential. The challenge to establish effective collaboration of the resources of families, communities, and the helping professions to better serve America's children.

Leon Chestang has eloquently addressed these issues:

> And so I ask, who, if not us will
> nurture our children?
> Who, if not us will protect them?
> Who, if not us will assume
> responsibility for them?
> And who, if not us will assure them
> of their birthright?
> Who?   (*Chestang 1974*)

REASSESSING OUR EDUCATION PRIORITIES

Burton White

Burton White, Director, Preschool Project,
Harvard Graduate School of Education

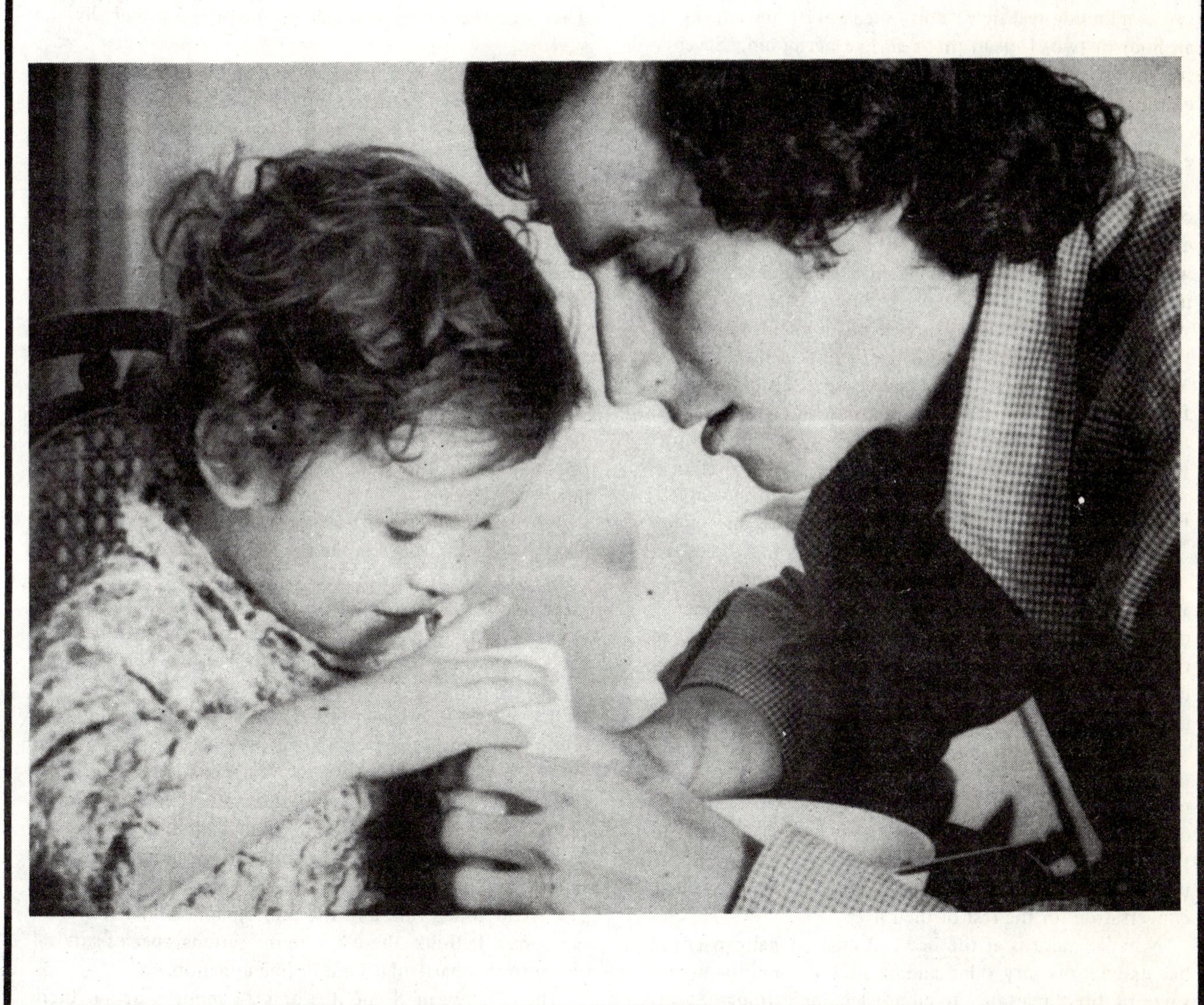

My purposes are to inform and attempt to influence you about a topic I think is of the highest priority in regard to national educational policy, our national resources and last, but far from least, the solidity of our young families. That topic is the role of the family in the education of a young child, particularly during the first three years of life.

My specialty is the study of what it takes to help each child make the most of whatever potential he brings into the world through the experiences of the first six years of life. That's my special role both as a member of the ECS Early Childhood Task Force and professionally. I believe that our current national educational policy is significant-

Reprinted with permission from The Education Commission of the States, Reprint No. 58, December 1974.

ly flawed in this particular problem area, that we're wasting much of our most precious natural resource — the people of the next generation — and that we're allowing the quality of everyday life for many of our young families to be far more stressful and far less rewarding than it could be. An awful lot of our most able young women have a miserable average day with two young children; very few people realize this, and the last ones to know are their husbands.

I've been conducting research on the early educational development of children for about 16 years now. When I say conducting research I don't mean every few weeks for an hour or two; I mean that's *all* I've been doing. Seventy-five per cent of my professional time has been on direct empirical research on this topic. I've come to some central conclusions that cry out for a new look at our national educational policy.

First of all, children start to learn long before they enter our education system. Traditionally, in this country and in every other Western country where there has been any writing on the history of education, the society first puts money into the job when the children get to be about 6 years of age. No society has ever put a lot of money into the first years of life, as far as I can find in the literature. Yet everybody knows that children are learning from the fitst day they come into the world. Although they don't usually learn to read, write or cipher much before 5 or 6 years of age, they do start, or fail to start, to learn in more fundamental areas that seem to determine directly how well they will later learn to read, write and cipher.

There are at least four fundamental learning topics that all children cope with before their third birthdays. These are not debatable points, by the way. First of all—language development. We have known for years that language growth starts and, in a large way, develops to a solid working capacity before the third birthday. Two- and three-month-old children don't process the meaning of words at all; at 6, 7, 8 months, they begin to understand the meaning of a few selected words — not surprisingly, words like their own name, Mommy, Daddy, kiss, bottle. That initial vocabulary is reasonably well understood. I think. By the time they're 3 years of age, most children have the capacity to understand most of the language they'll use in ordinary conversation for the rest of their lives.

Now language is at the heart of educational capacity. It has its own primary value and, in addition, an instrumental value of direct relevance to all intellectual learnings. Subtly, but just as importantly, it also underlies healthy social growth. Sociability in the first couple years of life depends for its good development on some capacities in the language area, particularly when it comes to other children.

The second major educational foundation that's undergoing development in this first three-year period is curiosity. What could be more important to whether a child learns anything — not just about academic subjects, but about the world at large, about what makes people tick, about how to become a good listener — than simple curiosity. It's the birthright of every child, with a few exceptions — the badly damaged children, for example, may have less of it. But even if a child comes from a bad home and is beaten regularly, it's very difficult to stamp out strong, basic, simple, pure curiosity in the first eight or nine months of life. It is, unfortunately, not that difficult to stamp it out in the next year or two or, if not stamp it out, suppress it dramatically or move it over into peculiar aberrant patterns. Take for example, the 2-year-old who looks at a new toy and, unlike other 2-year-olds, sizes it up mainly to see how he can use it to badger his mother. That's not sheer unqualified curiosity. That can also be very tough on a young mother, by the way.

Third major point — social development. In the last five or six years we've begun to apply a little more serious attention to the value of social goals for our educational system, although we're still limping along in this area. For years we've had soft-hearted early-education people saying a child is more than a brain, but they have seldom been listened to because most of them don't have doctorates and most of them don't have the gift of gab. I personally believe, and have a lot of research evidence to support it, that the social skills that develop in the first preschool years are every bit as important, every bit as instrumental, to the intellectual success of a student, for example, as the directly intellectual skills. Moreover, I think a lot of people in this country would be happier if the children we produced were not only bright but were people with whom they liked to live.

We are pretty clear now on the details of social development; we know that human infants won't survive without some sort of strong, protective attachment to an older, more mature, more capable human. And God or somebody else built into the creature a collection of attributes — tools, actually — that help in the cementing of a relationship to somebody.

For instance, that early social smile of the 3-month-old is not reserved for any particular person. It looks as if the child is using it on everyone who happens by. It's as if the species had a kind of first-stage guarantee of attractiveness. The 3- and 4-month-old child is an incredibly attractive, nice-to-live-with creature. He starts to giggle and becomes ticklish for the first time; he's given to euphoria a great deal. Now that's fun, and the photographers like it a great deal, but I think there's a more serious species-survival virtue to this particular kind of phenomenon.

Then, between 8 months and 24 months or so, there takes place one of the most gorgeous experiences you'll ever see. The child establishes a relationship—usually to the mother, because most of our children are still being brought up in homes by their own families. This is an incredibly complicated relationship, making most contracts pale in simplicity in comparison to it. The child learns thousands of things about what he can and can't do in his home, what he can and can't do in interactions with the primary care-taker, about how to read her different mood states, and an incredible number of other things. After all, little children have relatively little in the way of important obligations other than just enjoying themselves, and one of the few really overpowering interests of the child 8 to 24 months of age is that other key figure.

We have seen children at age 2 who are marvelous people to live with; they are free and easy; they are comfortable with their parents; they have gone by the negativism of the second year pretty well. They can play alone well. They are just a delight. On the other hand, how many times have you heard a mother of a 2-year old say he doesn't play alone well? That's synonymous for he's hanging onto my skirt or my slacks or my legs all day long. That situation can be very rough, especially if there is another child, 8 months of age, crawling around in the home simultaneously. When we see a child for the first time at 2 years of age, it's too late. They are crystallized into their basic social counters in the next year or two — to other children who come into the home, to older siblings, to other adults. A human personality is being formed during those first two years, and there is no job more important than doing that well.

Over and above that primal social development, we have the foundations of intelligence. There are all sorts of problems children can't solve in the first two or three years of life, but they are learning the tools of the trade, and this process is beautifully and brilliantly explained, in detail, in the work of Jean Piaget, the Swiss student of the growth of intelligence. From the very first years, children are very much interested in cause-and-effect relationships, in learning about simple mechanisms such as jack-in-the-boxes and flipping light switches on and off to see the consequences. Such events are trivial little things on the surface, but they indicate a very deep interest in how things work and in the various characteristics of physical objects. After all, these children haven't had a chance to examine many things first-hand, and most things, therefore, are new to them.

Now, these four topic areas are, I submit, the foundations of educational capacity. I'll repeat them: language development, curiosity, social development and the roots of intelligence. They are all undergoing basic formative development in the first three years of life, and the national education system essentially ignores that fact.

These fundamental learnings do not always go well. Indeed, there's reason to believe that failures in these learnings in the first years lead directly to underachievement in the elementary grades and beyond. We're getting there after the horse has left the barn.

Moreover, poor results or failures in the first years are extremely difficult to correct using any means we now have available. I'll repeat that because it's a very strong statement and I think I can support it — poor results or failures in the first three years are extremely difficult to correct using any means now available, be it $10,000 a year spent in a private tutoring situation or a Head Start or a Follow Through or a special education program.

In addition, relatively few of our children, regardless of the type of family that raises them—and that includes your families and mine, your grandchildren and mine—get as much out of the education of the first years as they might.

We are probably wasting substantial amounts of our most precious resource, the developed competencies of each new generation.

Can I back up these claims, or am I just another in a long list of education sensationalists?

Point one: Children who enter the first grade significantly behind their peers are not likely ever to catch up. There are exceptions, but the norm is that they fall further behind. This has been recognized educationally for a long time.

Let me tell you a little story about the origination of the Brookline Early Education Project. The superintendent of schools in Brookline, Mass., who's a very smart and vigorous fellow, called me one day and said, "I've been reading things like Benjamin Bloom's statement that most of intelligence is already developed by the time the child is 8, and that half of it is in by 4. I put that idea together with the experience we have in our school system [where, by the way, next year they have budgeted $2,600 for each child at the high school level and $2,000 for the elementary level]. I think I have a pretty good school system," he went on. "But I know that when I get a child in the first grade who already looks weak, I can't do much for him, even though I have one of the best special ed programs in the country."

Now as a reasonable man, he is driven to consideration of the topic of prevention. He has no choice. In fact, it's the same reasoning that led to the creation of Head Start. But here is a fellow who has no excuses — he has first-rate people, he has more money than God and he still cannot do the job.

He said, "I want to recommend that all kids get into our schools at age 4. What do you think of that as a good way to get into this problem?" I said, "That's a dumb idea." He said, "What do you mean? People have been telling me that public kindergarten is a great thing for all these years." I said, "Look, don't spend all your money on an expensive kindergarten program. Half or more of your kids are not going to get much out of it educationally, in my opinion. Take a look at what is going on in the first six years, not just in the fifth year. Try to get at the origin of educational deficits; try to prevent them. Try to help earlier in the game." And so we built the Brookline program.

Second point: The country has been working on prevention for nine years now in a very substantial way. Head Start's original central purpose, I remind you, was to prevent educational failure. Now, it has had lots of other purposes that have grown in emphasis in the last four or five years—better early health care, better social and emotional development. But don't you forget that the original rhetoric that sold Head Start was to try to prevent educational failure. That has been its core purpose. It has had a budget, most of you know, of several hundred million dollars a year, and it's been politically powerful. It has concentrated on the 3- to 5-year age period.

There are two conclusions I think can be easily drawn from the Head Start experience (so far) that are appropriate to this discussion: First, it doesn't often succeed in its prime goal (no matter what somebody working in a center tells you). The best objective evaluation of Head Start is that by and large, by itself, it hasn't had much success in preventing educational failure in the elementary grades. Second, serious deficits for many children are usually already visible at 3 years of age.

Point three: Except for the fewer than five per cent of our children born with serious defects or subjected to extreme abuse during the first year of life, serious educational deficits are not usually seen before 18 months of age. This point comes out of the educational and psychological research literature. The same children who are going to give you endless problems in the third grade look fine at age 1.

Point four: Educational failure begins to show itself toward the end of the second year of life. It is often very reliably detected at 3 years of age and nearly always detectable well before the first grade. Furthermore, educational underachievement by children who look average or slightly above average is quite likely, but has not really been investigated in a serious way as yet. After all, the emergency situation, as always, comes first.

What causes low achievement levels in children? Can we as educators do anything about this problem, or are genetics, for example, at the root of the problem? The question is a very complicated one, and I can't deal with it elaborately here. But I will summarize my position on the issue. We have no conclusive evidence as yet as to how much achievement is due to heredity and how much is due to environment. We have fragments of evidence, but nothing like the weight of evidence needed to resolve that issue on a scientific basis. My personal judgment is simply that both heredity and environment obviously play a role. Heredity certainly sets upper limits to development, but by itself it doesn't guarantee that those limits will be reached. If a child is seriously brain damaged, no matter how you work on his early education, he is never going to achieve the levels that an intact, well-educated child will. But if a child comes into the world with great genes, he is not going to make the most of that potential irrespective of what happens to him subsequently. By controlling his experiences, I can prevent any child in the world from learning to talk, I can prevent him from acquiring any of his skills.

Of course those are just the extreme cases. But my point is that so far we really haven't thoroughly understood what it takes to help each child make the most of the potential he has. We have no right to assume that, by hook or by crook, children are doing that. In fact, we have plenty of evidence that suggests that they are not. I've done more direct research on the role of experience in early development than all but a handful of people in the country, and I'm convinced of the power and relevance of early experiences in this area. Certainly until we have definite evidence to the contrary, the most sensible policy is to assume that early experience makes important differences and to do everything we can to make such experiences as beneficial as possible.

For now, let me point out that there seem to be at least three major obstacles that families face in doing the best job of educating their young children. But let me digress for just a moment. I very much endorse the concept that we are wasting resources and the need for public education. In terms of developmental day care it generally costs more than $3,000 per year, and it can go higher. I agree that this country is not going to make that kind of money available in the near future for all the kids who ought to have it or who need it.

The three major obstacles, then, that I see families coping with in trying to do the best they can for their children are: First of all, ignorance. They don't know how to do the job. They don't know, for example, about the poison-control data that says that most of our reported poisonings in childhood take place between 10 and 30 months of age. More importantly, they don't know why such poisonings take place at that age. They don't know that babies in that age range are incredibly curious, are inclined to use the mouth as an exploring organ and are unsophisticated about labels that have warnings on them.

Parents don't know the story of social development. They don't know, for example, that to be a 9-month-old *only* child means to live in a world that is full of happiness, sweetness, pleasant interpersonal relations. On the other hand, to have an older sibling at home who is 2 years old almost invariably means being on the receiving end of genuine hatred from time to time.

Now that sounds funny, but boy I'll tell you, it's a sad thing to watch a 9- or 10-month-old baby, when his mother isn't looking, trying to put up with the real physical threats of a 2- or 2½-year-old child who had previously thought the whole world was built for him. Now he's got to share it with this creature that's into his toys, that seems to have first place in his mother's affections, and so forth. It is painful for everybody. The older child is having a very tough time; the younger one is having a tough time and may be experiencing things that I don't think anybody should have to experience, if we can avoid it. The mother may be having the worst time of all. Some women spend the whole day trying to control two such children, trying to avoid the destruction of the baby; and the father comes home at night and wonders why the mother is tired. The simple fact is we don't prepare or assist people for this job. As long as you can mate, you are eligible to have a child and the responsibilities that go along with it. That's absolutely crazy.

The second major obstacle for parents is stress. The 8- to 24-month period is not only educationally critical, in my opinion, but it's also one of the most dangerous periods in life. I would guess that there is no period of life that is more dangerous in terms of maimings and accidental deaths.

Take, for example, an 8-month-old child who, for the previous three months or so, has had mature visual and auditory capacities, but hasn't been able to move his body anywhere. Move him to an upright posture, he can see out into the room. It's a new world for him; no matter how poor it is, it's all new to him, and somehow or other his species requires that he learn as much as he can during his early developmental years. Think of how much curiosity is building up inside that mind. Then all of a sudden he discovers he can get from here to there—and he goes. It's a very rare child who doesn't go. Children at this age are very much like puppies, kittens, even young horses I've been told, in their pure, unadorned curiosity. It's necessary for the species.

They go, but they don't know anything at all about the world. They don't know that if you lean on something very spindly, it will fall; they don't know that those beautiful rose-colored shards of glass from a broken vase are dangerous. Everything looks interesting, and one of the prime ways in which they explore something first hand is to immediately put it to the mouth. They are very impulsive at that age; they do not stop to smell, to savor or to sip; they just bring it quickly to the mouth.

We have to tell parents about these things. Why should they learn these things after they go to the pediatrician to have a child's stomach pumped? These aren't controversial matters. There's a lot of controversy in this field about some topics, such as how you should rear children, whether you should teach them to read at nine months, whether you should be stroking their limbs at four months for "tactile stimulation." There's a lot of controversy in that area, but there isn't any about safety.

Every family should know how to safety-proof a home for the child's first crawling efforts. Every family should know that a baby starts to climb at about 8 or 9 months of age, can generally only climb six or seven inches at that point, but by the time he's a year old will be able to climb units of 12 to 14 inches, which means that he can climb almost anything in a room. That sequence has very powerful everyday consequences for a family. It should be common knowledge. Why is learning to drive a car so much more important than learning how to parent a child? Does the high school curriculum have room for driver ed and no room for these topics?

Not only are the first years a dangerous period of life, but they mean extra work. The child crawling around the home makes a mess, and if your husband likes a neat home, that adds to the stress. In addition, if there's an older child who is less than three years older than the child, it's quite normal for there to be significant resentment on the part of the older child, and that also adds to the stress on the mother. Furthermore, when the child gets to be 16 or 17 months of age he starts testing his power with his mother. That's quite routine; almost everybody goes through it.

Some people find this very tough to take. So, there is a lot of stress involved in raising a young child, and raising two or three closely spaced ones creates almost an intolerable amount. Sometimes it is not tolerated, and women crack up and marriages crack up.

Third obstacle: lack of assistance. Mother usually faces this job alone.

So the three obstacles I see through our research are,

first, ignorance—they aren't prepared for the job, they aren't knowledgeable, indeed there's an awful lot of misinformation around; second, stress; and third, lack of assistance. That is a tough collection of obstacles to get through.

If there is a role for education, what is it? We must accept the fact that professional educators, working directly with children, especially children over 6 years of age, have much less influence on development than was previously thought. This is, by the way, the major implication of the 1966 U.S. Office of Education report by James Coleman, *Equality of Educational Opportunity*.

I remember a poignant story about a teacher in IS 201 in the heart of New York about six or seven years ago describing his classroom, a third-grade classroom. He said that at no time could he count on more than 30 per cent of the youngsters to be in their seats, and at no time could he count on more than half of them to even be in the room. And he said, "Somehow or other, I'm not doing well in that class." And I said, "How on earth can you expect to do well in that class?" I think teachers have been taking a terribly bad rap in this country. Educating a child is a partnership between the family and the professional educator. I think the senior partner is the family.

The second thing educators must do is recognize that the family ordinarily is the first educational delivery system for the child and seriously accept and face the consequences of that fact.

Third, we should prepare and assist the family for that fundamental educational job.

How do we prepare and assist the family to give the child a solid educational foundation? Here are a couple of suggestions.

Item one: Long before the child is born, we should teach each and every prospective parent all the known and accepted fundamentals about educational development in the first years of life. How do we do this? I would suggest through required courses in the high schools and, second, through public television. I would also suggest that neither of these vehicles costs a great deal. We might delete the geography of India for a year or for one semester.

Item two: Just before and soon after the baby is born is a special time. A lot of parents are traumatized. They suddenly come face to face with the reality that they've got the responsibility for this fragile little thing and they don't know what they're going to do. That can be a very tough experience. I've had lots of young parents express that fear spontaneously to me. Suggestion: Teach each and every parent whom you missed the first time around the same information and routinely provide refresher information to the remainder. How? Offer adult education courses, year in and year out, for pregnant women and their husbands. Perhaps provide the video-cassette or filmed minicourses in hospitals during the lying-in period. That's being done in Hawaii, by the way. Most of these things are being done somewhere in the country. Provide high-quality public television material on a continuous basis. There's no reason why it cannot be done. I'm involved in commercial television right now, talking about educating an infant. It works well. The viewing audience is dedicated; they watch that program like hawks. If I say something wrong, they're right on it. It can be done, and it can be fun, too.

In addition, just before or soon after the child is born, provide a low-cost education early detection and referral service to every family, with a promise that if a family participates, its children cannot go through the preschool years with an undetected educational handicap. You can make that promise and you can deliver on it for about $200 per year for a child.

Item three: After the child is born, for his first six years of life, especially the first three, I suggest the following: make available continuing, low-pressure, strictly voluntary training for parents. How? Through resource centers and a home-visiting program. I'm talking, you'll notice, about working through the family, not bypassing it and going directly to the child. Provide for monitoring educational development as an extension of that early detection and referral system, again through medical psychology and educational teamwork in resource centers, for about $200 a year.

Provide general assistance for parenting, again with a focus on education, in the following ways: Lend materials like toys and books out of your resource center. Have films and pamphlets available. Have professionals available for parents to talk with once in a while. Have other parents available so that people can talk to each other about their frustations and their joys.

Provide free baby-sitting for psychological relief for parents. This is not day care; I'm talking about a few hours a week when a mother can just leave her child without guilt, and just get away.

On the other hand, a home-visiting service, especially for families who want it and who have a little more difficulty with their children and fewer resources than average, again

does not have to be a frightfully expensive affair. We find if you go very often to a home, more than every two or three weeks, it gets uncomfortable. There is not enough to do for most families; so if you go for an hour or two every six, seven or eight weeks we guess that's plenty. These kinds of programs are nowhere near as expensive as running a conventional center; nothing like it.

Item Four: Provide referral service for special needs, an ombudsman function. How do you do it? Through neighborhood resource centers. Provide remedial assistance as soon as possible. If an early detection program finds a borderline hearing difficulty in a 6-month-old child, we can do things about that today. It's scandalous for this country to continue to let some fraction of our children go through primary language acquisition with untreated, unnoticed hearing deficits. The screening examination can be done for $15 or so and the occasional higher level diagnosis will cost $50 to $75. But what an investment!

I think it's fair to say that the entire task force of the ECS Early Childhood Project agrees with the general desirability of strengthening the family ofr its role as the child's first educational delivery system. Exactly how far to go in terms of dollars per year, of course, is not fully agreed upon. I suggested to you that for an expenditure of perhaps $300 or $400 per year we probably could do the bulk of what needs doing on this topic for most families (not for the very special-need families; they are a much more expensive proposition). Exactly which ideas to use, again, are not fully agreed upon, but I submit to you that there is a core of fundamental information about safety, about social development, about motor development that most people do agree on, and that such information could be very, very useful to young families. Much needed assistance is feasible today. You could spend $1,000 a year for an average family, but I think you could do it quite nicely for $400 or $500. And there just isn't a better way to spend that money than to invest in improving the quality of our earliest educational system.

ATTACHMENT AND THE ROOTS OF COMPETENCE

L. ALAN SROUFE

Some two-year-olds approach problems with great enthusiasm. They are eager, persistent, and flexible. They show obvious joy in the mastery of problems and are not easily frustrated. If they do get stuck, they seek help from their caregivers.

Other children present a different picture. They give up quickly or spend a great deal of time in activities that bear no relation to the problem. They may whine, pout, fuss, or become frustrated—stamping their feet, banging objects, or becoming petulant. Even in the absence of frustration some children show no joy in mastery, no eagerness in the face of challenge. They either ignore their caregivers' suggestions, refuse them loudly, or do exactly the opposite of whatever is suggested—even when it keeps them from solving the problem. Some throw tantrums or hit or kick their caregivers.

Do such wide differences among young children reflect the emergence of individual personalities? If we are observing characteristic behavior in these children, can we predict later developmental problems and later competence from what we have seen? Finally, have these children simply been different from birth, or has their early experience—including the quality of the relationship with their caregivers—played an important role in the development of their personalities?

The issue of whether a baby's early experiences affect the development of attitudes, fears, and expectations that will later influence the way he or she behaves as a child or an adult is important. Although some researchers profess to find little continuity in human development, the question is not settled. If it is possible to show strong links in the behavior of individual children over time and across situations, we clearly have captured something enduring in the child. And if we can predict which children are likely to show later developmental problems, it may be possible to intervene before the problems develop. At the same time, establishing continuity in behavior is important for understanding the roots of competence and the nature of human development itself.

But attempts to predict individual development are doomed if researchers simply measure the same behavior throughout a baby's growth. Infants and young children develop rapidly—they learn new behavior, and old behavior takes on new meaning. All behavior becomes increasingly complex. Two-year-olds, for example, are learning language and solving problems, running and climbing, and showing complex emotions like shame and defiance. None of these activities are characteristic of young infants. Babies babble, crawl, uncover objects, and push away the hand that wipes their noses, but we cannot assume that these actions are identical to later reactions, even when they appear similar. Attempts to show that particular behavior or capacities are stable have consistently failed.

Early attempts to show consistency in characteristics like dependency or aggression also failed—and for good reason. Dependency, for example, is a natural, universal state in infancy. Seeking physical closeness and contact is both normal and adaptive. Therefore such behavior in a baby cannot indicate whether he or she will be overly dependent as a four-year-old. Aggression, on the other hand, is not within the capacity of the infant, so preschool aggression cannot be predicted from an infant's vigor in nursing, an activity which might be used by researchers as an early measure of aggressiveness. Vigorous babies may or may not be vigorous toddlers, but if they are, they may be vigorous in climbing and in play without necessarily being aggressive. In general, all approaches that have assumed some simple identity between earlier and later behavior have failed.

In our work at the University of Minnesota we assumed that despite rapid advances in development, and despite dramatic changes in a child's behavior, there is continuity in the quality of a child's adaptation, in his or her personal style or orientation. The child who functions well emotionally and socially at one

1

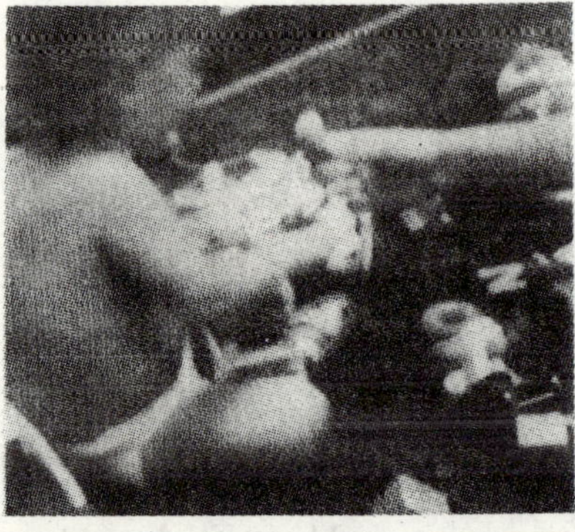

2

In an unfamiliar playroom a securely attached baby leaves her mother (1) and plays happily (2). The approach of a stranger does not bother her (3). Left alone in the room, the baby becomes distressed (4),

3

age will be likely to function well at the next, even though different areas of behavior might be examined. Although toddlers are much more developed, they are fundamentally the same people they were as infants, and four-year-olds are the same people they were as toddlers.

Thus by assessing how well a child functioned with respect to the important issues in one developmental period it should be possible to forecast the quality of the child's functioning in the next period. As complex and subtle as the task was, we sought to capture something basic about the nature of the individual personality as it emerged in infancy and as it was manifest in the preschool years.

The developmental issue we decided to study in infancy was the effectiveness of the attachment relationship between the infant and his or her primary caregiver. (In order to avoid confusing caregivers and babies, I will refer to the caregiver as "she," since in most cases the caregiver is a mother, and to the baby as "he.") Attachment refers to the special intimacy and closeness that develop toward the end of the first year between the infant and his caregiver. The infant feels comfortable and secure with her

and derives comfort and security from her presence. The baby who is doing well is the baby who has a healthy attachment to his caregiver, a relationship that promotes exploration and mastery of the environment. In studying the way infants used the relationship with their mothers to support their exploration and play, we felt we could capture the quality of their adaptation.

We predicted that the one-year-old infant who showed a secure, effective attachment would also be competent and successfully autonomous as a toddler, in terms of both his style in approaching problems and his emotional involvement in them. Such a link was entirely reasonable. The infant who uses the caregiver as a base for moving out into the world, and as a haven when threatened or distressed, develops motor skills and a sense of himself as effective. In sharing his play with his caregiver at a distance, the infant evolves a new way of maintaining contact while operating independently. The infant is free to invest himself in challenging the environment because he is confident that he can maintain his tie with his caregiver even while he is widening his world.

By the preschool years, children's capacity for independent functioning has vastly increased. They are concerned with developing peer relations, establishing their sense of themselves as boys or girls, expanding their skills at symbolic play and fantasy, and learning to manage their impulses. Children who have adapted well will look at challenging situations positively, and their expectations concerning people will also be positive. Such a child should be competent with peers and well liked by teachers, but this competence should be predicted not from measures of play between infants but from the quality of the attachment relationship between infant and caregiver.

If later personality can be predicted from studies made during infancy, then attachment is a likely starting point, for it is the focus of social, emotional, and

The attachment between mother and baby
can support or retard the later development
of healthy independence and personal competence.

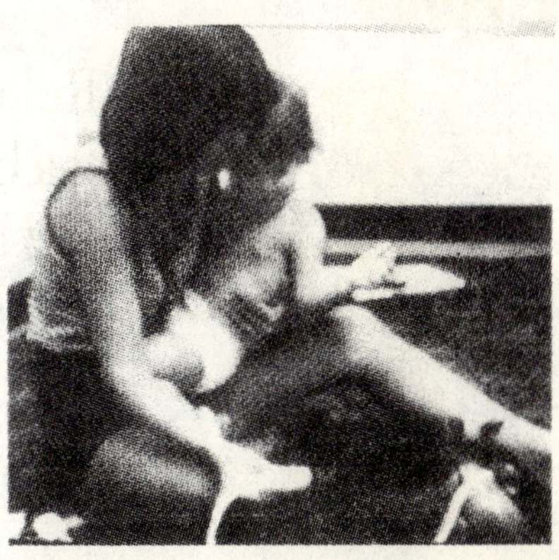

6

5

4

and the return of the stranger fails to pacify her (5). Only the mother's return can bring comfort (6), and the baby seeks contact as soon as her mother enters the room.

mental development in infancy. A great deal of the infant's experience occurs with, or is controlled by, the caregiver. The tendency to become attached to an available figure has been built into the infant through the course of evolution, and virtually all infants become attached. But the quality of the attachment relationship varies widely, and these differences must have a strong impact on the emerging person. We are all defined by our relationships with others. Within this first relationship, the child also learns a great deal about his impact on the world—about who he is.

In our studies we used Mary Ainsworth's system for assessing attachment. In this system the quality of a baby's attachment is defined in terms of its balance with exploration—the use of the caregiver as a base for exploration and as a source of comfort when distressed—and in terms of the baby's effectiveness in reestablishing contact following separation. The emphasis is on the organization of the baby's behavior across contexts that vary in their degree of stress. Separation and reunion experiences are especially critical for the one-year-old infant and are therefore central in assessing attachment. In Ainsworth's system there are three major patterns of attachment: securely attached infants; anxiously attached, avoidant infants; and anxiously attached, ambivalent in-

fants. Obviously, only the first group shows good adaptation.

If a securely attached baby comes into an unfamiliar playroom, he leaves his mother and becomes absorbed in the toys, though he may share his play with her. He rarely becomes wary in response to a stranger who chats with his mother before engaging him in play. Although he may hesitate at first, he soon warms up and begins to play with the stranger.

When his mother departs, leaving him with the stranger, stress is presumed to increase. Even so, some securely attached babies do not become upset. Distress at separation is influenced by a host of factors, including the baby's mood, hunger or fatigue level, health, age, recent experience, degree of involvement with the stranger, and understanding of the situation. Some babies do become upset. On reunion they go directly to their mothers, actively seeking contact and maintaining it until they are settled. They often cling, sink in, mold, or otherwise clearly show their desire for contact and its effectiveness in providing comfort. Securely attached infants who are not distressed by separation commonly do not seek physical contact on reunion; instead they smile, bounce, vocalize, or show a toy, actively seeking interaction instead of contact. They are happy to see their mothers.

When a securely attached infant is left alone, his stress is greatly increased. Many 12- to 18-month-old infants are obviously distressed, and almost all reveal

some degree of upset by subdued or otherwise altered play. Although such an infant may become more settled when a stranger enters, and may even promote contact with the stranger, he clearly shows that this contact will not do. He may continue to be distressed or he may mix contact seeking with squirming and pushing. When his mother returns, he immediately leaves the stranger and goes to her.

It is impossible to reduce the quality of attachment to a single kind of behavior. Securely attached infants may or may not seek physical contact with their mothers. They may cry a lot or a little. Sometimes they are friendly to strangers, at other times they are not. But securely attached infants do actively reestablish some kind of contact on reunion, whether physical or social, and they are able to use their mothers as a base for exploration and play.

Anxiously attached babies show quite different patterns of behavior. The ambivalent group does little exploring in an unfamiliar playroom, even when the mother is present. They may cry and seek physical contact before they are separated. They are obviously wary of the stranger and acutely distressed when the mother leaves—even when they are not left alone. Most significant, they cannot settle down when the mother returns. Some clearly reveal their ambivalence by mixing contact seeking with contact resistance, behaving much as distressed infants do with strangers. They may push the mother away, or hit, kick, or bat away offered toys. Others simply continue crying, fussing, or pouting. Such an attachment relationship obviously fails to support the infant in his

Relationships between the quality
of a baby's attachment at 18 months
and his adaptive functioning at two
years were dramatic and powerful.

1

2

3

To get the piece of candy from the plastic box (1), this two-year-old must weight the lever with a block. The problem is beyond her capacity, but (like other children who had been

exploration and mastery of new surroundings.

The other major group of anxiously attached infants is not so obvious. In an unfamiliar playroom, infants in this avoidant group separate readily from their mothers and do not seek contact. A baby from this group is not wary of a stranger and does not cry when his mother departs, unless perhaps he is left alone. But when his mother returns, he greets her casually, if at all, and commonly shows frank signs of avoidance. He may look, turn, or move away, or start to approach his mother and then turn or back off. He typically settles down when a stranger enters the room. His avoidance of his mother becomes extreme during a second reunion when he is under increased stress. The more these infants are distressed, the less likely they are to seek contact. The system is turned around and has become maladaptive.

In our research Everett Waters, Leah Matas, and I sought to determine whether the quality of an infant's attach-

ment would indicate the nature of his or her emerging personality. First we examined 108 infants, some at 12 and then at 18 months, others at only one of these ages. Each time independent coders rated them according to Ainsworth's system. Ninety percent of these suburban infants fit one of Ainsworth's three patterns closely. Of the 50 infants seen at both ages, 48 were placed in the same group at 18 months as they had been at 12 months. A baby may have become less (or more) upset the second time, may have smiled and vocalized more (or less), or may have sought less (or more) physical contact, but the quality of attachment had remained the same.

Demonstrations of reliability and stability are essential starting points for any attempts to show long-range continuity in development. In addition to our own results we had Ainsworth's data showing that a baby's attachment pattern at 12 months could be predicted from an assessment of his mother's behavior from his sixth to his 15th week of life, and that the baby's behavior in the laboratory was related to his behavior at home.

If these measures of attachment were capturing something essential about the emerging personality of the child, then the differences in the quality of attach-

ment should have clear consequences for autonomous functioning in the next developmental period. To assess the quality of these babies' adaptations as two-year-olds, we selected a situation in which each toddler had to solve increasingly difficult problems. The early problems, such as pushing a toy from a tube with a stick, were easy for two-year-olds to solve. But the final problem—which required the child to weight down a lever with a block in order to raise candy through a hole in the top of a plexiglass box—was well beyond the capacity of a two-year-old. When the child got stuck, however, his mother was nearby to help him. As when the infants had been subjected to separation and stress, this procedure taxed their capacities for maintaining organized behavior and for drawing on their own resources and those of their mothers.

How quickly a child solved the problem was unimportant, just as at 12 or 18 months an infant's level of cognitive development was not our central in-

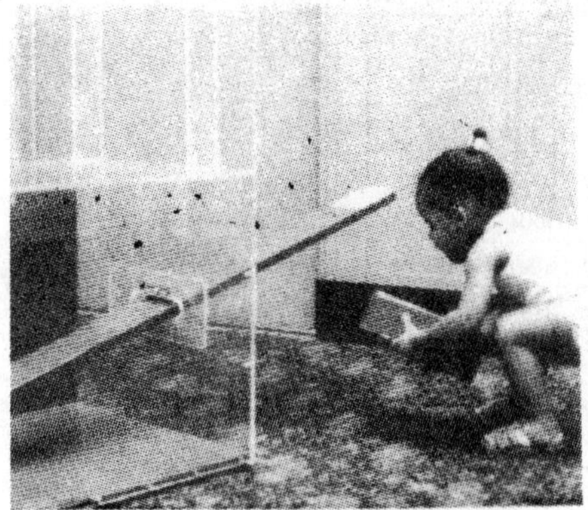

4

5

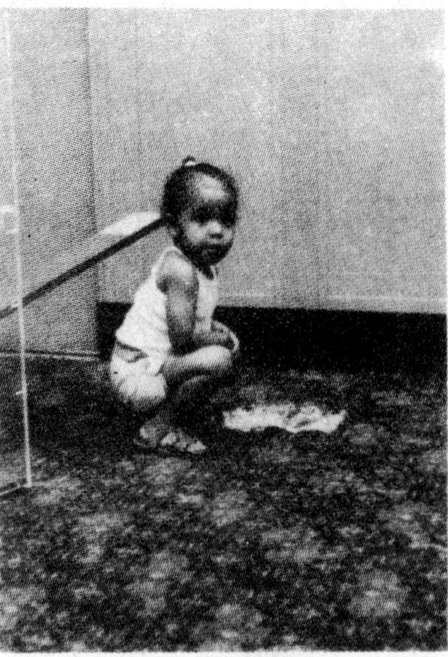

6

*securely attached as infants) she
accepts her mother's advice (2) and,
after testing the lever (3),
puts on the block (4), retrieves
the candy (5), and enjoys her treat.*

terest. We were interested in three aspects of competence: (1) emotional dimensions such as enthusiasm, positive feelings, and the ability to face challenges without becoming frustrated; (2) motivation, reflected by the time spent away from the task (the inverse of persistence); and (3) ability to use maternal assistance effectively, as shown by the child's compliance or attempted compliance, or by his ignoring suggestions, saying "no," acting aggressively, or throwing tantrums. We also assessed the quality of the mother's assistance (the timing, pacing, and clarity of her hints) and her degree of support (whether she encouraged, attended to, or was otherwise available to her child).

Relationships between the quality of a baby's attachment at 18 months and his adaptive functioning at two years of age were dramatic and powerful. Children who were assessed as secure in their attachment as infants were much more enthusiastic and persistent and showed more positive feelings than did children who had earlier been assessed as anxiously attached. The children who had been securely attached showed fewer negative emotions, and in a situation where assistance was essential, they were more compliant, threw fewer tantrums, and ignored or opposed their mothers less often. In contrast to the anxiously attached groups, they showed no aggression.

The relationships with the quality of maternal behavior impressed us even more. Mothers whose infants had earlier been assessed as securely attached were strikingly higher on both "supportive presence" and "quality of assistance" than were mothers of anxiously attached infants. The infant's attachment reflects the history of his interaction with his mother; and it is reasonable to expect that the caregiver of a securely attached infant will be similarly responsive in the child's second year. In our assessment of the infant's behavior we had apparently captured the quality of the mother-child relationship.

We had tested the children with the Bayley scales and knew that the three groups were similar in their general level of development, but we needed to make sure that we were not simply measuring intellectual capacity or some simple inborn trait of the infant. We also had to determine whether or not the continuity we observed was entirely a result of the mother's presence. Our final study was done in collaboration with Wanda Bronson of the University of California. As part of her studies of young children she video-taped 34 mothers and their 15-month-old infants in an unfamiliar setting, using a procedure similar to Ainsworth's. Bronson also had descriptive codings of these same children, which were made in a nursery-school setting when the children were three and a half years old. In the nursery school, two independent observers watched the children for five weeks and then arranged a series of statements according to how well they described each child.

We viewed only the infant-mother tapes and had no knowledge of the children's later behavior. But when our judgments of the infants' attachments were compared with codings of their behavior made more than two years later, relationships again were clear and powerful. Infants we assessed as secure in their attachment were distinguished by 11 of the 12 statements relating to competence with peers, and by five of the 12 statements relating to ego strength from the nursery-school study. As preschoolers, the securely attached infants were more purposeful, involved, and effective with peers than were the insecurely attached infants. There were no differences in the groups on a developmental level at 15 months or in IQ scores at three and a half years. Because mothers were not present when the children were assessed at nursery school, it was clear that the quality of infant-mother attachment indicated the child's emerging personality.

Why did we succeed in demonstrating continuity when others have failed? First, we assessed the child's overall quality of adaptation rather than particular capacities or behavior. Second, we emphasized emotions and motivation rather than intellectual abilities. Third, we linked our assessment to issues that are important in various periods of development. Finally, we began with measures having demonstrated power.

THE EMERGENCE OF PERSONALITY

PEER COMPETENCE	Securely attached babies	Insecurely attached babies	Level of significance*	Level of significance*	Insecurely attached babies	Securely attached babies	EGO STRENGTH
Sympathetic to peers' distress	16.7	8.3	.01	.04	10.2	13.2	Forcefully goes after what he wants
Spectator in social activities	8.2	12.2	.02	.05	10.0	11.8	Likes to learn new intellectual skills
Hesitant with other children	6.8	10.8	.03	.25	6.2	5.3	Does not persevere when goals are blocked
Characteristically unoccupied	7.3	9.4	.14	.36	9.6	8.8	Suggestible
Hesitates to engage	7.7	12.4	.007	.23	13.0	14.2	Becomes involved in whatever he does
Peer leader	10.4	6.5	.01	.15	11.4	13.2	Confident of own ability
Other children seek his company	12.4	7.5	.001	.01	7.4	4.8	Uncurious about the new
Attracts attention	11.2	6.8	.02	.01	8.3	12.8	Self-directed
Suggests activities	12.3	6.9	.005	.03	8.4	5.6	Unaware, turned off, "spaced out"
Socially withdrawn	6.7	12.1	.002	.19	11.0	12.5	Sets goals that stretch abilities
Withdraws from excitement and commotion	5.3	8.2	.03	.25	7.5	6.3	Samples activities aimlessly, lacks goals
A listener (not full participant in group activities)	8.3	11.8	.05	.38	7.0	6.4	Indirect in asking for help

*Any number lower than .05 reflects a statistically significant relationship. Numbers lower than .01 reflect highly significant relationships.

It should be pointed out that our studies and others demonstrating continuity have been the result of research with children in stable environments. In our study, infants came from two-parent families characterized by stable employment, a low divorce rate, and low mobility. Much greater change, toward both better and poorer adaptation, would be expected in studies of children from rapidly changing environments. Work by Byron Egeland and Amos Deinard, which is now in progress, shows this to be true.

Within our model of continuity, however, the issue is not stability but the coherence of individual development. We would not expect a child to be permanently scarred by early experience or permanently protected from environmental assaults. Early experience cannot be more important than later experience, and life in a changing environment should alter the quality of a child's adaptation.

Still, early experience may be of special importance in two ways. First, the child is engaged in active transactions with the environment. The child not only interprets experience, the child creates experience. As Alfred Adler has suggested, the child is both the artist and the painting. If because of early experience the preschooler isolates himself from the peer group, he removes himself further from positive social experiences. Second, if self-esteem and trust are established early, children may be more resilient in the face of environmental stress. They may show poor adaptation during an overwhelming crisis, but when the crisis has passed and the environment is again positive, they may respond more quickly. Even when floundering, some children may not lose their sense that they can affect the environment and that, ultimately, they will be all right.

In these first studies we did not explore temperament. Children also differ in their reactivity, their tempo, and their particular likes and dislikes. Children who are secure in their attachment may be highly active or placid, cuddly or stiff. Some toddlers are more interested in one kind of activity, some prefer another. Well-functioning infants and children do not fit one particular mode.

Moreover, every child will at times be difficult, irritable, or have tantrums. Even securely attached infants squirm, kick, and push away from strangers. It is not the capacity that distinguishes the children but when and how they show it. The securely attached infants who cooperated with their mothers in solving a problem were not so cooperative when they were asked to stop playing with attractive toys. In this situation they showed as much opposition as did anxiously attached infants.

The personality differences we stress cannot be reduced to temperament (though the influence of temperament is part of our current research). We emphasize the child's self-concept and his or her approach to problems and opportunities. A child who has a rapid tempo may be seething with anger, hostile to other children, unable to control his or her impulses, and filled with feelings of worthlessness. But a child who has a rapid tempo also may be eager, spirited, effective, and a pleasure to others, and may like him- or herself.

In our work we emphasize the quality of maternal care. This is not because care from fathers and others is unimportant. If a father provides consistent, high-quality care, we would expect the baby to become securely attached to that father. All of the people in the child's environment help to shape the development of his personality. Nonsocial experiences are clearly important as well. A baby needs to play with objects if he is to develop a sense of mastery. And inborn differences in babies certainly affect the quality of adaptation, especially in the case of the ambivalent, difficult-to-settle babies. But our emphasis on maternal care is based on clear and substantial evidence concerning the impact of maternal care on the quality of an infant's attachment.

*When observations of nursery school children were compared
with ratings of their attachment to their mothers
(measured when the children were 15 months old), strong
relationships appeared between the quality of the early
relationship and later personality.*

Certain behavior patterns among caregivers appear to be linked with later secure attachment and competence among babies. At least half a dozen studies point to the same key characteristic, which is best described as responsiveness or sensitivity. Ainsworth's research has shown that highly sensitive mothers who are neither interfering nor rejecting consistently have infants who are secure in their attachment at 12 months.

Good maternal care involves responding to the infant's signals promptly and effectively. When during face-to-face interaction the infant turns his head away, signaling that he needs less stimulation, the sensitive caregiver relaxes and waits. Not until the baby signals his readiness does she reengage him. When the infant cries, the sensitive caregiver responds promptly, and effectively puts an end to the infant's distress. When the baby seeks contact, the sensitive caregiver responds warmly and affectionately, teaching the infant that his signals are effective. The sensitive caregiver provides smooth transitions and meshes her (or his) stimulation or assistance with the infant's behavior. She does not thrust interaction on an unreceptive infant. Sensitivity requires that the mother respond to the individual needs and nature of her infant: This is why sensitive care generally promotes healthy emotional development in vastly different babies.

Through sensitive interaction the infant learns that he can have an impact on the world and that stimulation in the presence of the caregiver is not threatening. In the presence of the caregiver he can tolerate the excitement of new experiences because he has learned that the caregiver is available when needed. Ultimately the baby comes to believe that such resources lie within himself, and he develops a sense of trust in his caregiver. This trust eventually becomes a belief in his own competence.

As a child develops, the characteristics of sensitive care change, although responsiveness to the child's signals probably remains a central feature. Psychoanalyst Margaret Mahler has described how, during the child's second year, the caregiver must give her infant a gentle nudge to encourage his move toward independent functioning. In our study of two-year-olds the sensitive caregiver was not the one who immediately solved the problem for the child, nor the one who allowed him to become frustrated before assistance was offered. She was the mother who gave the child space to work, then offered minimal hints to help him solve the task and retain a sense of having solved it by himself.

The process of becoming an autonomous individual continues in different ways throughout one's life. It is reasonable to expect that difficult beginnings could be overcome by good social support during later development. And it is doubtful that good adaptation can be maintained without continued support. Competence in early years does not guarantee competence later in life. But it's a good start.

For further information:

Ainsworth, M. D. S., and S. M. Bell. "Mother-Infant Interaction and the Development of Competence." *The Growth of Competence*, edited by K. J. Connolly and Jerome Bruner. Academic Press, 1974.

Brazelton, T. B., Barbara Koslowski, and Mary Main. "The Origins of Reciprocity: The Early Mother-Infant Interaction." *The Effect of the Infant on Its Caregiver*, edited by Michael Lewis and L. A. Rosenblum. John Wiley & Sons, 1974.

Matas, Leah, R. Arend, and L. A. Sroufe. "Continuity of Adaptation in the Second Year of Life: Quality and Infant-Caregiver Attachment and Later Competence." *Child Development*, (in press).

Sroufe, L. A. *Knowing and Enjoying Your Baby.* Prentice-Hall, 1977.

Sroufe, L. A., and Everett Waters. "Attachment as an Organizational Construct." *Child Development*, Vol. 48, 1977, pp. 1184-1199.

L. Alan Sroufe *is professor of child psychology at the Institute of Child Development, University of Minnesota, and adjunct professor in the department of psychiatry at the University of Minnesota School of Medicine. He served four years on the Personality and Cognition Research Review Committee of the National Institute of Mental Health. Sroufe has written more than a dozen articles on early emotional development, and his book,* Knowing and Enjoying Your Baby, *emphasizes the infant's social, emotional, and intellectual development.*

THE PARENTAL LOVE TRAP

By Jerome Kagan

Is our notion that parental love is critical to a child's self-image and development simply a culture-bound belief? An eminent developmental psychologist suggests that it may be—and argues that this myth explains our apprehensions about day care.

One of the long-lasting structures that is supposed to be shaped during infancy and early childhood is a sense of emotional security—an idea closely related to the notions of trust, attachment, and love, and one of primary concern to mothers who are considering day care for their children. Many parents and psychologists assume that if the infant is loved, he will forever be protected from the slings and arrows of misfortune. If the young child is not loved, he will be continually vulnerable to the slightest threat or frustration. During a six-year study of day care, I found it illuminating to examine the history of cultural attitudes toward children, to search for the source of Rousseau's prescription that a mother's love will cure society's ills.

Why has this assumption been so strongly held by Western theorists and parents during the last 300 years? It was far less prevalent during the medieval period and is not part of the folk theory of many non-Western societies. One basis for this premise stems from the universal need to believe in a force that can protect the child from future threat. Some cultures assume that fate or benevolent, transcendental forces watch over the child; others assert that this protective power is either inherited or a function of growing up in a healthy and harmonious community. Our own society places its faith in a properly orchestrated set of parental actions that are supposed to insure

the child's future. Indeed, the originality in Freudian theory is the suggestion that parental practices with the young child can affect the adult profile of sexual experiences and behavior. This notion challenged the popular assumption at the turn of the century that sexual perversions were a product of either heredity or degenerate social conditions.

Faith in the protective quality of proper parental behavior is an instance of a more general Western belief that catastrophe can be averted by taking the appropriate prophylactic action, whether it be baptism or breast-feeding. We would like to believe in a prescription for caretaking that can inoculate the young child against future misery and failure. During most of this century, many American psychologists assumed that there was a set of specific parental behaviors that always signified parental love or rejection, for there was an enormous degree of commonality

among investigators in definitions of these concepts. Harsh physical punishment and absence of social play and of physical affection were typically regarded as signs of rejection, and few American psychologists would rank a mother high in a loving attitude if she also showed signs of aloofness. Yet Alfred Baldwin has reported that in the rural areas of northern Norway, one sees maternal behavior that an American observer would regard as rejecting but that the Norwegian children themselves apparently do not.

The rural Norwegian mother sees her four-year-old sitting in a doorway, blocking the passage to the next room. She does not ask him to move, but bends down, picks him up, and silently moves him away before she passes to the next room. Although a middle-class observer might view this lack of communication as indifference and hence a sign of dislike, most mothers in Norway behave this way, and the children do not behave the way rejected youngsters should by our theoretical propositions.

During the early 17th century, European and Colonial parents were advised to beat their children in order to tame their inherently evil character, and otherwise respectable and well-educated parents inflicted severe punishment upon their dependents, punishments that would be classified as extreme abuse today. Samuel Byrd of Virginia, for example, made a dependent of his drink a "pint of piss" because he wet his bed. Then, as well as in the present century, many children of upper-class English families were rarely at home with their parents. After birth, they were sent to a wet nurse in a nearby village until weaning, perhaps at two years of age. They then returned home for a period before being sent away to boarding school. Sir Robert Walpole, born in 1676, rarely spent more than a few weeks in his home each year between six and 22 years of age. Since this pattern was common, it is unlikely that parents thought they were being cruel or that their children felt unloved.

In his autobiography, John Stuart Mill describes his father as aloof, stern, and lacking in affection: "The element which was chiefly deficient in his moral relation to his children was that of tenderness." But Mill, unlike most modern adults, did not treat this combination of qualities as reflecting hostility. Rather, he assumed his father had repressed his tender feelings, and he added that he felt no sense of resentment toward the father: "I was always loyally devoted to him. . . . I hesitate to pronounce whether I was more a loser or a gainer by his severity."

Evaluation of a parent as hostile or accepting cannot be answered by observing the parent's behavior, for neither love nor rejection is a fixed quality of behavior. Like pleasure, pain, or beauty, it is in the mind of the beholder. Parental love is a belief held by the child, not a set of actions by a parent.

The view that a child's perception of parental love is like an immunization assumes a prominence in contemporary society that it may not have had in earlier periods, or may not have in other contemporary societies. Many American children are uncertain whether they are valued by their family, and parents are eager to communicate to their children that they love them. Unhappiness, failure, and psychopathology in adolescence and adulthood are often attributed to the absence of parental love during infancy and early childhood. Prior to the mid-17th century, it was far less common to find Europeans referring to the importance of the love relation between parent and child when they discussed the conditions that promoted optimal development. The child needed proper nutrition, physical protection, a good education, faith in God, and parents who were consistently firm in their discipline.

A wealthy Florentine aristocrat, Leon Battista Alberti, wrote an essay on the rearing of children in the middle of the 15th century that contrasts sharply with modern beliefs. Although Alberti acknowledged that parents exert a significant influence on the training of character and believed that early experience contributes to the formation of adult personality, he did not regard a mother's love as a major element in that process. Alberti suggested that it was the duty of the father, not the mother, to train the son to strive for honor and fame, and to develop the ability to de-

> **"Parental love or rejection are beliefs held by the child, not a set of actions by a parent."**

termine one's destiny through competence and power—a combination of qualities that constituted *virtù*. Attainment of those sacred attributes was accomplished through parental vigilance, identification with the child's victories, and provision of appropriate examples. When Alberti listed the qualities most important to a happy family, he failed to mention love: "The intellect, prudence, and knowledge of the old people together with their diligence are what maintain the family in a happy and flourishing state, and adorn it with praise, glory and splendor."

Alberti seemed indifferent to the mother's sentiments, confessing that he was not sure whether a mother or wet nurse was better for an infant; a woman's influence on the young child was mediated primarily through the quality of milk she provided, not through her attitudes or practices.

In all of Thomas More's *Utopia*, written nearly a century later, there is less than a page devoted to parental treatment of young children and no mention of the psychological relation between parents and children. More was not worried about foster care for an infant whose mother could not

nurse "since the child who is thus fostered looks on his nurse as his natural mother."

And children older than five years were supposed to serve adults in the dining hall or, if "they are not old and strong enough, stand by—and that in absolute silence." Since More was describing an ideal human community, the failure to dwell on the love relation between parent and child implies that this idea was not salient in the consciousness of some 16th-century men of letters.

The Dutch minister John Robinson, writing in the early 17th century, also felt that a child needed parental severity more than affection. Consequently, fathers were better for children than mothers "for forming virtue and good manners by their greater wisdom and authority and ofttimes also by correcting the fruits of their mother's indulgence by their severity." Robinson acknowledged that parents naturally are affectionate toward their children, but rather than celebrate that spontaneous emotion, he urged parents to suppress it. "There is running in the breasts of most parents a strong stream of parental affection toward some one or other of their children . . . either for its beauty or wit . . . or some other fancied good in it, which is always dangerous and oft harmful."

But by the end of the 17th century, explicit recognition of the significance of the love relation between parent and child had emerged. Locke advised parents to love their children: "He that would have his son have a respect for him and his orders must himself have a great reverence for his son." Rousseau warned that if parents—and he meant both mothers and fathers—did not establish affectionate ties with their children, vice was inevitable. Anticipating psychologist John Bowlby's emphasis on the infant's attachment to a single caretaker, Rousseau advised against the use of wet nurses or substitute caretakers. But if that decision had been made, then "the foster child should have no other guardian, just as he should have no teacher but his tutor. . . . A child who passes through many hands in turn can never be well brought up." And by the middle of the 19th century, the modern view that a mother's love was not only sensed by her infant but essential to his future welfare was being articulated by many essayists. Horace Bushnell, a Congregational minister in Hartford, Connecticut, advised: "If the child is handled fretfully, scolded, jerked, or simply laid aside unaffectionately, in no warmth of motherly gentleness, it feels the sting of just that which is felt towards it; and so it is angered by anger, irritated by irritation, fretted by fretfulness; having thus impressed just that kind of impatience or ill-nature which is felt towards it, and growing faithfully into the bad mold offered, as by a fixed law."

As the 17th century came to a close, Locke's writings reflected the growing sentiment against the assumption that man was naturally disposed to be subservient to divine and royal authority, and for the view that all are born free. That change in premise happened to be accompanied by an increased permissiveness toward the older child's independence from the family, and, concomitantly, an emergent concern with the importance of parental love. Now, for the first time, "it was increasingly common to hear that parents were obliged to love them and to prepare for the day when they would go out into the world as free and equal adults." In *Some Thoughts Concerning Education,* Locke advised parents to rely less on restriction and punishment and to exploit the child's capacity for shame and fear of parental displeasure as means of training character. Withdrawal of love was to be used as a strategy of socialization.

Thus, as unquestioned acquiescence to God and family lost their moral force to individualism and the development of an autonomous ego, parental love assumed a position of prominence. Is this correlation causal, the joint product of more fundamental factors, or an accident? We favor the second of these positions and shall try to support it.

The rise of an urban middle class during the late 16th and early 17th centuries was probably accompanied by the realization that children were less obvious economic advantages. Youth were not needed to help with agricultural work or to care for infants and very young children.

The middle-class father, feeling economically more secure than the 16th-century rural parent, was probably less concerned about becoming economically dependent on his grown sons when he was too old to work. It

is likely, then, that the child's role gradually changed from an object of utility to one of sentiment. Although the child could not contribute to the family's economic position, he could enhance the family's status by mastering academic skills and attaining prestige and position in the larger community. Now more parents would begin to identify with their children because of the latter's potential accomplishments. This change in the child's function in the family could have produced an enhancement of the attitude we call parental love.

A second basis for such an attitude

> "Many persons who had nurturant and devoted parents during the early years feel unloved as young adults."

may have been that 17th-century parents began to recognize that an aloof, authoritarian attitude, which seemed to be effective in producing obedience and conformity in children, was not conducive to autonomous achievement. Fear of authority is a potent incentive for inhibition, but it is far less effective as a goad for continued striving toward goals that require the invention of ideas and actions. The desire to maintain the positive regard of parents is a more appropriate incentive for such striving.

On the other hand, the economic and social changes that led to new parental attitudes may have also created new nodes of uncertainty in children. The 18th-century child could not point to a plowed field or a full woodpile as a sign of his utility. As a result, he may have been more uncertain about his value, more dependent on parental communications assuring him of his worthiness, more preoccupied with parental attitudes

We are suggesting that there is theoretical substance to the correlation between the emphasis on the child's independence and autonomous achievement (along with the decreasing concern with conformity

and the child's economic contribution to the family) and the awarding of formative power to attitudes of parental affection. The correlation reflects, in part, the growth of a folk theory implying that confidence, independence, and the drive for accomplishment require a belief in one's value and potency and a reluctance to lose parental love. We do not know whether the folk theory is valid empirically or merely believed to be correct by the community.

As hinted earlier, parental love may have become viewed as a psychological nutrient because a celebration of individualism implies that any protective amulet must be possessed by the individual. Since urbanization and industrialization made it likely that many adults would be distant from family and early friendships, the protective shield was of little value if it required proximity to family. Although strength, health, and endurance were less necessary for successful survival, uncertainty still remained a potential enemy. Loss of a loved one, temptation, and rejection were always possibilities in tomorrow's sunrise, regardless of one's position or wealth.

Anxiety gradually became the adversary against which one needed protection. Benjamin Franklin wrote that uneasiness was the basic human motive, and 19th- and 20th-century theorists from Sigmund Freud, Alfred Adler, and Otto Rank through John Bowlby, Mary Ainsworth, and Rollo May amplified that theme. The assumption is intuitively appealing, for our most unpleasant moments seem to occur when we are uncertain about how another will treat us, how our actions and products will be received, how to decide what to believe, and how to deal with possible danger. The popular belief is that early parental love, which leads to the private conviction that one is valued, can protect child and adult from distress.

I s it likely that there is a special set of treatments that, by itself, would lead any child to believe he or she was not valued? Adolescents who have been locked in a room for two to three years excuse their mothers' actions by confessing that, because they were such difficult children, their mothers were correct to restrict them. Many persons who had nurturant and devoted parents during the early years feel unloved as young adults. The belief that one is not valued does not lie in a particular set of parental actions, but in the child's construction of those actions.

In our society, characterized by dramatic variability in child-rearing practices, children have the opportunity to compare their treatment with those prescribed by the culture and those they see displayed by other parents. The child comes to discover what privileges, actions, and treatments reflect parental concern and affection. He compares his receipt of these symbolic prizes with the lot of siblings and age-mates. That information allows him to decide if he is loved. Rather than view this belief as relative and resilient, parents and psychologists have made it a material entity—a beauty mark that the child carries with him the rest of his life.

What evidence has sustained the belief that parental love protects the child from later pathology? Western psychologists define parental love in materialistic terms. The basic ingredients are physical affection, sacrifice of the self's interests for those of the child, consistency of care, and enjoyment of interaction with the child. All of these are reasonable definitions of parental affection. Some scientists then argued that children who did not have this set of experiences during early childhood were more likely to display dispositions in adulthood that they called psychotic, asocial, or neurotic. The syllogism was as follows:

Premise 1: If the child is loved, the adult will be psychologically healthy.

Premise 2: This adult is not psychologically healthy.

Conclusion: Therefore this adult was not loved as a child. This conclusion is valid, even though the truth value of the original premise may be questioned.

Consider the alternative, invalid syllogism, which has a retrospective first premise:

Premise 1: If this adult is psychologically healthy, he was loved as a child.

Premise 2: This adult is not psychologically healthy.

Conclusion: Therefore this adult was not loved as a child.

Many parents and psychologists have made the mistake of assuming that since the first argument is logically sound, the second must be also.

The intuitive appeal of the invalid second argument is one reason for the belief in the "power of parental love." There is no persuasive evidence, however, to show that most unhappy adults were unloved as children. We look at distressed adults and assume they were not loved, forgetting that many factors could have intervened between an early childhood full of love and an unhappy adulthood.

Many have assumed that the belief in "one's value" remains stable from early childhood through adolescence and adulthood. Of the millions of children who do not receive adequate amounts of early affection, only a

> **"An adolescent girl was strapped to her bed until she was 13. She did not behave as if she'd been rejected by humanity."**

small proportion develop pathology, and of the group with adult pathology, a large proportion may have been loved during early childhood. At the moment, we do not know if there is a strong relation between early child treatment and later adult pathology, even though there may be a strong relation between the adolescent's belief that he is not valued and the frequency of his bouts of distress.

It is useful to view a person's belief in his value as dynamic and continually subject to change depending on life context. If the adolescent or adult finds himself in an environment where his "traits" are valued, whereas in prior contexts they were not, the belief is subject to modification. By contrast, if he feels valued in one situation and finds himself in a context where all around him do not prize his extrinsic and intrinsic qualities, his prior belief may be subject to modification. One of us spent two days with an adolescent girl who had been locked in a room, strapped to her bed from 20 months of age until she was 13 years old. After a few years with a foster family, she did not behave like a girl who believed she was rejected by humanity. She approached strangers, initiated physical contact, and seemed to expect kindness, not hostility, from adults. Her extreme

isolation did not permit her to conclude that she was not valued. A subject cannot tell how large or distant an object is if he is looking at it through a box that prevents him from making any comparisons. Judgments of value, like size and distance, require an anchor.

It is not easy to ascertain whether lack of parental affection in childhood does indeed make a serious contribution to future psychic illness, but the reasons are not strictly empirical. When we ask, "Does temperature contribute to the probability of snowfall?" we only need gather easily obtained objective data to answer the query. But in the case of the contribution of parental love or rejection, we are in difficulty because we are asking, "Does a mental state in the child contribute to a future mental state in the adult?"

The first interpretation of the question is subjective and concerned only with the adult's belief about the validity of the functional relation. If the adult believes that a set of experiences influences the future state, he will act as if it were so. The second interpretation of the question is empirical and asks if there is an objective relation between the child's perception of favor or disfavor and adult outcomes. That version of the question has not been answered satisfactorily because parental rejection is not a set of actions by parents, but a belief by the child. The only way to exit from this frustrating position is to determine if there is any observable relation in a culture between the actions of parents and the child's belief that he is or is not favored.

There are no data that have demonstrated unequivocally the relation between specific parental actions and the child's belief, even in our culture. Working-class American parents punish and restrict the child much more than middle-class parents, yet there is no evidence indicating a class difference in perception of parental favor. Mothers of the Kipsigis tribe in Kenya have older siblings care for their young children, while Israeli mothers on kibbutzim use surrogate caretakers. There is no evidence indicating that Kipsigis- or kibbutz-reared children feel less in parental favor than others. We are tempted to suggest that each child constructs a theory of the actions that imply parental favor and disfavor. The content of the theory is based on local conditions and will not generalize to other communities in any detail.

What seems unique in modern Western society is the popularity of the thought that one might not be valued by one's family. Historical events may have been responsible for introducing this idea as a major node of apprehension, and therefore of illness, just as social changes have been responsible for new anxieties over nuclear waste, racial violence, and municipal defaults. Mayan villagers

> **"Many modern mothers share Rousseau's conviction that a mother should not give her infant to a substitute caretaker."**

worry about not having enough food, about slanderous gossip, and about the actions of gods. A society can create a new source of distress by introducing a new belief. Many modern mothers share Rousseau's conviction that a mother should not give her infant to a substitute caretaker. In violating that natural obligation, she believes she is not only placing her child's development at risk but also increasing the likelihood that she will produce a socially disruptive adult. It is reasonable, therefore, that American parents worry about the conse-quences of day care.

But need they worry? The results of several recent comparisons of young children attending day-care centers and those raised at home reveal little difference between the two groups. In our own study, we compared the psychological development of 33 infants who attended a specially run day-care center from three and a half months through 29 months of age with infants of similar ethnicity and social class who were being raised at home. We assessed them on eight separate occasions with a battery of procedures designed to evaluate attentiveness, sensitivity to discrepancy, fearfulness, language, memory, social behavior, and attachment to the mother. There were no important differences between the day care and home-reared children.

What appears to be important in good-quality day care is the ratio of staff to children, and, of course, the experience and conscientiousness of the staff. We believe that the ratio of children to staff at the center should be low—about three infants to one staff member during the first two years of life and seven to 10 children to one caretaker during the years from two through five. The caretaking staff should be reasonably knowledgeable about child development and be sensitive to the values of the families of their charges. Finally, the children should have opportunity to practice the linguistic, inferential, and social skills valued by their society. If these conditions are met, children raised in day-care centers and those brought up entirely at home seem to be equally mature, socially competent, and attached to their mothers.

Although it is our belief that good-quality day care does not have hidden danger, that the child is not robbed of his true potential, we must point out that modern psychological methods for assessing a child's talents, ideas, and emotions are not very sophisticated. Hence, it is possible that there may be subtle but important differences in personality and cognitive ability between day-care and home-reared children that investigators have been unable to detect. This issue still remains unresolved.

Many scholars from Plato to Bowlby are convinced that the infant and young child is best prepared for adulthood by sustained contact with its mother. Nonetheless, there are societies in which children are with surrogate caretakers for most of the day, and available evidence does not indicate that these children develop into more anxious or hostile adults. Much emotion surrounds this issue; hence, it is important that more exact information be obtained before final judgments can be made.

Jerome Kagan took his Ph.D. in psychology at Yale in 1954, and is professor of human development at Harvard. He is author of *Change and Continuity in Infancy* and *Understanding Children*, and coauthor of *Child Development and Personality* and of *Psychology: An Introduction*. Philip R. Zelazo and Richard B. Kearsley are codirectors of the Center for Behavioral Pediatrics and Infant Development, Department of Pediatrics, New England Medical Center and Tufts University Medical School.

Who Will Rear Our Children?

Glenn R. Hawkes

Glenn R. Hawkes is Professor of Human Development, Department of Applied Behavioral Sciences, University of California, Davis, California 95616.

Various kinds of institutional child socialization facilities have risen over the past decade in response to the demand for multiple options by women and other social circumstances. Tasks that were formerly assumed by the extended family are gradually being supplanted by bureaucracies due to changes in the extended family and greater emphasis upon the more mobile nuclear family. This paper examines Eugene Litwak's theory of shared function which attempts to establish a cooperative relationship between families and those bureaucracies created to help, and, in some cases, supplant the family in tasks traditionally tied to the family alone, such as socialization.

Nonfamilial programs for young children have burgeoned over the past five decades, primarily in response to war, depression, and a growing awareness of the importance of the early years in the cognitive development of children. In the past decade the demand for multiple options by women has become a primary factor in the rise of institutional care facilities for young children. These institutional programs generally take the form of Day Care for children of working mothers, nursery schools dedicated to early childhood education and play groups developed by groups of mothers. The last are designed to give some respite from the demands of young children, to free mother for other interests, and to share parenting concerns with peers. Thus, changes are taking place in the way in which families are ordering their priorities in the child socialization area.

In the past, the extended family was the major societal vehicle for the dissemination of knowledge on child rearing and parenting with limited assistance from schools, churches, social agencies and various groups concerned with the nurturing process. The extended family served as an apprenticing unit for the future parent. Through this mechanism children and adolescents learned the rudimentary knowledge of how children grow and develop and how to create an environment which would facilitate this development. Skills and attitudes were transmitted to new generations through *doing* with younger siblings and through the modeling provided by parents and parent surrogates in the extended family. But the extended family ties have weakened, making this opportunity less and less available as modern families have fewer personnel available. This adult withdrawal from the lives of children has been accompanied by a growing tendency for children, at every age and grade level, to depend on their peers and to be susceptible to group influence (Bronfenbrenner, 1974a). Further, the constantly changing notions of child rearing have largely invalidated generational knowledge.

In addition, little outside work activity is shared and the opportunity for family interaction is greatly lessened. Today's children, influenced by rich information garnered from television, comic books and the broad spectrum of periodicals and paperbacks, live an action-poor childhood. They are "book smart and life dumb" (Coleman, 1972).

As Bronfenbrenner (1974a) so succinctly puts it:

> The crux of the problem lies in the failure of the young person to be integrated into his society. He feels uninterested, disconnected and perhaps even hostile to the people and activities in his environment. He wants "to do his own thing" but often is not sure what it is or with whom to do it. Even when he thinks he has found it—and them—the experience often proves unsuccessful and interest wanes. This feeling, and fact, of disconnectedness from people and activities has a theme that has become familiar: alienation (p. 3).

It is clear that the family as presently constituted is not carrying out its traditional obligations, particularly in the socialization of its very young members. The concept of the family as a complete social unit, with the virtues of autonomy, self-sufficiency, and the capacity to solve all basic problems on living, is a carry-over from the idealized myth associated with the agrarian past; it little resembles the bureaucratic pattern evolved in this era of industrialization and technological development.

Independence and autonomy may be desired by and for families, but for some families such independence may lead to more problems than it solves since the family lacks the resources to capitalize on independence. Under conditions of father absence, economic instability, and isolation some external help may foster sufficient resources to keep the family from becoming a casualty in a complex and perplexing world. According to Bronfenbrenner (1974b), thousands of investigations in the past thirty years have linked developmental antecedents of behavioral disorders and social pathology to family disorganization. Circumstances that adversely affect the development of the child include: Familial relationships of distrust and emotional instability, impediments to the parental provision of care and education, and lack of support from the external world for the value of child-rearing.

Concept of Shared Function

What is needed is a theory (and a program growing from it) that fosters a *fit* between the family and bureaucracies created to help and, in some cases, supplant the family in tasks traditionally tied to the family alone, such as socialization.

This paper, then, explores a concept of shared function and applies it to the early part of the family life cycle, when the young family is expanding and also attempting to become an integral part of the social structure, that is, when the young family is usually operating with limited resources—both economic and psychological—and developing a sense of its own autonomous structure and function. The period is characterized by the need for young parents to develop themselves further and to shape their roles as individual adults as well as mothers and fathers.

The theory of shared function is the notion that formal organizations and families coordinate their efforts if they are to achieve their goals. It calls for mutual planning and articulation. It suggests clarification of goals and the development of mechanisms to achieve goals.

The early state of the life cycle is an optimum time for developing a notion of shared function in socialization—a function shared by the family and the bureaucracies which represent concerns from the larger society. This shared function should permeate the thinking of the family and the helping professions. Whatever scheme is developed, it must be clear that the bureaucratic structure and the family are not in competition with each other; in many cases, their concerns will conflict, but a sense of cooperation must prevail. It must be explicit that a family has not failed simply because it is assisted by the bureaucratic segment of society. A family pays a high price for help if the members are allowed to feel inadequate and subordinate to the professional expertise of the bureaucracy. Guilt and hostility, consequences of such lopsided partnership, are disabling to the family, not facilitating. Mediation, to be successful, must involve a reciprocal process of being able to influence as well as being influenced. It has to involve "action which results in compromise without an undue loss of position, integrity or power by participants" (Sussman, 1974, p. 586).

Bureaucracies and Primary Groups

Bureaucracies are social structures developed by society to achieve certain goals. They are instrumental-role oriented in operation and emphasize objectivity and impersonality. They are usually built on merit, stressing performance as a criterion for advancement in the organization and, for that matter, for perpetuation of the organization.

They are generally planned to have high stability and to exist for long periods. Codes and rules are part of their planned structure. They are also subject to public scrutiny. Whether part of the private or public sector, bureaucracies are developed with an eye to stability even though permanency of membership is generally not a common characteristic.

Families are primary groups usually described as a group of people living in a single household tied by bonds of marriage, blood, or deep commitment. They are expressive-role oriented and emphasize nepotism and subjectivity. The family provides continuing membership regardless of age or performance. It provides for primary face-to-face contact, and membership is retained merely through staying alive. Nepotism rather than objectivity characterizes its personnel policies. Because of its size and the diffuse nature of its function, it is well equipped to react with speed and flexibility to non-uniform events. It is a private operation and essentially not subject to societal scrutiny for efficiency or economy of operation. The family also provides a setting for the use of skills which a bureaucracy is ill-equipped to handle: feeding, elementary protection, exhibiting and reciprocating affection, etc.

The theory of shared function involves the notion that the family and bureaucratic organizations can be articulated in a way which maximizes the contribution each can make to betterment of the human condition. For shared function to play such a role, the functions of each interface must be developed in such a way that certain services are not overrepresented and therefore wasted. It is also important that the autonomy of each sharer be protected and that the dominance of either in given circumstances be related to its function. It would be very easy, for instance, for the bureaucratic structure to attempt to standardize families. One function of a bureaucracy is standardization to ensure uniformity of response, which tends to stifle the uniqueness and adaptability of the unit with which it is in primary face-to-face contact.

The theory of shared function assumes also that needed services are constantly being reviewed in light of changing social conditions. A mechanism for such review seems to be one of the most difficult tasks. Leaving the review to the bureaucratic interface may, indeed, tend to give dominance to bureaucracy. The family is at a disadvantage in that it has neither the expertise nor the resources to anticipate unmet needs and visualize ways in which these needs might be met.

It has been suggested that one compelling reason for citizen participation on boards and regulatory agencies is to make certain that the needs of the citizenry are not overlooked. Another useful way of informing planning groups of the needs of a population is the public hearing. A recent requirement that planned social-service programs and expenditures be advertised and hearings be held may be developing a model that can be exploited in a theory of shared function. Such developments should be watched to determine whether this model can bring the bureaucrat and the citizen together.

Shared Function of Socialization

How can a theory of shared function relate to the task of socializing the young? Socializing the young child means to equip him with the skills and attitudes basic to effective functioning in this culture. In Sussman's (1974) view, this functioning in adulthood would be predicated on competence in using bureaucratic organizations and being able to take advantage of options in education, leisure, welfare, and work. Socialization should focus on developing skills and fostering attitudes which will make a child a competent and productive member of society. Developing these competencies in the child calls for inculcating a strong learning drive, developing attitudes and skills which foster maximum physical growth and development, building a strong sense of emotional security, and laying a foundation for effective interaction with others. Individual priorities may vary, but they will generally contain elements of sound mental and physical health and techniques to foster their growth and development.

As men and women become parents they must develop roles for which they may have great or little preparation. Much disruption can be mitigated by the development of support systems in the bureaus of society. When support systems are nonexistent and families have dysfunctional child-rearing practices, familial stress can have a violent impact on young children. The disruptive potential that the birth of a child can have in a family is demonstrated in the 2,300 cases of abuse and neglect of infants under the age of one reported in New York City in 1975 (Bronfenbrenner, 1976).

Examples of support systems designed to ameliorate child socialization, already implemented in England and in the United States, include:

1. Parental Stress Hot Lines that are staffed by sympathetic volunteers trained to listen and refer clients to other social services.
2. Parenting groups that are facilitated by city and county agencies to provide an intimate forum for voluntary discussion of parenting problems.
3. Education for Parenthood programs sponsored by state and federal agencies to provide adolescents with child-development background and experience in interacting with young children (Kruger, 1973).
4. Adult Education Programs that are sponsored by school districts to provide parents with participatory nursery-school experience.
5. Extended Family Centers that provide resources for isolated parents who are acting out violence against their children (Broeck, 1974).
6. Health visitor programs so that parents with newborn and young children are provided with a professional expert (Health Programs for Newborns, 1976).
7. Developmental family centers, such as the Martin Luther King Family Center, that provide home visits and preschool facilities to help "families to help themselves" (Scheinfeld, 1969).

8. Child Care Services designed to provide for care for children, in and out of the home.

Bureaucratic support services for the early socialization process have traditionally been of very limited diversity even if physical/medical evaluation of the newborn is included. Public health, as an example, is concerned with eliminating children's diseases. Toward that goal they have developed programs to blanket the young with immunizing shots. Pediatricians, school nurses, mass media, and religious and social groups have been recruited to urge acceptance and participation of the public in such programs. Success has been great when a clear and immediate threat has been perceived, as with poliomyelitis, and less great when the threat has not seemed so clear and immediate.

Headstart, another example of intervention, initially limited its focus to the preparation of "disadvantaged children" for the mastering of middle-class educational achievement goals, *i.e.,* cognitive skills. Directed more toward parent education than to parent involvement, the program attempted to upgrade the competence and experience of the parents. Its early implementation did not recognize the important contribution that parents could have made to guidance and management of the program. Most evaluation research has concluded that although Headstart did not meet its objectives of "widespread significant cognitive gains . . . supported, reinforced, or maintained in conventional education programs in the primary grades" (Cicarelli, 1969, p. 10), the experience did suggest the importance that increased family participation could assume in early education.

A further example of the benefit gleaned from increased family participation is found in Levenstein's Verbal Interaction Project in which stimuli in the form of toys were demonstrated to mothers for use with their preschool children. Earlier findings by Bronfenbrenner, further supported by this experiment, implied that "reciprocal action between mother and child involves both cognitive and emotional components which reinforce each other" (Bronfenbrenner, 1974b, p. 30).

Ways to Expand Interface

Is it not possible that a clearer partnership between the bureaucracy and the family would have ensured greater success? If ameliorative programs and procedures can be developed in concert by those sharing responsibility, will their chances of success be improved? Or if the nuclear family clearly understands the shared-function concept and sees the social-services bureaucracy as having responsibility in certain measures, will greater success be assured? Research on such questions might be one way of testing the validity of shared function.

Figures 1-3 summarize essential differences between families and bureaucracies and suggests ways in which they might interface. Figure 1 conceptualizes public education's relationship to the primary group with Figure

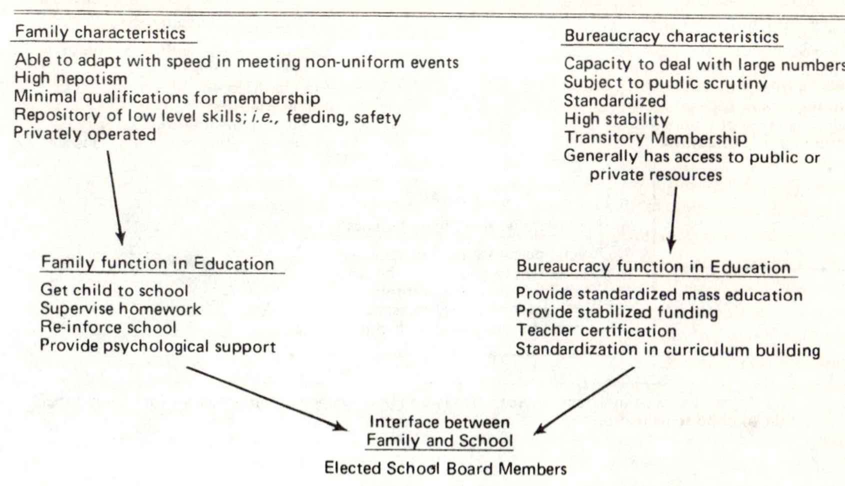

Figure 1. Shared function of education.

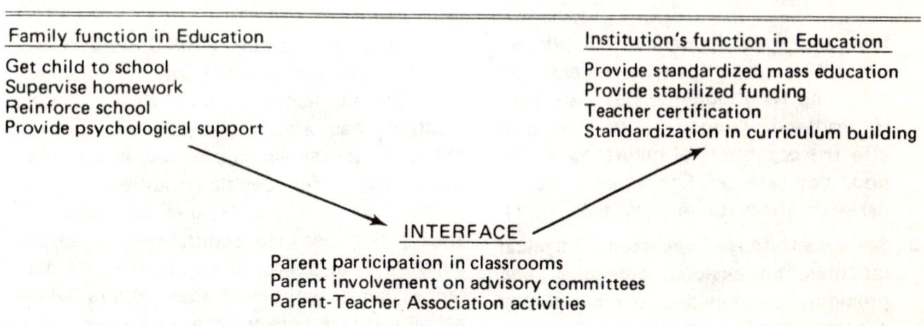

Figure 2. Expanded interface between family and schools.

2 representing an expansion of that interface. The third example suggests the interface with out-of-the home and home socialization. Both Figures 2 and 3 demonstrate the interrelatedness that these complementary groups must arrange to achieve satisfactory goals in child socialization.

They also illustrate that "thinking big about what kinds of children we want to have in the next generation" (Caldwell, 1971) will require careful examination of the structure of bureaucracies designed to facilitate child socialization and of the mechanisms that link the bureaucracy with primary groups. A national child-rearing social policy is an empty exercise unless a viable family/bureaucracy system of delivery is provided. Unless delivery is of good quality, bureaucracies may exacerbate some of the problems they are designed to solve.

Litwak's model (Litwak & Meyer, 1967) gives social planners of child care services a theoretical perspective for negotiating interfaces between bureaucracies and primary groups. His conceptualization of the structure of bureaucratic organization provides three alternatives that can be observed in child-care service organizations: (a) the rationalistic model, stressing impersonal social relations, detailed rules, and hierarchal authority; (b) the human-relations model, which permits personal relations, general policies, and colleague structure; and (c) the professional model, which incorporates attributes common to both the rationalistic and human-relations models.

Litwak's framework also predicts that complementary balance between the bureaucracy and the primary group is regulated by linking mechanisms that inhibit or promote social distance. Described in terms of communication from the organization to the primary group, social distance can be reduced if too great, or increased if too intimate. A balance at some point between isolation and intimacy allows optimum achievement of goals.

Litwak illustrates this balance theory with an approach that a formal organization might use in effectively influencing external groups. Bureaucracies that offer child-care services use at least six of these mechanisms:

1. *Detached-expert approach.* Relatively autonomous professionals from the bureaucracy participate directly in the primary group to influence members. They become trusted members of the group. Examples are England's program of health visitors to families of newborns, and Schaefer's Home-based Infant Intervention Program (Schaefer, 1972).

2. *Opinion-leader approach.* The organiza-

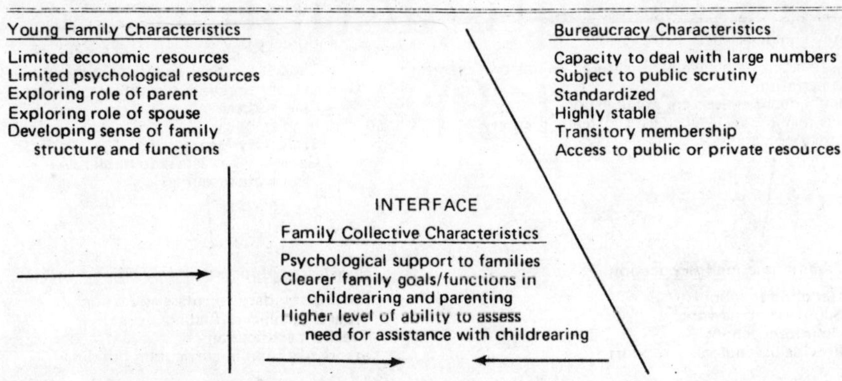

Figure 3. The Collective as an interface between family and bureaucracy as a mechanism for shared function of child socialization.

tion seeks to influence the primary group through indigenous leaders. The Matching Neighborhood Day Care Plan in Portland, Oregon, illustrates how effective organizers of natural neighborhood day care can link users of family care with givers (Emlen & Watson, 1971).

3. *Settlement-house approach.* Physical facilities, professional personnel, and proximity are provided to the potential clientele. The Extended Family Center in San Francisco demonstrates how this mechanism can provide respite and therapy for families where there is child abuse and neglect (Broeck, 1974).

4. *Common-messenger approach.* Individuals who are regular members of both the organization and the primary group transmit messages intended to influence one or the other. Serving this function are parents who participate in cooperative nursery-school programs.

5. *Mass-media approach.* The formal organization attempts to influence the primary group through newspapers, printed notices, and mass mailings. Examples are monthly newsletters from city-sponsored Child Care Services agencies.

6. *Formal-authority approach.* The organization uses a legal or strong normative basis to communicate with the primary group. An example is the Child Services Program mandated by state and federal law to protect children at risk.

Litwak has also proposed four general criteria to assess which procedures are most appropriate under specific conditions:

The first principle is one of initiative, stating that because coordinating mechanisms differ in ability to regulate social distance, some are better than others when social distance between the bureaucracy and the family group is too close or too far. Primary groups socially distant from the bureaucracy are more likely to be influenced if the mechanisms used for communication allow the organization to take great initiative in contacting these groups.

The second criterion is intensity. To reach very distant families, the bureaucracy must intensify relations with family members through a trusted individual, usually a member of the group or neighborhood.

The third criterion, focused expertise, states that the more complex the message the greater the need to provide feedback and flexible response. Face-to-face contact is a more powerful communication tool than indirect access. The fourth, maximum coverage, predicts that communication procedures will be more successful if they reach the largest number of families possible.

The functionality of Litwak's model is illustrated in a child-rearing program judged successful by its community and the people who organized it: a Day Care Neighbor Service sponsored by United States Children's Bureau and a group in Portland, Oregon. The Service was a project aimed at demonstrating that an informal family day-care system can operate in neighborhoods of all levels even when its existence is officially denied. The strategy was to capitalize on the potential of natural care givers. The interventions involved social workers (detached experts in Litwak's framework) who provided consultation to the opinion leaders, day-care neighbors. These leaders, in turn, helped potential users and givers of care to find each other and to make mutually satisfactory arrangements (Emlen & Watson, 1971). Through use of the consulting social worker, linkages were made from the day-care neighbor to the care giver and to the families. Generally, the day-care neighbor and the social worker functioned as powerful tools in closing the communication gap between the sponsoring agencies and the families being served. They allowed the agencies to take the initiative when families were distant; they allowed high intensity in the delivery of complex messages. Although their scope was limited, that disadvantage in this context was compensated for by the use of mass media, advertising of the service on bulletin boards located where families who needed family care would gather, *e.g.*, laundromats and grocery stores.

Conclusion

Shared function not only has strong implication for the way in which families and bureaucracies interface but also describes the interface between mother and father roles. In view of emergent life styles and dual-career marriages, shared parenting is becoming an important dimension in the present alteration of family structure and the articulation of social policy. Bronfenbrenner (1974a), Roby (1975), Schienfield (1969), and Wortis (1974) all argue convincingly and strongly for the expressive attributes that males (fathers, grandfathers, and uncles) can contribute to child socialization. Their argument follows Litwak's description of the expressive and instrumental attributes of the family and the bureaucracy. Males and females can be complementary, not competitive, organisms. Each sex has instrumental and expressive functions. Matching these functions to child-socialization tasks requires thoughtful attention to the profile of the individual family.

Parent-Teacher Interaction: A Developmental Process

R. ELEANOR DUFF and KEVIN J. SWICK

*Drs. Duff and Swick are affiliated with the
University of South Carolina, Department of
Early Childhood Education.*

A topic of great interest and concern for numerous educators today relates to the involvement of parents in the education of their children. Parents' active involvement in their child's growth experiences (both in the home and in the school) appears at the outset to be an elementary objective, one that should be easy to set in motion. The involvement process, however, is found to be a highly challenging system of human interactions, with effective implementation dependent upon careful attention to a number of sensitive variables. It is therefore not surprising that school systems having successful experiences in the development and implementation of this concept are still few in number.

This paper will attempt to examine briefly this concept from a developmental point of view. The first deals with the meaning and the second points-of-beginning. The latter section will focus on questions to be considered by both teachers and parents as they examine and analyze their feelings and attitudes about being a part of such a dynamic relationship.

Parent Involvement in Education: Meaning

Parent involvement, from a parent's point of view, may be perceived as involvement with the child's interests in the home setting, sharing fully, in collaboration with the school, all decisions related to the child's school experiences. It encompasses the parents' acknowledgement and acceptance of themselves as the child's most important teachers and a willingness to accept responsibility to try to understand their child's learning behavior. It further commits the parents to a collaborative supportive relationship with the child's teacher in the school.

From the teacher's point of view, parent involvement encompasses the recognition and acceptance of the parents as important teachers, and a willingness to encourage them to share in the educational decision making that affects their child.

With respect to how parents and teachers can be helped to deal with this highly challenging concept, it is reasonable to approach it from a developmental point of view. From a developmental perspective, it is suggested that parents be encouraged to recognize that the wide range of skills required for effective parenting do not appear automatically with the birth of the child. Instead, just as we acknowledge the stages of growth and development through which young children move, we should recognize that parents also move developmentally in their acquisition and refinement of parenting skills. In this respect, parents, as they learn how to be in touch with their child's development and at the same time be perceptive to the changes taking place in their own development, gradually come to realize the importance of their presence and influence on the total development of the child.

As a result of positive experiences or conditions which encourage parents to perfect their parenting skills, it is logical to expect that their role will become clearer and take on increased importance. The effective parent thus grows with the child.

The child's entrance into a group-care or school situation marks the beginning of a critical period for both the child and his parents. As parents confront new school related knowledge and understanding about their child's expanding skills and interests, effective parents will most likely seek encouragement to be involved in this dimension of the child's life. Such an involvement would hopefully make them more understanding, and thus more fully supportive of the child in his/her school-related efforts. It seems only natural that as the family approaches the school experience, the parents should not expect to abdicate the school-related portion of their association with their child. Instead, they should expect to add significant individuals to their family's total life experience—the teacher and other school-related individuals.

As parents continue to view themselves as important influences in their child's total development, their attitudes and feelings about their roles and their responsibilities for their child's school-related experiences may be expected to undergo still further change. With encouragement from the school the parents are likely to gain increased confidence in their ability to complement and support the professionally trained teacher, and hence, perceive themselves as productive members of the teaching-learning team.

While the parents' interactions with the school may take any of several different forms interchangeably (educational experiences, participation experiences, and/or highly involved experiences), it is likely that if these experiences continue to be of a positive nature, the parents will be able to gain greater insight into their own personal capabilities. From this point they will be able to move toward greater competence to be integrally involved in school related activities and decisions that affect the quality of that important segment of their child's growth experiences. Vital to the effectiveness of the interactions between parents and teachers, however, is an open trusting system of communication.

As in the case with parents, teachers, who for the first time begin to collaborate with parents, may find it necessary to make adjustments in their understandings, attitudes and skills related to working closely and cooperatively with other adults. In other words, they, too, must move developmentally in their relationships with parents. It is apparent that society (especially during the school-life of the individual) has done little to encourage the development of cooperation and teaming skills. Even today, as in years past, one of the behaviors most valued by the typical classroom teacher is that of *doing one's own work by one's self.* Seldom is there an expectation that children should collaborate, cooperate, and share responsibility for accomplishing anything. Furthermore, teacher preparation programs do little more than suggest the value of supportive interaction between parents and teachers; hence, adults who become teachers in our society lack the proper attitude and skills to work cooperatively with other adults. As a result, when teachers encounter the need for a close relationship with parents, they often find it necessary to make great changes in their feelings and beliefs with respect to the parents' role and responsibilities in school-related decisions.

In many cases, both parents and teachers lack the interpersonal skills required to function productively in such a collaborative fashion.

Recognizing the conditions, both personal and professional, which have influenced the attitudes often held by both parents and teachers (relative to each of their roles and responsibilities in the learning process), it is then obvious that the productiveness of the interactions between the parent-

teacher team will be contingent upon their compatibility of attitudes, combined with their competence in the use of interpersonal skills. Once parents and teachers are aware of their interactive behaviors as they strive toward the goal of enhancing the relationships between the child and his parents, parents and teachers can then begin to implement the involvement concept.

Parent Involvement in Education: Points of Beginning

For the teacher of young children who for the first time is willing to venture into a close, cooperative relationship with the parents, there are several questions which she should carefully and candidly consider. The responses made will come to serve as a beginning in an effort to examine beliefs about parents, their children and learning. As such, they will become a basis and guide for subsequent efforts.

I. Philosophical Statements

A. Teacher

- To whom am I, as a teacher of young children, personally and professionally responsible?

- Who was the child's first teacher?
- To what extent does the family influence the young child's development?
- Do I have the right to expect the parent to put his child's school experiences completely in my hands?

The same set of questions, considered thoughtfully and honestly, should yield responses which may also become the basis for the parents' concerned efforts.

B. Parents

- As a parent, what are my responsibilities both at home and at school in assuring the development of my child's learning skills?
- Who was my child's first teacher? Was I an effective teacher during his/her early years?
- To what extent does the home environment influence a child's development?
- Do I have the right to expect the school to take complete responsibility for my child's education?

The chief aim of this set of questions is to encourage the acknowledgement by both parents and teachers that they together are responsible for the development of the child's learning skills and that their responsibilities may be more effectively met if they begin to perceive their roles and skills as complementary and to behave in a supportive fashion.

The positions taken with respect to each of the following questions should lead both teachers and parents to assess logically the conditions of communications as they exist in the school. While both parents and teachers recognize the importance of concerned communication between themselves, many feel unsure about the appropriateness of questions or discussions concerning what may be perceived as sensitive areas to the other. At this point, attention must again be focused upon communication as a mode of interaction through which parents and teachers seek to learn more about and to understand more fully, in order to be supportive of the other. The chief purpose to be kept constantly in mind is to enhance the growth experiences for the children, the parents and the teachers.

II. Communication: How much do I know and understand?

A. Teacher

- How much do the parents of my children know about me as a teacher and how much do they understand about the school's program? How much do I really know about each of my children?

- How often, in what form, and under what conditions do communications take place between the parents of my children and me?

- How and by whom are decisions made as they relate to the school and its activities?

B. Parents

- What do I really know about my child's school program? How well am I acquainted with my child's teacher?

- Should I always wait for the teacher to initiate contact with me?

- I wonder how the school decides which programs of instruction it will select for my child?

Responses to the following questions by both parents and teachers should suggest directions that either may take to facilitate meaningful interaction between the school and the home. The most important step toward this kind of interaction will be the first step whereby the teacher or the child's

parents, in a caring, concerned yet sensitive fashion, extend genuine support to the other.

III. Springboards to Action

A. Teacher

- What kinds of instructional changes could be made for each child if I had additional personal information about each one?

- What kinds of instructional changes could be made if I had additional assistance in the classroom?

- In what kinds of activities could I involve parents that would give them greater insight into their child's learning behavior? How may I increase the parents' confidence in their child?

B. Parents

- In what ways and at what times could I be of assistance to my child's classroom teacher?

- What kinds of information could I provide the teacher so that she/he would have a clearer picture of my child?

- I wonder if my child is learning as well as she/he is able? I wonder if our home environment is of a quality conducive to maximal development?

As it becomes increasingly clear that "the most important influences on the development of young children arise within the context of their immediate environment . . . the family,"[1] it would appear that we have reached a point, socio-educationally, that professionally trained teachers (as well as teachers-to-be) must examine and analyze their system of beliefs and attitudes about the children they teach (and their families) in order to clarify and articulate their responsibilities to their needs.

By the same token, parents would do well to assess their developmental status as parents and, with such information, consider a realignment of family priorities that would place their child in a position of confidence and respect, with empathetic concern for the child's total development.

Only as a result of continuous growth experiences and a continued willingness to take the risks that close relationships require will teachers and parents be able to bring about their maximum influence on the child.

NOTE

1. The National Research Council. *Toward a National Policy on Children and Families.* 1976 (Washington, D. C.; National Academy of Sciences).

When a

by Luleen S. Anderson

This September more than six million 5- and 6-year-olds will make their first significant venture into foreign territory: they will leave home to begin kindergarten or first grade. That a large percentage of them adjust to school with a minimum of difficulty is a tribute to the resiliency of the young child. Unfortunately parents, who play a major role in this drama, seldom receive the support they need to help both themselves and their child effectively handle this new experience.

When the child leaves home comfortably and is eager for the new experiences school will bring, everything is lovely. But when the child becomes anxious and fearful or refuses to go to school—or if he or she goes amid such emotional scenes that both the child and parent are physically and emotionally drained—something has gone awry. Unless the situation receives immediate attention, a temporary crisis may become a chronic problem. (This may lead to what is usually called "school avoidance" or "school phobia"—terms which simply mean that for one reason or another, the child is anxious about the separation from home and is afraid to go to school.)

What can parents do to help their child take this developmental step forward? First, parents should understand that there are certain tasks which must be mastered at certain ages. No matter what our age, each of us has a job to do—a task or tasks to master. Each period of life brings its own challenges and stresses —from infancy, when the baby must

Child Begins School

learn to trust his world and the helping people in it, to young adulthood, when the young person must decide on career goals and lifestyles. The building blocks for sound personality development involve the successful mastery of these tasks at each level of growth and development.

Thus, the 5- or 6-year-old has a major job: to go to school. In order to do this—a task society has set for him or her—the child must successfully master three earlier tasks. First, he or she must make the shift from dependency upon parents and the home to dependency upon peers and other adults. This means that the school-age child must allow other people to meet many of his needs and to relate to him in meaningful fashion. How easily this task is mastered depends in large measure upon how secure and trusting his early relationships have been, and how unambivalent his parents are about supporting his new venture.

The second task of the child entering school is the management of separation anxiety. For most children this is accomplished with a minimum of anxiety or distress. For others, however, the threat of the loss of mother is terribly frightening and extremely stressful, both for the child and for the mother. Separation anxiety is one of the most painful experiences a child can have. Often for mothers, who can see no logical reason for it, it is a most baffling experience.

Finally, the school-age child must learn to accept the authority of other adults, namely, the teacher, principal and other support personnel in the school. This acceptance is made easier if the child has had a healthy dose of basic trust through his early relationships with other helping adults.

These, then, are the young child's jobs. But parents have their job, too, and that is to do everything they can to make it possible for the child to deal effectively with his or her new experiences. How can parents do this? In response to questions from many parents, I began three years ago, in late spring, to meet with parents of preschoolers to discuss how they could help prepare their children for entry into school. Here are some practical suggestions — some "dos" and "don'ts" — which we discussed and which have proven effective for many parents:

• Don't make the beginning of school a topic of daily conversation during the summer months. Don't belabor the issue—or, as one child said to his over-zealous mother, "Don't make a federal case out of it!"

• Do treat going to school as part of the normal course of events, something that is expected and something that parents casually accept that the child will be doing (with some support and encouragement).

• Don't allow older children to frighten or tease the younger child with tales of how awful school is. If necessary, speak with the older children privately about their responsibility in helping the younger child go to school without fear. Try to make the older children your allies. If a teasing child is a neighborhood bully over whom you have no control, invite your child to trust *your* perceptions about what school will be like, rather than accepting what the other child has to say on the subject.

• Do answer honestly all questions the child asks about school and what to expect. Knowing the number of days he will attend, the length of time he will be away from home, how he will get back and forth to school— all are important, for a child may be made anxious by uncertainty and needs to know details in order to master his anxiety. Many schools hold orientation sessions for parents and children to acquaint them with school staff members, the classroom the child will be attending and school procedures.

Working mothers and fathers will also want to make certain that the child knows the arrangement for before- and/or after-school care.

• Don't give the impression that there is any choice about whether or not to attend school. Children will often say, "I'm not going," or "They can't make me." These comments should be responded to calmly and reassuringly, letting the child know that you understand his concerns about this new situation but that you know he will be able to handle it— and that all children have to go to school. You may want to add that there is a law (or rule) which requires

Luleen S. Anderson, Ph.D., is coordinator of Psychological Services and Elementary Guidance for the Quincy Public Schools, Quincy, Massachusetts.

that children attend school. At five and six, children are already learning to respect and appreciate laws and rules. The point is not to waiver; the wise parent does not offer a choice which he cannot or will not honor. The mother who wants a child to eat eggs does not say, "Would you like an egg for breakfast?" Instead, she asks casually, "How would you like your egg this morning: fried, scrambled or boiled?" Don't argue the issue of school attendance. A calm, matter-of-fact, positive attitude is your goal.

• Do communicate to the child that you appreciate the effort he or she is making to do what is being asked, and that you will do your part to make it as easy as possible for the child to meet this new responsibility. There are many possibilities for communicating this support: "Would you prefer your new shoes or your sneakers for the first day of school?" "What dessert would you like in your lunch box?" "Think of something special you'd like us to do when you get home." The basic idea here is to find ways of acknowledging the child's efforts and to give the child some say-so—some control—over the situation, whenever possible.

• Do make transportation plans clear to the child. If he or she is to walk to school, walk the route together once or twice before school begins or walk him to school and meet him there after classes have ended the first day or so. If there are other children from your neighborhood who are his age and who are walking, see if your child and a friend could walk together.

Don't set a pattern of walking into the classroom and standing around while the child gets seated. This may lead to tears or clingy behavior, which gets the child off on the wrong foot with other children, who then may tease him, thus adding to the problem. Goodbyes are best said at home or in the school yard.

If a child is transported to school by bus, help the child identify the type of vehicle and, if possible, take a bus ride with the child prior to the first day of school to alleviate some anxiety. If there are other children whom you know waiting for the bus, introduce your child to them. Older children may be encouraged to watch over younger ones. Once the bus arrives, be direct; say goodbye and allow the child to board by himself. If the child does cry, be assured that in most cases the tears will usu-

ally disappear before the bus is out of sight.

• Don't try to force the child to be exuberant about going to school. It is natural for a child not to be ecstatic about giving up a comfortable and safe relationship at home for the uncertain territory of school. Allow, even encourage, him to express all his feelings about school. One good way of allowing children to let off steam is through fantasy—and you need not be afraid of granting in fantasy that which you cannot grant in reality. In other words, acknowledge a child's right to wish for things or to wish that things were different, even when you cannot allow the wish to be fulfilled. For example, when the up-tight 6-year-old says, the day before school begins, "I wish nobody ever invented schools or teachers," the wise parent will understand the underlying concern in such a statement and respond, perhaps in the following fashion:

"I wish nobody ever invented schools or teachers."

"It would be fun, wouldn't it, if we could just stay home and play all day and have nobody telling us what to do. Some days I feel that way, too. But we can't do all the things we'd like to, even though it's fun to think about the idea."
Sometimes just being able to say whatever is on his or her mind and to discover that the words are heard and the feelings are accepted is both calming and reassuring to a child.

• Many non-working mothers look forward to the free time they will have once their child enters school. However, don't tell the child how much fun you are going to be having while he or she is in school. Do let the child know that while he is doing his job at school, you will be doing yours. Mentioning of concrete tasks can be very reassuring to the child. "While you're in school today, I'll do the laundry and vacuuming so we can have some time together when you get home."
Working mothers often make special arrangements which allow them to be home the first day or two when their child returns from school. When

this is not possible, other ways of giving a little extra attention can be found, such as a telephone call from work to the child who has just completed his first day at school, or an arrangement to do something special with the child later in the day when the mother returns home from work.

• Do create a normal routine atmosphere at home the first few days of school. This does not mean that you deny or avoid the uniqueness of the first day of school but, on the other hand, don't give the child the impression that his leaving for his first day of school is of the same magnitude as Lindbergh's solo flight over the Atlantic. One such family of a 5-year-old arrived en masse at the school for the child's first day, formed a line on the sidewalk and waved and cried as their movie camera recorded his slow disappearance into the school! The parents' responsibility is to provide reassuring support when needed, but otherwise to "play it cool."

• Don't assume that all of the anxiety associated with a child's entry into school is the child's. Parents —especially mothers—may experience some anxiety of their own over their child's moving into a new era. This is understandable, for the mother has to give up some of her control of the child to school authorities and to share her child's teaching and upbringing with others. Often she also has major readjustments to make in her own life if she now has a large portion of her time free.

Mothers need to separate their own anxiety from that of the child's. A mother's worry and tension are highly contagious and the young child quickly perceives and responds to them. I encourage mothers to acknowledge and accept their own feelings and reactions, get the youngster off to school—and then to relax and share their feelings with a friend.

What I am suggesting here is that a child's going off to school represents a developmental phase for parents as well as children. Parents should be aware that sending a child off to school can be anxiety-provoking for them. Each parent maintains many childhood memories, both positive and negative, about school. A child's entry into school seems to reactivate for some parents the feelings they had when they started school themselves, particularly feelings associated with negative experiences—which, perhaps, leave the deepest impression. Therefore, remembering their school experiences, parents may have ambivalent feelings concerning their child's new experience. Since the parents' reaction to the child's early school experiences is of critical importance to his or her early school adjustment, parents might profit by reviewing their own anxieties and satisfactions regarding their school entry experiences.

By the time their first child begins school, most parents have been away from the educational system for a number of years. When their child enters kindergarten or first grade, parents see a school that has probably changed considerably from what they remember. It would be helpful if parents could see this as a positive opportunity to reacquaint themselves with the educational system and to get to know the school staff members and other parents involved in their child's school.

While the focus here has been on the child entering kindergarten or first grade, we must realize that, for increasing numbers of children, kindergarten does not represent their first school experience. Today many children attend nursery schools, day care centers and other preschool programs. A happy preschool experience may promote a comfortable transition into kindergarten; however, kindergarten is *not* a repeat of nursery school. As one very bright second-grader explained when asked about the differences between nursery school and kindergarten, "Well, most anybody can make it in nursery school. But when you go to *real* school, you're not so sure you can learn everything and make good grades."

Parents whose children have adjusted well to preschool are often surprised that they may experience separation anxiety when they approach kindergarten or first grade. This repetition of emotional experience is an important developmental

> **". . . most anybody can make it in nursery school. But when you go to real school, you're not so sure you can learn everything . . ."**

phenomenon. These children have endured the initial separation from home to receive the gratification of new experiences and friends, and they have dealt with their first major loss of persons outside their home. Children who have attended preschool and are entering kindergarten are, in effect, being asked to risk separation again for new horizons which have not been defined.

If parents do enroll a child in a preschool program, they should, if possible, select one which is as compatible as possible with the school their child will later attend. If the parents themselves are aware of whatever major differences exist, they can forewarn the child and, thus, help him to cope with them. The intention of preschool programs should be to provide a bridge between home and the world, one which might help children toward a kindergarten adjustment without infringing on local kindergarten experiences.

What happens if, after all this good planning and careful handling, the big day arrives and the child begins to cry or to complain of being sick? Parents should grit their teeth, fight back the annoyance and PUSH. This means that the child is to go even if tears flow. Usually the "moment of truth" occurs at the point of separation between mother and child. Once this separation is made, the child usually recovers quickly and has a successful day. Many a mother or father who feels terrible all day because the child left in tears would be reassured if they could know that the tears have usually subsided before the child had gone two blocks away, and that the teacher was unaware that the child had experienced difficulty in getting to school that day. In a situation such as this, the first few days are critical. With firm, patient, reassuring handling of the child by parents and teachers, this fearful, tearful behavior usually disappears within a few days. By then the child has learned to feel comfortable away from home; he has learned to trust his teacher and has made some new friends; and he has learned that some interesting, exciting things go on in his classroom. What is important for the child's *emotional* health is that with support he or she has mastered a fear—has learned to cope—and, in the process, has learned to feel good inside about himself and secure in his world.

In rare instances when this smooth process does not occur, when the anxiety does not abate after a few days and the child's fearfulness and feelings of distress continue to mount, the child may be developing a more serious problem. At this point, parents should seek professional advice by asking for a consultation with the school guidance counselor, if the school has such a person, or other school personnel. A consultation with the family doctor or pediatrician might also be considered. However, for most children who have experienced basically stable and supportive relationships prior to entering school, and whose parents have dealt successfully with their own ambivalent feelings about the child's entry into school, their upset—if obvious at all—usually disappears quickly, particularly if the techniques described here are used consistently by parents and other supportive persons.

Office of Human Development Services, Department of Health, Education and Welfare.

LANGUAGE DEVELOPMENT

Language is described as our primary tool for communication. It serves as the basis of all human interaction. Emphasizing the paucity of information really known yet today about how children learn language, Bruner in "Learning the Mother Tongue," suggests a "New picture of language learning which recognizes that the process depends upon highly constrained and one sided transactions between the child and the adult teacher." Language acquisition, according to Bruner requires joint problem solving by mother and infant, and her response to her child's language is closely tuned in a way that can be specified. With respect to language and reading acquisition, the question of critical periods emerges often. Conlon's paper, "Is There a Critical Period for Language and Reading Acquisition," attempts to bring research findings to the problem.

While language is unquestioningly the medium of learning, it reveals the conceptions and misconceptions held by the learner. Osburn's "Children's Language: What Does It Reveal?" provides a number of episodes to illustrate generalizations that researchers have found characteristic of the language of children. The author further suggests implications for further classroom experiences for enhancing language development.

One of the critical areas concerning classroom practices and language learning relates to the large numbers of commercially prepared materials in the form of kits. All espouse the guarantee to bring development of language skills. Patricia Huntinger's paper, "Language Development: It's Much More than a Kit" emphasizes the importance of interaction with people. She offers the teacher many suggestions for providing an atmosphere conductive to optimal language development.

In "Comments on Language by a Silent Child" Lillian Weber relates language learning experiences for today's children to her own personal experiences as a child. She illustrates not only how children learn language as infants, but how they do it as a part of the whole "time sweep," incorporating the supportive processes involved - who parents are and what they do.

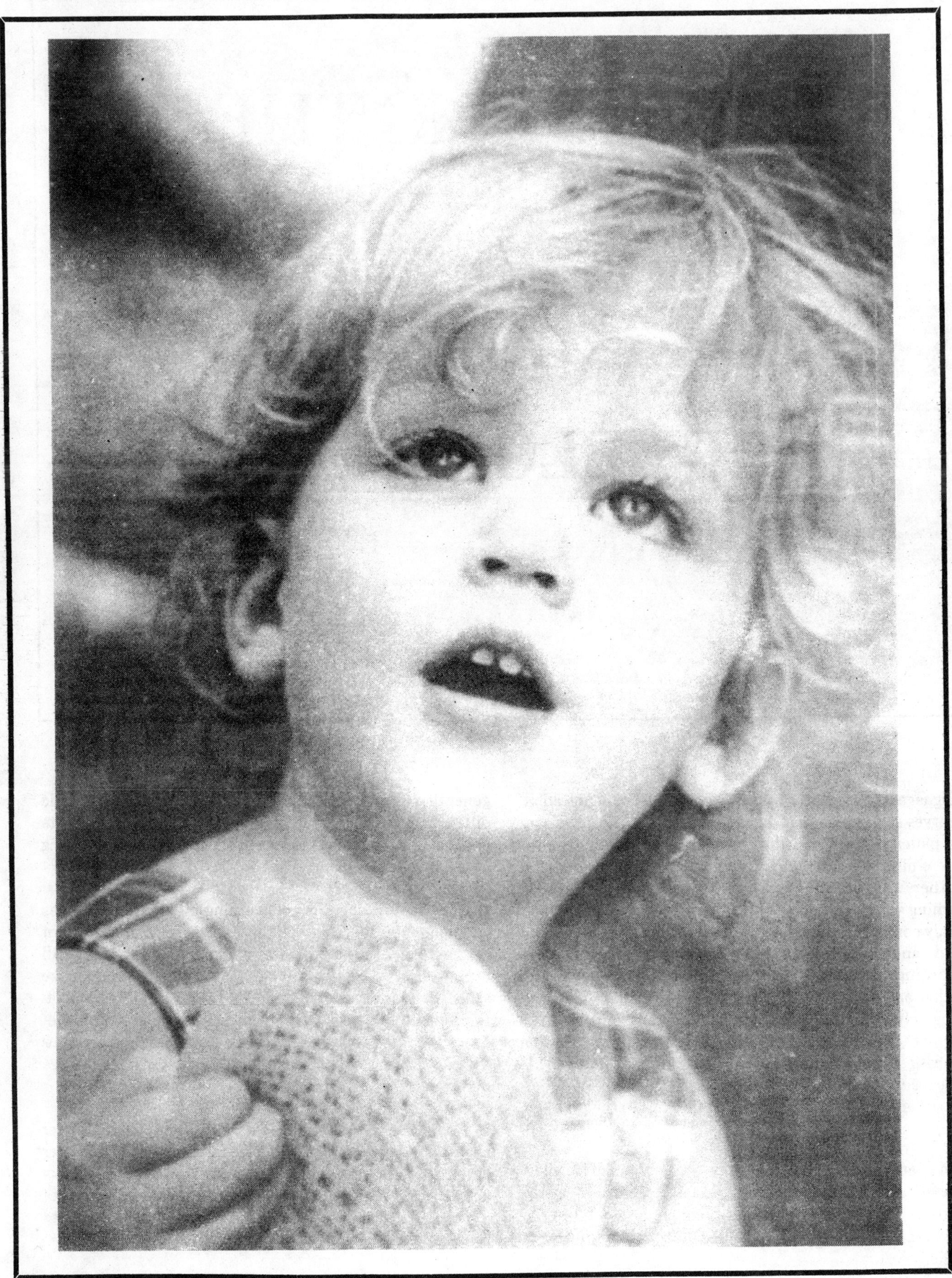

Office of Human Development Services, Department of Health, Education and Welfare.

LEARNING THE MOTHER TONGUE

Acquiring language appears to be either inexplicable or miraculous, but close observation indicates that baby and mother work together and the role of the mother is crucial.

JEROME S. BRUNER

Learning a native language is an accomplishment within the grasp of any toddler, yet discovering how children do it has eluded generations of philosophers. St. Augustine believed it was simple. Recollecting his own childhood, he said, "When they named any thing, and as they spoke turned towards it, I saw and remembered that they called what they would point out by the name they uttered. . . . And thus by constantly hearing words, as they occurred in various sentences, I collected gradually for what they stood; and having broken in my mouth to these signs, I thereby gave utterance to my will." But a look at children as they actually acquire language shows that St. Augustine was wrong and that other attempts to explain the feat err as badly in the opposite direction. What is more, as we try to understand how children learn their own language, we get an inkling of why it is so difficult for adults to learn a second language.

Thirty years ago, psychologies of learning held sway; language acquisition was explained using principles and methods that had little to do with language. Most started with nonsense syllables or random materials that were as far as researchers could get from the structure of language that permits the generation of rich and limitless statements, speculations, and poetry. Like G. K. Chesterton's drunk, they looked for the lost coin where the light was. And in the light of early learning theories, children appeared to acquire language by associating words with agents and objects and actions, by imitating their elders, and by a mysterious force called reinforcement. It was the old and tired Augustinian story dressed up in the language of behaviorism.

Learning theory led to a readiness, even a recklessness, to be rid of an inadequate account, one that could explain the growth of vocabulary but not how a four-year-old abstracts basic language rules and effortlessly combines old words to make an infinite string of new sentences. The stage was set for linguist Noam Chomsky's theory of LAD, the Language Acquisition Device, and for the Chomskyan revolution.

According to this view, language was not learned; it was recognized by virtue of an innate recognition routine through which children, when exposed to their local language, could abstract or extract its universal grammatical principles. Whatever the input of that local language, however degenerate, the output of LAD was the grammar of the language, a competence to generate all possible grammatical sentences and none (or very few) that were not. It was an extreme view, so extreme that it did not even consider meaning. In a stroke it freed a generation of psycholinguists from the dogma of association, imitation, and reinforcement and turned their attention to the problem of rule learning. By declaring learning theory dead, it opened the way for a new account. George Miller of The Rockefeller University put it well: We had two theories of language learning—one of them, empiricist associationism, is impossible; the other, nativism, is miraculous. The void between the impossible and the miraculous remained to be filled.

Both explanations begin too late—when children say their first words. Long before children acquire language, they know something about their world. Before they can make verbal distinctions in speech, they have sorted the conceptual universe into useful categories and classes and can make distinctions about actions and agents and objects. As Roger Brown of Harvard University has written, "The concept . . . is there beforehand, waiting for the word to come along that names it." But the mys-

"Learning the Mother Tongue," by Jerome S. Bruner, *Human Nature*, Vol. 1, No. 9, September 1978, pp. 42-49. ©1978, Harcourt Brace Jovanovich, Inc.

tery of how children penetrate the communication system and learn to represent in language what they already know about the real world has not been solved. Although there is a well-packaged semantic content waiting, what children learn about language is not the same as what they know about the world. Yet the void begins to fill as soon as we recognize that children are not flying blind, that semantically speaking they have some target toward which language-learning efforts are directed: saying something or understanding something about events in a world that is already known.

If a child is in fact communicating, he has some end in mind—requesting something or indicating something or establishing some sort of personal relationship. The function of a communication has to be considered. As philosopher John Austin argued, an utterance cannot be analyzed out of its context of use, and its use must include the intention of the speaker and its interpretation in the light of conventional standards by the person addressed. A speaker may make a request in several ways: by using the conventional question form, by making a declarative statement, or by issuing a command.

Roger Brown observed young Adam from age two until he was four and found that his middle-class mother made requests using a question form: "Why don't you play with your ball now?" Once Adam came to appreciate what I shall call genuine *why* questions (i.e., "Why are you playing with your ball?"), he typically answered these—and these only—with the well-known "Because." There is no instance, either before or after he began to comprehend the genuine causal question, of his ever confusing a sham and a real *why* question.

Not only does conceptual knowledge precede true language, but so too does function. Children know, albeit in limited form, what they are trying to accomplish by communicating before they begin to use language to implement their efforts. Their initial gestures and vocalizations become increasingly stylized and conventional.

It has become plain in the last several years that Chomsky's original bold claim that any sample of language encountered by an infant was enough for the LAD to dig down to the grammatical rules simply is false. Language is not encountered willy-nilly by the child; it is instead encountered in a highly orderly interaction with the mother, who takes a crucial role in arranging the linguistic encounters of the child. What has emerged is a theory of mother-infant interaction in language acquisition—called the fine-tuning theory—that sees language mastery as involving the mother as much as it does the child. According to this theory, if the LAD exists, it hovers somewhere in the air between mother and child.

So today we have a new perspective that begins to grant a place to knowledge of the world, to knowledge of the function of communication, and to the hearer's interpretation of the speaker's intent. The new picture of language learning recognizes that the process depends on highly constrained and one-sided transactions between the child and the adult teacher. Language acquisition requires joint problem solving by mother and infant, and her response to her child's language is close tuned in a way that can be specified.

The child's entry into language is an entry into dialogue, and the dialogue is at first necessarily nonverbal and requires both members of the pair to interpret the communication and its intent. Their relationship is in the form of roles, and each "speech" is determined by a move of either partner. Initial control of the dialogue depends on the mother's interpretation, which is guided by a continually updated understanding of her child's competence.

Consider an infant learning to label objects. Anat Ninio and I observed Richard in his home every two weeks from his eighth month until he was two years old, video-taping his actions so that we could study them later. In this instance he and his mother are "reading" the pictures in a book. Before this kind of learning begins, certain things already have been established. Richard has learned about pointing as a pure indicating act, marking unusual or unexpected objects rather than things wanted immediately. He has also learned to understand that sounds refer in some singular way to objects or events. Richard and his mother, moreover, have long since established well-regulated turn-taking routines, which probably were developing as early as his third or fourth month. And finally, Richard has learned that books are to be looked at, not eaten or torn; that objects depicted are to be responded to in a particular way and with sounds in a pattern of dialogue.

For the mother's part, she (like all mothers we have observed) drastically limits her speech and maintains a steady regularity. In her dialogues with Richard she uses four types of speech in a strikingly fixed order. First, to get his attention, she says "Look." Second, with a distinctly rising inflection, she asks "What's that?" Third, she gives the picture a label, "It's an X." And finally, in response to his actions, she says "That's right."

In each case, a single verbal token accounts for from nearly half to more than 90 percent of the instances. The way Richard's mother uses the four speech constituents is closely linked to what her son says or does. When she varies her response, it is with good reason. If Richard responds, his mother replies, and if he initiates a cycle by pointing and vocalizing, then she responds even more often.

Her fine tuning is fine indeed. For example, if after her query Richard labels the picture, she will virtually always skip the label and jump to the response, "Yes." Like the other mothers we have studied, she is following ordinary polite rules for adult dialogue.

As Roger Brown has described the baby talk of adults, it appears to be an imitative version of how babies talk. Brown says, "Babies already talk like babies, so what is the earthly use of parents doing the same? Surely it is a parent's job to teach the adult language." He resolves the dilemma by noting, "What I think adults are chiefly trying to do, when they use [baby talk] with children, is to communicate, to understand and to be understood, to keep two minds focussed on the same topic." Although I agree with Brown, I would like to point out that the content and intonation of the talk is baby talk, but the dialogue pattern is adult.

To ensure that two minds are indeed focused on a common topic, the mother develops a technique for showing her baby what feature a label refers to by making 90 percent of her labels refer to whole objects. Since half of the remainder of her speech is made up of proper names that also stand for the whole, she seems to create few difficulties, supposing that the child also responds to whole objects and not to their features.

The mother's (often quite unconscious) approach is exquisitely tuned. When the child responds to her "Look!" by looking, she follows immediately with a query. When the child responds to the query with a gesture or a smile, she supplies a label. But as soon as the child shows the ability to vocalize in a way that might indicate a label, she raises the ante. She withholds the label and repeats the query until the child vocalizes, then she gives the label.

Later, when the child has learned to respond with shorter vocalizations that correspond to words, she no longer accepts an indifferent vocalization. When the child begins producing a recognizable, constant label for an object, she holds out for it. Finally, the child produces appropriate words at the appropriate place in the dialogue. Even then the mother remains tuned to the developing pattern, helping her child recognize labels and make them increasingly accurate. For example, she develops two ways of asking "What's that?" One, with a falling intonation, inquires about those words for which she believes her child already knows the label; the other, with a rising intonation, marks words that are new.

Even in the simple labeling game, mother and child are well into making the distinction between the given and the new. It is of more than passing interest that the old or established labels are the ones around which the mother will shortly be elaborating comments and questions for new information:

Mother (with falling intonation): What's that?

Child: Fishy.

Mother: Yes, and see him swimming?

After the mother assumes her child has acquired a particular label, she generally drops the attention-getting "Look!" when they turn to the routine. In these petty particulars of language, the mother gives useful cues about the structure of their native tongue. She provides cues based not simply on her knowledge of the language but also on her continually changing knowledge of the child's ability to grasp particular dis-

tinctions, forms, or rules. The child is sensitized to certain constraints in the structure of their dialogue and does not seem to be directly imitating her. I say this because there is not much difference in the likelihood of a child's repeating a label after hearing it, whether the mother has imitated the child's label, simply said "Yes," or only laughed approvingly. In each case the child repeats the label about half the time, about the same rate as with *no* reply from the mother. Moreover, the child is eight times more likely to produce a label in response to "What's that?" than to the mother's uttering the label.

I do not mean to claim that children cannot or do not use imitation in acquiring language. Language must be partly based on imitation, but though the child may be imitating another, language learning involves solving problems by communicating in a dialogue. The child seems to be trying to get through to the mother just as hard as she is trying to reach her child.

Dialogue occurs in a context. When children first learn to communicate, it is always in highly concrete situations, as when mother or child calls attention to an object, asking for the aid or participation of the other. Formally conceived, the format of communication involves an intention, a set of procedures, and a goal. It presupposes shared knowledge of the world and a shared script by which mother and child can carry out reciprocal activity in that world. Formats obviously have utility for the child. They provide a simple, predictable bit of the world in which and about which to communicate. But they also have an important function for the mother in the mutual task of speech acquisition.

When a mother uses baby talk, her intonation broadens, her speech slows, and her grammar becomes less complex. In addition, baby talk virtually always starts with the here and now, with the format in which the two are operating. It permits the mother to tune her talk to the child's capabilities. She need not infer the child's general competence for language, but instead judges the child's performance on a specific task at a specific time.

A second major function of speech is requesting something of another person. Carolyn Roy and I have been studying its

development during the first two years of life. Requesting requires an indication that you want *something* and *what* it is you want. In the earliest procedures used by children it is difficult to separate the two. First the child vocalizes with a characteristic intonation pattern while reaching eagerly for the desired nearby object — which is most often held by the mother. As in virtually all early exchanges, it is the mother's task to interpret, and she works at it in a surprisingly subtle way. During our analyses of Richard when he was from 10 to 24 months old and Jonathan when he was 11 to 18 months old, we noticed that their mothers frequently seemed to be teasing them or withholding obviously desired objects. Closer inspection indicated that it was not teasing at all. They were trying to establish whether the infants really wanted what they were reaching for, urging them to make their intentions clearer.

When the two children requested nearby objects, the mothers were more likely to ask "Do you really want it?" than "Do you want the X?" The mother's first step is pragmatic, to establish the sincerity of the child's request.

Children make three types of requests, reflecting increasing sophistication in matters that have nothing to do with language. The first kind that emerges is directed at obtaining nearby, visible objects; this later expands to include distant or absent objects where the contextual understanding of words like "you, me," "this, that," and "here, there" is crucial. The second kind of request is directed at obtaining support for an action that is already in progress, and the third kind is used to persuade the mother to share some activity or experience.

When children first begin to request objects, they typically direct their attention and their reach, opening and closing their fists, accompanied by a characteristic intonation pattern. As this request expands, between 10 and 15 months, an observer immediately notes two changes. In reaching for distant objects, a child no longer looks solely at the desired object, but shifts his glance back and forth between the object and his mother. His call pattern also changes. It becomes more prolonged, or its rise and fall is repeated, and it is more insistent. Almost all of Richard's and Jonathan's requests for absent objects were for food,

Mothers' questions when children request nearby objects

Type of question	Age in months		
	10-12	13-14	More than 15
About intention ("Do you want it?")	93%	90%	42%
About referent ("Do you want the x?")	7%	10%	58%
Number of questions	**27**	**29**	**12**

Forms of early requests

Request for:	Age in months				
	10-12	13-14	15-16	17-18	20-24
Near and visible object	100%	74%	43%	22%	11%
Distant or invisible object	0	16%	24%	8%	24%
Shared activity	0	10%	14%	23%	36%
Supportive action	0	0	19%	47%	29%
Minutes of recording	**150**	**120**	**120**	**120**	**150**
Number of requests/10 minutes	**1.5**	**1.6**	**1.8**	**4.3**	**2.3**

Adult responses to children's requests

Type of response	Age in months				
	10-12	13-14	15-16	17-18	20-24
Pronominal question					
Open question (who, what, which)	78%	55%	36%	8%	1%
Closed question (yes, no)	3%	10%	18%	30%	22%
Comment/Question (yes, no)	6%	27%	36%	25%	36%
Comment/Question on agency	8%	2%	0	20%	28%
"Language lesson"	6%	6%	9%	14%	4%
Request for reason	0	0	0	3%	5%
Other	0	0	1%	0	4%
Number of utterances	**36**	**51**	**22**	**116**	**100**

As children's requests change with increasing sophistication (center), their mothers switch from establishing the sincerity of a request to identifying the object wanted (top). The sharp increase in replies having to do with who will get or control an action ("agency") reflects a demand for sharing and a difference in wishes (bottom).

drink, or a book to be read, each having its habitual place. Each request involved the child's gesturing toward the place.

When consistent word forms appeared, they were initially idiosyncratic labels for objects, gradually becoming standard nouns that indicated the desired objects. The children also began initiating and ending their requests with smiles. The development of this pattern is paced by the child's knowledge, which is shared with the mother, of where things are located and of her willingness to fetch them if properly asked. Once the child begins requesting distant and absent objects, the mother has an opportunity to require that the desired object be specified. Sincerity ceases to be at issue, though two other conditions are imposed: control of agency (who is actually to obtain the requested object, with emphasis on the child's increasing independence) and control of "share" (whether the child has had enough).

Requests for joint activity contrast with object requests. I think they can be called precursors to invitation. They amount to the child asking the adult to share in an activity or an experience — to look out of the window into the garden together, to play Ride-a-cockhorse, to read together. They are the most playlike form of request, and in consequence they generate a considerable amount of language of considerable complexity. It is in this format that the issues of agency and share (or turn) emerge and produce important linguistic changes.

Joint activity requires what I call joint role enactment, and it takes three forms: one in which the adult is agent and the child recipient or experiencer (as in early book reading); another in which there is turn taking with the possibility of exchanging roles (as in peekaboo); and a third in which roles run parallel (as in looking around the garden together). Most of what falls into these categories is quite ritualized and predictable. There tend to be rounds and turns, and no specific outcome is required. The activity itself is rewarding. In this setting the child first deals with share and turn by adopting such forms of linguistic marking as *more* and *again*. These appear during joint role enactment and migrate rapidly into formats involving requests for distant objects.

It is also in joint role enactment that the baby's first consistent words appear and, beginning at 18 months, word combinations begin to explode. *More X* (with a noun) appears, and also combinations like *down slide, brrm brrm boo knee, Mummy ride,* and *Mummy read.* Indeed it is in these settings that full-blown ingratiatives appear in appropriate positions, such as prefacing a request with *nice Mummy.*

Characteristically, less than 5 percent of the mother's responses to a child's requests before he is 17 months old have to do with agency (or who is going to do, get, or control something). After 17 months, that figure rises to over 25 percent. At that juncture the mothers we studied began to demand that their children adhere more strictly to turn taking and role respecting. The demand can be made most easily when they are doing something together, for that is where the conditions for sharing are most clearly defined and least likely, since playful, to overstrain the child's capacity to wait for a turn. But the sharp increase in agency as a topic in their dialogue reflects as well the emergence of a difference in their wishes.

The mother may want the child to execute the act requested of her, and the child may have views contrary to his mother's about agency. In some instances this leads to little battles of will. In addition, the child's requests for sup-

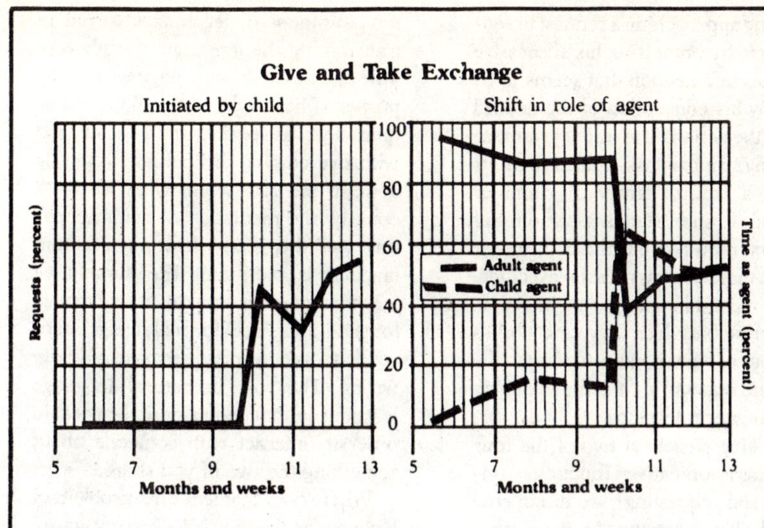

Toward the end of the first year the child gradually begins taking the lead in give-and-take games. Through such joint activity a child learns about sharing and taking turns.

port more often lead to negotiation between the pair than is the case when the clarity of the roles in their joint activity makes acceptance and refusal easier. A recurrent trend in development during the child's first year is the shifting of agency in all manner of exchanges from mother to infant. Even at nine to 12 months, Richard gradually began taking the lead in give-and-take games.

The same pattern holds in book reading, where Richard's transition was again quite rapid. Role shifting is very much part of the child's sense of script, and I believe it is typical of the kind of "real world" experience that makes it so astonishingly easy for children to master soon afterwards the deictic shifts, those contextual changes in the meaning of words that are essential to understanding the language. At about this time the child learns that I am *I* when I speak, but *you* when referred to by another, and so too with *you*; and eventually the child comes to understand the associated spatial words, *here* and *there*, *this* and *that*, *come* and *go*.

The prelinguistic communicative framework established in their dialogue by mother and child provides the setting for the child's acquisition of this language function. His problem solving in acquiring the deictic function is a *social* task: to find the procedure that will produce results, just as his prelinguistic communicative effort produced results, and the results needed can be interpreted in relation to role interactions.

For a number of years an emphasis on egocentrism in the young child has tended to blunt our awareness of the sensitivity of children to roles, of their capacity to manage role shift and role transformation. Although there is little doubt that it is more difficult for a young child to take the view of others than it will be for him later, this aspect of development has been greatly exaggerated. In familiar and sufficiently simple situations the child is quite capable of taking another's view. In 1975 Michael Scaife and I discovered that babies in their first year shifted their glance to follow an adult's line of regard, and in 1976 Andrew Meltzoff found in our laboratory that babies only a few weeks old appeared to have a built-in mechanism for mimicking an adult's expression, since they obviously could not see their own faces. More recently, Marilyn Shatz has shown that quite young children are indeed able to "take another's position" when giving instructions, provided the task is simple enough.

According to Katherine Nelson and Janice Gruendel at Yale University, what seems to be egocentrism is often a matter of the child not being able to coordinate his own scripts with those of the questioner, although he is scrupulously following turn taking (which is definitely not egocentric). They found that when "egocentric" four-year-olds do manage to find a joint script, they produce dialogues like the following. Two children are sitting next to each other talking into toy telephones:

Gay: Hi.

Dan: Hi.

Gay: How are you?

Dan: Fine.

Gay: Who am I speaking to?

Dan: Daniel. This is your Daddy. I need to speak to you.

Gay: All right.

Dan: When I come home tonight we're gonna have . . . peanut butter and jelly sandwich . . . uh . . . at dinner time.

Gay: Uhmmm. Where're we going at dinner time?

Dan: Nowhere, but we're just gonna have dinner at 11 o'clock.

Gay: Well, I made a plan of going out tonight.

Dan: Well, that's what we're gonna do.

Gay: We're going out.

Dan: The plan, it's gonna be, that's gonna be, we're going to McDonald's.

Gay: Yeah, we're going to McDonald's. And ah, ah, ah, what they have for dinner tonight is hamburger.

Dan: Hamburger is coming. O.K., well, goodbye.

Gay: Bye.

The child takes into account his or her partner's point of view, phrases his turns properly, and says things that are relevant to the script they are working on jointly. That is surely not egocentrism. But even managing the deictic function of language provides evidence that children realize there are viewpoints other than their own.

The last type of request, the request for supportive action, has a very special property. It is tightly bound to the nature of the action in which the child is involved. To ask others for help in support of their own actions, children need at least two forms of knowledge. One of them represents the course of action and involves a goal and a set of means for getting to it. The second requirement is some grasp of what has been called the arguments of action: who does it, with what instrument, at what place, to whom, on what object, etc. Once children have mastered these, they have a rudimentary understanding of the concepts that will later be encountered in case grammar.

The degree to which a child comes to understand the structure of tasks is the degree to which his requests for support in carrying them out become more differentiated. These requests do not appear with any marked frequency until he is 17 or 18 months old and consist of bringing the "work" or the "action" or the entire task to an adult: A music box needs rewinding, or two objects have to be put together. In time a child is able to do better than that. He may bring a tool to an adult or direct the adult's hand or pat the goal (the chair on which he wants up). He is selecting and highlighting relevant features of the action, though not in a fashion that depends on what the adult is doing. Finally, at about the age of two, with the development of adequate words to refer to particular aspects of the action, the child enters a new phase: He requests action by guiding it successively. The pacemaker of the verbal output is progress in the task itself.

Let me give an instance of this successive guidance system. Richard, it transpires, wishes to persuade his mother to get a toy telephone from the cupboard; she is seated (and very pregnant). Successively, he voices the following requests:

Mummy, Mummy; Mummy come.... Up, up.... Cupboard.... Up cupboard, up cupboard; up cupboard.... Get up, get up.... Cupboard, cupboard.... Cupboard-up; cupboard-up, cupboard-up. ... Telephone.... Mummy.... Mummy get out telephone.

His mother objects and asks him what it is he wants after each of the first two requests. She is trying to get him to set forth his request in some "readable" order before she starts to respond—to give a reason in terms of the goal of the action. Richard, meanwhile, achieves

something approaching a request in sentence form by organizing his successive utterances in a fashion that seems to be guided by his conception of the needed steps in the action. The initial grammar of the long string of task-related requests is, then, a kind of temporal grammar based on an understanding not only of the actions required, but also of the order in which these actions must be executed. This bit of child language is an interpersonal script based on a young child's knowledge of what is needed to reach the goal in the real world; it is the matrix in which language develops.

In looking closely at two of the four major communicative functions (indicating and requesting), we discovered a great deal of negotiating by the mother about pragmatic aspects of communication: not about truth-falsity and not about well-formedness, but about whether requests were sincere, whose turn it was, whether it should be done independently or not, whether reasons were clear or justified.

There is, of course, more to communication than indicating and requesting. Another major function of speech is affiliation, the forming of a basis for social exchange. This involves matters as diverse as learning to acknowledge presence, to take turns, and to enter what has been called the "cooperative principle" underlying all speech acts.

The final function is the use of communication for generating possible worlds, and it has little to do with asking for help or indicating things in the real world or, indeed, with maintaining social connection. The early utterances of the children we have studied show one clear-cut characteristic: Most of the talking by mother and by child is *not* about hard-nosed reality. It is about games, about imaginary things, about seemingly useless make-believe. What is involved in the generation of possible worlds is quite useful for both conceptual and communicative development—role playing, referring to nonpresent events, combining elements to exploit their variability, etc.

Had we gone on to look at the other two functions, affiliative activity during which mother and child learn the rules for interacting and the sort of play in which possible worlds are created, the case for mother-infant interaction would have been as strong. There is an enor-

mous amount of teaching involved in transmitting the language, though very little of it has to do with language lessons proper. It has to do with making intentions clear, as speaker and as actor, and with overcoming difficulties in getting done in the real world what we want done by the mediation of communicating. And this is why learning a second language is so difficult. The moment we teach language as an explicit set of rules for generating well-formed strings out of context, the enterprise seems to go badly wrong. The rule in natural language learning is that language is learned in order to interact with someone about something the two of you share.

Where does that leave the problem of language acquisition? Well, to my way of thinking it brings it back into the sphere of problem solving—the problem being how to make our intentions known to others, how to communicate what we have in consciousness, what we want done in our behalf, how we wish to relate to others, and what in this or other worlds is possible.

Children still have to learn to use their native lexicons and to do so grammatically. They learn this in use, in order to get things done with words, and not as if they were ferreting out the disembodied rules of grammar. I think we have learned to look at language acquisition not as a solo flight by the child in search of rules, but as a transaction involving an active language learner and an equally active language teacher. That new insight will go a long way toward filling the gap between the impossible and the miraculous.

For further information:

Clark, Herbert, and Eve Clark. *Psychology and Language: An Introduction to Psycholinguistics.* Harcourt Brace Jovanovich, 1977.

De Villiers, Jill G., and Peter A. de Villiers. *Language Acquisition.* Harvard University Press, 1978.

Miller, George A. *Spontaneous Apprentices: Children and Language.* The Seabury Press, 1977.

Snow, Catherine E., and Charles A. Ferguson, eds. *Talking to Children.* Cambridge University Press, 1977.

IS THERE A CRITICAL PERIOD FOR LANGUAGE AND READING ACQUISITION?

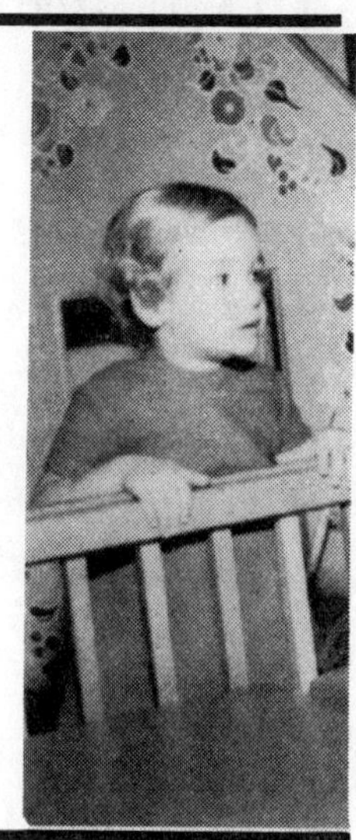

Pamela Conlon

Seven years ago a fourteen year old girl named Genie was rescued by the police and admitted to Children's Hospital of Los Angeles. From the age of 20 months she had been strapped to a potty chair, her movements restricted by a cloth harness. When she was not in the potty chair, she was confined to an infant crib covered over with wire mesh. Her room was separated from the rest of the house by double doors, preventing sounds from reaching her. She was physically punished by her father if she made any noise. Although her mother may have occasionally whispered to her during brief feeding sessions, no other family members spoke to her.

At the time of her discovery, Genie was suffering from severe malnutrition as well as general retardation. She appeared to have neither receptive nor expressive language skills. A background search and diagnostic tests performed upon her admittance to the hospital ruled out metabolic and neurological disorders. Her apparent extreme retardation seemed to be attributable to the intensity and duration of her physical and psycho-social deprivation (6,9).

The case of Genie provides an unusual opportunity to examine the issue of the existence of critical periods for the development of human behaviors such as language acquisition and reading. For unlike other cases of extreme deprivation, Genie's isolation extended beyond the age of puberty. Genie's ability to learn language will be considered later. First, it seems appropriate to discuss the origin of the critical periods notion, the controversy associated with it, and its relevance to language and reading acquisition.

It is generally agreed that the concept of the critical period has its roots in the literature on imprinting. Accord-

From the *42nd Yearbook,* 1978. The Claremont Reading Conference Center for Developmental Studies, ©1978 Claremont College, Claremont, California 91711.

ing to Sluckin (23), the term "imprinting" originally referred to the attachments built on approach and following responses of precocial birds (i.e., birds covered with down). Unlike conventional conditioning, imprinting does not depend on physiological rewards. A baby duck, for example, will follow others of its kind instinctively as long as it is exposed to the sight of its own species during a given time period of its life. The observation that the emergence of this and similar behaviors could be manipulated or entirely suppressed during a specific period early in the development of the organism led to the notion of a critical period. The term has been extended to other types of attachment responses and has since come to be used with reference to numerous behaviors in mammalian young.

A distinction has long been made in the literature between the term "critical" period and a weaker formulation, the "sensitive" period. The critical period hypothesis maintains that particular times exist in the early life of an organism beyond which certain capacities to acquire specific behaviors are forever lost if necessary conditions are not present. The sensitive periods hypothesis, on the other hand, posits the existence of certain time spans during which rapid acquisition of specific behaviors will occur with a minimum of stimulation. More intense stimulation to produce the same or less satisfactory results is presumed necessary in nonsensitive periods.

The debate concerning the existence of sensitive/critical periods in man is considerable and has naturally been colored by the theoretical positions of the various debaters relative to the nature of human development. For example, the nativistic and psychoanalytic views are both largely consistent with the critical periods concept. The cognitive-developmental view, on the other hand, appears to be more comfortable with the idea of sensitive phases in development during which the effectiveness of stimulation is contingent upon its optimal match with a given level of maturity (14). Finally, the empiricists have been most outspoken against either hypothesis. Gewirtz (10) observed that although some behaviors established early in life appear permanent, this is not attributable to the fact that these behaviors are irreversible, but rather to the constancy of environmental conditions that "lock in" these behaviors.

Much of the evidence for critical periods in the development of human behaviors is based upon the work of such researchers as Scott (22), and Harlow and Harlow (12), with mammalian young. It is precisely for this reason that many writers including Sluckin (23), Bronfenbrenner (4), Wolff (24), and Ausubel (2) have questioned the notion of critical periods for humans since its existence is largely extrapolated from studies with infra-human species.

What evidence do we have then that critical periods exist in the development of species-specific human behaviors? According to Bronfenbrenner (4), inferences related to critical periods and stimulus deprivation have been based on observation of affectional bonds between mother and child or on studies of children placed in foundling homes. Wolff (24) has called such evidence anecdotal rather than experimental. However, Ainsworth (1) reviewed the literature on I.Q. and maternal deprivation and concluded that a sensitive phase crucial to intellectual development exists for the first 6 to 12 months of life with reversibility of deprivation possible during the next 6 to 12 months.

Kohlberg (14) has suggested that the stability of human characteristics reported in Bloom's (3) longitudinal study did much to promote the notion of critical periods in human cognition. Although he did not specifically mention the concept itself, he reported that by age 9 at least 50% and by age 13 at least 75% of general achievement patterns such as reading comprehension and vocabulary had been formulated. In addition, 17% of the development of general learning growth took place between ages 4 and 6. A negatively accelerated curve of development reaching its midpoint before age 5 was reported for general intelligence and other characteristics. Bloom concluded from his data that preschool and primary grade experiences are extremely potent, since much of subsequent learning in the school setting is dependent upon patterns established in these early years. However, Kohlberg ascribed the stability of human characteristics to the constancy of influence in the home environment during the early years.

Schultz and Aurbach (21) examined evidence for a critical period related to the effects of sensory deprivation in the low SES environment. They reviewed studies by the Deutsches, Bernstein, V.P. John and Hess and Shipman and concluded that such research was marred by value bias and inadequate test measures. Kohlberg and Wolff have been particularly opposed to the stimulus bombardment orientation of preschool programs designed to counteract the so-called stimulus deprivation described in these studies. Limited specific training, they maintained, can never hope to replace the massive experience accrued with time.

In essence, it can be said that there is much conflict of opinion concerning the relevancy of the sensitive/critical period hypotheses to human behaviors in general. A number of experimental studies, though, have dealt specifically with critical periods in language development. It is to these studies that we now turn our attention.

Lenneberg (16,17), a major proponent of the nativistic thesis, and Ainsworth (1) present some of the most convincing evidence for a critical period in language development. Lenneberg believed that language development could be correlated with chronological age, motor development and certain physical indications of brain maturation. Both Ainsworth and Lenneberg observed that even without verbal stimulation, deaf children follow patterns of verbalization similar to those of hearing children up to the age of 6 months. According to Ainsworth, speech in the hearing begins to mirror adult sounds and intonation in the environment between 6 and 12 months of age. Ainsworth concluded that the preverbal substrata upon which language depends is both maturational and environmental with a sensitive period occurring around the second half of the first year of life.

Lenneberg, on the other hand, regarded the span between two and four years of age as the onset of the critical period for primary language acquisition. He documented this belief with evidence from cases of recovery of language functions following brain lesions of the left hemisphere during early childhood. He reported that even lesions occurring in the early teens did not result in permanent language loss. Lenneberg therefore hypothesized that the end of the critical period for language acquisition occurred between 11 and 14 years of age, an event he believed coincided with cerebral lateralization of function. This notion has recently been challenged by Krashen (15) whose research suggests that cerebral lateralization occurs around 5 years of age and is therefore not the neurological correlate of the end of the critical period for language acquisition.

Several other studies have found evidence that verbal behavior is perhaps more sensitive to environmental conditions than other types of human behavior. Rheingold and Bayley (20) modified the maternal care received by a group of institutionalized infants. Those children who received attentive care from one person from the 6th to 8th month of life showed significant differences in their verbal behaviors one year later. Pringle and Bossio (19) found that lower verbal scores on the WISC as well as poorer general language development for institutionalized children was associated with separation from families prior to 5 years of age and the degree of familial contact after initial separation. However, by age 14, these differences no longer appeared, indicating that effects of earlier separation are reversible. Finally, Irwin (13) demonstrated that spontaneous vocalizations of children could be significantly increased if mothers read and told stories to their infants 15-20 minutes daily. Although stimulation began at 13 months, differences first surfaced at 17 months and continued until 30 months. This would seem to support a critical period for verbal stimulation around the age of 17 months.

And now let us return to the case of Genie. If there is a critical/sensitive period for first language acquisition, then Genie's language learning should be severely limited. This is, in fact, the case. Although she is acquiring language skills, her production is syntactically and morphologically impaired, and her progress is much slower than that of normals. Her semantic and lexical abilities are ahead of other areas, and her vocabulary is much larger than that of normal children exhibiting the same level of syntactic complexity. Her cognitive development has exceeded her linguistic development as revealed by her comprehension of forms such as the superlative and comparative which are not evident in her own language productions (7,9).

It is interesting to note that dichotic listening tests have revealed that although Genie is right-handed and has the EEG patterns typical of left hemispheric dominance, it appears that her right hemisphere is doing all the work for both language and nonlanguage functions. It is believed that inadequate stimulation during her early life inhibited language aspects of left hemisphere development so that it is as if the usual language centers have atrophied. If this is true, then it may be that the left hemisphere of the brain must be linguistically stimulated during a specific time for it to participate in normal language acquisition. Failing this stimulation, normal language acquisition must rely on other cortical areas and will proceed less efficiently due to the previous specialization of these areas for other functions (9). Accordingly, Genie's capacity for language development will probably be permanently limited.

As far as reading is concerned, Genie reportedly has learned to recognize names, can print the letters of the alphabet, read words, assemble printed words into grammatically correct sentences, and can understand questions and sentences constructed from these words. However, she makes slow progress and has a great deal of difficulty learning and retaining new words as they are introduced.

A significant contrast to Genie is a case reported by Mason in 1942 (18). The child in this instance was discovered at age 6 1/2 and within 22 months had thoroughly acquired language. It would seem that evidence for a sensitive period is substantiated by the disparity in language ability related to the age differences in the two cases.

It is probably unwise to accept two case histories and the handful of experimental studies reviewed here as definitive evidence of a critical period for language acquisition. There does appear to be some convincing data, however, supporting the sensitive phase theory.

Reading acquisition is another matter. Although reading presupposes language ability, there are some major distinctions between the two behaviors that may make the establishment of a sensitive period for language development irrelevant to reading. Learning to read, much like learning a second language, is not motivated by the same sociological forces as first language acquisition. Like a second language, reading is taught rather than learned by exposure. Yet, educators act as though a critical period for reading acquisition exists. Interest in prediction and prevention of reading failure has expanded greatly in recent years. The rationale for early childhood education and early intervention in reading and language disorders clearly accepts the notion of a critical period. Indeed, based on a review of 10,000 cases, Goldberg and Schiffman (11) reported that 82% of potential reading disability cases diagnosed in second grade could be brought to grade level through appropriate intervention. By fourth grade, only 15% could be readily remediated, dropping to only 6% by ninth grade.

It is not clear that these data can be explained in terms of a critical periods hypothesis for reading acquisition. It does seem important, though, to recognize that the child who meets with repeated failure in his attempts to learn to read generally suffers untold and cumulative ego damage. The consequence of school failure is usually emotional and motivational disengagement from the learning situation. De Hirsch (8) has called intervention programs that reach children around the age of 4 remedial rather than preventive. There is evidence that short-term intervention is far less successful than intensive programs involving parents and children from the first year of life through the elementary school years, and that children enrolled in preventive programs at the age of 5 or later show few permanent gains (5).

Even if there are no critical periods for language development and reading acquisition, perhaps there is a crucial time for intervention in language-related disabilities. That time is as soon after difficulties are predicted as possible.

REFERENCES

1 Ainsworth, Mary D. Reversible and irreversible effects of maternal deprivation. In Helen L. Witmer (Ed.) *Maternal deprivation.* New York: Child Welfare League of America, Inc., 1962, pp. 149-168.

2 Ausubel, David P. How reversible are the cognitive and motivational effects of cultural deprivation? Implications for teaching the culturally deprived child. *Urban Education,* 1964, *1,* 16-38.

3 Bloom, Benjamin S. *Stability and change in human characteristics.* New York: John Wiley and Sons, 1964.

4 Bronfenbrenner, Urie. Early deprivation in monkey and man. In Urie Bronfenbrenner (Ed.) *Influences on human development.* Hinsdale, Illinois: Dryden Press, 1972, pp. 256-294.

5 _________________. *A report on longitudinal evaluations of preschool programs; Volume II: Is early intervention effective?* (DHEW Publication No. OHD 74-25) (DHEW) Washington, D.C.: Office of Child Development, 1974.

6 Curtiss, Susan, Fromkin, Victoria, Krashen, Stephen, Rigler, David, and Rigler, Marilyn. The linguistic development of Genie. *Language,* 1974, *50*(3), 528-554.

7 Curtiss, Susan. *Genie: the linguistic development of a modern day wild child.* New York: Academic Press, 1977.

8 de Hirsch, Katrina, Jansky, Jeannette J., & Langford, William S. *Predicting reading failure.* New York: Harper & Row, 1966.

9 Fromkin, Victoria, Krashen, Steven, Curtiss, Susan, Rigler, David, and Rigler, Marilyn. The development of language in Genie: a case of language acquisition beyond the "critical period." *Brain and Language,* 1974, *1,* 81-107.

10 Gewirtz, J. L. Mechanisms of social learning: some roles of stimulation and behavior in early human development. In D. A. Goslin (Ed.) *Handbook Socialization Theory and Research.* Chicago: Rand McNally, 1969. 57-212.

11 Goldberg, Herman K., & Schiffman, Gilbert B. *Dyslexia: problems of reading disabilities.* New York: Grune & Stratton, 1972.

12 Harlow, H. F. & Harlow, M. K. Social deprivation in monkeys. *Scientific American,* 1962, *207,* 137-146.

13 Irwin, Orvis C. Infant speech: effect of systematic reading of stories. *Journal of Speech and Hearing Research,* 1960, *3,* 187-193.

14 Kohlberg, Lawrence. Early education: a cognitive-developmental view. *Child Development,* 1968, *39,* 1013-1062.

15 Krashen, Stephen D. Lateralization, language learning, and the critical period: some new evidence. *Language Learning,* 1973, *23,* 63-74.

16 Lenneberg, Eric H. *The biological foundations of language.* New York: John Wiley & Sons, Inc., 1967.

17 _________________. On explaining language. *Science,* 1969, *164,* 635-643.

18 Mason, M. K. Learning to speak after six and one-half years. *Journal of Speech Disorders,* 1942, *7,* 295-304.

19 Pringle, M. L. & Bossio, B. A study of deprived children. *Vita Humana,* 1958, *1,* 65-91, 142-169.

20 Rheingold, Harriet L., & Bayley, Nancy. The later effects of an experimental modification of mothering. *Child Development,* 1959, *30,* 363-372.

21 Schultz, Charles B., & Aurbach, Herbert H. The usefulness of cumulative deprivation as an explanation of educational deficiencies. *Merrill-Palmer Quarterly of Behavior and Development,* 1971, *17*(1), 27-39.

22 Scott, J. P. Critical periods in behavioral development. *Science,* 1962, *138,* 949-958.

23 Sluckin, W. *Imprinting and early learning.* Chicago: Aldine Publishing Co., 1965.

24 Wolff, Peter H. Critical periods in human cognitive development. In S. Chess, & A. Thomas (Eds.) *Annual progress in child psychiatry and child development.* New York: Brunner/Mazel, 1971. Pp. 155-165.

Children's Language: What Does It Reveal?

E. Bess Osburn

Fairfax County Public Schools
Fairfax, Virginia

"Me 'n' Mike are going to the park after school," Fred announced to his kindergarten teacher.

"Mike and *I* are going to the park after school," the teacher corrected.

In a voice betraying amazement, Mike said, "Yeah, me and the teacher are going to the park after school."

Fred began to cry, "I want to go, too!"

Fred did not understand that the teacher was correcting his grammar. He interpreted the surface message instead of the underlying intent and concluded that the teacher was taking his place with Mike on the excursion to the park.

Teachers of kindergartners often experience such episodes and need to be on the alert to avoid misunderstandings. Indeed, teachers in all grades should be sensitive to the oral and written language of their students. Knowledge of language and how it is used is a prerequisite for instructional planning. Language is the medium of learning, but it also reveals to the teacher pupils' conceptions and misconceptions. The wise teacher will use the information in designing meaningful instruction.

Research on the language of elementary-school children has mushroomed. The expanding knowledge on this large and complex subject can in no way be completely explored in a short article. However, a few samples of classroom language may provide an introduction. Each episode described here illustrates a generalization that researchers have found to be characteristic of the language of children of elementary-school age.

Episode 1

John was hurt while standing in the hall. Mary, who was nearby at the time, was asked to tell that had happened. "He stooded by me at the water fountain when he was hurt," Mary, age six, replied.

Such mistakes as "stooded" and "bringed" are common among young children. These mistakes, research indicates, can be viewed as signs of language development. Children first learn many irregular verb forms, such as "came" and "went," Cazden's study found (1). Then children's grammar appears to deteriorate as they begin to say "comed" and "goed." How can the apparent deterioration be explained?

3. LANGUAGE

Do children unlearn the correct forms? Unlearning does not seem to account for what happens. Rather it seems that children internalize morphological rules such as the past-tense morphemes. Children tend to apply the rules appropriately—as well as inappropriately. Children say "walked" as well as "stooded." If one looks below the surface, these overgeneralizations indicate that children are indeed making progress in learning the complexities of their language. As they use language—as they listen or speak and write—they detect exceptions and incorporate them into their grammar. In learning language children acquire a set of rules that they apply to express meaning.

Generalization

Learning a language involves internalizing morphological rules and sorting out the irregularities and inconsistencies.

Other common examples of overgeneralizations can be cited:

Generalizations	Overgeneralizations
herself, myself,	
yourself	hisself
nobody	yesbody
ducks, cows, busses	sheeps

Episode 2

Dick, an eleven-year-old, was asked to explain the sentence, "Tom promised Mary to drive the car." Dick replied, "Well, I don't even know who's driving."

The sentence is unclear (2). Is the speaker saying that Mary will drive? Or that Tom will drive? In real life, the meaning of the sentence would pose no problem: the context of the situation would establish who was promising to drive. In isolation, however, the sentence is ambiguous. The listener must determine whether the sentence means: Tom promised Mary that she could drive the car or Tom promised Mary that he would drive the car.

Menyuk found (3) that by the time children enter school they have acquired most sentence patterns (syntax) that adults use. The child is able to express his ideas by using mature patterns of the language:

Tom hit the dog.
(noun–verb–noun)

Tom was sick.
(noun–linking verb–adjective)

Tom gave Mary a present.
(noun–verb–noun–noun)

Tom walked slowly.
(noun–verb–adverb)

Yet, certain complex syntactical patterns remain to be worked out. Brown (4) states that in learning the syntax of a language a child cannot possibly acquire a set of sentences, but must acquire a system of rules—a system that makes it possible to generate and comprehend an infinite variety of sentences. Several researchers have identified certain complex patterns that children are still acquiring from ages eight to twelve (5, 6).

Generalization

Learning a language involves internalizing certain syntactical rules and patterns that make it possible for one to express the relationships that exist in one's mind.

Other examples that illustrate children's syntactical development are described here.

Sally marked the wrong answer in her workbook. The picture in the workbook showed a boy and a girl. The caption read, "Tom was hit by Mary." Sally's task was to answer the question "Who was hit?" She was to respond by making a check mark under the drawing of the boy or the girl.

Explanation: Children, as they begin to use sentences, learn that the first noun is the subject and also the agent of the action. In passive sentences the subject is not the actor but the receiver of the action. Thus the early generalization is violated. Sinclair's research (7) points out a developmental pattern as children acquire mature comprehension of the construction of the passive sentence.

A first-grade teacher said, "Mary, ask Tom what to feed the fish." Mary cried, "But I wanted to feed the fish."

Explanation: Apparently, Mary did not understand that she was to go to Tom, find out from him what the fish were usually fed, and then feed that food to the fish. The sentence is short and seems simple, but, as Carol Chomsky's research indicates, short and seemingly simple sentences can be very complex. Her research also reveals that at early stages "ask" and "tell" are interpreted alike. A young child does not detect the subtle difference between "Mary asked Tom to go," and "Mary told Tom to go."

Doug began his story: "Once upon a time, there was a man and he . . ."

Explanation: One would expect the child to use the common sentence pattern, "Once upon a time there was a man *who* . . ." rather than "and he." The capability of expressing thoughts by relating one sentence to the next gradually increases as language ability develops. Research reveals that sentences are loosely connected at first: "There was a boy. He fell into the lake." Later sentences are drawn closer by the use of the conjunction "and": "There was a boy, and he fell into the lake." Still later sentences are drawn closer by the use of the relative clause: "The boy, who fell into the lake. . . ." Sinclair (7), Ingram (8), and Chomsky (2) suggest that complex sentence patterns are acquired after children begin school.

In a class in remedial reading a seventh-grade student read from a workbook, "Although it is not true that all animals are born blind, most newborn mammals do not begin at once to use their ________." To complete the sentence, the student had a choice of four words: "brains," "eyes," "legs," and "heads." He chose "eyes."

Explanation: The teacher asked the student why he chose "eyes," expecting the child to explain the meaning of the sentence. Instead the student answered, "Well, it says 'blind'." The complex relationships expressed in this difficult sentence pattern were beyond the grasp of the student, but often, as in this example, redundancy makes it possible for a child to understand a passage in spite of the difficulty of a sentence pattern (9).

Episode 3

While discussing the meaning of the word "alive," John, age seven, said, "I know the rock is alive because it needs fresh air and oxygen."

John's language reveals that he does not have meaningful, clear concepts for the word "alive." His ideas about fresh air and oxygen are mere verbalizations. Children in the primary grades are sophisticated users of language (3), and their verbosity often causes the teacher to exaggerate the child's understanding of abstract concepts. Attention to the child's comments and responses is necessary to ferret out the child's understandings or misunderstandings. The information can be helpful in developing appropriate instruction. The curriculum for John's class may include the study of air, oxygen, and the meaning of the word "alive," but John's glib use of the terms reveals that the science program is not meaningful to him. Through questions the teacher should be able to build on his existing knowledge. Ausubel (10) writes, "The most important single factor influencing learning is what the learner already knows. Ascertain this and teach him accordingly." Listening to the child's language is the quickest way to gain insight about a child's picture of the world and the relationships that she or he has abstracted from the world.

Generalization

A child's language can tell the teacher something about the child's knowledge and his ability to apply the knowledge to new situations.

Other classroom examples that reveal children's misunderstandings are discussed here.

Sue had practiced identifying words containing the short-vowel sound, but she was unable to apply this knowledge while reading.

Explanation: For some children phonics generalizations are so abstract that they are meaningless. To apply phonics rules, young children must hold many concepts in mind. Children must know that "a" has several sounds; children must know that "a" can look like *a*, A, a, *a;* children must know that "a" can fit into "b-a-t" to represent , into "c-a-k-e" to represent , into "c-a-r" to represent , or into "b-a-l-l" to represent . Furthermore, when sounds are treated in isolation the child does not have available redundant cues of syntax and meaning that are found in the total language.

A first-grade teacher asked Jimmy: "Which child in the picture has 'less' balloons?" She wanted to make sure that the child differentiated correctly between the words "more" and "less." Jimmy's incorrect answer was quite unexpected.

Explanation: Research (11) indicates that children learn the meaning of "more" before they learn the meaning of "less." Furthermore, at first children tend to treat "less" as a synonym of "more." Jimmy's answer revealed that he had not yet differentiated the concepts. He obviously could see which child had the fewest balloons even though he could not apply the correct label.

In an experiment the teacher asked James, age eight, "Why do you think this weight will make the balance bar go down?" He answered, "We saw a bar in class."

Explanation: Although James responded to the question, his answer revealed that he failed to understand the cause-and-effect relationship. He was unable to make the responses required by "why." Blank (12) found that mastery of a term such as "why" is a long and difficult process. To respond, a child must attend to the ideas suggested in the question, then recognize relationships from personal experience and, in this example, from the setting. Blank further suggests that a functional use of "why" is a cognitive requirement for success in school.

Episode 4

"I run to the room. Tom run too," Jed said. The teacher corrected Jed: "Tom runs too." Jed had failed to use "s" for the third person singular form.

As suggested earlier, children internalize grammatical rules of their language group. These rules are generated from the language—the dialect—the children hear in their environment. Therefore, it is important that teachers recognize linguistic rules common in dialect groups. In standard English the pattern, "I run, you run, they run," is changed in the third person singular, which requires that "s" be added. This rule does not exist in some dialects. The teacher corrected Jed when he said, "Tom run," but will she correct Jed when he says, "He go," "He talk," "He swim"? If the teacher corrects Jed everytime he uses nonstandard English the child will probably be unable to express a complete idea without interruption. Additional misunderstandings may arise. Jed may ask himself, "Isn't the teacher interested in what I have to say?" When to correct and how and when to teach standard English become important and complex issues (13, 14).

Consider another example: The book read, "The flower grew. It grew and grew." Nine-year-old Joan read aloud, "The flower growed. It growed and growed."

Three questions come to mind. Is this an overgeneralization of the past-tense form as described in the first episode? Is "growed" a word that is common in Joan's dialect group? Should the teacher correct Joan?

For a child of Joan's age and cultural group, the teacher may well conclude that "growed" is a common word in the child's dialect. Because Joan was apparently making sense of the reading—translating the author's "grew" into her own language—to correct her would be inappropriate. Confusions may be created if efforts for meaningful reading are tangled with efforts for correct grammar. Certainly, educators want pupils to acquire standard English, but teaching language usage must not be confused with teaching reading as a comprehension process. If teachers want children to know that reading is communicating with an author, such strategies as correcting "grew" would add misunderstandings about the purpose of reading.

Generalization

Human beings abstract the language rules heard in their dialect group. Correcting individual instances of a nonstandard internalized rule is often unproductive and confusing to young children.

Here are two examples of patterns that illustrate rules acquired by children from their dialect groups:

"I hope youse do your job so we can get these folks moving," the boy pleaded.

"Ya'll be sure to come to my party," the child called. Her mother corrected, "*You* come to my party."

"But how can I let them *all* know that I want them to come if I say 'You come' instead of 'Ya'll come'?" the child asked.

Explanation: In both examples the speakers have acquired a rule which indicated that "you" must be changed to show plural number. Because most English words require a plural indicator—"boy, boys"; "he, they"—it seems logical to conclude that "you" also requires a plural marker. Exceptions are easily acquired by native speakers as they hear standard English. Some dialects, however, use regular forms in "youse" and "ya'll."

Current research on the language development of young children promises to add important understandings that are useful to teachers. The child's language can indicate acquisition and use of grammatical units and sentence structures. The child's language can also reveal conceptual development and cognitive understandings. Research invites a new respect for the ability of young children to abstract from their complex environment. Children abstract the sound distinctions (phonology), the units of meaning (morphology), and the patterns that make it possible to communicate thought (syntax). Considering that most human beings, even those who are seriously retarded, learn to communicate through language, one must recognize broader and more pervasive possibilities for education.

No longer can elementary-school teachers accept the notion that children have acquired language by the time they come to school. Many complexities of English, it appears, are developed after age six. The elementary-school years are active and important for language development. As teachers become aware of developmental stages and dialect patterns, instructional possibilities come to mind. Teachers recognize that it is extremely important for children to have daily opportunities to produce language, through speaking and writing, and to receive language, through listening and reading. Through many and varied settings for communication in the classroom, children can make the differentiations and the generalizations that will enhance their language.

References

1. Courtney Cazden. "The Acquisition of Noun and Verb Inflections," *Child Development, 39* (June, 1968), 433–38.
2. Carol Chomsky. *The Acquisition of Syntax in Children from 5 to 10.* Cambridge, Massachusetts: MIT Press, 1969.
3. Paula Menyuk. *Sentences Children Use.* Cambridge, Massachusetts: MIT Press, 1969.
4. Roger Brown. *A First Language: The Early Stages.* Cambridge, Massachusetts: Harvard University Press, 1973.
5. Henry Olds. *An Experimental Study of Syntactical Factors Influencing Children's Comprehension of Certain Complex Relationships.* Cambridge, Massachusetts: Research and Development Center, Harvard University, 1968.
6. John Bormuth, J. Carr, J. Manning, D. Pearson. "Children's Comprehension of Between and Within Sentence Syntactic Structures," *Journal of Educational Psychology, 61* (October, 1970), 349–57.
7. Hermine Sinclair. "Piaget's Theory and Language Acquisition," *Piagetian Research in Mathematics Education.* Washington, D.C.: National Council of Teachers of Mathematics, 1969.
8. David Ingram. "If and When Transformations Are Acquired by Children," *Developmental Psycholinguistics: Theory and Applications.* Edited by D. Dato. Washington, D.C.: Georgetown University Press, 1975.
9. Frank Smith. *Understanding Language.* New York, New York: Holt, Rinehart, and Winston, 1971.
10. David Ausubel. *Educational Psychology: A Cognitive View.* New York, New York: Holt, Rinehart, and Winston, 1968.
11. Margaret Donaldson and G. Balfour. "Less Is More: A Study of Language Comprehension in Children," *British Journal of Psychology, 59* (1968), 461–71.
12. Marion Blank. "Measuring the Intangible through Language," *Developmental Psycholinguistics and Communication Disorders.* Edited by D. Aaronson and R. W. Rieber. New York, New York: Academy of Sciences, 1975.
13. John Carroll. "Language and Cognition: Current Perspectives from Linguistics and Psychology," *Language Differences: Do They Interfere?* Newark, Delaware: International Reading Association, 1973.
14. William Labov. "The Logic of Nonstandard English," *Proceedings of the Twentieth Annual Round Table.* Washington, D.C.: Georgetown University Press, 1970.

LANGUAGE DEVELOPMENT:
It's Much More Than a Kit

PATRICIA L. HUTINGER

Patricia L. Hutinger is Professor of Early Childhood Education at Western Illinois University, Macomb, Illinois 61455, and Director of the Macomb 0-3 Regional Project.

When those of us who work with children younger than 6 think about language development and the activities we should plan to enhance children's language development, sometimes we think only of adding more vocabulary. Although a wide vocabulary is useful for a young child, sometimes the child who is highly verbal, talking about "infinity" and other abstract concepts, is only demonstrating something Piaget calls "school varnish." It is misleading to assume that the child who has a fantastic vocabulary also has developed the underlying concepts that go with all the big words he or she uses. Language development is much more than the acquisition of new words.

While theorists do not agree about the relationship between language and thought, practically speaking, we know enough to plan activities for children that will help them develop a flexible use of language. Sometimes teachers and administrators are bombarded by educational-materials salesmen who promote their products as the answer to a

language program. But language development takes people, not kits. A good language program is not as complicated as is sometimes thought.

Simple Steps

We all use the language other people in our community use to communicate all kinds of information in most of our waking hours. So do the children in our care! Sometimes we don't feel like talking. Children feel the same way! Sometimes we don't want to respond to a question with a complete sentence; instead we respond with a short phrase. We are more inclined to carry on a long, complex conversa-

tion when we initiate that conversation ourselves. Children have similar inclinations!

Probably the most effective steps teachers and other caregivers can take toward enhancing children's language development are simple ones. They don't require a cash outlay, or new curricular materials, but they do make *time* demands upon you.

1. Accept each child as a very special, worthwhile, unique human being.

2. Listen to each child when he or she talks to you (and when a child doesn't talk, listen to the *behavior*).

3. Take the time to talk to each child, using complex, elaborated language.

4. Provide rich varied experiences so that each child will have something to talk about. Then, allow children plenty of time to observe what is happening.

5. Make sure the child has many opportunities to hear language from other *people,* rather than hearing language primarily from a mechanical source (radio, television, mechanical talking toys, and head phones).

After you've looked over the above suggestions, you will probably agree that they won't cost you or your school any more money. They may, however, mean rescheduling your time and your priorities. It is *more* important that you spend time listening to what a child is trying to communicate to you than it is to separate out the language patterns that are not yet "mature," correcting the child's grammar. *Communication is far more important than whether or not the young child uses the correct verb form each time he or she speaks.*

The Development of Syntax or Grammar

When linguists talk about syntax or grammar, they are not talking about the kind of grammar you studied when you were in elementary school or high school. Rather, they are talking about a *description* of the way the child puts words together—there is no right or wrong way. The child develops his or her own grammatical system. He or she learns language by imitating some things, but there is much more involved than that. The child learns a rule system for using language, even though no one points out those rules (in fact, the child's language may develop more easily if those rules are *not* pointed out). By the time the child is 5, he or she uses most of the complex constructions that adults use, but the communications are usually shorter and contain less information. Language develops in a predictable manner in most children.

In the beginning, the very young

child uses holophrases (one-word sentences)—when "mo" means "more milk," "more water," "play with me some more." Soon, the child begins to use two-word utterances for communicating a variety of ideas. Two-word utterances may differ in the meaning and/or intention of the speaker. Some examples follow: "dog cat" (*conjunction:* "I see a dog and a cat"); "John hat" (*possession:* "This is John's hat"); "party dress" (*attribution:* "This is a party dress"); "Chuck ball" (*subject-object:* "Chuck will throw the ball").

Children "operate" on their language. Sometimes you will hear a child correcting himself or herself, or sometimes he or she will expand an utterance, such as "Stand up . . . dog stand up . . . dog stand up table." When this happens, the child is showing progressive operation on his or her own language (but he or she won't be able to use words to tell you about what he or she is doing). Children filter what they hear through their own rule system: when children stop and correct themselves, we can infer that they are monitoring their speech against some form of correctness.

Around 3 or 4 years of age, sometimes a little later, the child begins to use over-regularizations of inflections, even though he or she

may have been using the correct (adult) verb forms earlier. These are to be expected, and will eventually be changed to correct forms. Examples occur when the child discovers that there is a way to make words express something that happened in the past—add an "-ed"! Then the child says "comed," "breaked," "goed," "doed," "feeded."

Something similar happens when the child begins to find out about the plural form. Then, he or she will generalize the plural rule to irregular nouns. Although the child may have been using "mice" correctly, when he or she begins to apply the plural rule, "mice" may become "mouses" and "feet" may become "footses." When the child acquires a flexible command of the rule for plurals, he or she will again use the forms correctly. Pay attention to what the child *means,* not the way in which he or she is saying it. Correcting may make you feel better, but it will not make much difference in the child's performance. Correcting can even be harmful to the child's sense of self-worth.

When the child begins to use negation (and it happens early!), expect to hear things like "No sit there" and "Wear mitten no." The correct form will appear without adult correction. The form the child's questions take also is interesting and will eventually be transformed into utterances that are much like adults'; but in the beginning, the child will ask questions such as "What the boy hit?" "Where I should put it?" and "What he can ride in?" Again, attend to the meaning, not to the form, or the way the child is asking a question. Questions that require a yes-or-no answer are much easier than the "Who," "When," "Why," "What" variety. The yes-no questions are usually formed correctly earlier.

Evaluation of the Child's Language Development

A measure of Mean Length Utterance (MLU) derived from samples of the young child's spontaneous speech may be more useful in diagnosing and prescribing than are scores on the various language scales of a more formal nature. Roger Brown's work outlines procedures for MLU (*A First Language: The Early Stages* [Cambridge: Harvard University Press, 1973]). The MLU and an accompanying analysis of the child's language patterns provides specific information about the child's communication. Language samples are individual measures, and are somewhat time-consuming. It is important to note, however, that an actual record of what a child *does* say gives you a lot more information for making curricular decisions than does a test score. Also of interest is the development of tests such as the *Say What I Say* test (developed by Madalene Barnett), which focuses on the child's ability to imitate various grammatical structures and also provides a fairly accurate assessment of the child's production ability as well as his or her syntactic patterns.

What Can Teachers Do?

There are several things you can do, and probably are doing already to some extent, that enhance the child's language development.

Use Expansion. When a young child makes an utterance that is not grammatically complete (for an adult), such as "dog bark," use the utterance, but expand it to an adult grammatical form: "Yes, the dog is barking" or "Yes, that dog barked."

Use Extension. Expand the child's utterance, as above, but add some new information, for example: "Yes, the dog is barking, but he won't hurt you" or "Yes, the dog is barking because he's mad at the other dog."

Use Questions That Are Open-ended (Divergent). For example, instead of asking, "Do you hear that noise?" (which requires a "Yes" or "No" from the child), ask, "What do you think might make that noise?" Ask questions that help the child begin to make predictions: "I wonder what would happen if we let these ice cubes sit here in the dish?" Practice using divergent questions, rather than those that have only one right answer (convergent).

Record Your Own Language. Use a tape recorder (or a video tape, if available) during the day, to record your own language. Play it back after school. Listen to your questions, to your sentence structure, your pronunciation. Consciously work on improving your ability to expand, extend, and ask questions. Do you use non-standard dialect, yet reprimand children when they speak in the same dialect?

Courtney Cazden is spending a great deal of time studying the language development of young children. She suggests that teachers ask themselves the following questions (the list below is taken, with some rephrasing, from her book *Child Language and Education* [Chicago: Holt, Rinehart & Winston, 1972]):

1. Is this a back-and-forth monologue on my part?
2. Are my questions open- or closed-ended?
3. Am I moralizing, that is, am I telling children how they should be thinking and feeling instead of accepting the way they do think and feel?
4. Do I really listen to children? Or do I jump in with an answer as soon as I think I've guessed what they mean, or even with an answer that fits my own preconceptions or needs for control?
5. Is my language production geared to the children's understanding, and does it at the same time expand the children's existing language, giving them new words for more complex operations?
6. Do I finish sentences, or do I leave children hanging?
7. Do I avoid using pat phrases over and over again?
8. Do I involve children in activities that lend themselves easily to promoting—and that might even necessitate—verbal interactions?
9. Is there a maximum chance for children to converse with each other?
10. Do I take action to involve children in verbal communications when there is the opportunity?
11. Is my verbal interaction related to the real world and the child's real world?

Cazden goes on to say: "Drilling children in linguistic forms can turn the kids off in a hurry, just as quickly as asking them to produce correct answers to questions. You can teach a child to use the correct words in the right places, such as 'under,' 'over,' 'around,' 'into,' 'or.' But if you want more than a mechanical repertoire of words, if you want understanding and transferability, be sure the words are attached to action or demonstrations of what the sounds actually mean in the context of the child's experiential field and are not embedded in abstractions" (*ibid,* p.116).

Finally, the most important question to ask yourself: Does the interaction between me and the child take place in the context of mutual trust and respect, based on my genuine friendliness, love, unconditional acceptance, warmth, empathy, and interest?

Some Experiences to Enhance Language Development

The activities listed below are usually a part of the early-childhood curriculum. They are simple, although they often require a great deal of planning. Nevertheless, they might be called "well-known but overlooked secrets" of language development. Classroom teachers often are doing the very things that will lead to enriched language development, yet fear that they are not doing enough directed work. Knowledge of what is expected in normal language development provides a justification for these activities.

1. Read to children every day. Be sure the stories are good ones, at the child's level. Ask the children's librarians if you need help. They have lots of good information.

2. Write down the things children tell you about their pictures. Remember, we don't talk in the same way that books are written.

3. Make books of each child's work, of photographs of the child's family, the class and its activities, and other things of interest. Fasten the pages together with rings, or sew them together. Use cloth pages sometimes. Talk about the books.

4. Take trips to interesting places: the bowling alley, the shoe-repair shop, the bakery, the zoo, a farm, a small airport and then a big airport, a trip on a train, a trip on a bus, different kinds of stores. When you get back, draw about the trip. Tell about it. Recreate it in creative dramatics. Effective trips can be quite simple but need careful planning.

5. Arrange things so that children have many opportunities to see operations from beginning to end. For example, make butter (shake up whipping cream in a sealed fruit jar, wash, add salt if desired)—it's more fun if you can visit the farm and bring back whole milk, but that might not be possible. Make applesauce from apples (better yet if you can pick the apples). Make cloth from yarn (woven, knitted, crocheted). Make peanut butter. Grow pumpkins, and make pumpkin pie or pumpkin bread, as well as jack-o-lanterns. Children often are not aware of the origins of things we take for granted.

6. Visit community affairs such as 4-H fairs, craft shows, antique-auto shows, new-car shows, farm-equipment displays.

7. Provide plenty of raw materials—paper, paint, crayons, clay, boxes—and time to work with them.

8. Encourage children to talk about whatever they are making, but don't keep asking them, "What is it?" Try Haim Ginott's "descriptive reinforcement" too (*Between Parent and Child* [New York: Avon Books, 1965]).

9. If you have a tape recorder, children can use it to communicate. Young children like to hear themselves talk when the tape is replayed. Young children's experience with CB radios can be an interesting dramatic-play starting point. Record group singing sometimes, too.

10. Encourage music activities. Children can make up their own songs as they are playing. Songs often use language in an expressive, exciting way.

Conclusion

Planning for the optimal language development of the children in an early-childhood setting requires interaction with *people*: children must be comfortable in communicating with adults and their peers. If the long-range objective is to raise children who can function in a democracy and communicate their ideas, then attention to the characteristics of developing language is important. Children must have many opportunities to use language and to have interesting experiences so that they really *do* have something to talk about. Teachers and other caregivers can provide conditions conducive to optimal language development.

Comments on Language by a Silent Child

Lillian Weber

MY commitment to the study of language has a long, natural history—personal and professional. First, in all the work I have done with small children since 1946, I have always had some who were what you would call slow to talk, and some, even, who were extremely slow, or what you would call language disabled. In working with these children, what I did from the start was respond to any bits of language they offered, and through one form of stimulation or another tried to create in them a need, a desire, to communicate. I have never wavered from that general approach.

When the Advisory Service was set up to work with teachers in the New York City public schools, the schools were preoccupied with issues of language and reading—remedial and compensatory issues. I knew from the start of that work—as I had known for a long time before then—that any involvement in school change would involve us not only in language development, but more specifically in language development considered from the stance we had taken during the whole of our work; namely, that we would deal with the language of *all* the children, without exclusion, for we had accepted responsibility for doing something about how schools could support children in all of their potentiality. The task we set for ourselves was to try to understand what was characteristic of children's language in general, and in particular, and do what we could so that children could use their language in the school, while working at different things, explaining their work, and being listened to.

In reorganizing the classrooms and schools in which we worked, we had new opportunities to observe language use. We also studied what was being written about language acquisition. It became clear that a better understanding of children's language would lead to a better understanding of children and, as we understood the parents' role in how their children acquired language, to a better respect for parents.

My focus, then, on what would support the emergence of stronger language in children has been a sharp and continuous one, in that each thing I learned further supported a deeper exploration, and this experience left me more than dubious about easy formulations.

Similarly, my own language experience, which goes back further than my professional work, leaves me—as I reflect on what I read about language—more than a bit doubtful

about the stereotypes and generalizations that people pose. I was called a "dumb doll" myself when I was a child. And that didn't mean that I was mute; it meant that I didn't answer questions, that I was not quick to talk, and that I was going to be silent.

Of course, we have all known lots of children who were described in this way in the past and not much was made of it, one way or another; it was not a terrible handicap to be considered "dumb," provided you *did* speak and *could* answer, because, after all, the school structure didn't really expect an enormous amount of performance. The teacher did most of the talking. The teacher asked the questions, and you answered to the point of the information. You certainly weren't expected to have every range of language function or to speculate or to be imaginative in your language.

It had not been a handicap to me in school to be a rather silent child (which was natural as the middle child in a large family), because I was the kind of child who was constantly stretching to catch on to what was going on, to comprehend. And there was a lot going on, because I grew up in a home with a lot of "language surround." My mother was a poet and my father was a kind of political arguer. There were always people there, at home, where big issues and ideas were being argued: there was immigrant talk and angry talk and this kind of talk and that kind of talk. It isn't that it came from us necessarily; we listened to it and we appreciated it.

On the other hand, if the talk puzzled you or was too much for you, you ran away, but you did not necessarily feel a burden of participating or an expectation to perform. Indeed, I remember that when I began to say anything, it would come out like an explosion—fueled by an enormous internal pressure to say something about something that I had given thought to and that didn't sit right with me—and this explosion would embarrass me. I would tremble inside. But children would always tremble; you'd fear that you would forget. It had nothing to do with dysfunction; it had to do with memory. You'd memorize things—other people's words, not your own—for a school assembly, and then when the time came, you'd have to go to the john, so extreme was your anxiety, and you'd get sweaty hands, and you'd shake. I know that other people have suffered from that, too.

I met many very silent children, even more silent than I was in my family, who were my classmates in the South. That silence was typical of my peers. There is a whole history of the two-or-three-word speech of the Vermont farmer or small storekeeper. When I was in Norway, I heard that the rural children there hardly speak; that was a widespread cultural phenomenon for children from working-class families on school entrance.

Perhaps for that reason, the academic description of disadvantaged children has never rung a bell in my head. These descriptions go on as if the limited answer on a test or in an interview is some strange new phenomenon. Both Courtney Cazden and William Labov have described the dynamics of these situations. I contend, though, that there's something more to it. Vera John-Steiner wrote recently about how Pueblo children grow up in a culture that treats the development of language as something that is wisdom.[1] In the Pueblo culture, language is made up of wise words, and one doesn't use it profusely and fluently and easily; it develops very slowly. Professor John's description evoked memories of language in my own home, evoked all of my own cultural experiences with language, and set my focus differently on a question that I want to raise as I discuss the importance of the study of language acquisition.

LANGUAGE DEVELOPS OVER TIME

The discussion that has emerged up to now in education has centered on the tremendous responsibility of the adult for bringing out language in children, on a one-to-one basis, even when it is acknowledged that children's language is freer when it takes place child-to-child. Such a focus disregards almost completely the cultural and historical influences on development, either in a single life, in a family, or in a time period. In other words, it does not take into account the continuities and transformations that people embody: that eloquence, for example, that often comes to women in their late thirties or forties, that is stronger in the paraprofessional who has worked in community control and has struggled politically for her rights, or in the undergraduate black who has fought, and continues to fight, in the civil rights movement. Language development is part of the whole cultural setting in which a person grows up; it is influenced by what is expected in the family, and a child's or adolescent's "silence" or shyness does not mean an incapacity for further development later.

That is part of what I knew had to be communicated in the understanding of language acquisition—not only how children develop language as infants, but how they do it as part of a whole time sweep, a whole cultural sweep. In understanding how children, and indeed people, have developed language over time, you begin to understand the dynamics of some of the supportive processes that are involved—what parents are and what they do. Questions about shared experience and language surround become central. You become capable of understanding the current controversies in education about learning theory, because the understanding of language is, I think, central to these controversies.

We must always remember that the functions of language are just that—functions.

There has to be a need for that function, and that function has to be there to develop. In other words, you're not going to get much "judgmental" talk if there's no need to make a judgment or if there's no power in your judgment. These kinds of things are comments on life. Basil Bernstein observed that the struggle for civil rights was a greater asset to the development of functional power in many blacks than anything that a school could do. It is extremely important to look at what is going on in a person's life if you are interested in language development.

As Courtney Cazden has written, summing up a broad range of research, there is no need for testing language acquisition, or assessing it.[2] Language acquisition occurs in the child, short of major troubles. It occurs if there's someone around who talks better than the child, if the child has a chance to speak, and if the child has something to talk about.

There are teachers, nevertheless, who say, "Oh, but you don't know these children. They have very limited vocabularies." You meet this barrier of perception about children's speech in student teachers and working teachers over and over again. Recognizing that teachers are enormously busy, I thought that one way to deal with this "blindness" was to ask them to spend exactly five minutes in a different area every day and to jot down the words that they heard there, whether of a particular child or of a group. The result was that it became entirely evident that a child does not simply have a vocabulary; each has various vocabularies. When a child, or anyone else for that matter, is working with clay, he has one vocabulary; and when he's building with blocks, he has another vocabulary and talks to the blocks with 100 other words that are related to what that's about; and when he's doing something else, he uses 100 other words; and so on endlessly.

That is a terribly important and very simple thing to build on. If the teacher wants to go into language lessons after that, then at least the teacher can say, "Do you know what I heard this morning?" and play back a tape five minutes after it's been recorded, bringing out the words that were spoken. The teacher can then say, "You know, those were the words that you were using as a block builder," so that the children can immediately correct and add additional words. This is a far more productive stance than that of seeing a child as an empty pot

whom you fill with words. It means the acceptance of the child's own agenda — what his parents have been doing for him naturally. It also helps the teacher understand what is so clear in the child's acquisitions of speech, that out of this big buzzing of speech going on around the child, speech clots out like cream in clumps around a context.

When I said "camping" to my grandson Teddy, who was two at the time and interested in camping, he said — and he had used few of the words before — "Ah, camping! Fifty dollars! Get the gas! Where's the sleeping bag?" The point is, his image of camping brought out a lot of unused words. If you were to ask him directly, "Teddy, tell me three words about camping," you would get nothing, unless your question tipped his magic point of interest, of context. Then all the words that are appropriate would be expressed.

"Appropriate" is the correct word; that's how speech clots out. The child doesn't suddenly say "raining chocolate pudding." He says "chocolate pudding" when he's talking about chocolate pudding, and he says "raining" when he's looking at the rain, and a mother understands that. She assumes intelligence and intent, and understands it. When a kid looks out the window and it's raining and the kid says "eh eh," the mother says, "yes, it's raining." The mother responds to all the gestural language that the child has, his eyes looking, his nose, hands, and body pointing to it, and she helps the child "clot out" by accepting his agenda, his intent, his purpose.

Language acquisition isn't a vocabulary list, a disconnected thing. It occurs around an object. When I said something about a baby to two-year-old Teddy, whose mother had just had a baby, his immediate response was, "Oh, the baby! The baby crying! Change the baby!" The baby was only four days old, but it didn't matter. He had already heard those words about changing diapers. And as a very enterprising, working child, he pulled up his shirt to demonstrate himself and said, "I feed him. Baby crying, I feed him!" It was not only the words that he had learned, but the intonation, the expression. Talking about the baby, his voice is mellifluous; talking about playing ball, it's big boy talk; and talking about something else, it's different.

The child clots out the words using all the drama of his existence, and that is exactly what you will hear if you go to where the child is working and listen in on the vocabulary. In school, you will hear it at a slightly older level than what I've described, but that's what you will hear, and it is that interchange, bounced back with a child, that helps the language capacity to grow further, because it's confirmed at that point.

It is this same awareness of, and concern for, context that has to inform the "sharing" session, where everybody sits in a circle and says what he or she did. This activity is supposed to encourage language — and I think it does, but only for the couple of children who are already very verbal. After all, why should children who cannot yet conserve in math be expected to recall the details of their experience when the details are no longer in front of them? How well do we recall the details of our own trips without the help of slides, journals, and the like? In far too many of these children, their recall comes to three words: "I played blocks"; "I did math"; "I did this." Three words over and over. The point is, if you are really aware that children do talk in their setting and that speech is very often contextual, then you support speech by showing slides, by looking at pictures, by the immediate excitement generated when someone else has, say, made the same trip and you recall it, piecing out each other's experience.

USING THE CHILD'S PATH OF DEVELOPMENT

In school, the tape recorder is a tool that can help children recall language. In addition, the teacher, having joined the discussion, can help by saying "You know, when I was watching you people, I heard somebody say something like this." You will then find a tremendous energizing of the children. We have done that a lot. In one instance, the same tape was played back four times to the children, at their request (and these were just four-year-olds), because they had become so interested in their own words. And they corrected themselves, saying. "Oh, no, it was three cups, not two cups"; "Oh, no, he wasn't doing that, he was doing this." So-called nonverbal children suddenly offered a profusion of words around the reality of the concrete.

The "rich life" is fostered in the school by these kinds of things; the "rich life" is what I'm saying teachers have to be aware of. As a teacher, you need to be aware of the fact *not* that the child has a limited vocabulary, which you, therefore, will fill up, but that the child has a richer vocabulary than you knew. Even if, indeed, the child's vocabulary is limited compared to someone else's, it is still richer than when you elicited it from the child just one-to-one; moreover, it can be built on. Nor is it simply a case of a child's syntax development, but the special nature of the way in which this child, or that child, has constructed a language that is common to all of us, and how the child uses it. If we don't respect that in children, we may actually be cutting across the path of their development, instead of using it.

At City College, all of our student teachers are asked, as part of their work, to do a language observation of one child. Since for the most part they're working with older children, only a few of them have come up with anything very striking. A meaningful observation requires very long case records. But one account that ran forty-five pages had at least six instances on every page that bore out what I'm saying.

The child being observed had a small visual focus in the way in which he used his language. Everything was "like a." All children will do some of that, but for this child it was special. That is the way in which he thought and saw. Using a curved block, he would say, "Oh, that's like a snake"; "Oh, that's like the letter in your name"; Oh, that's like this, isn't it?"; "Oh, that's like that." Everything was the small thing, not the global, whole contextual thing. I'm talking about a child who is not defective; indeed, he is rather bright. He was functioning, listening to stories, and so on, at the time. Yet 90 percent of his remarks were made in this way. So you say, "Well, maybe he's going to be an artist." Maybe he is. We don't know that. One thing we do know — he is not approaching his language phonetically but from the looks of the thing, like an e. e. cummings poem. I don't know what you do with that fact yet, but I say it's interesting.

Similarly, for the grandchild I mentioned earlier, the question of speech clotting out in clumps around contexts is more marked than for another child. Teddy is a storyteller. He puts together a whole thing and has from the very beginning. He is interested in how things work and creates folk songs to express his understanding.

For example, a year ago Christmas, I had fallen in a bad accident, and when I went to see him, my face was black and blue and looked quite interesting. He was, at that point, about three-and-a-half years old, and asked me about it. Like all children, he asked again and again and again and again, and each time I described what had happened. Finally he asked, "Would you like a song?" He had put together the whole story in a complete folk-song format that he had absorbed from the Mexican household where he stayed while his mother worked. In that household were a lot of teenagers, and he had become very interested in these big boys, whose guitars and folksinging were very attractive to him. He ran and got a block to be his guitar and gave me a block, and when he saw that I didn't hold it correctly, he gave me a short block so it could be my horn. "Well, it was raining." he sang, "and the wind was blowing cold, and my grandmother had an accident, and there was blood, blood, blood." "Now you make the music, olee, olee," he instructed me, and he went on to the next verse, and then the next verse, each time stopping for the "olee, olee" part.

Some of that ability exists in all children. They make up songs while they're building with blocks, and so on. My grandson, clearly, is at the extreme end of that continuum. Yet, a few months later, when his nursery school teacher decided that learning phonics was essential for a four-year-old, Teddy almost stopped talking. This extremely verbal child practically became handicapped in his speech because, although he is interested in almost anything an adult tells him, the phonics approach cut across the rhythm of how he looked at speech. He began to go "er, er, er, er," and he stopped having those big clumps of speech, which had rhythm and pattern and were held together tightly around a context, where every element was important.

On his own, quite probably, he would have approached reading, having first memorized the familiar, like "The Three Little Kittens," as many of us did as children. But phonics, which he would teach himself, would come later for him because at that point it segmentalized the language for him — it confused and cut across his perception of the language, which isn't words at all, but whole thoughts, with a rhythm and a pattern. Another child I know does it still another way, with great succinctness of observation: the relevant and very important word about a process is what he hits on, as well as a few little words around it.

3. LANGUAGE

In other words, there are many, many ways of putting together language, and the description of syntax is hardly the whole story for us as teachers, working to provide a supportive surround. One child with great deliberation savors the sounds, the syllables; another will chatter part of the time to hear himself. Another child is succinct, another child speculates, another child storytells. And none of this contradicts what has been observed about how children acquire syntax and grammar. Each is working within his or her style. Style is relevant to understanding children's language and how you support children; it must be. I don't know fully in what *sense* it is relevant, but I am certain that it is deeply important—and remains important. After all, we identify each other in part by the style of our speech—not only its pace and rhythms, but the characteristic ways we put speech together. This is something that's always been understood by novelists; it's what makes Shakespeare's work so enduring.

THE QUESTION OF PUBLIC SPEECH

To focus my remarks a bit further, let me turn to a question that I think has been too little studied—the question of public speech. There are children, even very young ones, who are highly socially related, who are fascinated with the expression of public speech, the manners of speech: "Oh, would you like to stay to dinner? I'd love to have you stay," Their grasp of what is absolutely essential in their environment is total. With the absolute truest kind of touch, the piece of public speech they bring out will be a very important piece of public speech in their particular household or in their school.

I have seen it again and again. When children have a chance to role-play and dramatic-play, they will try out many aspects of public speech, which also assists their further development and their taking on of other patterns. Children can be in a doll corner and you can hear them doing a take-off on how you yourself speak.

You can see this clearly in Kenneth Haskins's film about the Morgan School,[3] where the children have a language surround that includes a lot of discussion going on, a lot of meetings. In one part of the film, the children are in the cloakroom, and one of them, the bigger girl, is being Kenneth Haskins; she's "chairing" a meeting in the cloakroom, and one of the little kids reports to her and says, "Well, and he pulled up that girl's dress, and

he saw her pussy, and he didn't even say please." And I thought, shades of *High Wind In Jamaica;* it's so beautiful for the way it expresses the child's perception, for the basic sex education that is in it, for the manners that are in it, for the dead seriousness with which the chairman, the older girl, listens and says, "Well, Mr. Haskins says 'please' is a very important word." You can see what supports language development in that school.

You can also see this principle at work in a marvelous film about the Netsilik Eskimos, from Education Development Center's *Man, A Course of Study,* where they're building the ice house, on the ice cap, and the older children are playing back and forth with the baby, eliciting language from it. It is very clear that the children are in the midst of language that is about houses and jokes and this and that and the next thing. It is also clear that there is intergenerational support for language. It is deeply necessary for teachers to understand the significance of this kind of interchange and to let a great humility enter their souls when they see it. It is incumbent on them to study how parents, and others in the family, support language acquisition in the child. I'm not talking about a conscious effort; it is done intuitively, unconsciously, and it is not only the middle-class parent who does it.

There are community studies of black rural families in the South and of African families that show this process at work. There is one very beautiful account of a mother sitting on the floor in a Buddha position, nestling the baby against her, practically breathing in its breath and responding to every sound — hardly a picture of no language stimulation from the "disadvantaged." It is true, as is also reported, that when the baby is a knee-baby, it is no longer in this "breathing back and forth" situation of language response and elicitation with the mother. Nevertheless, the children are still on the edge of a great deal of talk, so that it is not that language stimulation has ended, but that very direct language stimulation has ended. Language then comes from a larger nexus. The child hears language on the street, in the store, at the washing machine, during the love process, the anger process, the landlord process, from older kids, and so on.

If you are concerned about a child having a range of language function, what kind of language do you suppose results if language is drawn *only* from the one-to-one contact — the adult talking back to the baby — essential as that may be? How much range is there in the language of the teacher, even when it goes beyond question and answer and giving orders? Function, diversified function, does not develop that way. It develops when the child hears higher level language, lower level language, street language, love language, this kind of language, that kind of language: contrastive language.

At a very early age, children hear contrastive language, and they understand it. "Grandma is coming to dinner; be sure you talk nicely for Grandma." The contrasts of language have to do with what is proper. The contrasts of language are, "Well, you know you don't talk that way at the table." Teachers need, constantly, to ask themselves whether they have offered enough life in the classroom to bring out discussion. They must question whether they have provided a language surround with sufficient contrastive elements, like the language of those wise experts that Vera John-Steiner has described, or, for that matter, the language of the not-so-wise experts, symbolic language, rhetorical language, and so on.

I'm not saying that the child is expected to use it. I'm saying that that is what he lives with, and is around. We provide it, in part, when we read poetry to children, when we read them stories. These activities introduce new language, new pauses, new phrases, new rhythms, extended phrases, all kinds of things, that are not in the spoken language. Frederick Erikson, in his "Politics of Speaking," discussed these different functions and described how narrow it is if a child is exposed only to standard Spanish. There's playground speech, for example. If a kid speaks pompously to all the other kids all the time, he doesn't fit.

For teachers, it is a question of looking at the range of possibilities, and what the situation elicits, in order to stretch the situation. Occasionally, poets will come into the classroom and present the image, say, of perfect English, but that isn't necessarily what the kids speak, or could be expected to speak. Similarly, if the adults in a child's environment are engaged in decision-making processes, in politics, or whatever, then the child will hear various linguistic functions. If his own living gives him a chance to hear people using their language to speculate, the child will use some of it on his own level, or at least it will be possible for him to do so.

That brings us to another question that Cazden raised in her recent *Urban Review* article—the power that adults wield in the classroom and how it affects the development of a diversity of function. Directiveness on the part of the adult is in the cards. I concur with Cazden on that. The informal educative experiences of the home include the very simple process of telling the child to sit down, to go to bed, to take certain nourishment. That's part of life, but that isn't the whole story. At home, a child has ample opportunity to express and define himself in other than a subordinate relationship.

But what happens in the traditional school? Is the "life surround" there strong enough in its elements of language surround? For instance, what responsibilities do children have in school? Are they part of the building of the school? When playgrounds are filthy, do they get a chance to clean them? It is difficult to answer these questions in the affirmative. The fact is that in most cases children aren't helped to define themselves; no one even thinks of it in that way—that we build an atmosphere and environment together. Collaboration like that—construction of a kiln or the care of younger children—would support further functional developments, a further kind of language, a further clotting of contextually generated vocabulary. So my response to the question of directiveness in the classroom is, yes, but toward what end?

THE SHARED HUMAN CONTEXT

Finally, let me comment on one other problem that Cazden reflected on—the difficulty she had generating language around a shared experience in her class because she lived in a community that was different from the one in which her pupils did, physically, culturally, and in terms of social class. In order to build up a shared experience, she took the children on trips and brought in other adults, all of which are wonderful things. But I would like to suggest that the shared experience really emerges from the human context that we share, and comes from very ordinary things. My experience is that the familiar encourages a tremendous use of language. You don't get a great language extension out of a new experience with, say, magnetism. You get a few additional vocabulary words; you don't get a

proliferation of the use of language or a diversification of function. It's too strange to do anything with, except name it: "Oh, yes. Magnetism!" But you don't have a whole story about it. What you have a whole story about is your own soap opera, and your own soap opera—the basic human drama—is something that we all share.

We all know about mothers, fathers, babies, harshness, illness, vomiting, sore throats. Children are not necessarily hypochondriacs, but a great deal of what they talk about is illness. That is not a difficult thing to share. It is not difficult to share tons of things that are just simply part of the human condition. That is the point made by Connie and Harold Rosen in their book, *The Language of Primary School Children.*[5] They describe shared experiences around simple aspects of the human condition and of human commonalities that, whether you have actually experienced them or not, you can empathize with.

I suggest that this point is very little understood. We keep thinking that new experiences are what's going to extend the child's language, and what we really mean is extending his vocabulary slightly. The Rosens, on the other hand, make the wonderful point that, in accepting the child, you take as a given that he has language. Then the question is, "Does he have the opportunity to use that language in increasingly complicated ways; that language, not another language that you're going to teach him." He will build the other language with connections to the language he already has, if he can use it. Indeed, there will be contrasts in the use because other children will use it in somewhat different ways. It is this that must be supported.

I am in no way derogating the value of new experiences. I'm simply saying that the basic factor must be the teacher's ability, using the classroom setting—its focus on ordinary natural materials and shared experiences— to evoke in children memories of their earlier experiences. These memories will clot out language that the teacher can extend. But the extensions have to come out of that reawakening instead of from something new.

THE QUESTION OF COMPREHENSION

I've been uneasy about many aspects of adult focus on children's language development. It is not only the question of stimulating function; it's also the question of comprehen-

"... in accepting the child, you take as a given that he has language."

sion, which seems to be the big worry currently, fed by all the testing and the emphasis on test scores. Actually, there are two sides to this question that trouble me: one is the way we worry about it, and the other is what we do about it—how we go about teaching comprehension.

In our worry, we seem to be afraid comprehension might not be there, or not be there unless we teach it. But, after all, what does that mean? When we question whether a child comprehends, are we questioning fundamental processing, that is, acting on a suspicion of malfunction or dysfunction? Surely, the number of such malfunctions must be very, very small—not a basis for a teaching approach to comprehension. Surely, if a child's comprehension is found to be faulty, it would be seen not only in an isolated aspect of that child's functioning—namely, in "reading," which is tested and scored—but would be seen throughout the child's functioning as inappropriate response. Clearly, children who have such inappropriate function need help, but the number nationally must be small. So why the pervasive big worry? Moreover, I cannot be anything but uneasy with the trend of the analyses that have been made of scores and the consequent focus on how much comprehension is being achieved, which seems constantly to be summoning up reference to groups—as in Arthur Jensen's type of analysis.

How can we be so sure of language acquisition and so unsure of comprehension? Surely comprehension is confirmed by language acquisition and must be treated as such. If language acquisition is assumed—if it is a given—so must comprehension be assumed. If the mother's assumption of intelligence and purpose is accepted as central for language acquisition, why shouldn't the same be true for the mother's assumption of comprehension, as her child uses language appropriately and acts appropriately? I end up thinking that we're asking the wrong questions, focusing on the wrong things in our efforts to assume a responsible adult role and to teach comprehension. I end up thinking that we draw from very limited, unclear, and confused meanings of comprehension. I end up thinking that maybe we shouldn't be focusing on the children at all, but on what we understand by the term.

Certainly, what is seen in low comprehension scores isn't the inappropriate response that implies noncomprehension or nonprocessing. In the first place, the scores are of reading comprehension. A child is asked to read something or do something. If he comprehends it and wants to do it or is obedient, he does it. If he doesn't comprehend, or won't, he doesn't do it. Does he comprehend when you tell him what the reading passage is about? Well, if he does, then the processing is all there and he *can* comprehend. If he doesn't, it may be because he has neglected to read the material. Or he wasn't focused on it and failed to get any cues from it. Or he couldn't read it. If he can't read, he needs help with reading. In the meantime, he requires information. If he can take in the information, he can comprehend.

Now, I stick with this argument because, though it is not stated quite that way, I think what is rubbed back and forth underneath the general discussion of lesser, or poor, comprehension is the issue of noncomprehension dealt with as something innate, rather than as an instance of poor experience, poor information, elision, getting mixed up, being bewildered, or having a different focus in one's response. Dealt with this way, the issue of comprehension is reduced to what? A matter of IQ?

I think that with each child we should stop a moment to make sure that, in our analysis, we don't confuse the process of reading with the basic process of comprehension. To the extent that, in fact, we do have comprehension itself as our central focus, we should, in our work, be drawing on meanings from the analysis of thinking, and thinking as it relates to language, in Piaget, in Vygotsky, and, of course, in the work of the psycholinguists who draw from these sources.

Piaget's discussion of clinical methods applies here. His analysis of the play or random response, the response that "cases" the interviewer's mind—the inevitably less-than-full match of thought with language—may give us some perspective on our attempts to reach out to the child's comprehension. With that perspective, we could analyze the validity of our efforts to get at the child's total comprehension, as well as judge our expectation of responses, which demands from the child generalizations and an understanding of the conceptual drift of the material.

Rather than emphasize generalizations and conceptualizing, we might better relate to the child's recall of concrete detail and begin to uncover what we understand about long-term memory links and the single or multiple threads of which they are composed. We might begin to observe more perceptively the times and situations that stimulate the sharing and organization of comprehension and the styles of comprehension. By uncovering our confused meanings, we might be able to move toward a closer analysis of what we understand by reading and toward a better critique of our approaches in reading. Either way, our approaches will be different — whether we concentrate on comprehension itself, or come to accept comprehension as a given and analyze why it is that we get rather poor responses from children.

I want to relate Basil Bernstein's analysis of restricted language to this issue. Bernstein not only analyzed the restricted language he ascribes to poor children as related to poor function in school, he analyzed the nature of restricted language — that it occurs within a set of common meanings and is, therefore, the language of primary relationships. Implicit meanings — where a gesture, a phrase, takes you into the heart of the matter, without the need for explication — are common to playgrounds, to the mother-child relationship, to a fraternity, to wherever the universe of discourse is already understood.

I think that much of a child's poor response and his poor "comprehension" falls within this description of restricted language — the assumption of a common frame in the universe of discourse and the lack of one in the school situation. This common frame allows us, as adult friends, to go to a movie, or to read a novel, and then discuss our shared experience, batting at each other sometimes totally different responses. But we recognize these responses and accept that their differences do not represent brain dysfunction, or lack of processing, or psychotic behavior, or something out of this world. One person says, "Oh, you know I thought this about the thing," and the other person looks a little startled and says, "You did? Oh, yes, I see that, but . . ." This is how conversations develop; people who are closely attuned to each other intellectually carry on such discussions for hours, even on a deep level, in exactly this way, catching the half-phrase that reminds them of something else. That type of brainstorming is enormously exciting.

Such conversations also go on with one's self and, on a higher level, this process is of the essence in the intuitive leap — the associa-

tive thinking — of the artist, in his poetry and in his painting. An analogy comes to the fore, possibly from the deepest recesses of one's being, yet it is recognizable, and because we recognize it, we don't exclude it from our universe of discourse.

Now, what happens when, in school, you ask a child a question to test his comprehension? With all the good will in the world, you are approaching that child externally, not from the restricted, in-group context of the common universe of discourse. You are asking the child to explicate to you, an outsider, his meaning. If you want to understand and share the child's meanings, then there are several ways of doing it. Certainly, what the Rosens describe — the informally shared experience — is a better way for the child to organize his thoughts for you, as a teacher, to know them. The social interaction emphasized by Piaget relates here, and, in direct adult-child interaction, an open-ended Piagetian interview that accepts the child's meanings may be far more appropriate: "That's interesting." "How did you get that?" "What were you thinking of?" and so on. If the child does process, and most of humanity does, then you can get pretty far — that is, if the child wants to talk with you and accepts the legitimacy of your interest.

If what you are trying to elicit is not the child's meaning but a reproduction of what specifically has been read — and there are times when you want to know whether directions are understood — well, then, if the child follows the directions, you know he comprehends. If you don't want his action as a demonstration, then if he is able to explain it to someone else, you know he understands. If the child can't read, but he understands the information when you give it to him, or read it to him, then, of course, he can comprehend. He may not have understood what "turn to the left, sit down three times, and exit" really means. Sometimes directions are quite hard to follow because they are so muddy, or simply because you don't quite know what they're about and you tune them out. Many of us have had this experience. We force ourselves to look at the directions on a machine, but we tune out. We stand there helpless in front of it, but not because we could not do it. Thus the issue of competence and performance also is raised. If the child really doesn't understand, then that is the relevant issue for the teacher.

I would like to go one step further to bring

a bit of personal history to bear on my perception that, in fact, what we can get from children's responses about their deep-level comprehension is, inevitably, only the tip of the iceberg. For me, as a middle child in a household with a lot of complicated things going on, the performance of those tasks that become the structure of one's life, whether in school or at home, had nothing to do with my sense of a whole world of meanings around me, which I was thinking about and taking in constantly. In this world, a whole swirling mass of not-quite-located, ordered, and categorized feelings, intuitions, understandings existed, of which only a few could possibly surface.

As a young "good" reader, I swallowed books sometimes almost as if in a dream, unable to verbalize my comprehension even internally, except in the most simple fashion, perhaps not even in any fashion. I can remember reading *Anna Karenina, Les Miserables,* and Dickens novels, all before I was thirteen. Of course, I skipped some bits; I searched for the conversations, the storyline; I wallowed in the pity of it all, and much of it I couldn't remember once I turned the page, even though I was reading it. The feeling of it and some of the story held me. If a thin enough question was asked me, or if I was asked a little bit about the book, I could say something about it.

Certainly, I was absolutely devastated when at thirty I reread some of those books. I had missed full essays in Victor Hugo. I had missed the entire political point in Fielding. I had missed the entire argument on the agricultural struggle in *Anna Karenina,* plus dozens and dozens of other things, where the wording was too difficult for me and I just swept on. But that's how I became a good reader, totally unaware of some of the issues that were important to me later—studying philosophy, contemplating the "critical line," discussing the tensions between good and evil, and the meaning of the image of the cave.

Metaphor didn't exist for me as a child, because meaning was all on the same level. I hardly caught on that there were other meanings to discern. Ah, but if my sister told me something more, did I take it in? If you tell something to a child, does that child take it in? Is it within his universe of discourse? Does he say, "Oh, yes, I see what you mean"? If that is the case, again, you have an understanding child. If that is not the case, perhaps the idea is too strange, not within the child's experience.

I think our task is to open up for ourselves these quite new questions, to uncover them for examination. We have not done this before. We have not really been aware. There has been a certain arrogance about teaching "open classrooms," or "other classrooms," or whatever, and a certain arrogance about the child's learning. We've talked in terms of children working up to capacity, or stimulating children, and so on, without a real awareness of the private spaces, of the river that must exist with much deeper meanings to feed the child's further progress, and which are not yet accessible to him. When we talked about comprehension, we actually thought we had something. Well, we do have something, but we are only beginning to understand what it is, and it is our understanding of this interesting phenomenon that needs to be examined, not the child's comprehension— as if that were an entity.

NOTES

1. Vera John-Steiner and Helgi Osterreich, *Learning Styles Among Pueblo Children,* Report to the National Institute of Education (August 1975).

2. Courtney Cazden, "How Knowledge About Language Helps the Classroom Teacher—Or Does It: A Personal Account," *The Urban Review* 9 (Summer 1976): 74-90.

3. *I Ain't Playin' No More,* Parts 1 and 2, 16mm film, distributed by Education Development Center, Newton, Massachusetts.

4. Paper presented at the Bilingual Leadership Training Institute, California State University, Los Angeles, 28 February 1974.

5. Connie and Harold Rosen, *The Language of Primary School Children* (Baltimore: Penguin Books, 1973).

"When we talked about comprehension, we actually thought we had something. Well, we do have something, but we are only beginning to understand what it is . . ."

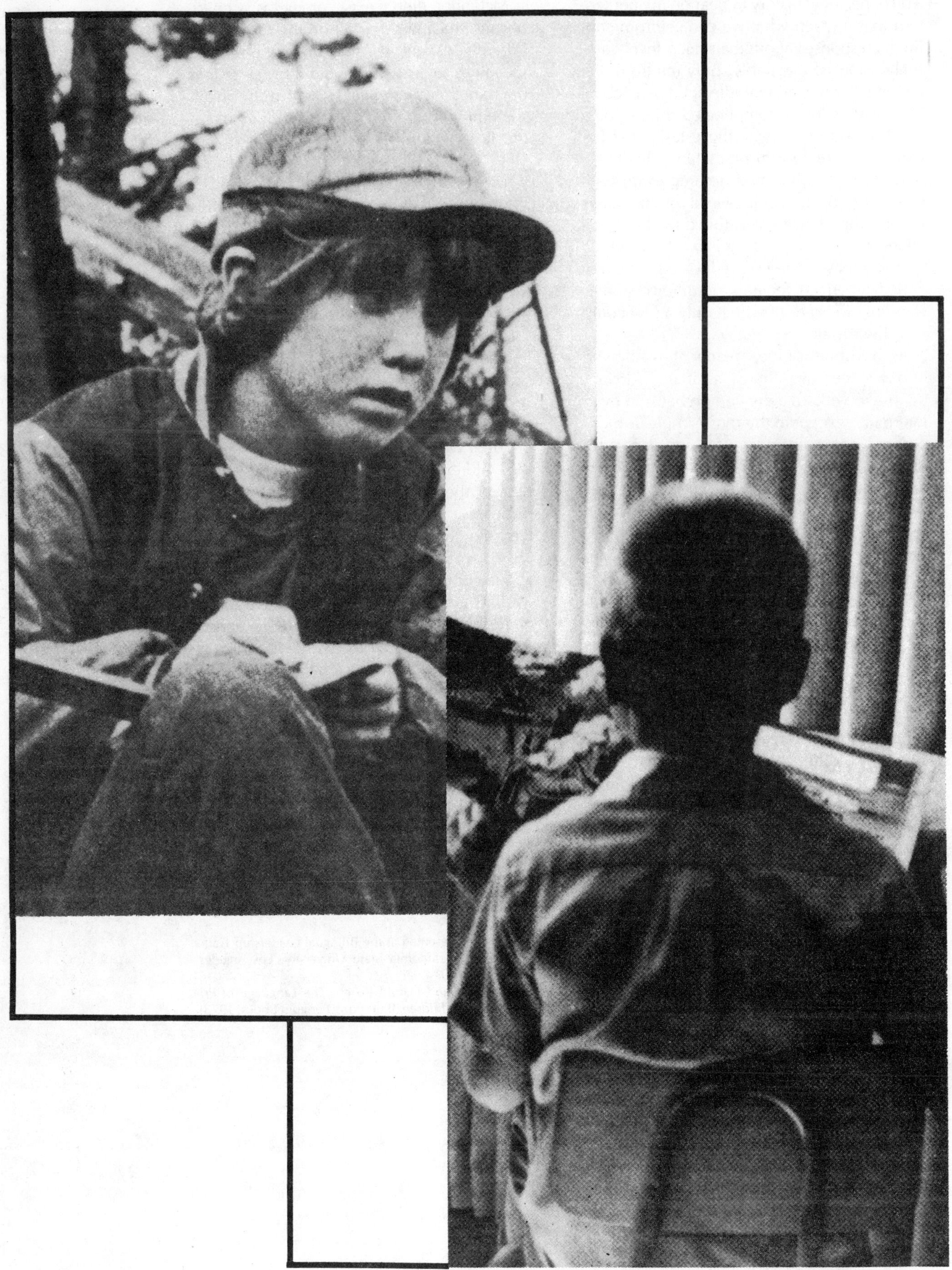

BEHAVIOR MANAGEMENT

One of the most critical concerns of both parents and teachers today relates to the area of discipline, child guidance, and ways of positively influencing the behavior of children. An area of extreme difficulty relates to aggressive and hostile behavior. Betty Caldwell in "Aggression and Hostility in Young Children," examines the question of how aggressive behavior develops, and effective methods of dealing with such behavior. She emphasizes the necessity of helping children acquire more prosocial behaviors, such as cooperation and altruism.

Temper tantrums is the topic of concern for many parents. Mary Stewart, in "How to Deal with Tantrums," discusses in down to earth terms effective ways of working with angry children. In a closely related article, Olum describes an approach for helping children release feelings through crying. In her paper, "It's Alright to Cry," she points out the value of cry for the hurt child, as well as the opportunity to care for another.

A good example is the primary function of adults in shaping behavior contends Dr. Benjamin Spock in "Teaching Your Child to be Responsible." Adults cannot teach responsibility, but can show how to care for other's needs as well as one's own.

The final two articles provide the teacher with ideas for positive social development. "How to Encourage Moral Development" and "Classroom Discipline Problems? Fifteen Human Solutions" illustrate the importance of understanding children's growth and psychological safety needs. This combined with good guidance techniques will give the teacher and parent the chance to influence behavior in a positive way.

Aggression and Hostility in Young Children

BETTYE M. CALDWELL

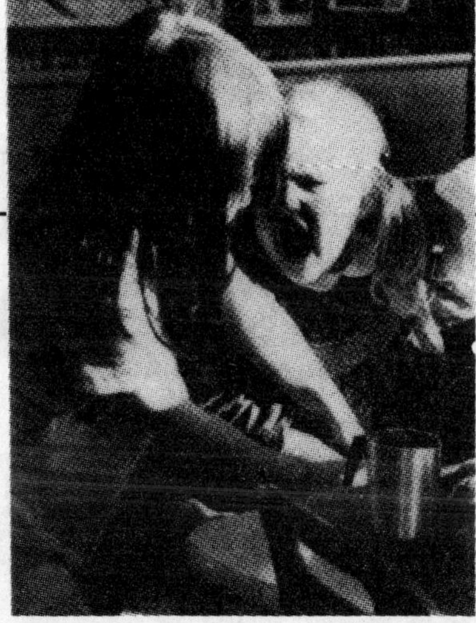

How does aggressive behavior develop? What are some effective methods for dealing with such behavior? How can we help young children acquire more prosocial behaviors, such as cooperation and altruism?

I have been active in early childhood education for half a generation now, and during that time I have seen my own professional interests turn almost 180°—from a primary concern with cognitive development (though that was never my only concern in working with young children) to an overriding obsession with how to foster the development of other-oriented, altruistic behavior in young children. This turn-around might not have occurred were it not for my personal style of working, namely, to be right in the thick of the action with teachers and children.

But what is there about my present life that has catalyzed this metamorphosis? For the past five-and-a-half years I have been the director of the Center for Early Development and Education. This is a research project funded during the first five years by the Office of Child Development and sponsored jointly by the University of Arkansas and the Little Rock School District. This year our funds come from the Carnegie Corporation; the Rockefeller Brothers' Fund; Title XX of the Social Security Act; plus financial support from our sponsors, the University of Arkansas at Little Rock and the Little Rock School District. The project originated out of my strong conviction that the experiences a child has during the first five years determine to a great extent later success or failure and the concomitant conviction that in the case of intervention with low socioeconomic children, there must be continuity between those first five years and later school experience if the early gains are to be maintained. We are housed in a Little Rock public elementary school, and our program of day care, health and family services, and home intervention is directed toward all children ages six months through fifth grade who attend Kramer School. Within that larger context, the particular experience which is most responsible for my own metamorphosis is that of being a public school principal—these three years have had tremendous and far reaching consequences in my way of viewing early childhood education and child development.

Just how has this way of life so significantly altered the way I feel about children and the process of education?

For one thing, I am now convinced that those of us in early childhood education have been unduly arrogant in our attitudes toward elementary education. There was certainly great arrogance (although perhaps unwitting and implicit) on my part in the thinking that led to the development of the Kramer Project. I was saying in effect, "Those of us who represent early childhood education could take care of America's children if you uncreative people in elementary education just wouldn't mess them up when we have finished with them."

Also I was saying—and there was nothing implicit in this, for I said it openly—"The techniques that we use in early childhood education would help to 'humanize' the schools if you would just watch us and learn from us. (*Why lines, physical punishment, schedules to go to the bathroom, desks in a row?*)" One of the things I have learned is that every one of those seemingly "inhuman" customs had its origins not in the emotional pathology of a distorted teacher but most likely in the gropings of a highly dedicated teacher trying to minimize the careless accidents and de-

liberate provocations that can be caused by children who have not, during earlier developmental periods, acquired sufficient self-control as to render such seemingly archaic customs unnecessary.

For another thing, I am persuaded by authors such as Toffler (1970) that changes are occurring in our society at an unassimilable rate, and that children are not exempt from the impact of these changes. For example, they are not immune to the impact of the media with its change in acceptable themes. The media demonstrate that "good guys" don't always win, and that quarrels are usually resolved by aggression and cunning. What does "All in the Family" teach about family life? Or about the equality of the sexes? What do children learn from the daily news? They learn that Whites and Blacks are fighting in Boston, but they do not learn that 20,000 children are being bused in Little Rock (where, supposedly, it all started) without incident.

There are many other opportunities for indirect or incidental social learning also—from Watergate, from the words emanating from a thousand songs that demand instant gratification, from such slogans as "do your own thing," from meetings in which adults might not be able to speak because of being shouted down, from direct and indirect forms of racial discrimination that persist in every segment of life, and from international indications that one can only settle disputes by resorting to aggression. While we need to be concerned about aggression and hostility in young children, we need even more to be concerned about these same behaviors in adults, and about the omnipresent indicators that ours is a society that apparently values such behavior.

What Do We Know about Aggression in Young Children

It is always disturbing to have someone say something like, "We really don't know too much about aggression and hostility in young children" —especially when you live with it every day. I am certain that every teacher and every aide is more of an expert on this subject than most of the researchers. But we necessarily have to say that about aggression, especially in young children, for a semantic reason if no other—namely, aggression is usually defined as behavior (verbal or physical) that has injury of a person or object as its *intent*. It can sometimes be very conjectural to try to assign intent to a young child's behavior. Did the baby who bit another child "intend" to hurt the other child, or was it to soothe aching gums? Did the toddler who pushed another child down in her eagerness to obtain a toy, causing the other child to cry, "intend" to hurt the pushed-down child or merely to get the toy? Does the child who calls his teacher a dirty name intend to defame her or to study her reaction for future reference or to try out words in an attempt to understand their meaning? Obviously, determination of intent is very difficult when we are concerned with very young children. Thus more people now are willing to define behavior as aggressive if it merely has the capacity to hurt or injure or damage, regardless of intent. The word hostility is even more difficult to define with reference to children, but most of us know what we mean by the term—the angry child whose behavior leaves little room for doubt as to its intent.

Although I do not like to labor too long on definitions, I think one more distinction is worth making. This is what Feshbach (1970) has called the difference between instrumental and hostile aggression. Instrumental aggression is the sort which is aimed at the retrieval of an object, territory, or privilege, i.e., that which results when a goal is blocked. Hostile aggression, on the other hand, is oriented to another person, as a person, following some sort of ego threat or a perception that another person has behaved intentionally: "He did it on purpose."

There is some evidence (Hartup 1974) that of these two forms, instrumental aggression is far more common in young children. In fact, the decline in overall aggression with age is largely a function of the decline with age in instrumental aggression. In one of the older studies concerned with children's aggression (Dawe 1934), most of the aggression shown by children from about eighteen months to almost six years of age was instigated by disputes over possessions, with the tendency most prevalent among the younger subjects. During these years person-directed, retaliatory, and hostile outbursts increased with age.

Another finding from these skimpy developmental studies of aggression was that the most aggressive children are sometimes the children who also show the greatest amount of prosocial (positive) behavior. This suggests that some children are simply more actively social than others; they engage in more of all types of interpersonal behavior. In spite of scattered "facts" of this sort, we still know precious little about age changes in aggressive behavior. Even more important, we know very little about time trends in incidence of aggressive behavior.

I think one thing we need to do in order to better understand aggression in young children is to develop some new ways of thinking about it. Because of the semantic problems centering around intent, I think it would be better to look at aggression as another manifestation of self versus other. That is, quite apart from whether the biting baby wanted to hurt his victim, we know that he was concerned with gratification of a self-based need. The child who suddenly took a toy from another might not even have noticed that another child was at that moment playing with it, so focused was she on her own desire to possess and manipulate the toy.

Elaine M. Ward

We need to be as concerned about the development in children of a healthy "other" concept as we do about the development of a healthy "self" concept. But how many of us are concerned with this task in our curricula? Not enough, I fear. We desperately need suggestions as to ways to help children develop empathy and concern for others, and our good thinkers need to be giving weight to this need equal to that of the importance of the self-concept.

Practical Suggestions for Those Who Must Cope

Those of us working with children cannot wait until all the data are accumulated and our good thinkers have reached their final conclusions. We are forced to deal with aggression daily and to use whatever bits and pieces of evidence are available to us at the present time—whether or not it is still inconclusive. We must evaluate the data as it comes in and do the best we can to wisely choose our methods of coping with the aggression expressed by the children in our programs. Therefore, I want to discuss some practical guidelines for all of us who must deal with aggression daily. Some of the guidelines are fairly well supported by research findings; others are based more on my personal way of viewing the problem and my attempts at seeking a solution.

Physical punishment of aggression is not the answer. One generalization that emerges with consistency is that there is a close relationship between high use of severe physical punishment by parents and high incidence of aggression by their children. "Spare the rod and spoil the child" is not borne out by data. However, it is difficult to get causative data. Though the two variables, physical punishment by parents and aggression by children, are closely related, it is still somewhat open to debate whether physical punishment "causes" the higher incidence of aggression. It might be possible to argue that high aggression on the part of the child causes more severe punishment by the parents and not vice versa. At this time we simply cannot say. We do know, however, that they are correlated. Further, it seems logical that the adult who uses physical punishment to deal with physical aggression is communicating: "You are just not big enough to get away with it and I am." The adult also is demonstrating to the child a certain belief in aggression as a viable solution to problems.

Ignoring aggression in children is not the answer. This is something I encouraged students and teachers to do for years. Ample testimony to my approach could be found by counting the number of times children at Kramer have been heard to say, "Mrs. Caldwell won't do nothing to you." I am now convinced that this is the wrong thing to do. Ignoring aggression will not make it disappear. The danger, it seems, in not responding to a child's aggressiveness is that the child may regard the watching adult's failure to deal with the aggressive behavior as adult approval of those actions. Siegel and Kohn (1970) have conducted an experiment which seems to support this interpretation of an adult's permissiveness by children. Working with pairs of preschool age children, they allowed half of the pairs to play with various toys for two sessions in the presence of a permissive (and noncondemning) adult; the other half of the pairs played in a similar setting but with no one else in the room. Most of the children in the adult-present condition exhibited more aggression in the second session than in the first; all of the children in the adult-absent condition decreased in aggression in the second session. The adult's permissiveness apparently was viewed by the children as approval of their aggressive behavior and therefore that behavior increased rather than decreased.

Permitting aggression or hostility to be expressed, and assuming that this will "discharge" the tension, will not work. Much of our current popular psychology, however, continues to promote this viewpoint. An article in a popular magazine recently listed the following consequences which can supposedly result from ignoring anger: taut, angry muscles; malfunctioning internal organs; migraine headaches; hives; pimples; itchy rashes; common colds; problems both mild and serious with the bladder, the stomach, and the bowels; ulcers; colitis; heart attacks; being accident prone; disastrous love affairs; and depression. Advice to openly express your anger and hostility in order to remain healthy and happy has been given for years and is still being given by some. Not only is the expression of anger and hostility supposedly preventive but it is also viewed by some as curative.

Yet this position is questionable in light of recent research findings. Berkowitz (1974) after an extensive review of research conducted on controlling aggression in young children concludes:

> He [the child] should not be encouraged to attack someone to express his hostility in the hope that he will drain some hypothetical energy reservoir. The catharsis notion is an outmoded theoretical conception lacking adequate empirical support which also has potentially dangerous social implications. Violence ultimately produces more violence. (p. 135)

With this principle in mind, there is one hint as to when "punishment" (but not aggressive punishment) should occur. According to a study done by Walters, Parke, and Cane (1965), it is most effective to punish or rebuke a would-be aggressor immediately after the aggressor has initiated the aggressive behavior rather than after the attack is completed or the goal is obtained. In their study, Walters, Parke, and Cane rebuked one half of a group of boys each time they reached for an attractive toy. For the other half of the boys, punishment (again in the form of a verbal reproof) came after the toy had been touched. Later the boys were allowed to play in the room with the desired toy but this time with the punishing agent absent. Those boys who had been rebuked before touching the toy demonstrated a greater ability to resist the temptation when left alone with the forbidden toy.

In order to minimize aggression, we need parent cooperation. One of my colleagues, Richard Elardo, and I conducted a study designed to determine whether or not teachers in day care programs and the parents of the children enrolled held differing values with respect to various areas of children's behavior. According to our research, one of the few important differences between parental values and teachers' values was in the area of aggressive behavior. Parents tended to believe that young children should be aggressive and fight in school, so others will not think they are sissies or cowards.

I have seen evidence of this attitude on the part of parents at our own school. We have had parents pick their son up from school and then drive around the school campus looking for another child who supposedly had insulted their son—in order that when the other boy was located, the son could get out of the car and beat the boy up. Similarly, we had a child whose parents had "dared" him to come home from school without having beaten up the little boy who threw sand in his sister's eyes while they were playing together the previous weekend.

Unfortunately, the school will remain ineffective in its efforts to control aggression in children as long as the parents support and even encourage such behavior in their children. If we are to minimize aggression, the school and the parents must work together.

In order to control aggression, we must strengthen altruism; we must emphasize helpfulness and cooperation as highly valued behaviors. In order to do this, however, we must have a society committed to these values. In 1974 I was a member of a U.S. delegation to the People's Republic of China. Our delegation spent most of its time observing in the Chinese kindergartens, which are for children between the ages of three and seven years. I saw no incidents of aggression on the part of the Chinese children. They did not push, shove, hit, kick, or in any way show hostility toward other students; further, there were no verbal attacks made against one another. The children were helpful and cooperative toward their classmates. At first I was somewhat amazed, but later such behaviors seemed the natural consequence of the societal values. The motto which guides the Chinese is "Serve the people!" and, as far as I could tell, the motto had become a way of life. The highest virtue is service to another person or to the collective, and the worst offense is selfishness.

Our society, I fear, lacks this emphasis on service and concern for other people. We, as a society, value competition and self-advancement. We profess belief in helping others, but usually it is considered secondary to the belief that people must help themselves. If we are to foster altruism in children, our society must esteem this quality. Even if the school and the individual parents agree, little will be achieved until the whole society values helpfulness and cooperation, and other attitudes which are inconsistent with aggression and hostility.

Non-permissiveness in our attitudes toward aggression may be as important as punishment for aggressiveness. We need to learn to communicate the attitude that says, "That sort of behavior is simply not going to be tolerated here." This was one of the major findings of the longitudinal study conducted by Sears, Maccoby, and Levin (1957) on patterns of childrearing.

4. BEHAVIOR

Our findings suggest that the way for parents to produce a non-aggressive child is to make abundantly clear that aggression is frowned upon, and to stop aggression when it occurs, but to avoid punishing the child for his aggression. Punishment seems to have complex effects. While undoubtedly it often stops a particular form of aggression, at least momentarily, it appears to generate more hostility in the child and lead to further aggressive outbursts at some other time or place. . . . Thus, the most peaceful home is one in which the mother believes aggression is not desirable and under no circumstances is ever to be expressed toward her, but who relies mainly on nonpunitive forms of control. The homes where the children show angry, aggressive outbursts frequently are likely to be homes in which the mother has a relatively tolerant (or careless!) attitude toward such behavior, or where she administers severe punishment for it, or both. (p. 266)

From my experience, I think the statement above would be just as true if we were to go back through it and every time the authors use the word "home" we were to substitute the word "classroom" and every time they use the word "parents" or "mother" we were to substitute the word "teacher." In our schools, we must communicate to the children a low tolerance of aggression while also using nonpunitive techniques for controlling it. Certainly this will not be an easy task. But all the evidence we have on the subject indicates that this is the most effective means for achieving our goal.

We must help children de-escalate their aggressive behavior. This is for me a relatively new concept which is of importance in helping to minimize aggressive behavior in children. It was born in this practical life I lead —observing the children at their play and observing how it is that most of the aggressive behavior develops. I couldn't begin to count the number of times I have seen a group of children running after each other, playing "monster," or "superman," or any of the other chasing games. Eventually one of the children gets knocked down, or trips, and gets hurt. The child becomes angry and blames a playmate—and the play becomes a fight. The same pattern is typical of play in the sandbox. The children begin innocently making pies, cakes, etc., until someone breaks a cake or pie and the "baker" gets mad and another fight occurs. Whenever these incidents occur and the question "why?" is posed to the children someone will answer, "We were just playing." Think how many times you have heard that explanation. I have come to realize how very often that is correct. Play, which began as positive social interaction, simply escalated too fast and in a manner not anticipated (and often not desired) by the children involved.

Our mistake is that we ususally read intent into the resultant aggressive behavior and reason: "The child should not get away with such behavior; he should be punished." We build intent into their actions, even though it might not have been there with the children (the tripping of a child or the breaking of a mud pie from the children's viewpoint were unintended accidents resulting from too much enthusiasm). If we can avoid being judgmental and simply help the children de-escalate back to the level of play, we will possibly have helped more than if we mete out punishment.

Children need to learn different alternatives to problem situations. It is relatively common for a child to tell me, "I hit him 'cause there wasn't nothin' else to do." Children do have a more limited repertoire of behaviors than adults. But it is up to us to work at providing more desirable alternatives for them. Unless we can help a child realize there are a variety of options, some more desirable than others, we cannot expect behavior to change.

We need to be more willing to play with children and to help them learn to play. How many children in your school know all the verses to London

Elaine M. Ward

Bridge? How many jump rope to the verses we chanted as children? (All their memorization is taken up with commercials.) Or how many of you rationalize that children need to be alone during free play time? The more adults withdraw from children, the more they expose them to peer influence. And the more children interact in the absence of adults (whose behavior they could model), the more likely they are to engage in fights and quarrels over property and privileges.

Summary

Our number one objective as teachers should be to facilitate the development of children's behavior that is cooperative and supportive of one another, altruistic and prosocial rather than aggressive. Those of us who work with children know that we must cope with a great deal of aggressive be-

havior, which is essentially self-centered. Although this is a phenomenon of our age and our culture, it is quite possible that we have been contributing our share to the apparent increase in such behavior. The isolation of our educational endeavors from schools for older children has in the past deprived us of the opportunity to follow the careers of children and obtain the necessary feedback we should have to enable us to adapt our own techniques to the realities of life histories.

For over a generation now we have been taught essentially to let children express their aggression both to "get it out of their system" and to prevent the development of symptoms of emotional dysfunction. As we now look at this practice, it appears to have been misleading. Aggression breeds not contentment and subsequent cooperation; aggression breeds more aggression. Severe punishment for aggression—especially punishment that mirrors the aggressive act itself —apparently does little to decrease the frequency of such behavior.

Nor does ignoring such behavior help; unfortunately, it does not just go away, and there is very little evidence that a child "grows out of it." Apparently children simply grow into more sophisticated manifestations of aggressive behavior, unless the environment in which the child is developing (home, school, community, nation) communicates that such behavior is not valued, and will not be tolerated. If that environment values cooperation and service to others, and if all segments of society support one another in that valuation, apparently children can learn to develop self-control and concern for others.

We, as parents and teachers, need to give some thought to helping children learn to de-escalate their aggressiveness back down to the level of play, where much of the behavior starts. De-escalating play is different from defusing the hostility which is often theorized as causing aggressiveness. As part of this de-escalation, a plea was made for more, rather than less, involvement of adults with children in their play. The price of liberty is supposed to be eternal vigilance. Vigilance by and extended contact with adults who model nonaggressive behavior is indeed one necessary precondition for the development of children who can cooperate with one another and with adults—and be happy in the process.

References

Berkowitz, L. "Control of Aggression." In *Review of Child Development Research, Vol. III*, edited by B. Caldwell and H. Ricciuti, pp. 95-140. Chicago: University of Chicago Press, 1973.

Dawe, H. C. "An Analysis of Two Hundred Quarrels of Preschool Children." *Child Development*, 1934, pp. 139-157.

Elardo, R., and Caldwell, B. M. "Value Imposition in Early Education: Fact or Fancy." *Child Care Quarterly*, 1973, pp. 6-13.

Feshbach, S. "Aggression." In *Carmichael's Manual of Child Psychology*, edited by P. H. Mussen, pp. 159-259. New York: John Wiley & Sons, 1970.

Hartup, W. W. "Aggression in Childhood: Developmental Perspectives." *American Psychologist*, 1974, pp. 336-341.

Sears, R. R.; Maccoby, E. E.; and Levin, H. *Patterns of Child Rearing*. Evanston, Ill.: Row, Peterson, and Co., 1957.

Siegel, A. E., and Kohn, L. G. "Permissiveness, Permission, and Aggression: The Effects of Adult Presence or Absence on Aggression in Children." In *Child Development and Behavior*, edited by F. Rebelsky and L. Dorman, pp. 234-242. New York: Alfred A. Knopf, 1970.

Toffler, A. *Future Shock*. New York: Random House, 1970.

Walters, R. H.; Parke, R. D.; and Cane, V. A. "Timing of Punishment and the Observation of Consequences to Others as Determinants of Response Inhibition." *Journal of Experimental Child Psychology*, 1965, pp. 10-30.

Temper, Temper... How to Deal With Tantrums

What erupts like Vesuvius, wails like a banshee, and kicks like a mule? Your child — if he's having a tantrum. Here's how to cope with these alarming outbursts.

By Martin Stewart

You're strolling down the aisle of the supermarket, heading for the check-out, your usually complacent three-year-old in tow. All is going along peacefully enough, when suddenly your child expresses a desire for that sugar-coated, multi-colored, marshmallow-nugget-filled cereal he has seen advertised on TV. To your answer of "No," your child, as though possessed, hurls himself to the floor and commences to howl and kick, while his face turns first crimson, then blue. What should you do? If you relent, do you also run the risk of spoiling both his teeth and his respect for parental authority? If you ignore his shrieks—or forcibly restrain him—might you be doing him some terrible psychic damage? And how concerned should you be by this outburst? Is this merely another phase through which he will pass, or does this behavior warrant consultation with a psychiatrist or child-development specialist?

"A temper tantrum is a description, not a diagnosis, given by parents to a common behavior pattern seen in very young children, two and three years old, maybe older," says Dr. Melvin Lewis, professor of pediatrics and psychiatry and director of medical studies at the Yale Child Study Center. "Usually it occurs when you start putting curbs on the child and not in very young children whose every whim is more or less gratified."

Temper tantrums are not inevitable in the development of young children, but they are not necessarily abnormal or unusual, either. There's no reason to be alarmed if a preschooler has a few

Martin Stewart writes frequently on child-related subjects.

temper outbursts. Children feel things intensely, and the process of making a child into a social human being often calls those intense feelings into play.

"A child and parent are in a delicate negotiating stance with regard to emotion and frustration," says Dr. James Egan, chairman of the department of psychiatry at Children's Hospital National Medical Center in Washington, D.C. "If the child has had significant frustrations in the first year of life, then it will be increasingly difficult for him to submit to social demands, in part because he has not developed a capacity to do so with relatively minor frustrations." Dr. Egan gives as examples of significant frustrations in the first year "multiple prolonged separations from caretakers and frequent changes in caretakers. Phenomena such as those in the first year increase the reservoir of aggression and decrease tolerance for further frustration.

"What the child ideally requires is relatively complete gratification in the earliest months of life to build up a sense of pleasure, pride, optimism, self-esteem, and good feelings about the world, trust, and hope. By skillful parenting, one ever so delicately increases the capacity for frustration."

"One of the things that increases frustration is delayed language," says Dr. Egan. When a child learns to speak he can articulate his needs and in that way avoid frustration. Also, developing the symbolic capacity to use language is a similar process to that of learning to control frustration.

Dr. Egan also believes that the presence of tantrums is ordinarily no reason to worry. "Some temper tantrums are universal. They are analogous to nightmares; every kid has them and one

cookies
crackers
snacks
club
CHEEZ-IT
SPY

shouldn't get concerned. But when they are chronic or severe and interfere with his functioning, then professional help is needed."

Temper tantrums can create other problems for the child when they persist too long. "Kids usually work their way out of tantrums by the time they enter school, or you hope they do. If they have them in school, they're in trouble," says Dr. Bertrand L. New, director of child and adolescent psychiatry at Westchester County Medical Center in Valhalla, New York, and associate professor of clinical psychiatry at New York Medical College. The problems arise in school because the child "disrupts a classroom. He's not learning and is preventing others from learning." But the child also leaves himself open to ridicule, which compounds the problem. "Other kids have a low tolerance of temper tantrums. They react more punitively than an older person does. Any stage newly mastered is apt to be treated with rigidity and inflexibility," he says.

Adults also take a dim view of school-age children who throw tantrums. "Take an eight-year-old who has temper tantrums," says Dr. New. "He's not going to be welcome in too many homes. The parents of his friend may say, 'He's a nice kid but I just don't want the hassle of having him around.'"

Because he believes the person having the tantrum is temporarily out of touch with the world and is "at the mercy of these things going on inside of him," Dr. New disagrees with the approach of handling the child's tantrum by isolating him. "A child depends on responsible adult strength to contain his antisocial destructive behavior and impulse."

"If the child is really worked up, probably the best thing is physical contact," says Dr. New, who suggests a "gentle but firm hand on the shoulders" with the words, "Stop. I can't understand what's bothering you when you're behaving like this." A long explanation of why this is unacceptable behavior is unnecessary, he believes. "Be short and sweet and direct. Communicate that although you might understand the child's anger, this is unacceptable behavior."

Picking up the child and holding and hugging him can also be effective if the child is not kicking and flailing wildly. Spanking, on the other hand, is not a good idea.

"Spanking provides a model of an adult giving forth to his anger through a physically violent act," Dr. Lewis explains. "The child doesn't understand what he's done, so it doesn't make sense to him. He doesn't learn from it, he just fears.

"What he needs is to feel protected, understood, even to get some understanding of why he is feeling and behaving as he is. Praise the child when he shows control so as to reinforce positive control. But don't punish the child because punishment simply lowers his self-esteem."

Dr. New says that, "parents have to distinguish between discipline and punishment," and defines discipline as presenting the child "with challenges and new situations and options in small increments, in little bits. Prevention lies in effective discipline, providing small increments of freedom."

"Many mothers and caretakers are very good at knowing when their child is tired, that 5 P.M. is not the time to make major new serious demands of the child, such as toilet training," says Dr. Egan. "The smart parent complies if his two-year-old wants his peanut-butter sandwich cut in triangles and not in squares. By allowing the child to exercise that element of control over his environment, he is more likely to be submissive on other issues."

Taking a child shopping can be a real invitation to a tantrum. If he's tired, it's worse, which is why going shopping with a child in the morning or after his nap is preferred.

"The first step should be just not to take the tantrum-prone child with you to the store at all," says Dr. Lewis. "If you do take him, make sure he gets some gratifications immediately so that he's happy." If those aisles where he wants things can be avoided, they should be. "If he starts having a tantrum, the simplest thing to do is leave," says Dr. Lewis. "Don't punish him there and then as if he can control himself. It's not fair to him."

Tone of voice is also important. Says Dr. New: "If, for example, the child says, 'Mommy, I want that cereal,' a mother can calmly explain, 'I don't want you to have it because it's sugar-coated and sugar is bad for your teeth.' If, however, you snap, 'That's a sugar cereal. You have to eat oatmeal,' you make oatmeal sound like a punishment.

"If parents are honest with themselves," he says, "they can determine which ways of handling a question are likely to frustrate a child and which ways are apt to satisfy the child. Parents should raise their kids, not by formula, but by their own judgment."

That's not to say it's easy. Temper tantrums are as complicated and as contradictory as the human desire to express oneself. The attitude that parents take toward tantrums is critical, however. Are you conveying to the child the attitude that it's not acceptable to express anger? Does the child believe that you disapprove of him rather than that you disapprove of his angry behavior? Does the child know that you mean it when you say you don't want him to do something? A temper tantrum deserves to be dealt with firmly, but with understanding.

"Don't just dismiss it as attention getting," says Dr. Lewis. "Sometimes if a child has repeated temper tantrums, there is also a message. There is a signal. If the child has to do that to get attention, he's not getting the attention he needs."

It's All Right to Cry

Joyce Olum

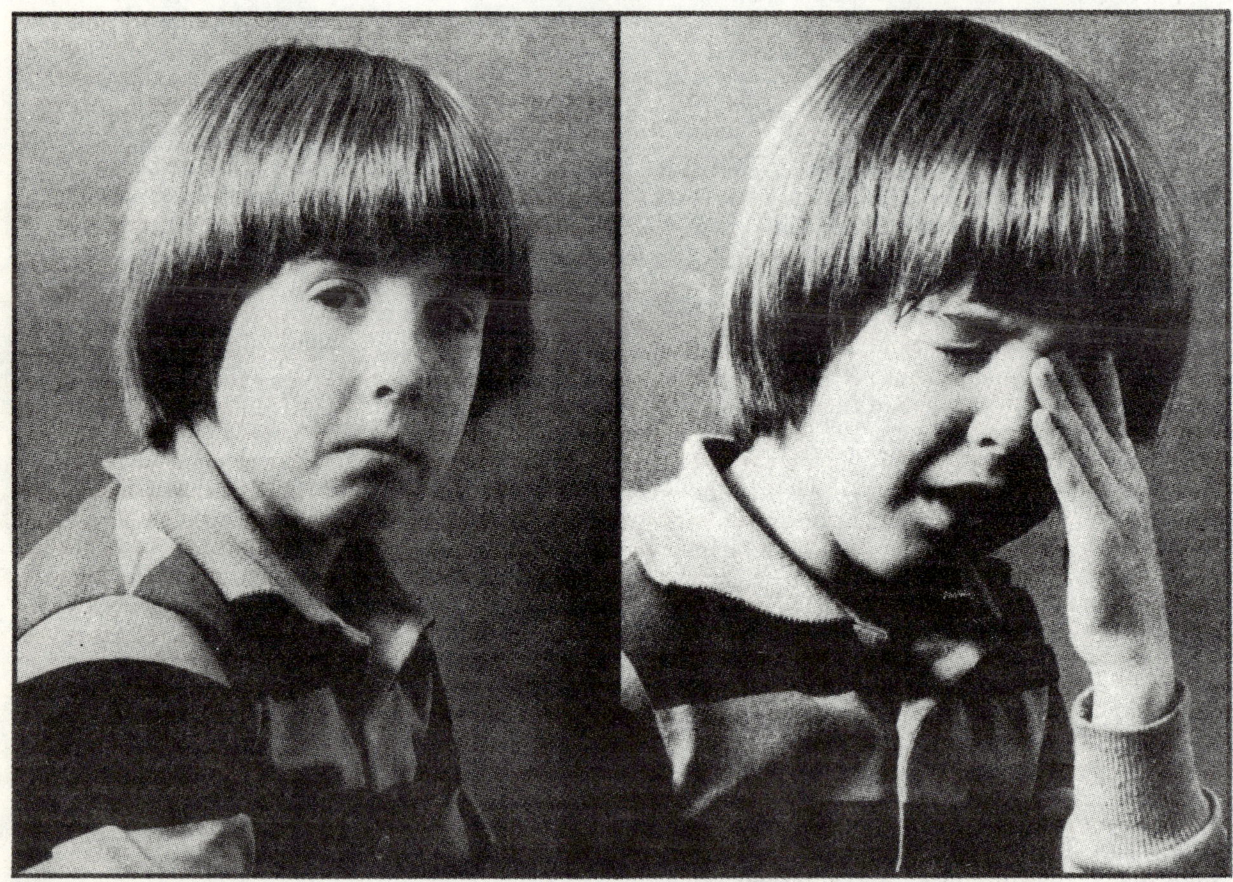

"You're a big boy, Johnny. Big boys don't cry!"

"There, there, Susie, there's nothing to get so upset about."

"Cut that crying out right now, Tommy. Can't you see the other children are trying to work?"

"Crying won't do any good."

What do you say when a child in your classroom bursts into tears? Often, we, as teachers, try to quiet crying children down as quickly as possible to avoid the disruption and distraction. Sometimes we comfort them; sometimes we cajole them; sometimes we're firm with them; occasionally, we lose our tempers with them. But one way or another, kindly or roughly, we try to get them to shut off the tears.

And yet, children often need to cry.

"In my classroom I try to be with children who need to cry— to hold them in my lap or just to sit with them"

Crying is a way of getting rid of hurts or angry feelings. As the song says—"It's all right to cry/Crying gets the sad out of you/It's all right to cry./It might make you feel better."

Song excerpted from "It's All Right to Cry" by Carol Hall, from "Free to Be . . . You and Me," Arista Records and the book published by McGraw-Hill © 1974. Ms. Foundation for Women; Inc., used with permission.

Crying does make children feel better. There is a widely held notion that if you stop children from crying, you'll stop them from feeling sad or hurt. However, the hurt is there, whether or not the child expresses it in tears. A child who isn't allowed to cry or who doesn't let himself or herself cry will bottle up the hurt and carry it around all day. It may not seem obvious, but the hurt will get expressed some other way—in sulking, in being unable to concentrate on schoolwork or in fighting.

But in a classroom where it feels safe to cry, when Tommy skins a knee or his feelings have been hurt, he'll run to the teacher or the nearest person he feels safe with and burst into tears. He'll cry and cry until he's all cried out and then go back to playing or working as if nothing had happened. He will have cried out the hurt feelings, and he'll really be rid of them.

Caring for Kids Who Need to Cry

In my classroom, I try to be with children who need to cry—to hold them in my lap or just to sit with them. They seem to need the safety of another person reassuring them that their feelings really are OK. This is very different from saying, "There, there, dear, everything's OK," which communicates, however subtly, that their feelings aren't OK and that something is the matter with them for feeling so upset.

What do you do, though, if you're one teacher with a class of 30 kids? What's happening with the other 29 while you're holding Susie on your lap and letting her cry? There are several possibilities. One is to ask the rest of the class to pay attention and watch you. After all, that's exactly what happens if we lose our tempers with one child; we interact with that child while the whole class watches. Why not ask the class to do the same when we're giving support to a child who's hurt or upset?

Once children get the idea that crying is OK, another possibility is to establish a specific procedure for children to follow to occupy themselves quietly while you're busy with the child who is crying. Depending on the age level you teach, and the type of classroom you have, you could say, "Everyone choose a game or puzzle to do quietly," or "Everyone find a book to read," or "Everyone do the next page in the workbook." The important thing is to have a prearranged procedure. It's useful to have such a system anyway, in case there's an emergency.

Finding the Time to Pay Attention

A teacher just doesn't have enough time to pay attention to *every* child *every* time he or she feels hurt and needs to cry. And there are times, such as when there's just been a fight on the playground, when several children need attention at the same time. One solution is to teach children to give support to each other. Even quite young children can learn to do this.

Russ Jones, a kindergarten teacher in Groton, Mass., told me of a time when one of the girls in his class was very upset. He sat with her while she cried, but after a time he felt he had to go work with some other children. So he called one of the other girls in the class over and said, "Linda, Judy needs someone to sit with her and hold her hand while she cries. Could you do that for her?" She did, and during the next 15 minutes several kindergartners

took turns holding Judy's hand and sitting with her. After that, Judy stopped crying and went back to playing, feeling fine. In addition to Judy being able to get the attention she needed and the teacher being able to go about his work, several children had learned something important about caring for other people.

Some Children Cry Over Anything

How about children who cry whenever they don't get their way—the one who cries because someone else got to play with the game he wanted to play with, or the one who gets upset because you didn't let her go on the trip that day? The best solution I've found is to let the child cry but not give in. Some children learn to cry in order to manipulate adults, and it works because some grown-ups will do practically anything to stop a child from crying. Children need to learn that crying is all right but that they can't use it to manipulate their teachers or anyone else.

There are also some children who seem to cry over practically anything. I've taught one such child. He'd burst into tears and cry and cry every time he bumped his knee or stubbed his toe, which was rather often. My first reaction was that he was "making a big fuss over nothing." But when I held him in my lap and let him cry and told him I cared about him, he started saying, "No you don't. No one cares about me."

After a while I realized that he was upset about all sorts of things—problems at home, frustrations with schoolwork, feeling rejected by classmates. The bumped knees and stubbed toes just provided an opportunity for him to cry about all the other hurts that he'd been bottling up. I spent quite a lot of time early in the year holding him and letting him cry. As the weeks went on, he started smiling more, laughing more, playing more with other children and doing better in his schoolwork. He stopped bursting into tears whenever he fell down and bumped himself; instead he'd laugh and pick himself up.

If we allow children to cry whenever they need to, will they distract other children who are trying to work? Crying children are sometimes noisy, but there's a difference between crying and screaming. Once the children have gotten used to the idea that it's OK to cry in school, most instances of crying won't bother the rest of the class. However, if you're doing an activity for which the room needs to be very quiet, the child who needs to cry can go to a corner of the room or some other quiet place with you or another child.

Learning to Care, Not Laugh

It does take the children a little while to learn to care for rather than laugh at a classmate who's crying. And no matter what we teachers say, children are never going to feel safe enough to cry in our classrooms if they're afraid their classmates are going to make fun of them. It can be very painful to be ridiculed, especially for a child who's already feeling hurt.

Right from the beginning, it's important to teach our students to respect each other's feelings. If the children start to tease someone for "being a crybaby," we can explain that crying is natural and healthy and nothing to be ashamed of. We can explain that instead of making Kathy feel even worse by teasing, they can help her feel better by showing they care about her or just by sitting with her for a few minutes. I've found that this kind of direct approach works well and that the teasing soon disappears.

But how about all the other things that have to be done in school, besides dealing with children's feelings and upsets? Will all this attention to children's feelings distract us and our students from teaching and learning basic skills, such as reading and math? The answer is emphatically no. Every teacher faces the problem of how to teach children who are perfectly intelligent but can't seem to keep their attention on what they are learning. One reason for this is that a child who's upset about something and is bottling up feelings has trouble paying attention to anything.

Every teacher also has difficulties with children fighting and saying cruel things to each other. Children who are upset themselves are likely to try to get the hurt out by hurting someone else. It's rare for children to get into fights when they're relaxed and happy with themselves.

At first it may seem like more work to pay attention to children who need to cry than to quiet them down as quickly as possible. But in the long run, taking the extra time will make the job easier. There will be fewer "discipline problems" and less difficulty with kids who "just can't seem to get interested in learning." Giving children the opportunity to get out their hurts, rather than bottling them up, will not only help make them happier with themselves and help them get along better with each other, but also help free their attention for learning reading, writing, math and all the other things that teachers are in the business of helping children to learn. Allowing children their feelings and their tears can make our classrooms happier, more relaxed places.

TEACHING YOUR CHILD TO BE RESPONSIBLE

BENJAMIN SPOCK, M.D.

In the first of my recent columns on the managing of small children, I pointed out that the fundamental factor in motivating them to good behavior is not punishment or scolding or threats or urging, or even setting them a good example. It is the parents' love of their children. This engenders in the children a love of their parents, which makes them want—more than anything else in the world—to grow up to be mature, responsible people like them and to be approved of by them—at least most of the time. This foundation for good character and good attitudes is laid down mainly in the first two or three years of life. Children who have not been loved during this formative period usually grow up to be shallow, demanding people who have no desire to conform or to please. Punishment has no beneficial effect.

But children who *do* experience love during their earliest years don't grow into well-behaved children and responsible adults by some kind of magic. They do it by watching closely and imitating their admired parents—every hour of the day. As a matter of fact, this is the principal way by which kittens and puppies and the young of many species learn to conform and to survive.

You can see the imitative process beginning even before babies are a year old, when they learn to "patty-cake" by copying their fathers and mothers. By the time they reach the one-year mark, they are trying to take hold of the spoon, to feed themselves; and wise parents encourage these efforts. For with such encouragement their babies will be feeding themselves by about a year and a quarter. But if the parents, fearing a mess, say, "No! No!" for several months, their babies may outgrow this particular ambition and insist on the privilege of being fed for a long, long time.

By two years of age, children want to dust the furniture when a parent dusts, brush their teeth when Mother or Father does, put on and pull off their socks and underwear the way they've seen their parents do these things.

When they are between two and three years of age, their vocabularies grow by leaps and bounds through imitation alone.

And by about three years of age, children aren't learning to behave just by imitating their parents' actions. The process goes deeper. Their affection and admiration for their parents is now intense. They want to *be* like their parents as people and they want to *feel* like them.

Another development is that the boy, sensing now that he is destined to become a man, watches his father, particularly, and tries to act like him in every respect. He assumes his tone of voice, cusses if his father cusses, pretends to drive the family car, pretends to go to the shop or to the office.

A little girl now pays more attention to her mother and models herself after her in activities and manner. When she dresses up in her mother's clothes—skirt dragging, gloves drooping off her little hands, high-heeled shoes falling over—she giggles with delight to be feeling so much like a woman.

Years ago, when I brought a group of medical students to observe in a nursery school, we happened to watch a bossy four-and-a-half-year-old girl giving instruction in doll care to a mousy three-year-old. As the older child undressed the baby doll, bathed it, dried it, powdered it, diapered it and dressed it again, she kept saying to the younger one, "See how I do it, dear? Watch me carefully, dear." Finally she said, "Now you try, dear." The three-year-old stepped forward and very carefully began the doll care. But the older one soon interrupted. "No, dear, not like that. Now, dear, watch me more carefully." Her tone was always condescending, slightly scolding.

By four years this child knew just how to do most of the things her mother did; she had adopted her mother's attitude in all respects and turned herself into very much the same kind of person her mother was. When she is 24 years old she will treat her real child in just the same spirit and manner in which she treated the three-year-old. She will have much the same attitude as her mother toward men and women, toward work, toward morals. In other words, at four and a half she already had a sharply defined, well-disciplined character—though a somewhat irritating one. (Incidentally, most children at that age are not yet quite so adult in attitude or so eager to be the spit and image of a parent; they are only partway along the road. It's more often first children who become adult so fast.)

What all this means is that young children themselves do a major part of the work of learning to adapt and behave. Most of the time they want to be "good" because they want to be grown-ups like their parents. The motive is in them, operating most of the time they are awake. In automobile terms, the engine is inside them. The parents still have lots to do, as all parents know, but their job is to supply the guidance —what you might call the steering and the gear shifting.

For parents to be able to steer and shift gears, they have to have some sense of how this machine works. They must know that shifting into a lower gear is the way you keep the machine from stalling when going uphill and that brake linings will burn out if you depend on the brakes alone in coming down a steep mountain. They have to know something about road signs, about the dangers of blind intersections and going the wrong way up one-way streets.

In other words, there is lots that parents have to know and do; but if the drive to be grown up were not in the child already, there would be no progress.

What are the implications for parents of children's eagerness to grow up to be like them? In a sense, all they have to do is set a good example. But of course, that's a lot harder to do than to direct and correct.

Of first importance, I think, is that parents have—and show—a generally friendly and trusting attitude toward their children, rather than the predominantly critical attitude that has been more or less traditional in past generations.

For if parents, however devoted they are to their children, usually speak to them in a critical and bossy manner (and that's a common combination), their children, though tending in the long run to become the same responsible kind of people as their parents, are likely from hour to hour of the day to act as pesky as they think they can get away with. (When parents are masterful in their domination, their children have to bottle up their rebelliousness. Commoner today are cross or bossy parents who lack assurance, and so without realizing it stimulate their children to argue every point—endlessly and pointlessly.)

When I say that parents should have a "generally friendly and trusting attitude," I want to make it clear that I don't think they should be submissive to their children or take rudeness or abuse. This is an important distinction. A fair number of parents today who want to be friendly rather than oppressive have trouble finding a middle course; they permit or unconsciously invite their children to be somewhat oppressive with them.

Now let's think of examples of how you can manage your children, especially in the three-to-six-year period, by taking advantage of their drive to be like you.

Since a girl is now most intensely motivated to become like her mother, the mother has the greater opportunity with her. If the mother has a job outside her home, she may take her daughter to visit her place of work once every year or two if this is permitted, letting the child pretend to carry out some of her mother's activities—sit at her desk, make telephone calls, stand behind a sales counter or talk with a make-believe client or customer. It's not that the girl is ready to begin practicing a profession. But it's good for her to feel identified with her mother in as many ways as possible, and especially in an activity that is ordinarily invisible to the child. To pretend to be a parent at an outside job, even once every few years, is a potent stimulus.

It is good for the mother to take her daughter shopping—for the mother's clothes as well as for the child's and for other things. Or the mother can take her on a visit to a friend, whether or not there is another child for her to play with. A child taken alone on an expedition with one parent gets an inspiration entirely different from when she is taken with other children; and she tends to be better behaved than when taken with both parents. Rivalry with one parent for the attention of the other is eliminated and companionship is accentuated.

A boy will be excited by a visit to his father's work place even if the work itself seems dull. Every few years my father, who was a railroad lawyer, took me to his office, where the walls were lined with identical-looking law books without illustrations and where the conversations were unintelligible to me. But on the bookcase was a model of a freight car, about three feet long, with sliding doors and brakes that actually responded to a hand wheel that protruded above the roof. I always secretly hoped that my father would give me that car someday, but of course, it wasn't his to give. My deep fascination with railroads has persisted, in spite of my having got into very different work.

It's particularly important for boys and girls to be *allowed* to help with table setting, with dish and silver drying, bedmaking, room cleaning and even cooking when they begin to take an interest, usually between two and three years of age. (They should be able to roll and cut cookies by four or five.) It is good for girls as well as boys to pretend to help with leaf raking and car washing. Girls will be likelier to volunteer if their mothers do these outdoor chores too.

I say "allowed to help" because children at this age will want very much to help. But many parents—because of their own upbringing—assume that chores must be assigned to children and will be resented by them. They forget that children start out *wanting* to do these things. So parents are apt to keep children from "helping" at first, sometimes for fear that objects will be broken or that the child will be more of a nuisance than a help.

Later these parents may begin assigning jobs. But remembering how much they themselves disliked these tasks in childhood, they assume that their children too will balk and evade. So they often take on a commanding or scolding tone to start off with, which, of course, promptly turns the children's feelings against the work.

Another aspect of chores for young children that seems important to me is that parents continue—for months and years—to do these jobs along with their children. Very often when parents find that their children can perform a task satisfactorily, they promptly delegate it to the children while they themselves turn to something else. That may be sound when children get older and perhaps even ask to take over a job completely, but not when the children are very young.

On the other hand, children under 12, 14 or 16 don't usually have enough persistence or sufficient joy in completing a task. So they tend to procrastinate after a while, or fool around or quarrel over which one is not doing her or his share. Then the parents have to nag. But if the parents continue to participate in jobs, the children will continue to be inspired by their example—and by their companionship. It will still be a grownup's job that they're allowed to share in rather than a child's unpleasant chore.

The value of the parents' continued participation applies to all kinds of duties at home—and it's particularly important, I think, in getting young children into their baths or into bed. If the parents get up to lead, young children tend to follow automatically. But if the children are told "Go," they feel that they are being banished from the area of light and sociability and fun into the lonely outer darkness. So they pretend not to hear, or they begin arguing and continue to argue as long as they think they can get away with it, short of provoking the parents into a rage.

In a similar spirit I think it's wise for at least one parent to be around the children's bedroom area, while all get dressed in the morning, to be a good example and a reminder, rather than for both parents to go to the kitchen or dining room while prodding the children from a distance.

It is also well for parents to remember—though it is extremely difficult—to set an example by not taking out on each other tensions that are coming from elsewhere.

I believe that children quarrel for two main reasons: They fear that a brother or sister may get more attention than they, and they feel and pass on the irritability that the parents direct toward them and toward each other.

We live in an unusually tense, competitive, insecure society. I had not realized how true this is until I traveled in countries where, for example, extended families are tightly knit and take care of their members materially and emotionally, or where the community outside the family is stable and nurturing, or where there is little unemployment, or where illness presents no financial problems, or where there is little striving to get a higher position or higher salary, partly because these differences are slight anyway.

We in America are proud of our material progress, but we forget what a stiff price we pay for it. We parents bring home tensions from our jobs, from neighborhood and national problems, from our financial and health worries. We take them out on each other and on our children. Then the children fight each other.

We can't solve the major problems of our society in this discussion. But it helps a little to realize that there are valid excuses for some of our tensions.

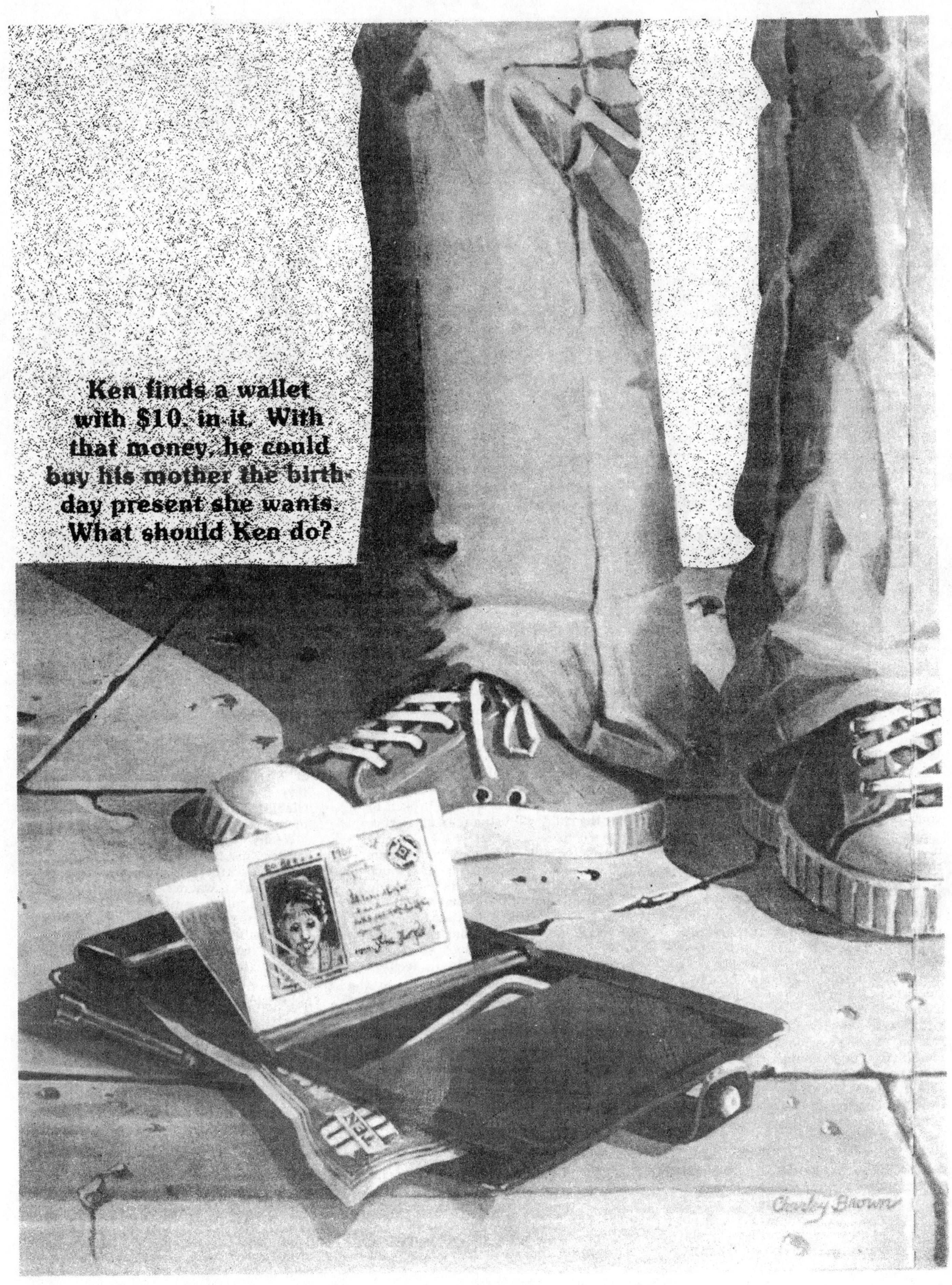

Art by Charley Brown

How To Encourage Moral Development

THOMAS LICKONA

"With us an order was an order. . . . Where would we have been if everyone had thought things out?"

"I believed he had the authority to do it."

"The success of this man proved to me that I should subordinate myself to him."

"I was there to follow orders, not to think."

Statements one and three were made by Adolph Eichmann at his trial for crimes he committed in Nazi Germany. Statements two and four were made by defendants in the Watergate trials.

Well before Watergate, social psychologists knew that most people faced with a tough moral decision prefer to pass the buck—they will do what they're told to do. That was the conclusion of Stanley Milgram's well-known experiments at Yale. A sizable majority of subjects, representing all walks of life, were willing to give what they believed to be intensely painful electrical shocks to protesting victims—simply because the experimenter instructed them to do so. Watergate and studies like Milgram's are not, however, the whole story. Unthinking conformity may be one form of moral bankruptcy, but the spreading violence in society seems to indicate that we don't have *enough* conformity to the most basic norms of human decency.

Can schools do anything about these moral problems? Should teachers get involved in the potentially murky waters of moral education? In one Gallup poll, 79 percent of the people interviewed said yes—schools *should* offer instruction in morals and in moral behavior. If you agree with these people, your next question probably will be the crucial one: How do we teach morals?

Understanding Moral Development

Developmentalists like Lawrence Kohlberg of Harvard have argued that the only objective definition of psychological maturity is one based on knowledge of how people actually do develop. Piaget's apparently universal stages of cognitive development provide a definition of maturity in the intellectual realm. Thinking at Piaget's concrete operational level, for example, is more mature than thinking at the preoperational level; thinking at the formal operational level is more mature than thinking at the concrete level, and so on.

So it is, Kohlberg maintains, in the realm of moral development, where similar stages of maturity can be identified. Over the last 20 years, Kohlberg and his colleagues have mapped stages of moral reasoning by presenting children, adolescents and adults with hypothetical moral dilemmas. One dilemma used with children, for example, describes a situation facing ten-year-old Holly: Should she climb a tree to rescue the stranded kitten of a small boy, or should she keep her promise to her worried father not to climb any more trees?

The five stages that Kohlberg's research has identified are described in the chart on page 38. The child at stage 1 believes that the people in power—adult authorities—are the arbiters of morality. The authorities determine what's right and what's wrong. Because the child doesn't yet understand the practical need for moral rules in human relationships, his only motivation to obey rules is his fear of getting caught if he steps out of line. If Holly were at stage 1, for example, she might reason that she shouldn't save the kitten, because if she climbs the tree, she might get in trouble with her father.

With stage 2 comes the first awareness that morality has something to do with human relations and needs. There's an understanding of reciprocity or, a tit-for-tat level. One girl in second grade said that Holly should save the kitten because some day Holly might be tied up and the kitten would remember and would come and loosen the ropes for her. Stage 2 reasoning *against* climbing the tree might focus on all that Holly's father has done for her in the past; this might convince Holly that she should pay him back by keeping her promise.

At stage 3, the child grasps the golden rule. Holly should save the kitten—or keep her promise to her father—because it's the "nice" thing to do, not just because of what's in it for her. People are counting on her. With stage 3 comes the ability to put yourself in the other person's shoes and to know simultaneously that they can put themselves in your shoes too. Perhaps Holly's father will understand if she climbs the tree to save the kitten; he'll know that she didn't want to disappoint him but that she felt she just had to help.

At stage 4, concern for others is ex-

Kohlberg's Stages of Moral Development

PRINCIPLED LEVEL (Concern for fidelity to self-chosen moral principles)	**STAGE 5** *	**MOTIVATOR:** Internal commitment to principles of "conscience"; respect for the rights, life and dignity of all persons. **AWARENESS:** Particular moral/social rules are social contracts, arrived at through democratic reconciliation of differing viewpoints and open to change. **ASSUMPTION:** Moral principles have universal validity; law derives from morality, not vice versa.
CONVENTIONAL LEVEL (Concern for meeting external social expectations)	**STAGE 4**	**MOTIVATOR:** Sense of duty or obligation to live up to socially defined role and maintain existing social order for good of all. **AWARENESS:** There is a larger social "system" that regulates the behavior of individuals within it. **ASSUMPTION:** Authority or the social order is the source of morality.
	STAGE 3	**MOTIVATOR:** Desire for social approval by living up to good boy/good girl stereotype; meeting expectations of others. **AWARENESS:** Need to consider intentions and feelings of others; cooperation means ideal reciprocity (golden rule). **ASSUMPTION:** Good behavior equals social conformity.
PRECONVENTIONAL LEVEL (Concern for external, concrete consequences to self)	**STAGE 2**	**MOTIVATOR:** Self-interest: what's in it for me? **AWARENESS:** Human relations are governed by concrete reciprocity: let's make a deal; you scratch my back, I'll scratch yours. **ASSUMPTION:** Have to look out for self; obligated only to those who help you; each person has own needs and viewpoint.
	STAGE 1	**MOTIVATOR:** Fear of getting caught; desire to avoid punishment by authority. **AWARENESS:** There are rules and consequences of breaking them. **ASSUMPTION:** Might makes right; what's regarded by those in power is "good"; what's punished is "bad."

*(Kohlberg recently has redefined his stages so that stage 5 incorporates much of what used to be in a stage 6.)

panded to a wider scale. One begins to have a concept of society, law, and one's role within a larger social and legal system. You want to do your duty, to set a good example, and to insist that other people do too. Stage 4 is still a morality shaped by external expectations, however. Not until stage 5, the level of principled moral reasoning, can you stand apart from the social framework and say that some things are morally wrong in the system —that some laws or institutions, for example, need changing to protect

the rights of individuals. Not until stage 5 can a person understand the moral basis for the Bill of Rights.

At stage 5, universal moral principles define right and wrong. That's what we told the Nazis at the end of World War II: they had an obligation to universal moral laws respecting human rights, and this obligation should have superceded the commands of their superiors. That's what, in effect, we told the Watergate defendants who said they were only carrying out what they believed to be presidential

orders.

Over the last two decades, Kohlberg and his associates have conducted substantial research: they have followed for 20 years the moral development of 50 individuals who are now 30 to 36 years old; they have compared moral reasoning in diverse cultures (Taiwan, England, Turkey, Yucatan and the United States); they have experimented with various techniques to stimulate advances to higher developmental stages. Their central findings:

1. The stages of moral reasoning appear to be the same for all persons, regardless of social class or culture.

2. Stages can't be skipped, because one stage builds onto another.

3. Stage change is gradual, because a new stage can't be instilled directly but must be constructed out of many social experiences.

4. Stage and age can't be equated, because some people move much faster through the stage sequence than others; some also get further (only about 25 percent of American adults reach stage 5 of principled morality).

5. Although an individual's stage of moral reasoning is not the only factor affecting his moral conduct, the way a person reasons does influence how he actually behaves in a moral situation. Persons at higher stages, for example, are more likely to help others, more likely to honor a commitment, and less likely to cheat.

6. Experiences that provide opportunities for what Kohlberg calls "role-taking" (assuming the viewpoints of others, putting yourself in another's place) foster progress through the stages. Children who participate a lot in peer relationships, for example, tend to be at more advanced moral stages than are children whose peer interaction is low. Within the family, children whose parents encourage them to express their views and participate in family decisions reason at higher moral stages than children whose parents do not encourage these behaviors.

How Not To Apply the Moral Stages

At first glance, the moral stages might suggest that you should be aware of a child's stage, adapt your behavior to that level, and at the same time provide impetus for the child's advancement up the developmental ladder.

This easy recipe for applying Kohlberg's theories has several problems:

1. It's often hard to diagnose a child's stage of functioning in a specific situation (although diagnostic ability does improve with practice).

2. Keying one's behavior to the child's stage is complicated by the fact that children, like adults, typically operate simultaneously at several different stages.

3. A teacher must come up with an approach to rules and responsibilities that works for the whole class; there can't be two or three different "moral curriculums" in the same classroom.

4. Focusing on the single aspect of a child's dominant stage of moral reasoning results in a kind of tunnel vision that can limit a teacher's perception of the multidimensionality of any child's moral personality. Lois Murphy's extensive naturalistic observations in the 1930s found that preschoolers frequently came to each other's aid—shoving an attacker away from the victim, for example, and showing intense concern for the hurt child. Such sympathetic emotional responses and prosocial actions, like children's early flashes of a sense of fairness, run ahead of their systematic moral reasoning. Teachers who dwell on a child's dominant pattern of moral reasoning may miss these positive moral flashes, which must be noticed and nurtured, because they are the seeds from which a more consistent moral orientation will later grow.

Teachers also can run into difficulties if they assume there's a direct link between age and moral stage. It is true that, in general, the moral reasoning research shows that stages 1 and 2 dominate in the primary school years and persist in some individuals long beyond that. Stage 3 gains ground during the upper elementary grades and often remains the major orientation through the end of high school. Stage 4 begins to emerge in adolescence. Only one in four persons moves on in late adolescence or adulthood to stage 5, the morality of equal rights, justice and democratic process underlying the American Constitution.

Even so general a statement of the research findings, however, can be misleading. For one thing, these norms are based on interviewing subjects on hypothetical moral dilemmas. Piaget points out that children's "theoretical moral thought" on fictional stories may lag behind their "active moral thought" in real-life situations. Thus a child may demonstrate the upper reaches of his moral reasoning—say, stage 3—only if you catch him in his natural environment acting upon a problem that he really cares about. Muddling the picture even more is the fact that a self-interested stake in the outcome of a moral problem may have just the opposite effect, causing a child to reason at a level lower than what he is capable of.

But there *is* a practical value in knowing Kohlberg's moral reasoning stages. They define a natural, nonrelativistic goal for moral education: progress through the developmental stages. Kohlberg's stages also provide rough indicators of what kind of moral understanding you can expect from children during broad developmental periods, and they underscore the idea that becoming moral, like becoming logical, is indeed a developmental process involving step-by-step stage changes and requiring the child's active construction of these stages.

Teachers don't need to worry, then, about tailoring their every behavior to a child's moral stage. It's much more important to provide an overall moral environment that is in harmony with the broad themes of moral growth, such as fairness and a concern for others. This moral environment should provide opportunities for the role-taking that Kohlberg's research suggests is so critical. Consider, for example, this finding: Children who grow up on an Israeli kibbutz—with its intense peer-group interaction, shared decision-making and intermeshing work responsibilities—typically reach stage 4 or 5 in adolescence. By contrast, children reared in situations where there is limited social interchange are often still at stage 1 and 2 even in late adolescence.

Developing Morals Discussions

Moral dilemma discussions were the first method for putting Kohlberg into the classroom. At the elementary level, I've gotten some animated discussions going with commercially prepared dilemmas—Guidance Associate's *First Things: Values* filmstrip series, for example. The most popular of these is "Cheetah (What Do You Do About Rules?)." A schoolteacher in ordinary life, Cheetah is a superhero who must decide whether to keep his solemn oath of secrecy as a member of the Cat-People or reveal his identity to his nine-year-old son, Marcus, who suspects him of being involved in a bank robbery. One third grade class was unanimously in favor of Cheetah's keeping his oath, so I role-played Marcus to dramatize what he would be feeling and to get the kids to think about other ways of looking at the problem. "Cheetah promised never to tell," they said.

"That's an interesting reason," I said. "Tell me, do you think it is ever right to break a promise? Did any of you ever break a promise?"

Most admitted to having done so, and we got into a good discussion of the reasons for breaking promises and for making them in the first place. We moved to other issues, such as whether Cheetah had a responsibility to keep fighting crime, and after 45 minutes the discussion still was going strong.

Sometimes children will say things during a moral dilemma discussion that are textbook examples of Kohlberg's stages, but most of their statements are not so easily pigeonholed, nor do they need to be. What's more important is getting students to think hard about a moral issue, to give reasons for their opinions, and to listen to the reasons others give. The teacher's job is to lead a good discussion: clarify each child's contribution, raise challenging questions, ask for reasons behind opinions, and stretch children's moral awareness to consider the viewpoints of all characters involved in a dilemma.

Phyllis Hophan, a third grade teacher in Lansing, New York, and a participant in Project Change (see resource list at the end of this article), has experimented with several approaches to dilemma discussions and says the following guidelines work best for her:

1. Keep the discussion group small; six is ideal.

2. Encourage children to respond to each other. Ask: "What do you think about what so-and-so said?"

3. List children's opinions and reasons on the chalkboard. Says Hophan: "Under each of the solutions the group mentions, we have many 'becauses' and it's the 'becauses' that we spend our time talking about."

Along with commercially prepared dilemmas, situations from the classroom can provide good stimuli for moral discussions. Teachers often say that they and their students get more involved in trying to solve real moral problems: How should teachers and students deal with a rash of fistfights, pencil jabbings and kickings in the classroom? How can cleanup be organized so all do their fair share? Is it right to revoke everyone's free-time privileges because a few have abused those privileges?

In Phyllis Hophan's classroom there is a chart with an unfinished sentence that anyone may complete: "This was the week when _________." Every Friday the class tackles whatever problems have been logged that week. Examples: "There were three fights on the morning bus." "Someone had money taken." "Another teacher kept the projector too long and we couldn't see our movie." Having these complaints recorded on the chart, Hophan says, gives her and the children a longer time to think about various sides of a problem and its solutions.

Real classroom conflicts are open to many solutions and can offer students the important moral experience of hammering out a fair compromise. Coming to grips with real problems and following through on group decisions help children take a crucial step in their moral growth: *acting* on the basis of their moral reasoning. Follow-through is critical; the solutions that you and your students come up with should be put into practice. As part of the class discussion, students should share the responsibility of determining just how a solution is to be implemented and its success evaluated.

Fostering Cooperative Learning

Moral discussions—whether of fictional dilemmas or of actual problems —can aid greatly in moral development, but they won't do the whole job. The deeper moral curriculum is the day-to-day life in the classroom— the quality of the relationships between the teacher and the children and among children.

Teachers can foster positive moral relationships among children by encouraging cooperative learning. At its best, this kind of learning involves what Piaget calls *co-operation*: doing operations or work together in a way that forces children to stop centering exclusively on their own viewpoints and to coordinate their ideas and actions with those of their co-workers.

Teacher Hophan's third grade class embarked on a cooperative learning project that spanned four months. Phase one of the project had the children working in pairs trying to figure out how to make dried beans grow without soil. At class meetings, each team shared its conclusions with the rest of the class. If there was general agreement that a reported "finding" was a fact, it was entered in the "Class Bean Book."

The children divided their labors well and showed respect for each other's ability. Said one child to his teammate: "You write in the Bean Book, OK? You write neater than me. I'll empty the water 'cause I don't care if it smells."

In phase two of the project, the class planted beans in soil. At this point, Hophan reports, unexpected competition erupted among the teams. "Partners blamed each other for over- or underwatering. Teams taunted each other and bragged about their plants growing faster or larger. There were even several cases of sabotage; in one instance the class discovered that many containers had been virtually swamped in water and that a book had been placed squarely on top of a lush crop of soybean plants. One team even blamed the death of their lima bean plant on other children's 'talking bad' to it."

The teacher used the class meeting, a regular feature of the classroom since the beginning of the year, to deal openly with the issues of cooper-ation, competition and jealousy. About half the children said they wanted to work alone, to care for their own plants, rather than having to work with a team member. The teacher agreed to this change.

About a week later, almost all of the children, acting on their own initiative, were back with their partners again. One boy explained that he needed his partner because, "I can't hold this paper [on which he had been recording his plant's growth rate] and mark it too." The members of one reunited team said that when they were apart they forgot to water their plants, but together they could remember.

The third phase of the project took the children on a visit to a greenhouse at Cornell University, which inspired group efforts to build their own greenhouses. As the culminating step in the project, the teacher created an opportunity for the children to engage in an altruistic act that would benefit the whole school: "I asked the principal to speak to the students, telling them that he had heard of their work in growing things and asking their help in beautifying our school by planting flowers. The response was so overwhelming that a parent contacted me that night, wanting to know if I really needed the shovels tomorrow as her son had claimed!"

Not every effort to foster cooperation in the classroom needs to be so ambitious. Ann Caren, who taught a combined second and third grade class in Ithaca, New York, found a class newspaper to be an excellent way to develop cooperative effort and group cohesion. In addition, she recommends stocking the classroom with materials—blocks, Lincoln Logs, Lego, animals, plants, clay, scrap materials, and plenty of paper and pencils—that naturally stimulate children to work together on activities that are meaningful to them. Craft activities are also good; one boy learned how to macramé and for three days straight taught other children how to do it.

The Class Meeting

To create a strong sense of community among children, which is a critical ingredient in a good moral climate, the teachers I've been describing rely heavily on class meetings. A time is set aside—typically 20 minutes at the end of the morning and sometimes again at the end of the afternoon— when children talk about what they enjoyed doing and what they didn't enjoy, discuss how they can make the classroom a better place to learn, share important personal experiences, plan a project, or exchange views about how to solve a problem that has arisen. Every teacher I know who has worked at developing this kind of regular communication among students reports a marked improvement in students' relationships and in the general moral atmosphere of the classroom.

Debbie Wilcox, a substitute teacher, uses a class meeting to begin her first day with a new class. She tells something about herself, asks the children to do the same, and explores with students the question: "What is a substitute teacher?" This discussion makes it possible to establish that a substitute teacher is a "real teacher" (most children do not think so initially) and to talk about problems that could arise during the day. The approach has proved to be very effective in creating rapport and in heading off the "let's-see-what-we-can-get-away-with" games that many classes use to make miserable the lives of substitute teachers.

Teacher Wilcox has also found that it's effective to call an impromptu class meeting during the day to clear the air and nip a problem in the bud, as she did recently when three boys threw spitballs in violation of an explicitly agreed upon rule. No discipline problem, she finds, is too tough to solve if she uses the meeting to compel children to be accountable for their own behavior.

Class meetings don't always work immediate magic, but they are always a step in the right direction—a step toward a fair exchange of perspectives, a willingness on the children's part to take responsibility for their conduct, and a group sense of caring. "This is the time of day," says Anne Roubos, a first grade teacher in Homer, New York, "when I relish the feeling of unity. At our meeting we're all together, becoming more aware of our place within the group. We're individuals, yet part of the whole. We are becoming more aware, little by little, of what respect means, what tolerance means, what sharing means. We have time to reflect, to wonder, to talk about what it feels like when someone laughs at us, or sits at our desk without asking, or crowds in line, or tells on us unfairly."

Developing a climate of moral respect in the classroom may also require directly teaching children how to communicate respectfully with one another. Often they simply don't know how. Peggy Manring, a former second grade teacher in Skaneateles, New York, recounts what she did

when the children in her room were using violence to express their feelings: "I brought in a bag of wood scraps from the local toy factory and dumped these on the rug within everyone's reach. I asked the children to make a model of the classroom as they saw it, and I concentrated on their cooperation skills when these became a problem."

Here is an excerpt from the dialogue that took place between this teacher and her students:

David: "That is the dumbest chalkboard, Martha. You put it in a stupid place."

Teacher to David: "You think Martha should put the block in a different place? Would you like to suggest to her where she might put it?"

David: "Yeah, right there. The chalkboard is behind the table!"

Teacher to Martha: "If you accept David's suggestion, you may move your block. If you like it where you put it, you may leave it right there."

Teacher to David: "When you don't use the words 'stupid' and 'dumb,' people like to listen to you. You had an interesting point to make about the chalkboard."

Manring reports: "The next time David wanted to say something, he said, 'Paul, I *suggest* you look where the art table is. It's next to the teacher's desk.' Paul picked up on the 'I suggest'; so did Eddy and Alan. All the children in the class seemed to be stretching to cooperate."

The kind of direct intervention this teacher used can teach children the social skills they need to enter into the positive interactions that foster progress through the moral stages.

Uncovering the Hidden Curriculum

Even more basic than teaching children how to respect each other is setting a good example—practicing what we preach. This may mean a change in the way we use our moral authority with children. Let me give you a personal example: When our son Mark was four, he began issuing commands to his mother and me: "Daddy, read me a story." "Mommy, fix my dinner." Get me this, get me that. After not very much of this, we sat him down for a moral lecture on the virtues of saying "please" and "I would like" and so on. The next day, during the morning hassle of getting him off to nursery school, I barked, "Mark, get in the bathroom and brush your teeth and wash your face!" He took two steps, turned around, and said solemnly, "Daddy, I don't like getting orders either." As a moral educator I could hardly squelch this

appeal to reciprocity and fairness, so I negotiated a bargain: I wouldn't give him orders and he wouldn't give us orders.

Piaget says that adults can have an enormous positive influence on a child's moral development if they will place themselves on an equal footing with children and stress mutual obligation with regard to at least some rules. Adults who use their authority in a way that is unilateral and that appears arbitrary to children may retard the child's growth toward understanding that morality is for everybody, big and small.

Kohlberg speaks of the influence of the "hidden curriculum"—all the ways that teachers and other adult authorities transmit, usually unwittingly, moral lessons to children. Most students, for example, must compete for grades with their classmates; helping another person may be defined as cheating. Most kids go to schools in which rules are laid down by authority; children never have a chance to participate in formulating, revising or enforcing moral requirements, and they're expected to obey without question the adult in charge.

I recently came across two stories, each about an incident in which a student called the teacher an obscene name. In one case, a second grade boy called his teacher a "son-of-a-bitchin' whore." The teacher marched the boy down to the principal's office and demanded that the child be expelled, which he was. The lesson that student learned was almost surely: the only reason to respect others is to avoid punishment (stage 1).

In the second incident, reported in Haim Ginott's excellent book *Teacher and Child*, a fifth grade boy was asked by his teacher why he persisted in talking out of turn. "None of your business, you motherfucker!" the boy replied. The teacher answered sternly, "What you have just said makes me so angry that I feel I cannot talk to you." The boy, obviously surprised at not being punished, came up after class and apologized for his behavior.

To punish a child, as Ginott points out, is to arouse resentment and to interfere with education. The essence of discipline is finding effective alternatives to punishment—alternatives that leave the child's dignity intact, show him how he has violated another's rights, and motivate him to change for the better. William Glasser's strategy for dealing with discipline problems [see "A New Look at Discipline," *Learning*, December 1974] by requiring the child to devise a concrete plan for self-improvement is another example of a discipline approach that stimulates a child's moral development and avoids wielding the club of stage 1 authority.

Teachers and parents needn't go overboard, however, worrying if they're retarding a child's moral growth every time they use their authority. Research shows that the parents who have the most morally mature children are those who assert their power with discretion—often by calling a halt to undesirable activity and directing children's attention to considering the moral problem at hand. What counts most is the overall climate an adult creates: Is there a concern for fairness? an opportunity for regular communication and collaboration? a spirit of pulling together and caring about others?

We must make education for moral development as important a part of the curriculum as is education for the intellect, because sharpened intellects alone will not prevent future Watergates and will not instill a respect for the rights of others.

Classroom Discipline Problems? Fifteen Humane Solutions

Marjorie L. Hipple

Organic alternatives . . . "It is so easy to take ourselves too seriously, to get lost in the welter of problems, to lose our sense of humor— and our sense of perspective."

Marjorie Hipple is a Preschool Teacher at Bent Twig School, Gainesville, Florida.

Concern about how to guide children effectively and humanely is common to all teachers whether they are veterans or beginners, young or old, male or female. Some teachers, however, seem to have less difficulty with child guidance or "discipline," as it is often called, than do others. The reasons for the differences are no doubt varied; the personality of the teacher or the size and composition of the class, for example, can readily affect the choice of approaches used and the success of these methods. Yet there are approaches that seem to work well for many teachers and that are based upon knowledge of child development, learning theories and sound pedagogy. The purpose of this article is to suggest some of these for your consideration.

The approaches are grounded upon some basic assumptions. One is that *it is preferable to try to identify causation whenever possible in guiding child behavior rather than to treat the behavior in isolation.* We know all behavior is caused—by internal needs of the child, by external factors, or by an inter-

"Classroom Discipline Problems? Fifteen Human Solutions," Marjorie L. Hipple, *Childhood Education*, Vol. 54, No. 4, February 1978. Copyright 1978, Association for Childhood Education International, Washington D.C. 20016. All rights reserved.

action of these forces.[1] An awareness of causation can enable us to respond more effectively and intelligently to specific behaviors. For example, if we realize that the aggression children display is the result of frustration they feel because a task is too difficult for them, we might want to modify the task rather than simply treat the symptom, aggression.

Second, it is assumed that *the use of positive or at least neutral techniques is more productive when guiding children than the use of negative methods.* Although various schools of psychology diverge on other points, most agree about the value of positive responses in maintaining productive human interaction. Self theorists claim that as we deal in positive ways with children, we bolster their self-concepts and thereby enable them to develop emotionally in growth-promoting ways. Behaviorists assert that positive reinforcement of behavior tends to increase the occurrence of that behavior. On the other hand, when we resort to *negative* techniques, including not only punishment but also the threat of punishment, we may create a mood of hostility that can transform classrooms into battlegrounds. And, once this pattern begins, we may be unable to turn it around as easily as we would like. Stated more simply, the difference between the use of positive and negative approaches often accounts for "the teacher who never scolds, but has such a good class" and "the teacher who has to yell and scream at her children, who still do not behave."

A third assumption is that *versatility in the use of guidance approaches is more effective than reliance upon any single technique.* No doubt you have experienced the frustration of using a method that works well one day only to note its ineffectiveness the next time it is tried. This inconsistency is not difficult to understand when we consider the variations of mood, motives, personality and situational factors that enter every human interaction. What works one day may fail another. What works with one child may fail with another. What works for one

teacher may fail for another. Versatility—or eclecticism if you wish—is vital if we are to be responsive facilitators.

Finally, it is assumed that, over the long haul, *approaches that foster the development of internal behavioral controls and problem solving are more productive than those that rely upon external controls or authoritarianism to keep the immediate peace.* Said another way, our goal is to foster self-discipline.

The following approaches and illustrative scenarios are offered as suggestions rather than as prescriptive cure-alls. They are a tiny part of the universe of guidance approaches that can make teaching and learning more humane and enjoyable.

1. Accentuate the positive. If a child's behavior is unacceptable, suggest appropriate alternatives—positive substitutes—rather than focus negative attention on the inappropriate behavior.

Scenario: A child is throwing building blocks. Intervene by suggesting that the blocks are for building but that, if the child wishes to throw, he may work with bean bags or balls. Two positive alternatives are offered the child: either to build with the blocks or to throw with other objects.

2. Be a "model" model. As a teacher you are assuredly a significant model for your students—yet quite inadvertently you may model the very behavior you wish to modify. Still, it is rather encouraging to also realize that when you model desired behavior that, too, is emulated. Note how much more effective Scenario 2 is likely to be.

Scenario 1: A child pushes another child in order to cut into line. You shake her violently while exclaiming, "I won't have you pushing other children around."
Scenario 2: Having in hand a leaking paint container, you need to use the classroom sink. You ask if you may *please* use the sink out of turn rather than simply cut in front of the children who patiently await their turns. They agree to your request, and you remember to thank them.

3. Spotlight behavioral consequences. Young children are egocentric. And their egocentrism can prevent them from being able to put themselves in another person's place. You can help children move from egocentrism to socialized behavior by having them analyze the consequences of their actions. In spotlighting consequences, try to discuss the child's behavior in a nonjudgmental way and encourage him to think about its impact on people, objects and

---

[1] For reasons of clarity and brevity, this article will deal specifically with ways to guide children. The analysis and modification of situational factors that affect behavior are also necessary when we deal with the ecology of the classroom. That aspect of management is, however, beyond the scope of this article.

events with the intent of developing his consideration of cause/effect relationships.

Scenario: A child continually damages equipment . . . take him aside for a probing discussion about "What will happen if all of the toys get broken?" Encourage him to think about the various effects of his behavior and to suggest alternate behaviors himself.

4. Send "I-messages." The use of I-messages is an approach developed by Thomas Gordon (1974) to deal with behavior that is causing problems for the teacher.[2] An "I-message" is a personal statement by you, the teacher, that has three components: your nonjudgmental description of the problem, its tangible effects upon you, and your feelings about it. The sending of "I-messages" is an intimate form of communication in that it bares your feelings in order to raise the child's consciousness about the effects of his behavior. For this reason, you may feel uncomfortable about using this technique and, if so, you may be better advised not to use it. Like the rationale for spotlighting consequences, this approach is based upon the belief that many children are unaware of the impact their behavior has upon others.

Scenario: Discuss a problem with your class concerning, say, clean-up behaviors: "When you leave the clay uncovered, it dries out and I have to mix a new batch which takes a lot of time. I really hate having to make new clay every day." Then facilitate a discussion of how the problem might be worked out.

5. Help children hurdle. Sometimes you can help a child avoid frustration or the loss of his or her self-control by simply offering a suggestion, a question or a gesture at the right time. This approach may sound alien to ears that have long received the message that teachers should encourage autonomy. Assuredly you do want to support this attribute. But you also need to foster interdependence when the situation calls for it. Everyone needs a helping hand sometime.

Scenario: A child stamps his feet in exasperation as he tries for the umpteenth time to pull on an unwieldy boot. Sensitive to his plight, give him a reassuring start with a pull on the stubborn footwear.

6. Instruct. Children often behave inappropriately because they do not know what is expected of them. Even that which appears to be obvious or simple to you may not be at all apparent to the children. A good dictum is: When in doubt, teach them how.

Scenario: A new set of manipulative math materials arrives. In introducing the equipment, demonstrate a few of the many possibilities for its use, and then observe children using the materials to determine whether further instruction is necessary.

7. Limit options. Sometimes children are overstimulated by the number of choices available to them or, once they have made a choice, they may not handle it well. They may have too much time, too much space, too many materials, or too many activities on their hands. This overload is often the case with children who enter school for the first time. Ultimately children must learn to make choices and, as they mature, they do. But their immediate problems may require the limiting of those choices.

Scenario: A child has great difficulty staying with a task. He moves from one learning center to another, staying only long enough to take out materials, then moving on. Request that he choose one activity, help him get started with it, and, if necessary, monitor his behavior until the activity is underway.

8. Divert behavior. Some unacceptable behaviors are fleeting or situation-specific. In these instances it is often most effective to alter the social environment by diverting the child to another activity.

Scenario: Two children, best friends, sometimes rub each other the wrong way. On these occasions, step in before their conflict gets out of hand, directing each child to different activities.

9. Ignore behavior. Sometimes the best thing you can do is to ignore inappropriate behavior. Although this can be difficult to do, ignoring some behaviors has positive outcomes worth considering. First, behavior that is ignored is *not* reinforced. And behavior that is not reinforced tends to subside or stop. (At least one exception to this generalization should be noted: Aggressive behavior does not necessarily lessen when it is ignored. It may, in fact, increase. For this reason, it often must be dealt with directly by other methods.)[3] A second value to ignoring some behaviors is that children will often solve their own problems when left to do so, utilizing worthwhile personal or interpersonal skills in the process.

---

[2] Gordon espouses this technique for dealing *only* with behavior that causes the teacher problems. Behavior that is causing problems for the child (e.g., fear, worry) are more effectively dealt with in other ways which he outlines. Readers interested in learning more about Gordon's approach are urged to consult the references that follow this article.

---

[3] See Restraining Behavior (Point No. 15).

4. BEHAVIOR

Scenario: Two children argue over the use of a toy. Silently observe them and decide not to intervene when they work out a method of taking turns that is satisfactory to them.

10. Reinforce appropriate behavior. Teachers continually reinforce behavior, either consciously or unconsciously, for good or ill. An important task for you is to become conscious about reinforcing behaviors you wish to see repeated. Unfortunately, if you are not aware of your impact as a reinforcing agent, you may reward the wrong kinds of behavior.

Scenario: A child who usually "acts out" during group activities interacts productively today. Immediately reinforce his long-desired behavior with either tangible or intangible rewards.

11. Reinforce adjacent behavior. Sometimes it is exceedingly difficult to reinforce desirable behavior because it appears so seldom. The next best approach may be to reinforce acceptable behavior of adjacent peers in the hope that the misbehaving child will imitate those peers so as to obtain similar reinforcement. This technique should *never* involve a direct comparison of one child with another (e.g., "Why can't you sit like John?")!

Scenario: Although a few children behave disruptively during a class activity, most of the children participate well. Praise the group of "good workers," commenting on the businesslike way most of them are working today. (Possibly suggest that those who complete their work might utilize the extra time to pursue activities of their own choosing.)

12. Cue behavior. Young children need and want a sense of order in their lives. Routines can provide the security that enables children to adapt with confidence to new situations. Everyone responds, often unconsciously, to environmental cues. Cues can be helpful in signalling fairly regular events such as transition periods between classes or activities. A flick of a light switch, a chord on the piano, or an upraised hand communicates messages in an effortless way.

Scenario: It is time to clean up materials used during the activity period. The children finish their work as they hear a familiar "Clean Up" tune on the piano.

13. Monitor behavior. Teachers monitor behavior in a number of ways, many of which take the form of body language or other nonverbal communication. An uplifted eyebrow or a surprised glance can sometimes relay messages to children more effectively than words. Physical proximity—placing a hand on a child's shoulder, moving about among the students, standing quietly in a potential problem area—can say, "I am here if you need my support."

Scenario: Two girls enjoy each other's company so much that they sometimes forget the task at hand in their happy socialization. A glance in their direction may clearly say, "It's time to get back to work, girls."

14. Give a breather. Occasionally it is necessary to remove a child from a provoking situation. The removal or breather is a neutralizing, tempoarary event—a time out—that is ended when the child indicates that he has the desire and control needed to reenter the group. Giving a breather is *NOT* punishing a child, placing him in a dark or otherwise frightening situation, or demeaning him. Instead it is providing him with an unprovoking alternative activity which he pursues by himself.

Scenario: Coming to school charged up with frustration, a child continually aggresses against her peers until adult intervention is imperative. Guide her to a quiet part of the room where she can work at an activity of her choice until she feels better about herself and can work productively with the group.

15. Restrain behavior. It is sometimes necessary to restrain children from continuing their behavior. When children are in the throes of anger that can make their actions potentially dangerous to themselves or others, restraint may be the only workable approach. Verbal restraints are simple, nonjudgmental statements that say, in effect, "I can't let you harm yourself or another child. You are angry now, but once you calm down, you will be better able to handle the situation." It may be necessary to accompany the verbalization by physically restraining the child. Physical restraint should never be a punitive or aggressive response: It is NOT hitting, shaking or pushing a child about. Instead the child is calmly but firmly held in a neutral way until regaining self-control.

Scenario: A playground altercation quickly escalates to a fight between two boys. Part them, but hold the one who will not stop until he calms down.

A FINAL WORD— WHEN ALL ELSE FAILS . . .

It is so easy to take ourselves too seriously, to get lost in the welter of problems, to lose our sense of humor—and our sense of perspective—especially on those days when everything goes wrong, our mood is a bit rocky, and we *know* the barometric pressure is affecting both ourselves and the children. Why not accept those days with humor rather than fighting them? Why not revise those plans so carefully made, laugh a bit, and find ways, with the input of the children, to salvage the day? After all, some days *are* like that, aren't they?

References

Galambos, Jeannette. *A Guide to Discipline.* Washington, DC: National Association for the Education of Young Children, 1969.

Gordon, Thomas. *Teacher Effectiveness Training.* New York: Wyden, 1974.

Greer, Mary, & Bonnie Rubenstein. *Will the Real Teacher Please Stand Up?* Pacific Palisades, CA: Goodyear, 1972.

Hipple, Marjorie. *Early Childhood Education: Problems and Methods.* Pacific Palisades, CA: Goodyear, 1975.

Pringle, Mia Kellmer. *The Needs of Children.* New York: Schocken, 1975.

Office of Human Development Services, Department of Health, Education and Welfare.

PIAGETIAN INFLUENCES

The study of developmental psychology with its growing body of knowledge related to growth and development is imperative for classroom teachers as they attempt to make appropriate and effective instructional decisions related to specific learning needs of young children.

Developmental stage theorists such as Piaget, Freud, Kohlberg, and Erikson provide the educator with information concerning the unvarying series of progressively complex stages of child development. They define appropriate expectations relative to behavior of the individual child. However, the information provided by these individuals serves only as a developmental framework upon which the educator may plot the developmental status of individual children. Lavach and Ries' paper "Ages and Stages: Child Development Revisited," emphasizes several of the leading theories and their relationship to institutional planning.

Piaget has provided an extensive and carefully documented analysis of the child's intellectual development. Too often teachers do little to apply Piagetian theory when planning and implementing learning experiences in the classroom. This is often due to the fact that Piaget did not prescribe educational techniques or instructional materials to be used in the classroom. Other reasons Piagetian principles of development are often not heeded is that they tend to run counter to the principles followed in the traditional classroom environment that often emphasize learning as a passive process. In the paper, "Take a New Look at Your Classroom with Piaget as Your Guide," Bingham-Newman and Saunders provide a first hand view of the learning centers to be found in a well planned classroom for young children.

Piaget's theories are finding applications in reading and language instruction. Teachers have come to gain "awareness of the sequential stages of the child's developing intelligence and look at the thinking processes characteristic of these stages," suggests Kirkland in "A Piagetian Interpretation of Beginning Reading Instruction."

Contrary to much of the education literature which suggests a structured, cognition based programing which emphasizes linguistic and conceptual skills for "disadvantaged" children, Parker, in "Usefulness of Piagetian Theory in Formulating a Preschool Program for Black Children," contends that the Piagetian approach is a more appropriate "base from which to construct programs for Black children."

The final article in this section discusses a lesser known work of Piaget's, *The Child's Conception of Physical Causality.* "Piagetian Stages in Causality: Children's Answers to 'Why?' " makes accessible valuable ideas from this book. It illustrates the wealth of information Piagetian theory provides the early childhood educator in planning and implementing effective environmental planning and classroom instruction.

Ages and Stages: Child Development Revisited

JOHN F. LAVACH
AND
ROGER R. RIES

JOHN F. LAVACH and ROGER R. RIES are Professor of Education and Associate Professor of Education, respectively, at College of William and Mary, Williamsburg, Virginia.

Developmental psychology has not been absent from the educational process. Teachers have long displayed curiosity about children. "What makes a child tick?" "How can I promote learning?" "Do children learn differently at different ages?" "What are the best ways to teach?" We find teachers continually asking these and many other questions about children and teaching. In their search for answers to these questions, teachers quickly recognize that children change with age. They know that kindergartners do not behave like high school seniors; nor do second graders act and think in the same way as students in the sixth grade. While most male six-year-olds claim to "hate" girls, few twelve-year-olds view girls in the same way. Understanding the characteristics of the age-group they teach has been a major goal of teachers.

The Quest for a Super Theory

Unfortunately, as teachers attempt to learn more about developmental differences of children, they tend to assume that existing somewhere is a complete and comprehensive theory that will authoritatively answer all their questions.

Too often the teacher has expected the psychologist to produce prescriptions that can be easily memorized and readily translated into classroom practice. All of us search for the final answers, the ultimate truths. We feel uncomfortable with ambiguity. We want the "right" answers.

However, historians can point to countless examples of frustrating and unsuccessful attempts by scientists in their search for these "final truths." In the 4th century B.C., Plato explained the nature of the universe by formulating a geocentric (or earth-centered) theory. Celestial bodies moving in perfect circles around a heavy, stationary earth was a pleasing concept and also provided explanations for many natural occurrences. Not all investigators elected to follow a geocentric theory of the universe, but the explanation posed by Plato was to influence astronomy and physics for hundreds of years. Scientific theories and laws seen as final answers in one century are frequently challenged, modified, and refuted in the next.

"Psychologese" and "Isms"

The tendency to seek a super theory is not entirely the fault of educators. Psychologists have not helped the situation. In their attempts to apply scientific strategies in gaining an understanding of children and their world, psychologists have dutifully followed the tradition of earlier scientists, committing the same mistakes in their search for the final truths. In attempting to articulate their ideas, they have frequently confused the teacher with their language of "psychologese" and complex statistical designs. They have organized into "schools" representing particular viewpoints. All too commonly, psychologists have taken the narrow one-sided view that their particular approach has an exclusive monopoly on the study of the nature of children and their development. Thus, we have "behaviorists," "gestaltists," "cognitivists," "humanists," and other "ists" representing their parochial viewpoints, seemingly talking "through" or "past" each other. Psychologists, like all of us, have a tendency to be prejudiced in favor of their own ideas. They have frequently oversold their ideas in an attempt to outshine their competitors. They have stated their ideas in the form of "laws" and guaranteed success in their application to the classroom. Psychologists have tended to think that they could produce a dramatic revolution within education that easily would solve the many problems confronting teachers.

The long-sought revolution in education has not occurred as forecast by the psychologist. Consequently, teachers have become more wary of psychologists who peddle their "wares" as the panacea for education. However, developmental psychology does have a body of knowledge—not infallible laws, but theories that have important implications for educational practice. Agreement rather than controversy can be culled from multiple and diverse theoretical positions. A teacher does not have to reject one viewpoint in order to accept another. This is particularly true of the developmental stage theories. Advocates of the stage development approach maintain that all children pass through an unvarying series of progressively more complex stages. Each stage is qualitatively different from the others. Physical growth, development of language and thinking, and personality and social adjustment have been described in terms of stage theories formulated by Jean Piaget, Sigmund Freud, Erik Erikson, and Lawrence Kohlberg. Although it is not possible to present each theory in detail with specific implications for teachers, it may be helpful to sample these approaches. By identifying and emphasizing agreement among the theorists, we can remind ourselves what children are like. An understanding of the developmental phases proposed by these theorists is essential if we are to interact with children meaningfully and see the world from their perspective.

The Pre-school Years

During this period, physical activity is of particular importance. The pre-school child is making steady gains in height and weight. Both gross and fine motor coordination have improved. The children are bursting with energy and thrive on activity. However, pre-schoolers are easily distracted and have difficulty attending to one activity for a long period of time, whether it is running and climbing on playground apparatus or listening to a story. Activities should be planned which allow the exercise of large muscles and do not require long periods of fine motor coordination. At the same time, alternating periods of rest are necessary since physical development is in its early stages; pre-schoolers' muscles are not strong, and they are generally unaware of their own limitations.

Observation of two- to three-year-old children at play reveals a growing capability of story-telling and emerging counting concepts, as they begin to enjoy social interaction with peers. It is at this point in life, the Freudians with their emphasis on psychosexual stages of development would argue, that children will learn to submit to the will of their parents, eventually generalizing this to the will of society. This submission, according to Freudians, is primarily due to the process of toilet training, and therefore they use the term anal stage.[1] Kohlberg looks at the same age levels and states that at this age (two to three years) the child begins to experience Level I reasoning in a six-stage pattern of moral development.[2] Level I reasoning is characterized by "Obedience and Punishment," as seen in the child's submission to parental or teacher standards and rules in order to avoid adverse consequences. In an analysis of life's stages as viewed by Erikson in his "Eight Stages of Man," he describes this same developmental milestone as a struggle on the child's part to achieve "autonomy" as opposed to "Shame and Doubt."[3] Inherent here is the assumption that while the child is still dependent on parents and parental controls, well-guided experiences must be provided which foster independence and self-reliance. An overly restrictive environment, whether at home or in school, inhibits the growth of autonomy and leads to the development of shame, doubt, and a sense of inability.

During these pre-school years, children rapidly develop their ability to communicate. While two- to three-year-old children have not mastered the syntax, phonology, and lexicon of language, they have learned several hundred words, and can communicate in primitive sentences. According to Bruner, they perceive the world in visual image fashion and are capable of thinking about objects, although the objects themselves are not present.[4] However, children's thinking is still bound by the physical characteristics of objects. For example, a young child is apt to say that an apple is red, while an adult would tend to think more in terms of its function and quality and describe it as "food," or "fruit."

Piaget would place these children at the preoperational stage, which is characterized by rudimentary symbolic thought, imagination, make-believe, and pretending.[5] They can think ahead and proceed systematically with a sequential task. However, their thinking is egocentric and, according to adult standards, frequently illogical. The child has not yet developed the ability to see things from other people's perspectives. The children confuse cause-and-effect relationships and are not capable of classifying objects and events into conceptual categories.

For parents and pre-school teachers, the growing coordination, language development, self-sufficiency, intense curiosity and interest of this age level are welcomed but frequently misunderstood. As children behave in more adult-like ways, it is easy to lose sight of the fact that they are still children, not miniature adults. For example, it is not uncommon for children to contradict themselves without even realizing it, and they appear to see no need to justify the views that they have expressed.

The Early Elementary Years

As children approach school age,

[1]S. Freud, *General Introduction to Psychoanalysis* (New York: Doubleday, 1949).

[2]E. Erickson, *Childhood and Society* (New York: W. W. Norton, 1963).

[3]L. Kohlberg, "Moral Education in the Schools: A Developmental View," *School Review*, 74 (1966): 1–30.

[4]J. R. Bruner, R. Olver, and P. Greenfield, *Studies in Cognitive Growth* (New York: Wiley, 1966).

[5]J. Piaget, *Science of Education and the Psychology of the Child* (New York: Viking, 1971).

they have matured muscularly, can skip, jump, copy geometric shapes, and, for most, even dress themselves. They are beginning to assume a sense of pride in their emerging responsibilities. Play with other children is becoming sex-typed, and signs of competition begin to evolve. Language blossoms as children master the linguistic system of their culture. Their sound system matures, vocabulary expands, and their syntax becomes ordered.

How children are treated during this period influences their emotional and social development. To Freud, of great significance to children are events associated with increasing awareness of their sexuality, boy-girl differences, and the pleasures as well as inhibitions and constraints placed on them by society. To a teacher this may appear farfetched; but overly harsh and restrictive treatment regarding the child's innocent and unsophisticated pursuit of sexual knowledge and experience, usually through immature manipulation and "peeping tomism," may very well inhibit further curiosity, ambition, and self-confidence. The "Initiative versus Guilt" stage of Erikson testifies to the importance of formulating a personal identity during this period. At this same time children are in the early stages of moral development. According to Kohlberg, their interpretation of rules appears to be ego-centered and result-focused. They are more concerned with satisfying their own needs, and display only an occasional concern for the needs of others.

The logical thinking processes which are now apparent provide a new source of encouragement for teachers. Concepts which a short while ago were too perplexing and confusing for children to master are emerging. They are able to deal with more than one aspect of a problem at a time. Children are readily capable of using symbols to describe objects in their environment. However, their direct perceptions still dominate their thinking, and they have difficulty going much beyond the literal content of whatever they are told. Additionally, they cannot understand the

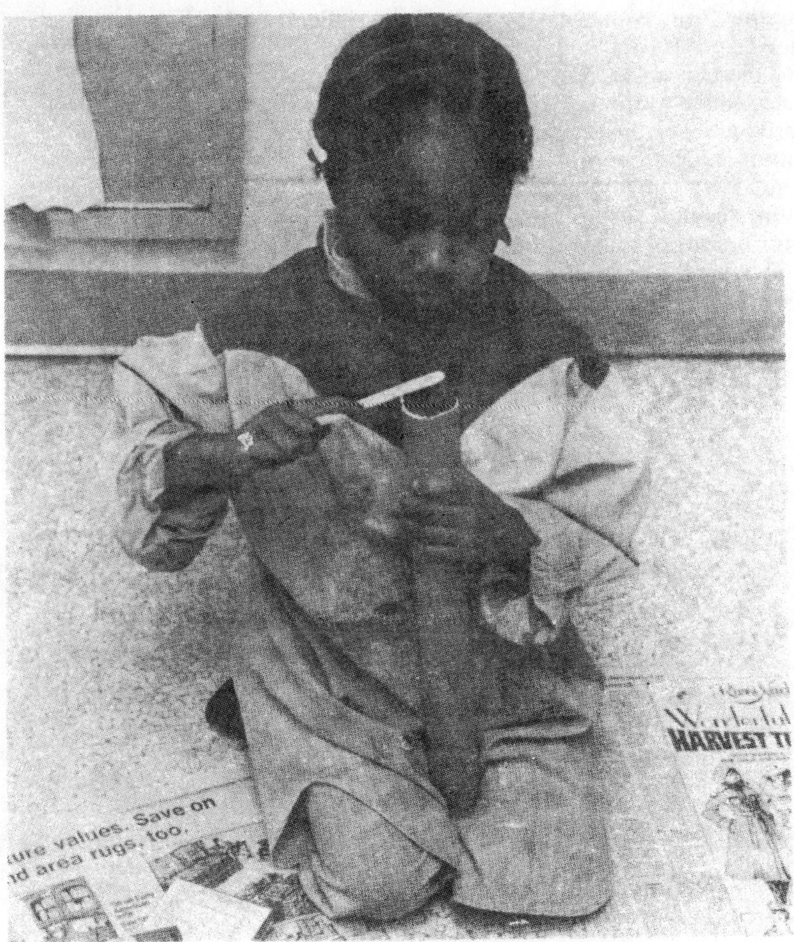

process of reversibility or abstract relationships. For example, a child cannot comprehend that a given quantity of liquid remains the same regardless of the shape or size of its container.

As children progress through the early elementary school years, dramatic changes occur in their affective and social development. Children turn outward. Clubs, television, and comic books become important. Social games dominate, and immersion in school work and play take over. Gradual independence from parents and adults grows. This gradual letting-go by the parents, according to Erikson, will permit the child to experience the pleasures of self-accomplishment and "Industry," as opposed to the limitations, restrictions, and criticisms of "Inferiority." According to the Freudians, the Oedipal complex of the preceding stage is resolved and repression of sexual or erotic impulses takes place until reawakened sometime during adolescence.

Intellectually, children are still in what Piaget would term the Concrete Operations stage. They can reason in terms of concrete objects, although they cannot think abstractly. During this period, children master the process of "conservation" and now know that a quantity of liquid remains the same even though it is poured from a short, wide glass into a tall, thin glass. They realize that concepts such as darker, taller, or heavier refer to relationships and not absolute qualities. They can classify and order concrete objects and differentiate between part and whole. For example, younger children think they are receiving more candy when it is broken into pieces, but the older elementary-age child is not perceptually "fooled."

Upper Elementary and Beyond

Finally, the complex and sophisticated final cognitive, emotional, and psychomotor aspects of life become apparent. To the Piagetians, Formal Operations become achieved. During this stage children begin to think logically, scientifically, hypothetically, and organize data going well beyond concrete material and opinions presented to them by their peers, teachers, and other adults.

While cognitive processes mature, so too does morality; for, as Kohlberg points out, the youngster now establishes "contractual, democratic" relationships and a sophisticated "Conscience or Principle" orientation. To Erikson, "Identity versus Role Diffusion" means that roles in life are recognized as we attempt, during adolescence particularly, to assume the responsibilities of student, family member, game player, sportsman, and lover.[6]

Conclusion

In this article we have presented a brief overview of the course of certain aspects of child development as seen from various perspectives and theoretical points of view. No attempt was made to present a given theory in detail, or to represent any single one as comprehensively explaining all aspects of child development. Rather, an attempt was made to provide at least a source of current developmental thinking which teachers may pursue. By emphasizing the similarities among the theories we have attempted to attain an integrative perspective which will help us to understand better how children become what they are. It is hoped that, by examining typical patterns of development that are associated with each developmental phase, we have helped teachers gain some idea of what to expect from the particular group with which they are working. These expectations can be helpful in formulating appropriate objectives and arranging realistic experiences conducive to the needs of the child. □

[6]E. Erickson, *Identity: Youth and Crisis* (New York: W. W. Norton, 1968).

Take a New Look at Your Classroom with Piaget as a Guide

Ann M. Bingham-Newman and Ruth A. Saunders

Ann M. Bingham-Newman, Ph.D., is Coordinator of the Interdisciplinary Child Development Program, California State University, Los Angeles. Formerly, she was Coordinator of the University of Wisconsin Early Childhood Center and Child Development Lecturer at the University of Wisconsin. Her areas of experience include Piagetian theory, observational methods, values clarification, infancy, and parent education.

Ruth A. Saunders, Doctoral Candidate, is Project Specialist for the Wisconsin Research and Development Center for Cognitive Learning at the University of Wisconsin, Madison. Previously, she has directed and taught day care, Head Start, and nursery school. She is currently working on a project for developing, implementing, and evaluating a Piagetian-based preschool program.

Often the search for solutions to the problems facing educators today reminds one of Pooh's hunt for the Woozle in *Winnie-the-Pooh*.[1] Recall that delightful episode in which Pooh and Piglet follow a set of footprints with increasing alarm as they notice new sets of tracks added to the first. Pooh's original problem of identifying who made the footprints almost immediately becomes the overwhelming problem of finding the mysterious Woozle (or Woozles). In hastily designating the unknown footprint-maker as a Woozle, Pooh overlooked valuable observational data. Only when Christopher Robin, from his perch in the big oak tree, points out that Pooh and Piglet have been going in circles does Pooh take a new look at the situation. He realizes that he has indeed been going round and round the thicket and, as a matter of fact, his own feet fit the prints perfectly.

Has the same thing happened in education as we become so enmeshed in our tracks (the problems in applying various methods) that we forget our original concern—the children whose thinking and learning abilities have led us to devise those methods? If so, Piaget's theory can be our Christopher Robin in leading us to look again at some of our assumptions. Let's go back to the classroom with Piaget as our guide for a new way to look at children and their intellectual development.

Like Freud's analysis of the emotions and Gesell's description of physical development, Piaget's work stands as a massive and carefully documented analysis of one aspect of human development. For nearly sixty years he has observed and interviewed children, seeking to understand the origins of logical thought. Perhaps his most important conclusion for teachers is that

---

[1] The inspiration for the use of the "Woozle episode" came from a similar use of this episode made by J. F. Wohlwill in an article entitled "Piaget's System as a Source of Empirical Research," published in *Merrill-Palmer Quarterly* 9 (1963): 253-262.

logic *develops*. Young children cannot use the reasoning we depend on in the adult world. Logical thought develops slowly and with certain recognizable steps in every normally developing child. The implications of this for education, though not elaborated on by Piaget, are tremendous. Young children are unaware, not only of specific facts but of the very tools of rational thought adults depend on for useful application of those facts. Adults cannot assume that their logic will convince children of a truth if only the terms are simple enough.

Because Piaget's theory represents an attempt to understand logical reasoning and is not a theory of education,the implications drawn from it have been varied. They range from revisions of specific subject areas such as science and math in many British infant schools to the creation of whole programs based on the theory, such as the preschool program of Kamii and Devries in Chicago or that implemented by the authors at the University of Wisconsin. The application of Piaget's theory to education is very difficult because it consists neither of prescribed materials nor techniques, but rather it describes how children think. What the theory does give to teachers is a framework from which to be creative.

Principles of Development

Several principles from Piaget's theory provide a basis for classroom atmosphere, curriculum development, and teacher role:

1. Learning is an active process;

2. There is a fixed sequence in development with individual variations in pace;

3. Language, alone, is not the answer—one cannot assume that because a child can say a word, the concept has been learned, or that simply teaching the word will teach the concept;

4. Intellectual development is fostered by social interaction with peers and adults.

First of all, Piaget states clearly that learning is an active process, both physically and mentally. Thought is the internalization of action. This indicates that children should be able to actively explore and manipulate materials in their environment. By so doing, the child is constructing his or her own knowledge. Therefore, teachers must create an environment in which children will be active and initiate their own activities. This environment includes not only the materials and equipment but also the teacher-child and child-child relationships. Interest centers where children may choose from a variety of activities, with or without teacher inolvement, can encourage active problem solving and valuable interchange with peers.

The second principle, that there is an invariant sequence to development and that individuals go through this sequence at their own pace, means that teachers can have a fairly clear picutre of a child's present reasoning capacities and what can be anticipated in the near future. Knowledge of the stages of development in a child's thinking helps teachers to plan with appropriate expectations. We can be aware of the limitations at a particular stage and of the new possibilities offered when the next stage is reached. t must be emphasized, however, that all children are not at the same place at the same time.

Children think about the world very differently than adults do—they make different interpretations and draw different conclusions. This is because each successive stage in the development of thinking or intelligence is characterized by the emergence of new ways of thought. A young child looking at a figure similar to Figure I might come to a very different conclusion than an adult would when asked, "Do both of these rows have the same number of circles?"

Figure I

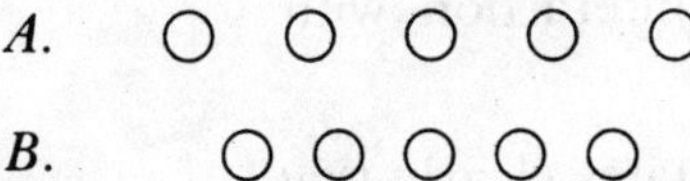

A child between four and seven years of age might say *A* has more. The preoperational child tends to focus on one attribute only—either the length of the row or the amount of space it takes up. Or this child might say *B* has more because the circles are so close together. Even if the child counted the circles and could say there were five in each row, before age six or seven, he or she would still probably say one or the other has more.

The third principle is that language training alone does not lead to intellectual development. Language helps to focus on concepts and to retrieve them or sort them out, but it does not in and of itself build concepts. We all have known the child who could say the word *five* but didn't know what *fiveness* was.

The final principle is that intellectual growth is fostered by social interaction with peers and adults as well as interactions with the physical environment. It is precisely this social interaction which enables the young child to begin to take into account different perspectives. The fact that children usually are only capable of seeing, understanding, and feeling things from their own individual viewpoints is what Piaget terms *egocentrism.* Consider, for example, the child standing up when other children are sitting. He or she is unable to understand why someone in back can't see. After all, it may be explained, "I can see perfectly well." Or reread some of the Winnie-the-Pooh stories by A. A. Milne. They are filled with examples of egocentric thinking. Egocentrism decreases with age as new types of thought appear, but it never completely disappears. Did you ever sit at a red light saying, "1, 2, 3—change!"?

By hearing different ideas, by having their ideas challenged, children begin to evaluate and reexamine their own ideas. Knowledge is gradually reshaped and reconstructed—going from one wrong answer to another and gradually coming closer to an adult view of reality. Remember the many times you have thought a child's answers to questions were absurd. Far from being absurd, the child has answered correctly the question as it was perceived. The cause of the ''error'' is that the child did not ask himself or herself the same question that you asked.

When asked if one set of beads is in the same order as another, for example, the question may be reinterpreted to mean whether one set has a bead to match each of those in the other set, regardless of order. It takes skill and patience to be accepting of those seemingly absurd answers so that the child's confidence is built up instead of destroyed. Many opportunities for guiding the child toward reality will occur on other days. Children's answers, though, can provide excellent information about their thinking, that is, where they are and where we can help them go. By accepting children's egocentric answers, we also encourage them to be intellectually honest rather than to be looking, listening, or waiting for us to give the right answer. As teachers, we must listen *to* an answer, not *for* an answer. Be on the lookout for the unexpected answer and use it advantageously as another starting point.

Children between four and eight years of age are in transition from what Piaget calls the *preoperational* stage to the *concrete operational* stage. They can use mental symbols to think about things which are not present; they can use language to represent objects; but they are perceptually oriented—their thinking is still dependent on how things appear. Piaget calls this thinking *intuitive.* That is, they believe things are as they appear to be rather than considering them from the adult's logical perspective. For these children, if it appears bigger, it is bigger. Even if their thinking tells them the correct answer to a problem, they become uncertain if what they see looks otherwise, and they will usually rely on the way it looks rather than on their thinking.

In other words, not until the age of six or seven does a child exhibit what Piaget speaks of as *conservation*—that is, understanding that some properties or attributes remain invariant despite perceptual changes. A friend has related to us a memory of her feelings before she developed the concept of conservation. She remembered her fear of going down into a deep canyon after having seen other people down at the bottom and noticing how tiny they had become. Not absolutely convinced that size was an invariant property, she didn't want to risk becoming any smaller than she already was. Like other children, she ignored one variable (distance) and focused only on apparent size. Until the major breakthrough of conservation, children's answers to questions and their solutions to problems are constantly shifting as their perceptions take precedence over their thought.

The Teacher's Role

What does all of this mean for our role as teachers? In her application of Piagetian theory to an early childhood classroom, Kamii (1972) has identified three kinds of knowledge which children acquire. Each type of knowledge is learned differently by the child and involves a correspondingly different teacher role. This division, of course, is arbitrary—it is impossible for one kind of knowledge to exist without the other two. As a guide for work with children, however, the distinction is an extremely useful tool. The three kinds of knowledge are:

I. Social Knowledge—acquired through feedback from people.

II. Physical Knowledge—acquired through feedback from objects.

III. Logico-Mathematical Knowl-edge—acquired through relationships which the child must invent or reconstruct, e.g., relationships between and among objects, people, and events.

Social Knowledge

The first of these includes the cultural use of language, social conventions, and social expectations. This kind of knowledge can be communicated directly to children, and the right answer reinforced. For instance, we can tell a child to ask for something instead of simply taking it, that a particular color is called red, or that a certain object is called a table. Social knowledge, then, is acquired directly through feedback from people. This type of knowledge should not be confused with what we typically think of as "social development."

Physical Knowledge

Physical knowledge includes a knowledge of properties or attributes of objects (such as hardness, flexibility) and of physical phenomena (such as causality and gravity). Physical knowledge can be effectively learned through feedback from objects and the effects of one's own actions on the objects. Children learn by dropping, folding, squeezing, stretching, smelling. In other words, they must be actively involved in doing things to objects and observing the results. As they learn that an object reacts in different ways in accordance with their actions upon it, they build a repertoire of actions which can be used in solving problems. In this repertoire will be many actions, and the reverse of each. In addition, children are accumulating a data bank of facts about what objects can do. Eventually this information can be used to accurately anticipate and predict outcomes.

5. PIAGET

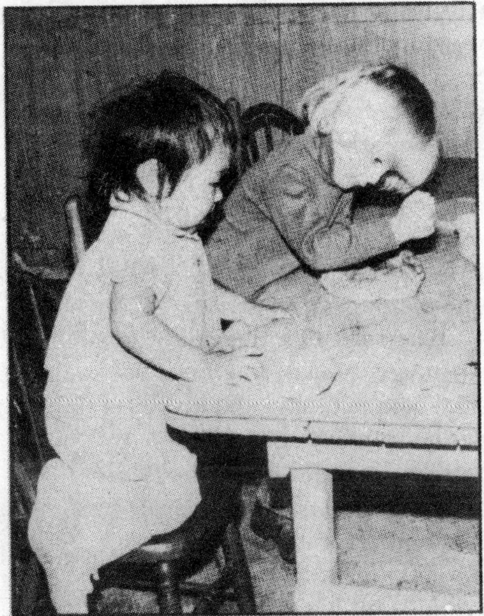

JOHN KIRK

The teacher's role in the area of physical knowledge is to encourage the child to become actively involved with objects—to find out what can be done with them, what can be done to them, and what kinds of questions can be asked about them. The teacher attempts to stimulate the child's curiosity and to encourage exploration of materials. For instance, one might ask, "What would happen if you didn't put the ice cube tray back in the freezer? How can you find out?" or "What can we do to this clay—squeeze it, tear it, . . .?" or "I wonder if this marble will stay at the top of this incline you're building. Hm, I wonder why it did that?" The teacher has to create an environment, present materials, suggest activities, and assess what is going on inside the child's mind from moment to moment. An on-the-spot curriculum developer, the teacher can interact with the child according to the kind of knowledge involved and the level of the child's thinking. Without intruding or interrupting, the teacher can respond to the child in a way which encourages the extension of the child's ideas. This extension of the child's own activity will be the most meaningful learning situation.

Logico-Mathematical Knowledge

The third kind of knowledge is called logico-mathematical knowledge. This consists of an understanding of relationships between and among objects, people, or events. This knowledge comes as a result of the child's own actions and thoughts about those actions, and must be constructed by the child.

Social knowledge involves names for things and social conventions—the kinds of information that come from people. When the question or problem involves physical knowledge of attributes and actions, the answer can be found in the physical environment. When the question is in the area of logico-mathematical knowledge, however, only the child's thinking can construct the answer. The child makes use of knowledge of actions, attributes, and properties in formulating logical relationships such as "more," "same," "some," etc. A solid foundation of physical knowledge based on the child's active involvement with the environment is vital to the construction of logico-mathematical knowledge.

Let's use some of the things a child knows about clay as an example. Felicia's *social knowledge* includes knowing a variety of related words (such as *clay, pound, roll, sticky*) and knowing what she is and is not allowed to do with it (such as that she must not throw it at other children). Her *physical knowledge* of clay probably includes an awareness of a wide variety of properties of clay (such as that it dries and gets hard when left out in the air or that it gets soft when water is added) as well as a rather extensive list of what she can do with the clay. For example, a ball of clay can be made into a flat pancake and the pancake can be made back into a ball.

The child's understanding that there is the *same amount* of clay in the pancake as there was in the ball which was flattened involves *logico-mathematical knowledge*.

She draws this conclusion after much experience in acting on the clay (flattening a ball of clay), reversing her action (remaking the ball), and observing that the re-formed ball always has the same amount as the original one. Eventually, she no longer interprets that somehow the pancake has more clay "because it's wider" or less clay "because it's so thin," or that whenever it is reshaped into the ball it "magically" reverts to its original amount. She begins to coordinate the increase in width of the pancake with the decrease in thickness and constructs for herself a notion of compensatory effects.

Teachers can help children formulate questions by interacting with them or by changing the environment so that previous interpretations are challenged. For instance, when children have been sorting red and white objects, the teacher might introduce some objects which are half red and half white; or if children are classifying liquids and solids, the teacher could introduce some Silly Putty. In addition, teachers can select materials that make the children become conscious of a problem and look for the solution themselves.

Teachers must be particularly careful to refrain from telling or reinforcing the "right" answer. The "pasting on" of logico-mathematical knowledge often tends to confuse children, who can't understand why they are wrong and you are right. They merely become unsure of their own powers of reasoning. Unlike social or physical knowledge where a correct answer can be accepted as fact by the child, logico-mathematical knowledge involves inference. You can correct a child who consistently calls you by the wrong name; you can demonstrate how easily glass breaks or water spills; but how do you explain why it's true that if all spiders have eight legs, and A is a spider, then A has eight legs?

As another example, recall for a moment the two rows of circles in Figure I. A child may have the social knowledge of counting to five and the physical knowledge of how the cirlces can be spread out or moved together, yet fails to understand why there are just as many circles in row A as in row B. We may patiently explain that one row just looks like more, but in the logic of the preoperational child "if it *looks* like more, then it *is* more." It takes time for the child to construct the concept of numerical equivalence.

Another reason for avoiding a heavy emphasis on the right answer in logico-mathematical knowledge is that one "right" answer doesn't necessarily mean the child's way of reasoning has changed. Remember, young children are in a period of transition, of constantly shifting answers. What they answer correctly at one time (whether by chance, because of specific perceptual factors, or because os a glimmer of our adult way of thought) they may well answer disferently the next time.

Gradually children move closer and closer to our logical, adult thought— or, as Piaget calls it, to an operational approach to the world. *Operations* are

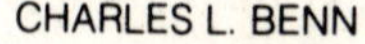
CHARLES L. BENN

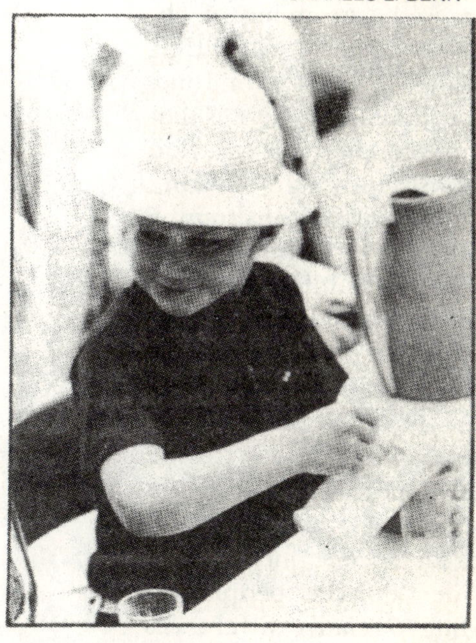

5. PIAGET

flexible, reversible thought processes which enable the child to understand that a person can be a doctor and a mommy at the same time or that the amount of water is the same no matter what the shape of the container into which it is poured.

Types of Logico-Mathematical Knowledge

The time between kindergarten and fourth grade is the time the child establishes operational intelligence. It is this kind of reasoning ability which enables children to master content. The education of young children, therefore, must concern itself with the child's ability to reason *before* the typical concern with content. This is where we have much to learn from Piaget's work. With this in mind, we can look at logical knowledge in more detail.

This type of knowledge is of primary interest for Piaget. In order to handle its many aspects, he breaks it into five distinct (but still overlapping and interactive) areas. These include three areas of strictly *logical thought (classification, seriation,* and *number)* and two areas of what he calls *infra-logical thought* (these being *space* and *time*).

Classification, Seriation, and Number
Classification is the grouping of objects according to similarities or differences, i.e., color, shape, size, or function. The important aspect here is that children be able to choose a criterion and use it consistently. Very young children tend to sort inconsistently, starting perhaps with one color, forgetting it in the middle of sorting, and then finishing the sort using a different criterion. Gradually, children begin to form hierarchies of classes and to see that one object may belong to two classes at once—that it can be both red and round; or both a daddy and a teacher.

A second area, *seriation,* includes the ability to order objects, people, or events according to relative differences (e.g., biggest to smallest, most fun to least fun, or loudest to softest). Here, again, children become aware that an object can be two things at once—it can be bigger than one object and at the same time smaller than another.

For a little practical experience in dealing with classification and seriation, take out a handful of change. (1) Group everything into two piles. What criteria did you use? Possible criteria include the kind of metal, the date, the place it was minted, the amount (less than a dime or more than a dime), size, or how well worn they are. Are there others you think of? Is one way of sorting better than another? What if you were a coin collector or were melting them down for the metal or looking for sizes which would fit in your piggy bank? Would you still do it the same way? (2) Now mix them up again and seriate them—order them according to a relative difference. How did you do it? A variety of ways can work and are equally valid—depending on your thoughts and your needs. The same is true for children in their activities. They often come up with unusual criteria which teachers have not

152

DONNA J. HARRIS

thought of but which are equally valid.

So classification and seriation are legitimate areas of reasoning ability, but what does that have to do with the real world? We are constantly using our ability in these two areas to organize and cope with our world. Just for a moment, think of your closet, your kitchen cupboards, or your workbench. You have probably classified and seriated most of the objects in these places. Big nails are separated from small ones; screws are separated from nails; screwdrivers are seriated by size. How about kitchen cupboards—are all the big plates stacked together, then the next size plate, and then the saucers? How complicated our everyday chores would be without an easy system for finding what we need.

As Piaget views it, ability in the areas of classification and seriation are vital for an understanding of number relationships. Counting is one of the first number ideas taught to children, but the numbers themselves have little meaning for them—and the relationships between the numbers are even more difficult. The child must come to know that each number contains the number preceding it (that five contains four, for example). Before understanding this, the child must know that number is not an attribute of the objects themselves but an abstraction applied to objects. For example, a young child often will refuse to be counted as number seven in a group of children, insisting instead that he or she is four years old. Conservation of number must be acquired in a manner similar to conserving amount in the example with the clay.

What kinds of experiences can you provide for children which will help them construct an understanding of number? Instead of counting two groups of objects, children could be encouraged to put the objects into pairs, one from each group, to check for equivalency. This type of task will be repeated over a period of time with many different kinds of materials before the concept of equivalency is understood. Materials in units (e.g., Cuisenaire rods, unifix cubes, unit blocks, or Dienes blocks) which can be ordered, grouped, arranged, and disarranged provide experiences in seriation and classification. Again, encouragement of peer interaction and peer teaching provides challenges to young children's thinking.

Space and Time

Spatial understanding is another concern in Piagetian theory. This involves concepts of linear order, distance, part-whole relationships, right and left orientation symmetry, and spatial judgment. Realizing that there are several ways of perceiving the same spatial arrangement depending on one's vantage point is one such spatial concept.

Young children may often have difficulty copying a sequence of more than four objects, as they might attempt in bead stringing. The problem here is similar to that of the unconscious shifting of criteria in classification. A child may start out copying the order from left to right and in the middle reverse to copying the order from right to left without realizing a reversal in direction has been made. A sequence of beads such as red, blue, orange, green, yellow may be copied as red, blue, green, orange, yellow.

A related spatial orientation problem exists when children have difficulty distinguishing *b* from *d*. Activities which invite children to move consistently in one direction either up to down, right to left, left to right, or northwest to southwest will give them experiences in spatial orientation which may apply to reading skills. Practice in making judgments about distance and whether one object will fit inside another contribute to a child's understanding of measurement as well as being useful for everyday living. Imagine the spatial problem-solving when learning to drive a car, or when packing a trunk for a trip.

Concepts of time involve much more than telling time by the clock. They involve both the sequence of events and the estimation of time intervals. Recalling story sequences and the order of activities in a cooking project or scientific experiment help young children better understand time relationships. Time intervals could be measured or estimated in minutes, in number of claps, by distance walked, by the number of verses which can be sung, or by amount of work achieved.

Summary

It is evident that these understandings of space and time, as well as of classification, seriation, and number all overlap and seldom operate in isolation. In fact, most activites can involve all ts thehh This is another good aspect of a Piagetian curriculum—no need to buy expensive kits, or new materials, or make drastic changes in the classroom. Instead, activities with children can be viewed in terms of the three basic kinds of knowledge and the five areas of logical thought. This knowledge may be separated for ease in explanation and study, but in Piaget's view, development proceeds simultaneously in all the arbitrarily separated parts. Growth in classification, for example, is accompanied by and enhanced by growth in any or all of the other areas.

With Piaget as a guide, take a look at your classroom and the activities you have planned. With an understanding of the development of young children's thinking the principal goal of education can be pursued, which in Piaget's view

is to create men who are capable of doing new things, not simply of repeating what other generations have done, men who are creative, inventive, and discoverers. The second goal of education is to form minds which can be critical, can verify, and not accept everything they are offered. The great danger today is of slogans, collective opinions and ready-made trends of thought. We have to be able to resist individually, to criticize, to distinguish between what is proven and what is not. So we need pupils who are active, who learn early to find out by themselves, partly by their own spontaneous activity and partly through material we set up for them; who learn early to tell what is verifiable and what is simply the first idea to come to them.[2]

---

[2] Ripple, R. E., and Rockcastle, V. N., eds. *Piaget Rediscovered: Report of the Conference on Cognitive Studies and Curriculum Development.* Ithaca, N.Y.: Cornell University School of Education, 1964, p. 5.

A Piagetian Interpretation Of Beginning Reading Instruction

Eleanor R. Kirkland

TO UNDERSTAND how a child learns to read, from a Piagetian point of view, one must be aware of the sequential stages of the child's developing intelligence and look at the thinking processes characteristic of these stages.

Piaget views the growth of the child's "structures of knowing" as beginning in early infancy and ending in adolescence, and believes that the stages of intellectual development follow each other not in strictly chronological order but in a sequential and orderly manner. These phases may be accelerated by manipulating the environment, but only up to a certain point. The environment is important only as a child is able to pay attention to it, and this ability depends on the degree of assimilation which has taken place. However, the greater the variety of experience children cope with, the greater their ability to cope.

Thanks to Piaget, we have a rationale and a sequence of typical experiences to help us better understand child learning, help correct children's inadequacies, and give them a more mature approach to learning. Most importantly, Piaget has encouraged us to stop imposing adult standards of logic on children's thinking. He insists that we move "out of ourselves" and our traditional levels of expectancy and take a good look at the child's logical thinking, which reflects the child's developmental progress.

The teachers of young children getting ready to read must understand what tasks are involved in reading. One must ascertain a child's stage of development, determine whether the child possesses the logical reasoning ability to perform the task, and then plan teaching strategies to allow the child to acquire the logical abilities necessary for the task. If the child does not display mature enough logic, then the teacher must set up an environment that will allow the child to learn the necessary logico-mathematical operations.

Necessary skills

There are many skill areas, interrelated both in function and development, in which a child must reach a certain level of maturity before reading can begin. The three main categories are: first, organic development (sensory, for receiving information; perceptual, for understanding, organizing, and integrating information; and neuromuscular, for using information physically); second, social development (development of interpersonal relations); and third, symbolic development (concept formation, verbal language, visual language).

Assuming that the child has the necessary organic and social maturity—and keeping in mind that Furth and Wachs (1974) indicate that even some seven year olds are not yet physiologically mature enough for traditional school demands—it is in the area of symbolic development that Piaget's work takes on special meaning for the teaching of reading. Specifically, reading requires a level of cognitive maturity that enables the child to deal with a variety of rules, abstractions, and classifications of more or less "concrete" objects.

These abilities include: directionality (ability to perceive and orient oneself to the top, bottom, sides, front, and back of an object); ability to perceive the distinguishing characteristics of small and capital letters, words, and pictures, and the ability to classify or recognize common characteristics of words, pictures, numerals, letters, etc.; ability to understand concepts presented in the text; ability to focus hearing upon and repeat phonemic sounds in words, in order to associate these sounds with their visual counterparts in reading.

To the above, add the ability to focus listening upon verbal instructions of the teacher; general ability to focus attention upon the task at hand.

Many children are introduced to formal reading during the preoperational stage of development, approximately age two to seven. What are the implications of the development of language and thought at this stage for the learning/teaching of reading?

Preoperational thinking

Throughout the early sensorimotor period, the child has been unable to use an image or word to represent an object or event not actually present. As the child moves into the preoperational stage of thought, s/he can differentiate a word from what it stands for (for example, use the sound "dog" for what it represents—a dog). Now, thought is lifted to an entirely new level.

Since thought comes before language, the latter is fitted on to thought that already exists. But once the child can use language, thought is extended over an immensely increased range.

Nevertheless, between two and five years of age, thinking tends to "center" on one striking feature of the situation. It is also irreversible in that the child is unable to move back mentally to the starting point from which the immediate thinking began. At this age, in Piagetian conservation tasks (which involve seeing objects in different transformations), a child can for example focus only on the length of a row of pennies and not also on its spatial relationships. Thus the "centering" child cannot be expected to learn rules and also to apply them.

Several characteristics of the child's thinking process may prevent this preoperational child from easily learning the alphabet and its phonemic representations: egocentrism, inability to follow transformations, limited concentration, and irreversibility of thinking.

By roughly three or four years of age, children have copied the adult model of language, but we must not overestimate their level of thought from the new maturity of their speech. We have a tendency to think they understand more than they do. One fundamental lesson for parents and teachers from Piaget is that while language is important, mere verbalization and verbal knowledge are of little value. Children can only see an event from their own viewpoint; they are unable to conceive the viewpoint of others.

As children are exposed to more social interaction and find other children's perceptions conflicting with their own, they begin to accommodate to others' egocentric thoughts. Children of five or seven will begin to seek verification for their thoughts as they must consider others' viewpoints (peer pressure). However, a child still dominated by egocentrism may not be very interested in learning to read other people's words and thoughts.

By seven or eight, children's thinking becomes more systematized; that is, their thought now conforms to certain rules and their thinking becomes more like what we adults call logical. The sequence and structure of actions in the mind, or the schemas now available, are altogether different in kind. The ability to reason and "understand" demands higher order schemas which permit a simultaneous grasp of the successive sequences of actions taking place in the mind. Most children of seven or eight years are aware of these sequences. They can see the part they themselves play in ordering their experiences and controlling their thoughts, and that they can use different schemas at will.

Piaget's observations led him to believe that it is schemas in the process of organization that children tend to repeat playfully and with seeming pleasure. Further, when such schemas have become organized, the apparent pleasure disappears and the schemas cease to be repeated unless they are combined to form new schemas or serve as a means to some end.

Learning, then, seems to start from the child, from the schemas already available to the child. Actions—such as exploring, discovering, using new ways to solve old problems—all have an intrinsic interest for the young child and are self-expanding. We must always bear in mind that there must not be too great a gap between the schemas available to the child and those demanded by the situation. Elkind (1969) reported a study where the researchers showed kindergarten, first, second, and third grade children a card with 18 pictures pasted upon it in the shape of a triangle. The children's task was simply to name every picture on the card. The kindergarten children named the pictures according to the triangular pattern in which they were pasted. They began at the apex and worked around the three sides of the triangle. This same pattern was employed by the third graders and to some extent by second grade children. First grade children and some second graders, however, read the pictures across the triangle, from top to bottom and from left to right. Elkind concluded that these children were in the process of learning the top to bottom and left to right swing which is essential in reading English. Because they had not entirely mastered this swing, they spontaneously practised it, even where it was inappropriate.

Children of two to four years of age (preconceptual period) cannot reason inductively or deductively, but instead reason transductively, going from particular to particular without apparent logical connection. Transductive reasoning prevents children from forming true concepts because they cannot cope with general classes. They are unable to distinguish between "all" and "some."

In the succeeding concrete operational stage (generally around age six to eight), children have made considerable progress. They are able to classify more consistently and can give reasons for their actions and beliefs. Language too progresses rapidly and assists internalization of behaviour through representation, which acts to speed up the rate at which experience takes place. Yet thought at this stage is restricted in quality and effectiveness by two things. It is dominated by immediate perceptions—by the dominant aspect of what is attended to, and by the fact that the child is unable to keep in mind more than one relation at a time. These limitations have clear implications for those who deal with preschool and lower primary school children.

When a six year old was asked, "What makes a car go?", he responded, "The wheels. The motor. The petrol. By the steering wheel." This set of explanations, although related to the movement of the car, does not constitute an ordered explanation. Piaget in his earlier works used the term "juxtaposition" to describe this phenomenon, which in effect involves an inability to see any relationship among the parts which constitute a whole.

Paradoxically, young children also

engage in a type of reasoning (syncretic) in which they tend to connect a series of separate ideas into a confused whole and assign to quite different things a similarity which to an adult is illogical. The child reasoning syncretically perceives the whole but does not see the differences within it. For example, in word recognition, the child would have difficulty discriminating between *cat* and *cut*, *wash* and *wish*, *came* and *come*. These children focus on one aspect of a situation at the expense of the other. They are unable to attend to differences among things and to their similarities at the same time.

The schoolchild who is still preoperational also cannot attend to transformations from one state to another. Although these children can anticipate cause-effect relationships, they cannot think about all the steps in between.

Such "faulty" logical thinking is directly involved in difficulties during learning to read. We teach children letter-sound associations and then expect them to miraculously put the sounds together into a word and words into meaningful sentences. Instead, we must prepare them for logical thought.

Learning to attach a phonemic equivalent to a graphemic symbol can be taught to young children— they can memorize. Thus, the small child may know the letters *c*, *a*, and *t*, but letters are transformed by their surroundings (*cat*) and they then denote a different grapheme-phoneme relationship—the separate sounds of *c*, *a*, and *t* do not sound like *cat*, even if you "say it fast."

Children taught by memorizing the sound-symbol relationships only appear to have difficulty in comprehension. The preoperational child who is not able to perform analysis on transformed words would have difficulty producing the phonemic equivalent of, for example, the *a* in *mat*, *mate*, *mark*. That same preoperational child would have difficulty deciphering the "long a" sound in *great*, *grate*, *eight*.

Piaget emphasized that children must have a rather large conceptual base acquired from firsthand experience before words will have meaning for them. In classroom practice, this means all children must acquire experience by interacting with others

and the environment, not merely memorize details.

The "centering" child, as mentioned before, can easily memorize rules but is usually unable to keep the rule in mind while applying it. Thus children from two to seven should not be expected to pursue a reading program based on naming the grapheme-phoneme correspondence at the same time they are putting letters together to form words and words together to form sentences with meaning. Decentration is crucial to successful reading comprehension.

In summary, the preoperational child can center on or pay attention to only one aspect of a situation at one time; s/he reasons not inductively or deductively, but transductively; s/he is not able to hold various attributes of a situation in mind at one time while searching for some common characteristic; and s/he reasons by proximity.

Reversing thought

Reversibility of thought processes allows the child to follow an operation from its conclusion back to its beginning and vice versa. A preoperational child, who cannot reverse thought processes, should not be expected to convert graphemes to phonemes by memorizing the sound that goes with the symbol (in reading) and also validate his or her "knowing" by attaching the right grapheme to the phoneme (in writing). That takes reversibility in thinking.

When children are presented with both uppercase and lowercase letters, different type faces, manuscript and cursive writing, and variations in assigning phonemes to particular letters, the nonconserving, transductive, preoperational child (generally from two to seven years of age) may experience failure in beginning to read. This indicates that it takes "concrete stage" thinking to deal with parts and wholes of words, and to think about all the possibilities one letter of the alphabet might denote.

Thus, in order to deal with the transformed letters and hold rules of relationships in mind while synthesizing meaning, a child must be a conserver, a concrete thinker. Millie Almy found a rather high correlation between the ability to "conserve" concrete substances and beginning

reading achievement. This indicates that the abilities to reverse thought and decenter perceptions, which underlie conservation, might be prerequisite to successful beginning reading instruction.

Taking some of the Piagetian tasks into consideration, reading requires representations (the evocation of vivid mental images). From the mechanical point of view: Discrimination of letters (*p* vs. *q*, *b* vs. *d*) and conservation of directions (left to right) require a well structured concept of space and awareness that the letters are also arranged linearly (for example, *saw* vs. *was*). The grouping of letters into words and sentences requires classificatory schema, and in addition, classificatory rules state when a capital letter is required, and that most of the time only an empty space is required between words.

As far as content is concerned, the child must have not only mental images of static unrelated objects but also the mobility of thought to coordinate the relationships among objects in space, time, and logic. For example, the passage "John went to the circus with his sister and father; there he saw elephants and clowns" involves space, time, classification, seriation, number, social knowledge, and physical knowledge.

One of the most important issues is whether language influences the development of thought or whether thought influences the development of language. This question has far-reaching consequences for planning programs for preschool and the lower primary grades in particular, for there is no dispute as to whether language influences the development of thought when the formal level is reached in the middle school years. Piaget's position is that up to the formal operational stage, the development of thought (logical structures) influences the development of language, and not the other way around.

Granted that the evidence is running in favor of the precedence of thought, what does this imply for the teaching of language skills in the early years? Perhaps it implies what at first seems the extreme view of Furth and Wachs (1974), who assert that the message the child who begins school gets is, "Forget your intellect for a while, come and learn to read and write; in 5 or 7 years' time, if you are successful, your reading will catch up with the capacity of your intellect, which you are developing in spite of what we offer you."

Furth suggests postponing the teaching of reading in favor of providing opportunities to develop thinking. His argument runs as follows: "Young children (5-7) are capable of operative intelligent thinking well in advance of spoken language and 'light years' ahead of what they can read or write.... Piaget's work suggests that it is thinking that should be strengthened so that the child can use the verbal medium intelligently."

Furth recommends that reading be relegated to an elective activity, encouraged but never imposed, and that this postponement would have no serious effect on the child's eventual capacity to read. This hypothesis remains to be thoroughly tested, but Furth's emphasis on providing an environment for the encouragement of thinking certainly follows from Piaget.

There would certainly be reaction against such a proposal. Perhaps learning to read is that kind of skill which develops best if begun when the child is first ready, which usually means the early primary years. It may also be that there is merit in Furth's contention that not enough effort is spent in the early years to encourage thinking.

It is not unreasonable to expect (but also not proven) that children can make use of the same strategies used in acquiring language and thought in order to become skilled readers. In fact, the proposed similarity of process in reading and language may be an important tool for teachers. Remember that some important concepts about reading must be learned before reading begins. First children need to know what reading is—meaningful communication between writer and reader. Children should understand that what they say can be written down, and what can be written down, can be read by them. Second, children need to know what a word is. Why should we expect an illiterate youngster to know that "want to" is two words when s/he usually hears "Do you wanna help me?"

Of course, meaning is the final goal for beginners just as it is for skilled readers. If written material represents the living language of children, early concentration on the context of language as a cue to words may shorten the procedure. Apparently, use of the language experience method, in which stories dictated by children are the material of instruction for the first stages in reading, has some long-range positive effect. This agrees with Piaget's emphasis on children first having experiences with words, opportunity to interpret what they have experienced, and interaction with others and the environment.

There is evidence that language which represents the language systems of children is more comprehensible to them than syntactic patterns that are unlike children's language. For the first stages of reading, this means that stories children dictate from their own experiences will provide the best written materials for reading instruction. This is the essence of the language experience approach.

If a child is not succeeding with the activities generally expected of kindergarten and first grade children, the teacher well versed in Piagetian theory can take a careful look and see at what developmental level the child is operating. Teachers are becoming increasingly adept at prescriptive teaching—pinpointing a child's deficits and providing activities especially selected to help him or her overcome them. The teacher must provide many kinds of concrete experiences from which the child gradually learns to generalize, developing an abstract concept needed at that child's particular level of intellectual functioning.

We need a great deal more research in order to know precisely what to teach when, and how best to fit our teaching to the individual child. But we are making progress and it is indicative of the genius of Piaget that his theories are finding applications in reading language instruction in early childhood education.

References

Almy, Millie and others *Young Children's Thinking: Studies of Some Aspects of Piaget's Theory* New York, N.Y. Columbia University, Teachers College Press, 1966

Elkind, David and J Flavell Eds *Studies in Cognitive Development* New York, N.Y. Oxford University Press, 1969

Furth, Hans G and Harry Wachs *Piaget's Theory in Practice: Thinking Goes to School* New York, N.Y. Oxford University Press, 1974

Kamii, C K "Preschool Education: Socio-emotional, Perceptual-motor and Cognitive Development" *Handbook on Formative and Summative Evaluation of Student Learning* Benjamin S. Bloom and others, Eds. New York, N.Y. McGraw-Hill, 1971

Lavatelli, Celia Stendler *Piaget's Theory Applied to an Early Childhood Curriculum* Boston, Mass. American Science and Engineering, Inc., 1970

McNally, D W *Piaget, Education and Teaching* Sydney, Australia: Hodder and Stoughton, 1973

Pulaski, Mary Ann *Understanding Piaget* New York, N Y Harper & Row, 1971

Roberts, Kathleen Piegdon "Piaget's Theory of Conservation and Reading Readiness" *The Reading Teacher* vol 30, no 3 (December 1976) pp 246-50

Wadsworth, Barry J *Piaget's Theory of Cognitive Development* New York, N.Y. David McKay Co., Inc., 1975

Usefulness of Piagetian Theory in Formulating a Preschool Program for Black Children

Robin N. Parker, *Doctoral Candidate in Child Development and Early Education, Stanford University*

Present early education literature suggests that a structured, cognition-based preschool program emphasizing linguistic and conceptual skills will enable the "culturally disadvantaged" Black child to better achieve in public school.[1] This suggestion, if taken literally, however, is diametrically opposed to the unique needs of the young Black child. A step in the right direction will have interested and concerned educators utilizing Piagetian theory as a more viable base from which to construct a preschool program relevant to the Black child.

It is extremely important to note that Piaget's work has reaffirmed the oft-forgotten idea of the child's reality differing greatly from that of the adult. Piaget has amply demonstrated that the child is not a "little adult." Through an intriguing series of experiments, he has mapped the course of human intellectual development. Piagetian theory divides intellectual development into four major periods: sensorimotor (birth to 2 years); preoperational (2 to 7 years); concrete operational (7 to 11 years); and formal operational (11 years and beyond). Defining intelligence in terms of content, structure, and function, Piaget's experiments are documented examples of the child's qualitatively different reality.

ADAPTING TO THE CHILD

In Piagetian description, the young child is egocentric. The child is unable to assume the other point-of-view. He is tied to

---

[1] C. Bereiter and S. Engelmann, *Teaching Disadvantaged Children in the Preschool* (Englewood Cliffs, N.J.: Prentice-Hall, 1966); M. Blank, "Some Philosophical Influences Underlying Preschool Intervention for Disadvantaged Children," paper presented at the American Psychological Association Convention, Washington, D.C., September, 1967; and M. Blank and F. Solomon, "How Shall the Disadvantaged Child Be Taught?" *Child Development*, XL (1969), 47-61.

concrete situations, centering his attention on limited amounts of information. The preschool child can only deal most reasonably with that which is immediately available to him and is unable to entertain possibilities. For the preschool education of Black children, this general notion has two important implications. The educator must sensitize himself to the child's level of functioning. He must make a consistent effort to understand the child's cognitive and linguistic world. Through continuing pupil-teacher interactions, the educator can become aware of the child's world. By careful observation and placing himself in the young child's point-of-view, the educator can come to understand the child. Of course, in order for the educator to accomplish the goal of understanding his pupils, the pupil-teacher ratio must be small. Then, too, because of specified linguistic differences between Blacks and the white mainstream, it becomes necessary that the preschool educator be Black himself, or someone trained in and sensitized to the Black Experience.[2]

For Piaget, optimal intellectual functioning is dependent upon inherited physical structures, a few automatic behavioral reflexes, and two general principles of functioning—organization and adaptation (assimilation and accomodation). While the first was probably contemplated to account for the latter, Piaget has carefully described the interactions of his own children with their environment from birth until about the fourth year. His research has demonstrated that the young child actively seeks contact with his environment. The preschooler welcomes stimulation and excitation and actively searches for it. Piagetian theory stresses that intellectual development results from hereditary and environmental interaction. It views the intrinsic activity of the young child as a major source of learning. The child's use of sensorimotor schemes in the manipulation and exploration of his environment serve to stimulate budding intellectual processes.

UTILIZING THE PRINCIPLE OF ACTIVE LEARNING

With regard to preschool education, Piaget's active learning principle requires that Black preschoolers be encouraged to manipulate and explore a wide variety of objects. The educator must level a constant persuasion, encouraging the preschooler to act on both physical and mental levels. One task of the educator is to insure the development of motoric, mental, and verbal understanding in a diversity of settings. Because Piagetian theory states, however, that later mental and verbal understanding is dependent upon motoric understanding the educator's essential task becomes insuring the Black preschooler's continual engagement in concrete manipulation. The educator should strive to present those experiences that are relevant to what the Black preschooler already knows, but are still sufficiently novel to arouse his interest. The word relevant here, holds a special significance for the preschool education of

[2]J. Baratz, "Language and Cognitive Assessment of Negro Children: Assumptions and Research Needs," *ASHA*, XI (1969), 87-91; W. Labov, "The Logic of Nonstandard English," J. Alatis (ed.), *Georgetown Monographs in Language and Linguistics* (Washington, D.C.: Georgetown University Press, 22, 1970); and F. Williams, "Language, Attitude, and Social Change," F. Williams (ed.), *Language and Poverty* (Chicago, Ill.: Markham, 1972).

Black children. Relevant means related to the experiences of the Black child—related to *his* sociocultural perspective and not that of the dominant white mainstream.

Piagetian theory also lays stress on the importance of social experience for the young child. It is thought that social interaction between peers and adults helps the young child shed his egocentrism. Such interaction brings the child to begin focusing on that outside of self. Through regular social interaction, the Black preschooler can become acquainted with another's point of view. This concept implies that little restriction should be placed on spontaneous classroom conversations. Moreover, for the Black preschool child, it is vital that older Black students representing elementary, junior high, and even senior high grades interact with him. Older Black children, spending some amount of time in the preschool setting can provide significant interaction with preschoolers. The presence of these children and teens in the preschool will positively contribute to the young Black child's affective development, while at the same time providing teaching assistants in the school setting.

INCORPORATING A PLURALISTIC MODEL

The work of Piaget on intellectual development has also affirmed the idea that all children of a given age should not be forced to learn the same material in the group mode. Piaget lays a singular emphasis upon allowing each child to progress at his own pace. Individual differences in cognitive development make it necessary for the child to regulate his own learning and impossible for any one lesson to arouse the interest of the entire class. Ginsburg and Opper have succinctly summarized the implications of Piagetian theory for education in general:

> What the student needs then is not formal teaching, but an opportunity to learn. He needs to be given a rich environment, containing many things potentially of interest. He needs a teacher who is sensitive to his needs, who can judge what materials will challenge him at a given point in time, who can help when he needs help, and who has faith in his capacity to learn.[3]

This passage also accurately describes the implications of Piagetian theory on the education of Black preschoolers. The young Black child does not need titles as "culturally disadvantaged," "cognitively deficient," "linguistically impaired," "culturally deprived," and corresponding preschool programs which strive to raise cognitive achievement level, using such titles as a base. In a way, Piagetian theory utilized as a base for Black preschool education actually liberates Black children from the oppressive, ethnocentric nature of traditional public education. For one thing, Piagetian theory suggests tailoring the curriculum to the needs of the child. It is not, then, that the child must change to fit the school, but rather, the school must change to fit the child— shades of Hunt's "problem of the match." It does not, then, become the concern of a preschool program to raise IQ points, or to

---

[3]Herbert Ginsburg and Sylvia Opper, *Piaget's Theory of Intellectual Development* (Englewood Cliffs: Prentice-Hall, 1969), p. 225.

get the Black child to say, "Am I doing this right?" instead of "Do I be doin' dis right?" Piagetian theory as applied to education takes it away from its middle-class, normative mental test approach and consequent heavy achievement orientation, toward a more humane, culturally pluralistic orientation, with an emphasis on all skills, cognitive and affective. Piagetian theory applied to the pre-school education of Black children will insure the presence of classroom teachers who are indeed sensitive, who do have faith in Black children, and who continually strive for curriculum relevance.

Piagetian Stages in Causality: Children's Answers to "Why?"

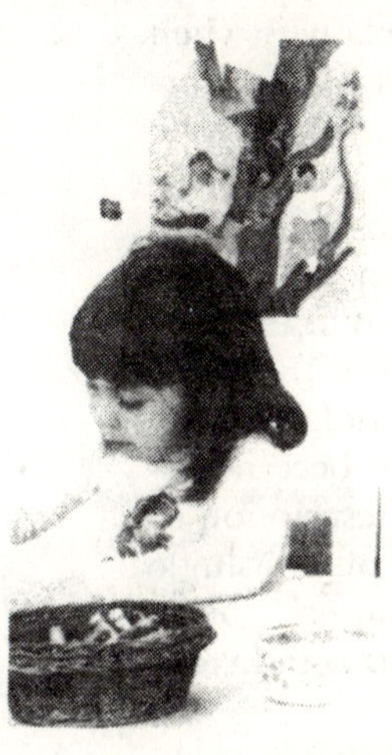

Karen Fuson
Northwestern University
Evanston, Illinois

Piaget's book *The Child's Conception of Physical Causality* (1) has ideas of interest to many educators. But the ideas are not readily accessible. Piaget's writing is difficult to understand, so difficult that few teachers read his works. Of the few who do read Piaget, only a small number ever read *The Child's Conception of Physical Causality*. To compound these obstacles, books about Piaget's theories rarely discuss the ideas in this particular work. The present article seeks to make accessible some interesting and helpful ideas from this little-known book by Piaget.

The most widely discussed features of Piaget's theory usually involve large, organizational constructs or small details about attainments in particular areas. These features are helpful to teachers in constructing an overall model for cognitive growth or in testing and teaching specific concepts. However, the features do not help a teacher understand children's actions or thoughts.

The first part of this article discusses the progression of children's thought from realism to objectivity, to reciprocity, and to relativity. An awareness of this progression can help teachers understand many aspects of children's behavior.

The second part of this article describes seventeen types of explanations children give to explain the causality of physical occurrences in the world. The types should be of interest to elementary-school teachers, for children use explanations of this kind every day. Teachers of adolescents and adults might also take note of the early types of explanations, for they crop up in social studies and science and seem to persist throughout adulthood, particularly in areas where the individual lacks expertise (2–5). Most readers will recognize some of the types, for they turn up in adults' discussions of religious, social, and political questions. Readers familiar with primitive cultures will note characteristic "primitive" modes of thought. Finally, readers who have some knowledge of the history of science will notice important historical currents of scientific thought in the causal explanations in Part II.

Piaget's book *The Child's Conception of Physical Causality* was first published in English in 1930. Many early experimenters in the USA stressed the similarity of children's and adults' ideas and attributed the differences to differences in experience and sophistication of verbal ability. Several recent studies in the USA corroborate Piaget's findings that there is a positive relationship between levels of explanations and age (6–9). It does appear, however, that specific experiences can lead to higher levels of explanations in specific areas (8, 10–12). In addition, the wording of questions can influence the level of the explanations given (11, 12).

In 1971 Piaget published a new book on physical causality, *Les Esplications Causales*. An English translation entitled *Understanding Causality* (13) was published in 1974. Although the new book reexamines some of the phenomena examined in the earlier work, there is practically no overlap between the two volumes. The new book is a summary of results of many research studies. The brief descriptions of behavior at various stages agree with Piaget's earlier descriptions. The theoretical discussion in the newer book focuses on the relationship between the child's acquisition of concrete operations (conservation, seriation) and the child's acquisition of concepts of physical causality. The earlier volume offers more concepts that have clear implications for education.

Part I: From realism to objectivity, reciprocity, and relativity.

According to Piaget, from age three to age eleven a child's thought shifts from realism to objectivity, from realism to reciprocity, and from realism to relativity (1: 241–58). This shift begins early in the child's life, continues slowly throughout his development, and remains incomplete at the close of childhood. Remnants of the early realism survive throughout the intellectual development of the adult.

Realism is the initial stage of the child's thought. At that stage the child does not distinguish between the different kinds of events that stimulate thought. Perceptions and feelings—and thoughts about perceptions and feelings—are all undistinguishably "real." Nor does he think about his perceptions or feelings; he merely has them.

The child who is capable of objectivity is able to distinguish what comes from the self and what forms part of the external reality observable by others. With realism, the world and the self are one. Reciprocity exists when the child places on others' points of view the same value that he places on his own point of view; reality is what is common to all points of view taken together. Thus a child moves from realism of perception (what I perceive is real: "The moon follows me when I walk.") to interpretation and thinking about perception ("If two people walk in opposite directions, can the moon follow them both?"). The interpretations become more logical as a child builds mental structures that help him to organize his world. Among those mental structures are spatial orientation and conservation of length and number. The child is using relativity when he perceives relationships between different objects or substances. Initially, the child views all objects as separate and distinct. He sees all objects as having certain independent characteristics or attributes. Gradually, he recognizes and uses relations between objects. He sees the wind and the clouds as related; the isolated sinkings of two pebbles in a pond become related; "sister" is no longer a description of a single person (in children's play, a single child or a doll is often "the sister"), but a name for a relation between two individuals.

Children who are not yet capable of objectivity are unable to differentiate between the external world and the internal world. This lack of distinction results in what Piaget calls "adherences"; adherences are fragments of internal experience that still cling to the external world. Adherences provide insights into children's thinking and often persist in adults' thinking on social, political, and religious problems. Piaget classifies adherences as feelings of participation, animism, artificialism, and finalism. The examples cited here are taken from *The Child's Conception of Physical Causality*.

1. Feelings of participation.

The child thinks he participates dynamically in the actions of nature. These feelings of participation are sometimes accompanied by beliefs in magic.

> Juli (age ten): "What makes the clouds move along?—*It's when you walk*" [1: 62].
> Nai (age four and a half): "Can the moon go where it likes, or is there something that makes it move along?—*It's me, when I walk*" [1: 74].
> Leo (age seven): "How do we make one (a shadow)?—*You make it when you walk, be-*

cause every step you make, it follows us behind"
[1: 187].

2. Animism
The child endows things with consciousness and life.

CAM (age six and a half): *"The clouds walk, and the moon goes with them, too"* [1: 67].

NAI (age four): Balloons go up *"because they want to fly away"* [1: 110].

Mos (age eight): "Why do they (clouds) move along?—*Because they feel cold"* [1: 67].

MART (age eight): "Why is it [a shadow] on this side?—*It likes best to be on this side"* [1: 187].

Box (age six and a half): *"When it's going to rain, the sun goes home quickly"* [1: 76].

3. Artificialism
The child thinks that everything is willed and intentional and organized for the good of man.

BONJ (age six): "How does the sun stay up there?—*Because it wants to give us light"* [1: 107].

BAR (age nine): The clouds move along *"by themselves, because if they didn't move along, there would never be any rain." "Why do they not fall on our heads?"—"Because if they fell, why, we'd be dead"* [1: 68].

FRAN (age nine): ". . . Why [does the sun shine]? *Because sometimes there are ladies and gentlemen who are going for a walk and they are pleased when it's fine. . . ."* [1: 77].

GIAM (eight and a half): ". . . *When people feel cold it [the sun] warms them, and for the people who are not, it makes shade . . ."* [1: 83].

4. Finalism
The child believes that everything has an explanation. Any explanation will do.

PIE (age nine): The sun does not fall *"because it is used to staying in the sky"* [1: 107].

HANS (age five): A book is let fall. "Why does it fall?—*Because you don't hold it.—But why does it fall?—Because it doesn't stay up in the air.—Why?—Because there's nothing* (to hold it) . . ." [1: 110].

M. To (age eight): "And the little boats without sails, why do they stay on the water?—*Because they are light.—And why do the big boats stay?—Because they are heavy* [1: 138].

BAR (age nine and a half): "How does the water in the Arve flow?—*Because if it didn't move along, you wouldn't have any water!"* [1: 100]

In the examples of animism, artificialism, and finalism, note that animism is often coupled with artificialism and with finalism. The deep stubborn finalism of the child ("There must be reasons.") creates a need for the first three types of adherence.

Piaget discusses a fifth type of adherence, force, in which children assume that things make efforts analogous to our own muscular force, but force appears to be a kind of animism.

In a fascinating article Jerome Bruner and Patricia Greenfield discuss the predominance of particular adherences in certain cultures (14). These two authors assert that artificialism is typical of individualistically oriented societies and that unself-conscious realism is present in several primitive cultures. They report that schooling, even for a short time, reduces realism considerably.

Piaget says that the shift in the child's thought from realism to objectivity, reciprocity, and relativity requires social interaction and intellectual growth. Social interaction compels a child to become conscious of his "I" (objectivity). Conflicts between his "I" and the "I's" of other children arise and must be resolved. Such a resolution requires that a child become aware that the other child has different thoughts and desires. These must be taken into account in trying to resolve a conflict. Intellectual growth insures that the child will have the mental structures to discern relations between objects; such development makes it possible for the child to relate phenomena that he previously considered unrelated. These mental relations also make it possible for a child to relate thoughts, feelings, and external happenings, and thus find some pattern among them. In this way external reality is slowly stripped of its subjective elements and becomes more objective.

These effects of social interaction and of intellectual growth have significant implications for elementary-school classrooms.

To sustain the shift to objectivity and reciprocity, a child must be given many opportunities for seeing and hearing different opinions of other children. Exposure to the different opinions of a teacher is not enough, for a child usually adopts "authoritative" opinions instead of comparing them with his own views. Thus social interaction among children is essential for intellectual growth as well as social-emotional growth.

5. PIAGET

Children's work in mathematics, science, social studies, and even reading and writing needs to be based on work with real things. Piaget's research on the development of the mental structures for relations indicates that they arise from a child's interactions with objects in the real world. Happily, activities that involve a child interacting with objects also lend themselves to social interaction, for the work done by one child is observable by other children and can serve as a focus of discussion. In addition, activities with real objects are usually better done by small groups of children than by the whole class. In smaller groups each child has more opportunities for social interaction.

Some educational environments encourage the shift from realism to objectivity, reciprocity, and relativity, while others do not. A comparison of open classrooms and individualized instruction is useful. A well-structured open classroom offers children many opportunities to interact with real objects and to work in small groups. In contrast, most individualized classrooms use printed media—dittoed sheets, workbooks—as the chief activity for pupils, and pupils ordinarily work alone. Of course, each pupil must learn for himself, and learning sometimes requires working alone. Any classroom must offer opportunities for independent work. Likewise, pupils need to learn to interact with printed media. However, a classroom that provides no opportunities for children to interact with the real world or with one another fails to use the most motivating and the most natural way—indeed, Piaget would say the only way—for children to learn. Such a classroom is not helping children to move out of their childish realism.

Growth in objectivity, reciprocity, and relativity is easy to observe if children are interacting with one another and with real objects and verbalizing about these interactions. One good way to collect data about growth in individual students is to record observations. The records can serve to remind the teacher to arrange experiences and to ask questions that will promote the shift out of realism. This shift is not limited to specific subject matter areas, but can and should occur in many areas. A teacher can be proud if she has seen her pupils show growth out of realism, for this growth is as important as the acquisition of academic skills, indeed, probably more important in producing mature, responsible adults.

An understanding of childish realism, in children or in adults, can shed light on many behaviors. Human beings are only imperfectly objective. They must learn to separate their thoughts and their feelings from their judgments about happenings in the world. Teachers can help children accomplish this separation by encouraging them to express their thoughts and feelings and to see the relation of the thoughts and feelings to the conclusions children are drawing. Reciprocity develops only when a child can freely compare his thought with that of another. An unequal distribution of power between two individuals (child-child or child-adult) precludes this kind of comparison. Teachers can encourage the development of reciprocity in children in two ways: by creating a classroom atmosphere in which the thoughts of all children are valued and by refraining from using their authority to validate their statements.

Part II: Seventeen types of causal relations

Piaget distinguishes seventeen types of causal relations in children's thought. The types, which are based on children's explanations of causality (1: 253–67), are divided into three stages. The first two stages are precausal; the third stage is true causality. Children simultaneously exhibit types of adjacent stages for a long time. Gradually primitive explanations are replaced by explanations of a more advanced type. Recent studies indicate that specific experiences can lead to more advanced explanations (8, 10–12).

Many examples of the seventeen types of explanations are combinations of several types. The exact dividing line between types is not always clear.

The research done in the USA cited earlier indicates that American children, like Swiss children, exhibit these stages. This research does not report verbatim explanations, however. To decrease the ethnocentricity of the Swiss examples, some Russian examples are given from Chukovsky's *From Two to Five* (15). To save space, the examples given earlier for four of these types (participation, animism, artificialism, and finalism) will not be repeated here.

Stage I: Precausality

Stage I begins when children first ask "Why?" and continues in some children as late as age ten.

1. Motivation or psychological causality.

This type includes any explanation that attributes mind or intention to objects or to happenings in the real world.

> MART (age eight): "Why is it [the shadow] on this side? *It likes best to be on this side*" [1: 187].
> LIALIA (age three): On first sight of a ship: "*Mommie, Mommie, the locomotive is taking a bath!*" [15: 1].
> "*The winter got so cold it ran away somewhere*" [15: 23].
> GIRL (age five) watching mother making pie dough: "*I know how stars are made! They make them from what is left over from the moon*" [15: 29].

2. Finalistic causality

Everything has an explanation. Any explanation will do. Children seemingly possess a compulsion to explain things, but do not examine their explanations. They are content with absurd, illogical, or vacuous explanation.

3. Phenomenistic causality

A child makes associations at random and takes these associations as causal.

> A mad dog was shot just at the time of a flame-red sunset. From then on two-and-a-half-year-old Maia would say, whenever she saw a red sky, "*Again they killed a mad dog!*" [15:20]
> PAQ (age four and a quarter): "And what makes the wheels go?—*They turn by themselves. It's when you are on top of the bicycle. It's the street that makes the bicycle go*" [1: 202].
> GRIM (age five): "*The clouds are smoke from the chimneys.*—Why do they move along?—*It's the moon that makes them move*" [1: 65].
> STEI (age five): A box of matches makes a shadow "*because it is yellow and there is some black*" (lettering) [1: 184].

4. Participation causality

A child participates in the actions of nature. Also, two phenomena that have resemblance or general affinity can act on one another.

5. Magical causality

Relationships are established in a child's mind between specific actions, thoughts, or objects and some desired end. Piaget gives no examples that are magical only. Most examples of phenomenistic and participation causality have magical overtones. Magical causality is common in primitive human cultures.

6. Moral causality

These explanations contain an element of moral necessity.

> GAV (age eight and a half): "Can it (the sun) set where it likes?—*No.*—Why?—*Because there are places which aren't good*" [1: 80].
> EILL (age nine): "Does the sun move along? *Yes, because it has to light us*" [1: 82].
> DEL (age six and a half): "*The waves are only at the edge of the lake. Why?*" "*Are waves on the lake naughty?*" [1: 88]
> VERN (age six): "*The boat is cleverer than the stone* [i.e. it doesn't sink].—What does it mean to be clever?—*It doesn't do what it ought not to*" [1: 136].

Stage II: Precausality

Stage II begins to appear at age five or six and is common until age eleven or twelve.

7. Artificialist causality

Everything is willed and intentional and organized for the good of man.

8. Animistic causality

The child endows things with consciousness and life.

9. Dynamic causality

Even after children eliminate most aspects of animism, they still attribute to objects internal forces that explain their activity or movement.

> MOC (age ten): The sun moves along "*by itself.*" "Does it know it is moving?—*Of course. It turns itself round. Of course it knows it!*" [1: 82]
> HEI (age eleven): "Why does it [the river] not go up?—*Because it hasn't enough strength to go up*" [1: 102].

Stage III: True causality

Stage III begins at age seven or eight and predominates by age eleven or twelve.

Piaget reports few detailed examples from children at this stage. Examples reported here are given by Piaget in various places in his theoretical discussions of this stage. Descriptions of these stages are the author's summary of Piaget's much more extensive discussion.

10. Reaction of the surrounding medium

This is the first genuinely physical explanation. It is the first attempt, though primitive, that considers the need for continuity and contact with the moving object. This explanation was used frequently by Greek and medieval physicists. According to this type of explanation, projectiles (clouds, airplanes) are "pushed by the air they make in moving"; boats, "by the waves they make."

11. Mechanical causality

Dynamism is the assumption that things make efforts analogous to our own muscular force. When a child realizes that this explanation is not adequate, he replaces it with a mechanical causality. The child has no detailed knowledge of the mechanisms by which various things work; he merely makes crude connections. Things are moved by contact and transference of movement. For example, the wind pushes the clouds, and pedals make the bicycle go. Thus the internal motor of something (its "force") is replaced by an external force.

12. Causality by generation

Generation implies that one thing is born of another. The clouds make wind by melting, or smoke makes the clouds. These explanations usually involve transmutations of substances.

13. Substantial identification

This type is similar to generation, but the animism implied in generation is now gone. Objects are not considered as being born from something else, but as the result of the fusion or burning of objects. The sky is made of clouds: "There are lots of little clouds close together."

14. Condensation and rarefaction

In this type, the qualities of objects are explained by the relative density of materials that compose it. The clouds are "well packed" to make the sun. The hardness of stone derives from the "closeness" of the bits of earth that compose it.

15. Atomistic composition

Eventually an object comes to be viewed as being composed of tiny particles. If these particles are packed closely together, the object is dense. If the particles are packed loosely together, the object is less dense.

16. Spatial explanations

Principles of perspective to explain shadows, ideas of volume to explain immersed bodies—these and other advanced forms are occasionally used by children.

17. Explanation by logical deduction

From experiences in the real world, a child eventually induces principles or laws. He then uses these deductively to explain that a certain phenomenon "must happen." Most of the causal explanations tend toward this kind of explanation eventually.

It should be noted again that many explanations that children give are a combination of the types listed. The growth from stage to stage is gradual and varies with the phenomenon being explained.

If a teacher knows how strong a child's finalism is and is aware of the stages through which a child's explanations move, she can avoid some negative effects of the traditional classroom. Finalism is evidence of the strong drive that impels children to find reasons for things, to organize their world. Any attempt at an explanation, which is an organization of data by the child, is better than no attempt. The explanation is evidence that at least the urge to explain is still present in that child. The child's answers should not be corrected. The teacher should accept them with some neutral phrase: "That is an interesting idea, Juan." Later some attempt can be made to give the child additional data to help him come to a more advanced answer. A specific experience with real objects or a talk with other children are two possible sources of data. The teacher's "telling of the answer"—giving verbally the correct explanation—is unlikely to help. The child will adopt the verbal explanation at the verbal level, possibly remember it, and even regurgitate it on command. But the explanation will not be assimilated into the child's mental schema of that phenomenon.

This is not to say that it is never helpful for the teacher to provide simplified explanations of phenomena, particularly if these explanations come in the wake of some kind of experience of the child in the world. But verbal explanations rarely produce the understanding that teachers assume they do. In an American study (16) sixth-grade children described complicated physical phenomena correctly using grown-up "textbook" words. But when asked for information in their own words, the children demonstrated incredible ignorance and gave explanations at primitive stages. The coexistence of primitive assimilated (meaningful) and advanced unassimilated (unmeaningful) levels of thought is common when instruction is at a verbal level only.

Often schools or teachers are so unaccepting of primitive answers that they extinguish the child's eagerness to find answers. The child gives up trying to find explanations on his own because his explanations are never accepted, are never "correct." He waits for the teacher to give him the reason for things. Often the teacher does not feel capable of simplifying a reason at the child's level and says to the child, "You're too young to understand that" or "You'll learn that in high school." This kind of response is particularly common in certain subject matter areas in which a teacher's background is weak. In elementary-school mathematics, "Why?" has been and still frequently is a forbidden question because the teacher does not know the answer. What effect do these negative experiences have on the child? The answer is obvious—he ceases to ask "Why?" or at least ceases trying to answer his own "Whys?"

Teachers who are aware of the types of explanation that children usually give at various ages are in a good position to accept these answers as reasonable for a child of that age. The knowledgeable teacher can assess a child's level and try to provide experiences to move the child to a slightly higher level.

Do adults give children animistic and other primitive explanations? The question deserves some research. The literature is clear that mothers modify their language patterns in speaking to young children. Adults in general might modify their explanations of complicated physical phenomena, using more primitive types of explanation with children.

In summary, education should aid the transition from childish modes of thought to more advanced modes. The progression from realism to objectivity, reciprocity, and relativity remains incomplete in most adults: every day adults do or say things that result from a lack of objectivity, reciprocity, or relativity. Awareness of the shift out of realism and of the various types of causality can aid educators at all levels, but particularly those in the elementary schools, to change the educational environment so that it promotes the development of more advanced modes of thought and fosters the pupil's powerful urge to ask "Why?"

References

1. Jean Piaget. *The Child's Conception of Physical Causality.* Totowa, New Jersey: Littlefield, Adams and Company, 1960.
2. T. M. Abel. "Unsynthetic Modes of Thinking among Adults: A Discussion of Piaget's Concepts," *American Journal of Psychology, 44* (January, 1932), 123–32.
3. Henry P. Cole. "An Analysis of the Effects of a Structured Teaching Approach Developed from the Work of Piaget, Bruner, and Others," *Dissertation Abstracts International, 29A* (March, 1969), 2997.
4. V. Hazlitt. "Children's Thinking," *British Journal of Psychology, 20* (April, 1930), 354–61.
5. M. E. Oakes. "Children's Explanations of Natural Phenomena" in Teachers College Contributions to Education No. 926. New York, New York: Teachers College, Columbia University, 1947.
6. James Harding. "Organizer Influence on Children's Responses to Questions Involving Physical Causality," *Dissertation Abstracts International, 31A* (February, 1971), 3981.
7. Harvey Morris Lesser. "The Development of the Perception of Causality in Children," *Dissertation Abstracts International, 31B* (May, 1971), 6878.
8. M. Mogar. "Children's Causal Reasoning about Natural Phenomena," *Child Development, 31* (March, 1960), 59–65.
9. Edna Ward. "A Study of Causal Thinking in Elementary School Children," *Dissertation Abstracts International, 31A* (December 1970), 2749.
10. Michael David Berzonsky. "Factors Influencing Children's Causal Reasoning," *Dissertation Abstracts International, 31A* (February, 1971), 3946.
11. Michael David Berzonsky. "Role of Familiarity in Children's Explanations of Physical Causality," *Child Development, 42* (September, 1971), 705–15.
12. Martin L. Nass. "The Effects of Three Variables on Children's Concepts of Physical Causality," *Dissertation Abstracts International, 15* (December, 1954), 1119.
13. Jean Piaget. *Understanding Causality.* New York, New York: W. W. Norton and Company, 1974.
14. Jerome Bruner and Patricia Marks Greenfield. "Culture and Cognitive Growth," *International Journal of Psychology, 1* (1966), 89–107.
15. Kornei Chukovsky. *From Two to Five.* Berkeley, California: University of California Press, 1971.
16. B. R. Joyce. "Children's Verbalisms and the New Curriculums," *National Elementary Principal, 45* (April, 1966), 23–25.

Office of Human Development Services, Department of Health, Education and Welfare.

ISSUES IN EARLY CHILDHOOD EDUCATION

Early childhood education is of paramount importance to this nation. The impact of early learning experiences on later development is widely acknowledged. As the number of working mothers and single parent families increase, the need for programs and day care facilities increases. John Von Hartz urges us to reexamine our national attitude towards children in "The War Against Kids." Support and understanding are being eroded by the effects of tax cuts on public schools. We have chosen to ignore the implications of our changing family structure on child development.

"Infant Nurturance and Early Learning Myths and Realities" by Mary Aaronson emphasizes that an infant has psychological needs over and above physical ones. Parent involvement is necessary -- and yet they are not always prepared for this important period, or capable of devoting the time needed.

Two articles address the need for, and availability of day care. "Who's Taking Care of the Children" presents the disturbing results of a national survey of working mothers. One answer, supported by the American Federation of Teachers (A.F.T.) promotes federal legislation to fund services through public schools. James Greenman in "Day Care in the Schools" responds to the A.F.T.'s position.

Additional issues of major concern to early childhood educators is the influence of television on the child's total development, and child abuse. Dorothy Cohen covers the issues surrounding the effects of television on the child's perception of reality in "Through a Glass Darkly: Television and the Perception of Reality." The widespread problem of child maltreatment and abuse is discussed in the paper "Child Abuse and Neglect in the American Society.."

The concluding article extends the A.F.T.'s position of federal involvement to the state level. Kevin J. Swick describes the findings of a national survey in "Needed: More State Leadership in Preschool Education." The results show state leadership nationwide to be "static, confused and lacking in substance." Federal and State intervention may not be the answer. But we need to move quickly to protect the rights and fullfill the needs of young children, our most valuable resource.

THE WAR AGAINST KIDS

Children are the forgotten members of our society—victims of taxpayers' revolts, government cutbacks, and everyday indifference.

By John von Hartz

John von Hartz, a freelance writer and playwright, is also the father of two young children.

The letter from the irate businessman smoldered with indignation. During a supersonic jet transatlantic flight, he fumed to the editor of a major American newspaper, the cries of a babe-in-arms had distracted him from his paperwork. What's more, the man moaned, he had paid the full fare while the offending baby traveled for free.

The number of adults who nodded in agreement while reading the businessman's letter might shock the majority of American parents. After all, this country boasts that it is youth-oriented. Parents are motivated, even driven, by an urge to improve the lot and lifestyles of their kids. The quintessential advertisement for the American way of life is a gang of carefree, bronzed teenagers disporting themselves in some healthy pastime.

This admiration for youth has a dark side, however, one that is never apparent in the media blitzes aimed at well-off teenagers with their pockets full of disposable income. Taken as a class, America's children are the victims of a war waged on them by society—a conflict that many parents do not fully perceive.

Society's disdain for children is rooted in the nervous realities of today's attitudes toward life. In an age when existence often seems an unremitting series of hassles and high costs, kids symbolize two unwelcome entities: trouble and money. As every parent knows, kids complicate life. Supporting children in schools, playgrounds, libraries, and the array of public services that enrich growing bodies and minds costs dearly in public tax dollars. None of this is lost on self-aware Americans who have transformed the 70's into a decade aimed toward ego-gratification and self-fulfillment, and away from the responsibilities of child rearing and heading families.

Statistics confirm the swing away from kids. Some 60 percent of all American households have no children, according to figures based on the U.S. Statistical Abstract, 1977. Today the national birthrate is only 1.9 children per family, a figure below that rallying cry of the issue-oriented '60's, Zero Population Growth. (ZPG is achieved when the birth and death rates are equal in a given year.)

We should welcome the news that America is facing up to the catastrophic peril of overpopulation. And we do. Concern about the wisdom of bringing children into the world, however, is fostering the unwanted side effect of questioning the rights of kids in general. As the childless households determine national policies, views toward children are becoming frosted with antagonism.

This negativism toward youngsters reveals itself in dozens of obvious and subtle ways. Rental housing, particularly new complexes, is becoming the domain of adults without children—swinging singles, young marrieds, and older people. The basis of this exclusionary stance is rationally explained: younger and older people prefer to conduct their lives away from the noise and demands of kids. Children, however, constitute a significant portion of America's population; almost one third of the country is under 18 years of age. Segregating this large and lively percentage of Americans from housing is a loss for all of society. It is perilously close to self-destructive for men and women without children to isolate themselves from the questing, restless, and constantly curious personalities of the young.

Society also shows kids the back of its hand with its pernicious rejection of school budgets. This past summer, the voters of Ohio rejected more than half of the 200 community-tax-increase requests aimed at financing the public schools. Only with outside aid from state and federal coffers could some of these schools be opened in the fall. Nor does Ohio stand alone in this rebellion against the costs of public education. Across the country community school boards and taxpayers find themselves in pitched battle, with referendums for school monies more often going down to defeat than being approved.

The sharpest recent attack on children came with the passage of Proposition 13 in California. It may be years before the full effect of this limiting of property taxes can be assessed, but already one thing is certain—the kids aren't any better off because of it. Summer-school sessions were canceled across the state. After-school programs, including many sports activities, were slashed, and such disparate courses as drivers' education and Latin were lopped off the fall schedules. Library staffs and hours have been trimmed, and state-funded summer jobs—so crucial to the budgets of working families—were eliminated.

The causes of this tax revolt are as complex and interwoven as the fabric of American life. Property-tax payers are bowed under the fiscal burden of community services, particularly the expense of running the schools. Anti-tax feeling reflects a disenchantment with busing and classroom desegregation, with an educational system that often turns out poorly educated kids, at ever-higher cost. Whatever the causes, the casualties are the kids. Lower budgets for local governments certainly won't produce better education or child-oriented services. The kids realize this and regard society's cut-backs as a series of frontal attacks.

Kids in trouble can expect little succor from states in these flint-hearted days. In Nebraska, for instance, foster homes which take in delinquent teenagers are granted only $4 per child per day. Unable to maintain children on this minimal payment, many foster homes in Nebraska must return their wards to reform school where the costs for caring for a child are twice that of sending him through college. And these children are not violent criminals; most of them are runaways from troubled homes, petty thieves, and incipient alcoholics. Since reform schools—like prisons—are little more than training grounds for crime, small wonder that our country's juvenile crime rates are streaking off the tops of most police graphs.

In daily life, the war against kids often consists of guerilla skirmishes. Restaurateurs have been known to turn ghostly white when confronted by a mother and her young brood wanting a table. The supply of high chairs or comfortable seating for children is limited in most dining places, perhaps to restrict the number of child patrons. Department stores and other commercial operations make no accommodations for nursing mothers, who are relegated to crowded restrooms for periods of breast-feeding their babies. Parents must suffer if they wish to expose their children to the great artworks of man; museums either deny admittance to children or place a sanction on strollers, the one convenient method of transporting a child around the vast marble halls.

Kids even have a hard time finding clean and safe recreation areas in most urban communities. Playgrounds are commandeered by derelicts or gangs of toughs who drive the kids and mothers away. The playgrounds that are safe are regularly visited by untrained dogs who use the sandboxes as lavatories, exposing babies and young children to flagrant health hazards. Older kids must often stand by in despair

while urban ball fields literally go to seed because park departments suffer retrenchments in maintenance personnel.

Even vacation trips with babies give no respite from the fray. A simple amenity like a diaper-changing table is a luxury no American air terminal seems able to afford (by contrast, many European airports provide them routinely). And passengers generally view young children boarding a train or plane with the affection cotton growers have traditionally accorded to an advancing boll-weevil swarm.

America's ambivalence toward children is based in large part in a conflict between our myth of the family structure and its reality. This was one of the insights gleaned by a five-year study of the family by the Carnegie Council for Children, headed by Kenneth Keniston. Most Americans see the typical family as headed by a working father with a dutiful wife who remains at home with the kids and pets. Facts uncovered in the Census Abstract challenge this cozy concept. For the first time in America's history, more mothers work outside the home than stay in the kitchen and nursery. Only 40 percent of American households with kids are "typical," i.e., have a husband who serves as the sole wage-earner. (Even in this typical household, more than one-third of the wives plan to reenter the labor market.) In a larger percentage of American households with children —45 percent—both parents work. Some 14 percent of all American families are headed by a working woman.

The concept of a male-dominated family as the prime building block of American society refuses to perish. This nation grew and prospered on the belief that the individualistic male wage-earner held the family together. With his helpmate wife, he pushed aside the roadblocks that cluttered the path of the children.

This idealization of the family leads many taxpayers to refuse aid to families led by a male wage-winner. Yet many families, even those with two jobholders, require more help from the state than ever before. One reason for this is that families have grown smaller, and there are fewer people to share the load. In 1948, only one in 14 children under six years old was brought up in a single-parent family, according to the Carnegie study. By 1973 that proportion had doubled to one in seven children. Relatives who once aided in child raising are retiring from the family circle. And the number of children produced by each family is dwindling. At the peak of the post-World War II baby boom, the average child had almost three siblings while today he has less than one.

A composite picture of the modern family shows a small unit with one or two working parents, and few—if any—relatives, brothers, or sisters to lend a hand. While the parents are out working, the kids are left with babysitters who often do little more than plop themselves in front of that baleful eye that never sleeps: the TV. Or the kids are remitted to the daily custody of the state through public schools and day-care programs.

Since the 1960's, the government has created an outburst of services for children—Head Start, after-school programs, medical, counseling, and day-care services. Some of these programs, such as the model parent-child center reported in *Parents'*, July 1978, are exemplary. Other programs however, have unfortunately fallen victim to misdirected goals and to the severe budget cuts of the 70's.

In spite of their deficiencies, these government programs for kids and their parents are a national priority. Ask any working mother to name the government service most useful to her and her reply is automatic: "Day-care programs." While government has taken the lead in this field, private industry could well follow suit. Any parent whose child is protected, nurtured, and well cared for during working hours is sure to be a better and more productive employee.

Similarly, working parents of both sexes would profit enormously from a more flexible work schedule that would free them to attend the needs of their kids. Far from being a utopian dream, flexible work time relieves the minds of the workers about their children, thus increasing their concentration and, ultimately, their effectiveness when on the job.

Attitude remains the most frightening weapon in the war against kids. Americans persist in making it difficult for parents to raise their young, then faulting them if they fail. Every funding reduction in programs for kids and every rigid rule that prevents a parent from giving his kid his undivided attention is a direct attack on the kids themselves. Parents must be responsible for the actions and behavior of their offspring. But it serves no discernible purpose to heap blame on a parent if a child is dragged through an indifferent society which is unwilling to open its wallet to supply the programs that add dignity to life.

Today, society has been entrusted with the task of helping to raise its children—this includes all the children from the littered streets of the ghetto to the sylvan glades of restricted suburbia. Without a thorough reexamination of the national attitude toward kids, the war will only escalate and worsen.

On reflection, any thoughtful American will realize that kids require support and understanding. Not only are these two commodities free, they restore the giver and receiver. Providing these precious human considerations is an undisguised gesture for peace. The next time a harried businessman is disturbed by a baby's cry, he might neglect his work for a moment and give the child his hand. It may not quiet the baby, but it will work wonders for the man.

Infant Nurturance and Early Learning: Myths and Realities

MAY AARONSON

May Aaronson, B.A., is Program Specialist, Early Child Care Research, Center for Studies of Child and Family Mental Health, National Institute of Mental Health, U.S. Department of Health, Education and Welfare, Rockville, Maryland. She thanks Doris Aaronson for consultation on the paper. The opinions expressed are those of the author, and do not necessarily reflect the official policy of the National Institute of Mental Health and HEW.

Editor's note: This update of information on "earliest child development" will be of special interest to practitioners in several areas of child welfare.

An understanding of the interdependency of infant nurturance and early learning is of utmost importance to the new parent and to those who provide services to parents and infants. Cultural myths are transmitted along generational lines in ways that interfere with the optimal development of a nurturant relationship between the caretaker and the newborn infant. Providers of services to parents and infants, including those involved in maternity care, are in an excellent position to help parents and other caretakers differentiate between myths and realities.

One myth is that the infant is totally helpless at birth and that the caring adult is wholly responsible for the developing relationship. This is far from realistic. It is a reciprocal affair with the baby in full participation. It follows that there are no instant relationships with newborns, no matter how skilled or motivated the adult caretakers. A relationship develops gradually as the two learn what to expect of one another and become a twosome. [11:429-442].

It is repeatedly stated today that the parent is perhaps the most influential teacher the baby will have. But in many ways the baby becomes an important teacher of the parents. If the parent can't learn what the baby is trying to teach, both will come to grief. That passive little bundle who in the hospital spends most of the time eating and sleeping may at home become a challenge to deal with and to understand. The infant has many ways of communicating, of which crying is the most forceful. He (or she) screams, and usually the parent comes. In this way he initiates many transactions between himself and his caretaker. In the beginning it is a guessing game and requires a great deal of patience, for at first the infant's cries are undifferentiated. What is he crying about? Is he hungry? Cold? Wet?

Does he have cramps? Or is he just restless and trying to get to sleep? He could be lonely and need to be held, touched, cuddled, fondled, stroked, to feel another warm human body next to his. It's a puzzle, but it will usually be possible to satisfy his needs after observing and listening, and engaging in trial and error.

Quieting the Newborn

One method of quieting a newborn is by swaddling, a practice from ancient times that has been largely ignored in modern society. Swaddling, or wrapping the baby snugly to restrict him, helps to soothe and comfort colicky babies and has a quieting effect on those who are irritable or wakeful, or who startle frequently. Its efficacy was demonstrated in an experiment in which 2- to 5-day-old infants were tested 1) when swaddled with a diaper and blanket, and 2) when free to move, unclothed except for a shirt. The swaddled infants slept more and cried less. They had more stable heart rates. The swaddling seemed to comfort them, reduce their crying and thrashing, and to act generally as a pacifier. At 2 months of age infants were no longer happy to be swaddled, and resisted swaddling attempts [7:57-65].

Years ago, pediatricians advised mothers not to pick up a crying baby lest it spoil him; that if it is not feeding time and there are no discernible reasons for baby's complaint, the screaming should be ignored. Most researchers today take the opposite view. According to Bell and Ainsworth, when a mother ignores or delays responding to the infant's cries when he is tiny, he is likely to cry more frequently later on [1:76-77]. This initiates a growing problem. The more the baby cries, the less the mother feels like responding, and the more irritable the baby becomes. Bell and Ainsworth found that babies whose cries were heeded cried the least, and developed many other ways of communicating by 8 to 12 months of age. Picking the infant up and holding him may be the most effective way to calm him throughout the first year. However, parents have to find ways to balance the needs of the baby with those of the rest of the family, and evolve a regime that all can live with. No humans can expect to have all their needs met all of the time; while the family tries to accommodate to the new baby, it is hoped that he is gradually learning to tolerate delays.

Learning in Newborns

Another myth is that during the first few months infants react hardly at all to the outside world, that all that matters to them is food and comfort [9]. Nothing could be further from the truth. The infant is actively learning from birth. Newborns, seemingly helpless and uncomprehending, perceive a good deal. For example, they can "track" with their eyes a bright object moving across their field of vision. Their sucking behavior shows that they can taste the difference between drinking water, acidulous liquids, sugar, salt solutions, and milk. They respond to touching. Touch a newborn's hand and he will move it. He may also move his other limbs in response, and perhaps sneeze, suck or swallow [2].

Many studies with newborns demonstrate that their senses are sharper at birth than had been supposed, and that their capacity to learn and adapt is amazing. This was illustrated in an experiment

conducted by Ilze Kalnins in Jerome Bruner's laboratory at Harvard
[9]. She projected onto a screen a movie of a mother playing with her
child, and positioned 4-week-old infants to watch while sucking
special pacifiers. The infants quickly discovered that they had to
suck to keep the picture from fading out or from blurring, and they
increased their sucking effort. Another day the situation was reversed. They had to stop sucking to keep the picture in focus, and
they reversed their sucking behavior accordingly.

Forming a Relationship

So it is known that the infant is not helpless; he has ways to communicate, even though the ways are crude at first, and he can learn
from the minute he is born. What has this to do with the relationship
forming between the parent or caregiver and the infant?

What seems to develop rather quickly between the infant and
adult is a code of mutual expectancy. For example, when a mother
responds to an initiative on the part of the infant—say, crying—he in
turn learns that if he calls, his mother comes. There are other circu-
lar communications taking place between the two. The parent and
infant send messages through eye-to-eye contact, smiles, and sounds
other than crying. From as early as 4 months, an infant will smile
more to a face that smiles back than to one that doesn't. If the adult
stops smiling back, the infant will look away. He may even struggle
bodily to look away. He is "turned off," and withdraws. A child's attempts at learning can be similarly warped when his expectancy is
thwarted, and things stop making sense to him [9].

Responsiveness in the adult-infant relationship is an essential ingredient making it possible for the parent or other caretaker to become the infant's teacher. As the adult's behaviors become more predictable to the infant and in line with what he has learned to expect,
and as he becomes more skillful at vocalizing and using a variety of
signals to attract attention, his crying behavior decreases. Also, as he
gets older and builds up trust in his caretaker, he learns to wait a bit
without signaling at all. In other words, he learns to delay gratification, secure in the feeling that he is not going to be neglected.

The adult-infant relationship becomes so reciprocal, each learning from the other and responding to the other, that it has been lik-
ened to partners in dancing. As the infant develops more skills and
becomes a bit more independent, the steps become more varied and
complex, but the two must keep in step with one another for the
teaching and learning to proceed.

The increasing responsiveness that develops between the caring
adult and the infant is rewarding to both. A thriving and responsive
baby causes the adult to feel successful and competent, gratified
with the infant's growing ability to learn and adapt. An emotional
bond develops that makes the drudgery connected with infant care
seem inconsequential, and all the effort worthwhile. The love and
admiration shown to the infant make him feel "special"—the beginning of a feeling of human worth and self-esteem. The infant becomes confident that he can exercise some control over his environment; after all, he is getting his caretaker to satisfy his needs. He
gradually attains the courage to increase his independence and the
competence to develop new skills.

The ideal caretaker described here also talks and sings to the infant from birth. The infant's babbling is encouraged by vocalizing
back to him whatever sounds he makes, until there is a vocal "tennis

match." Accidentally the infant makes an "mmmmmm" sound or "dddd" sound, and the caretaker becomes enthusiastic, breaks out in smiles and applause, and encourages him to say "mama" and "dada" by pronouncing the syllables back to him. With such reinforcement, the infant is soon saying and comprehending many words, and communication through language has begun. Exaggerated reinforcement for small accomplishments in the very early years enhances the parents' potential for becoming influential teachers of their children.

Though caretaking in our society seems currently in a state of transition, with fathers or outside caretakers playing an increasing role, the infant's first caretaker is still most likely to be the mother. It follows that development of a nurturant relationship and emotional bond by the mother with her infant remains of utmost importance. Some researchers and clinicians seeking to facilitate development of this bond assert that it can be achieved by altering maternity care and hospital procedures and practices. Changes of this nature are unlikely to occur until some myths about childbirth have been dispelled.

Childbirth Practices

With the advent of modern medicine and the construction of modern hospitals, childbirth was largely removed from the home. What was formerly a natural family occurrence, assisted by a midwife and others, became a "surgical operation," with all of its frightening overtones. The mother-to-be is separated from her family and familiar surroundings. The full hospital technology comes into play. The "operation" is accompanied by analgesics and anesthetics, by the hospital staff in white, the hospital equipment in gleaming stainless steel, the operating room, and the recovery room. The infant is brought to the mother for inspection and feeding, then whisked away for "expert" nursing care by professionals.

Currently there is a growing countermovement for transfer of childbirth from hospitals to either special maternity facilities or back to the home, with midwives in attendance, if no complications are foreseen. Advocates of this change contend that giving birth in a hospital is not essential, if there are no contraindications. It is not clear what is proposed if unforeseen needs for expert medical assistance and facilities arise. However, many persons are in training today for the profession of nurse-midwife, and the American College of Nurse-Midwives, a national association for registered nurses with special training, has more than 1200 members. Additionally, there are practicing midwives who are not registered nurses.

A growing number of families are enrolling in special courses to educate and train parents for family-centered maternity care, whether or not a hospital delivery is planned. Haire defines family-centered maternity care as individualizied maternity care that permits the parents to share the child-bearing experience and to have access to their baby during the postpartum period to the extent they desire [3:171-191]. The goals are 1) to ensure that the mother has a good experience during labor, birth and the postpartum stay; 2) to enable the father or other involved person to share in this experience, if there are no contraindications; 3) to insure that the mother leaves the hospital confident of her ability to care for her baby; and 4) to accomplish these goals without jeopardizing the health and well-being of mother and child.

Establishing the Bond

According to Klaus and Kennell, studies demonstrate that the degree of interaction permitted between mother and infant at childbirth and during the postpartum period influences maternal-infant bonding and infant development [5]. Kennell states, "Extra hours of contact could have a more decisive effect than many hours of health education and volumes of child-rearing advice [4]." Haire asserts that for the mother to be able to receive and interact with the infant immediately after birth, she has to be alert and relatively free of drugs [3:171-191]. Educating mothers for the child-bearing experience and improving the emotional support given to mothers during labor and birth, she says, have been demonstrated to lessen or eliminate the need for obstetrical drugs and obstetrical intervention during labor and birth. She adds that drugs administered to the mother may be risky for the baby's health. Some of the subjects in the Klaus-Kennell maternal-infant bonding studies have been followed up by Ringler, measuring the effects of early and extended contact on the speech and language comprehension of the children [10]. In her small sample she found that the altered hospital practices at birth improved the mothers' language communication with their children at age 2. And at age 5 the children's IQs, speech, and language comprehension were significantly superior to those of a control group.

Leboyer, the French obstetrician, in *Birth Without Violence*, goes a step farther in calling for changes in hospital procedures in childbirth [6]. He contends that the emotional well-being of the newborn child is ignored in the bright, noisy atmosphere usual in a hospital delivery room. Leboyer advocates requiring dim lights and hushed voices in the delivery room, massaging the baby on the mother's stomach, cutting the umbilical cord only after it stops pulsating, and then giving a brief, relaxing water bath to the baby. He cautions:

> There should be no misunderstanding. Whenever there is a feeling that breathing is not perfectly all right, or there is difficulty in oxygenation, put on the lights and do whatever you want—use suction, give oxygen. I am not denying the progress of obstetrics. I am only saying birth is both a physical and emotional affair.

Leboyer's book appeared "at a time when the relationship between mother, hospital, and obstetrician is being re-evaluated and such accepted practices as early separation and hospital delivery are being questioned with new intensity, according to Medical World News [8]. The periodical quotes T. Berry Brazelton, pediatrician-researcher at Harvard University, as stating: "It's catching the public's fancy because everybody feels we have been treating childbirth as if it were a disease. It should be a happy normal event, but it isn't."

To enhance the possibility of an emotional bond and a nurturant relationship developing between the mother and the newborn, providers of medical services appear to be moving toward communicating facts to parents-to-be and allowing them to make informed choices on how the baby will be delivered and cared for at childbirth. There's no denying the life-saving advances in modern obstetrical procedures and practices, or the need for their employment where necessary. However, researchers and clinicians alike are beginning to accept the idea that prolonged and intimate contact between mother and infant from the moment of birth gives the mother-infant bonding process a head start, affecting the mother's nurturant and language behavior and the quality of the infant's early learning.

Conclusion

To enhance the possibility of an emotional bond and a nurturant relationship developing between any caretaker and the infant, providers of services should make certain their clients understand that: 1) the infant is not helpless; 2) he is capable of acting, reacting and learning from birth; 3) he will be enabled to respond in more consistent and predictable ways if the caretaker's responses are consistent and predictable; 4) over and above survival needs, he needs the emotional gratification of exercising some control over his environment; 5) he is capable of shaping the behavior of his caretaker even while the latter shapes his; 6) crying and other vocal sounds, eye-to-eye contact, facial expressions, and body contact are the earliest forms of communication, with the repertoire gradually increasing in variety and complexity; 7) the infant's language learning stems from language hearing and early vocalizations, bolstered by much encouragement and many expressions of approval; 8) the infant has the capacity to adjust and adapt gradually to family needs as his own abilities and self-control increase; 9) as a human being, he has psychological needs over and above the physical ones, can experience loneliness, and needs human interaction—to be held, touched, cuddled, fondled, stroked, to hear human sounds, and to feel another warm human body next to his.

References

1. Bell, S.M., and Ainsworth, M.D.S. "Infant Crying and Maternal Responsiveness." Paper presented at meeting of Society for Research in Child Development, Minneapolis, April 1971. Abstract in M. Aaronson and J. Rosenfeld, Baby and Other Teachers. Washington, D.C.: Day Care and Child Development Council of America, 1974.

2. Brown, B.S. "New Clues to Your Baby's Secret World," Parents Magazine and Better Homemaking, February 1975. Reprinted DHEW Publication No. (ADM) 76-253, 1975.

3. Haire, D. The Cultural Warping of Childbirth. International Childbirth Education Association, Seattle, Wash. 1972. Reprinted in Environmental Child Health, XIX (June 1973).

4. Kennell, J.H. "Extra Postpartum Contact Strengthens Mother's Tie to Baby," Pediatric News, VI, 7, (July 1972).

5. Klaus, M., and Kennell, J.H. Maternal-Infant Bonding. St. Louis: C.V. Mosby, 1976.

6. Leboyer, F. Birth Without Violence. New York: Knopf, 1975.

7. Lipton, L.; Steinschneider, A., and Richmond, J.B. "Autonomic Function in the Neonate," Psychosomatic Medicine, XXII, 2 (1969).

8. Medical World News. "Taking the Violence Out of Birth: French Obstetrician's Best-Selling Book Stirs Delivery Room Debate," May 1975.

9. Pines, M. "The Development of Intelligence in Babies," in The Mental Health of the Child. Program Reports of the National Institute of Mental Health, PHS Publication No. 2168, June 1971.

10. Ringler, N.M. "Mother's Language to Young Children and the Effects of Early and Extended Contact on the Speech and Language Comprehension at Five." Paper presented at annual conference of the National Association for the Education of Young Children, Dallas, November 1975.

11. Yarrow, L.J. "The Development of Focused Relationships During Infancy," Exceptional Infant, I (1967).

WHO'S TAKING CARE OF THE CHILDREN?

A Crisis in Child Care

Is anyone minding the children of working mothers? Yes and no, according to the results of Family Circle's survey on day care taken last year. The findings, based on responses from working mothers themselves, are disturbing and sometimes shocking. What they reveal not only shatters some popular notions we've held about the family, but indicate that we may have reached a crisis in child care. It is a crisis that affects the middle class for the first time, and its consequences have profound implications for the future of our children and the future of the American family as we know it. Consider some of the findings and the urgent questions they raise:

● Nearly 30% of working mothers' children age 6 to 13 are either home alone after school or with brothers and sisters—that's almost a third of the mothers responding who have pre-teens left to fend for themselves while mothers work. What is happening to these children?

● Only one mother in five has a husband or relative who helps with child care when she is at work. Yet only one mother in ten would leave her child in the care of a relative if she had a choice. Apparently, working mothers don't want grandmothers, aunts or other family members caring for their children while they work. What is happening to the family?

● Fully 98% of working mothers with children under six use day-care mothers, sitters, family homes and day-care centers for child care. Who are these new people now caring for the infants?

● Three out of five working mothers have changed child-care services in the last two years. What is wrong with our present system of child care?

● Fewer than one in ten working mothers favors Federally funded, free day-care services. What do working mothers want? What do they need?

JANE WHITBREAD

JANE WHITBREAD is a prize-winning author, with Stella Chess, M.D., of books about children, most recently, "Daughters: From Infancy to Independence," a complete guide to bringing up girls. Researchers Mark Clements, Laurie Beck, Mary Mohler and Ann Tilson screened and analyzed the data for this survey.

Seventeen million mothers with children under 13 years of age are at work today. *Who's taking care of the children?*

When FAMILY CIRCLE asked readers (half of whom are employed) that question last year, 10,000 working women replied —filling out the detailed child-care questionnaire and writing hundreds of long, thoughtful letters about their child-care problems and the solutions they've found or still hope for.

Their answers (processed and analyzed by Mark Clements Research, Inc., in New York City, from a representative sample of 3,000 responses), provided the first comprehensive survey of working mothers' child-care practices and needs since mothers started flooding the job market in the '60s to become the fastest-growing segment of the working population.

The picture that emerges shatters popular notions about who's taking care of the children, and clearly documents the need for a better system of child-care services.

The women who answered the questionnaire are a good cross section of the country's working mothers: young (median age 30.8), with infants and children still too young to be left alone. They come from every state. They work full-time, every workday, averaging 35 hours a week and earning $8,300—a bit more than the average woman who works.

What they bring home boosts family incomes to the $10,000 to $25,000 or solidly middle-class range, and makes the difference between "survival and security," as one writer put it. If they are single, divorced, separated or widowed—as one in five of them is—their earnings provide the essentials of life for themselves and their children.

The critical importance of their earnings to family security lends a special urgency to their child-care reports. They answered out of concern for their children, their own needs and for the nation's future.

What did they say? One woman, an accountant, back to work after divorcing, and anxious about having to leave her six children—ages 5, 6, 8, 9, 10 and 14—home alone after school, wrote: "There are just too many things that can and do happen. Sometimes when an ambulance or fire engine passes the office, I tremble. There must be lots of women out there like me. I have no one to listen to my fears, and I worry a lot. If I paid a sitter, it wouldn't make sense for me to work."

There are indeed other women "out there" like this worried mother. Nearly 30% with children age 6 to 13 reported leaving their children home alone or with brothers and sisters after school. Another 15% left the question unanswered, suggesting that they had no appropriate child-care arrangements to report, and that their children, too, may be home by themselves.

What is happening with this new generation of middle-class youth left alone and on their own? It is still too soon to tell, but as one mother wrote, describing her neighborhood as filled with "bands of kids just at the age when they want to be 'in' with their friends, alone with temptations and dozens of empty houses—I wonder what society will be like when these children who have grown up with so little care and guidance are in charge of the country."

The basic problem is one of supply and demand: too many children needing child care, and too few qualified people to supply it at reasonable rates. Double-digit inflation and the high divorce rate are driving mothers back to work. The same pressures—plus the growing mobility of the American family—have all but taken out of circulation the relatives and neighbors mothers used to depend on to look after the kids when they had to work. Grannies and aunties, mothers write, often live hundreds of miles away, or—like the next-door neighbor—are holding down jobs themselves.

Contrary to a 1976 Department of Commerce report which said that three-fourths of working mothers' 3 to 13-year-old children were cared for by husbands or other relatives when they are working, only one mother in five in our survey reported having such help. And interestingly, only one mother in 10 would by choice leave her child in the care of a relative—a finding that strongly contradicts the popular opinion of child experts who claim that the next-best thing to child-rearing by mother is child-rearing by a child's relative.

Many mothers (40%), our survey found, take their infants and preschoolers to either day-care mothers who care for one or two other children, often along with their own preschoolers; or to family homes, where, typically, an older woman cares for as many as 20 or 30 children with some help from her own grown children or a paid assistant or two.

About the same percentage (45%) use nursery or pre-schools (21.4%), day-care centers (18.8%) or Head Start or public kindergarten programs (5.7%), and must arrange additional care for the several hours per day when preschools are not normally in session. One in 10 seems to rely on a baby-sitter or housekeeper coming to the home.

Care for babies and for toddlers who are not toilet-trained is so hard to find that mothers of babies say they look forward to first grade when their kids will be safely in school with trained, responsible teachers. However, mothers whose kids have reached that landmark report that "older is not easier." As one wrote, "Even if they are trustworthy and responsible, seven-year-olds should not be alone every day

---

SIX THINGS TO DO TO KEEP CHILDREN WHO ARE HOME ALONE SAFE AND CONTENT

1. Tape on the inside of the telephone receiver cradle a list of important phone numbers: your work number, your husband's work number, the doctor, fire and police department, a neighbor, one or two relatives. Let your child know that when necessary it is all right to call you at work. 2. List productive things your child can do until you get home. These might be "brainstormed" together over the weekend and written in on a special "after school" calendar. Include fun activities such as making a dessert or assembling a jigsaw puzzle, as well as homework assignments and household chores. Remember to leave careful instructions for using the stove and to review them occasionally with your child. 3. Make use of a tape recorder for taping last-minute instructions that your child can play back when he or she returns from school. 4. Have a favorite nutritious snack ready when your child gets home. Try to vary the snack. 5. Have an emergency procedure established for your child in the event of an accident or other mishaps. 6. Set guidelines for what your child should do about phone calls or people coming to the door when you're not home, and practice these procedures.

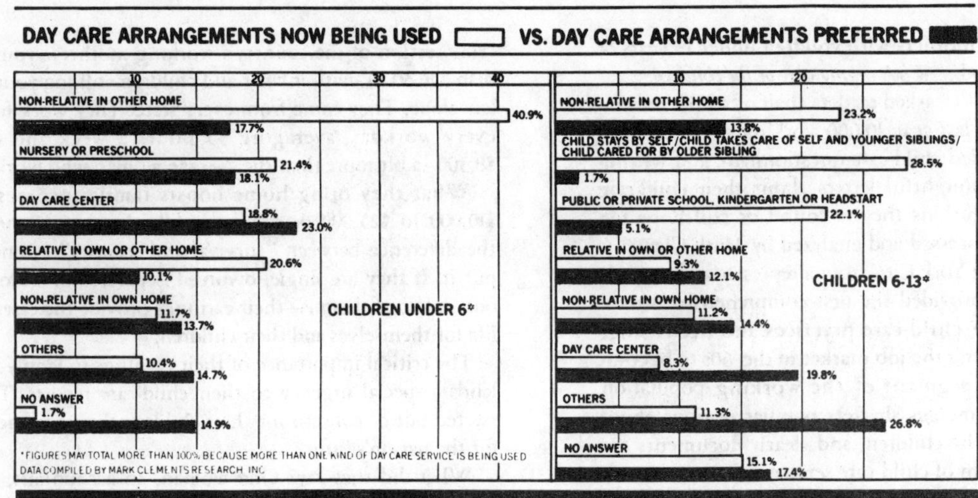

WHAT TO LOOK FOR WHEN CHOOSING A DAY CARE CENTER

The Early Childhood Education Administration Institute of Trinity College in Washington, D.C., a nonprofit organization that specializes in training day-care personnel and also assists parents who are looking for day-care facilities, has compiled the checklist below for parents to use in judging day-care centers. Try to evaluate at least two day-care centers for comparison before making a selection, advises Cynthia Jones, director of the Institute. Here are her other suggestions for making an accurate evaluation:

OBSERVE THE CHILDREN 1. Do the children in the day-care center seem relaxed and sure of themselves, or do they appear to be tense and anxious? 2. Do they seem to like each other? 3. Are they interested most of the time in some activity? 4. Do they seem comfortable talking, and asking questions easily, or are they often silent? 5. Are they using all of their senses to discover and explore their play materials and surroundings?

OBSERVE THE TEACHER 1. Does the teacher in the day-care program welcome each child and seem to be aware of what each is doing? 2. Does she speak naturally and directly to a child, stooping to his or her eye level? 3. Does she step in to stop fights or change activities before behavior becomes disruptive? 4. Does she become upset and judgmental when accidents occur? 5. Does she show respect and genuine interest in a child's work, or does every project get a meaningless "That's nice," or, worse, a damaging critical evaluation such as, "Trees don't have green trunks!"?

OBSERVE THE PROGRAM 1. Does the day-care program follow a rigid time schedule, or a natural sequence? 2. Are there activities for individuals and small groups as well as for the whole class? 3. Do some activities offer quiet experiences and opportunities to explore and manipulate objects? 4. Are all children expected to take part in all activities every day, or is there opportunity for individual choice? 5. Are the children's interests and comments taken into consideration in the planning of activities, or are all the activities planned by teachers? To get all the information you need, don't hesitate to ask the teacher questions such as: What specific activities are being offered? How does she plan to carry them out? And what are her professional credentials?

from 2:30 until 6, and during vacations. It's too lonely. They're much too immature to be by themselves that much."

By far the largest group (over a third) who have after-school care for their young school children use non-relatives—often the day-care mother or woman in the family home the child stayed with before he or she started school. And at this stage, only one mother in 10 has help from relatives.

Child care during vacations and when children are sick is harder to find than regular day care for babies. Parents simply can't "afford" sick children, and they report that fear of a child becoming ill is one of their greatest concerns. For two mothers in every three, the only solution is to stay home themselves. Only one mother in seven reports that her husband can or does share sick child care.

In what ways do these women assess their child care? A very solid majority (70%) say that adequate child care helps their job performance, suggesting that working mothers function better on the job when they know their children are being cared for. Another 62% say child care helps their children and 84% say their children are doing well in child care. Just as many (72%) say they have the child care they want.

But their answers to other questions, and the letters they write, tell a different story. Though mothers say they are fairly content, they voted for quite different types of arrangements when we asked them to select the child care they'd prefer if they had a *choice*.

Significantly, not one mother in a hundred would leave her children home alone if she had any choice, although almost a third of them reporting do so now.

It was day-care centers with *trained staff* that headed the list of preferred child-care service by our survey mothers. Many more mothers would use such care if they could, and many fewer would have their children with day-care mothers or in family homes. Only 18% would take their infants and preschoolers to day-care mothers and family homes—down from 41% now using such care. Specifically, 23% would enroll their children in day-care centers if they could, up from 19% whose children now go to such centers.

Evidently, well-staffed day-care centers are not perceived as cold, sterile institutions by working mothers (dispelling another commonly held notion), but as comfortable, pleasant places run by trained people who will properly take care of the children. More than half the mothers using family homes and day-care mothers for their preschoolers would switch to day-care centers if they could, which indicates that day-care mothers and family homes may not be doing the best job possible.

Mothers themselves report as much. Many complain that their children who are with day-care mothers or in family homes are often kept pacified with junk food and television. "It's nothing but custodial chaos," one mother says. Another tells of a day-care mother who left her infant charge strapped into a car seat for several hours while she went shopping.

Mothers with young school children age 6 to 13 would also prefer day-care centers to non-relatives for care during out-of-school times. While fewer than 1 in 10 now uses a day-care center, one in ten says she would if she could; and only 14% would have their school children with day-care mothers or in family homes when school is out—down from 23% now relying on these kinds of care.

These discrepancies between what working mothers say they want and what they are in fact forced to use indicates that good, reasonably priced day care is simply not readily available. Mothers complained in their letters about day care's high costs (averaging $29.35 per week per child), inconvenient locations, and the bureaucracy of licensing regulations that they say forces good day-care operations out of business and discourages others from starting. They also plead for changes to eliminate "Catch-22" welfare regulations which purportedly deprive them of federally funded day care as soon as they begin to earn enough to make ends meet.

Engineering any change in child-care arrangements usually involves so much stress and strain for both the parent and child that no working mother undertakes it lightly. But three out of five FAMILY CIRCLE mothers made such changes in the past two years. Many changes are naturally inevitable (45%): Children outgrow care, work schedules change, families move. But it was undependability and poor quality of care that forced half of the survey mothers to look for new arrangements.

Answers to other survey questions confirm that for more than 60% of these mothers, tender, responsive and dependable people caring for their children is more important than any other aspect of child care. And lack of these qualities gets to the heart of their child-care problems. Responded one working mother who decided to stop working and stay home after her 16-month-old had been through nine child-care services in one year: "I can't risk our most prized possession any longer."

Yet most working mothers have to and want to continue working but they need financial help for child care in order to do so. They don't want *free* child care, however. Fewer than one in ten favors Federally funded, no-fee day care for all. Most (68%) want to pick the kind of care that suits their children and pay on a sliding scale based on earnings. Helping to pay for their childrens' care, they feel, will give them a voice in the child care, thus ensuring the kind of care they *want*.

Some FAMILY CIRCLE mothers favor a child-care system based on Federal subsidies to all mothers of young children, so that those who want to stay home can afford to, while those who want to work can afford the cost of child care.

Others propose more generous tax credits for child care, and some say that child-care services set up at companies where mothers work—supported by employers, workers and Federal subsidies—could, alone, solve the child-care problem.

Clearly, there are no satisfactory answers for everyone. But it is also just as clear that more and more mothers are starting to work, will continue to work, have to work, and want to work. They apparently also intend to try to solve their child-care problems.

But as the number of mothers joining the work force increases, the question of child care may become the most pressing one facing the next generation. The child-care question will require new answers—not just from working mothers, but from employers and the Federal Government. The future of our children demands that the answers be swift in coming.

Day Care in the Schools?

A Response to the Position of the AFT

A fast developing awareness of this country's expanding need for day care services is meeting head on with recent conditions of staff surplus and underutilized space in public schools. (American Federation of Teachers 1976, p. 2)

James Greenman

James Greenman, M.A., is Day Care Consultant/Instructor in Child Development at Iowa State University, Ames, Iowa. He has taught in day care, Head Start, and parent education programs.

That observation begins *Putting Early Education and Day Care Services into the Public Schools* (1976), a carefully constructed, extensive argument that the schools are the logical sites for day care, prepared by an American Federation of Teachers (AFT) task force. The AFT is pushing the notion that any new large child care funding proposals, successors to the vetoed Child and Family Services Act, have as a feature the "presumed prime sponsorship" of public school systems. That is, unless a particular school system was unwilling, or unable and declined, all federally-supported child care programs would be administered by local school districts. The potential implications of a mass institutionalization of child care in the schools requires a close examination of all of the issues contained in the AFT position. What is at stake is not only jobs and power, but the course of childrearing in our society.

The AFT Position

There are two main lines of argument in the AFT report. The first and least controversial argues the need to greatly expand early childhood education and day care services. The second line proposes that school systems are the natural overseers for this expansion.

The Need for Expansion

The task force marshalls the familiar arguments for expansion: changing demographics, the inadequacy of current children's services, and the importance of early experience. There is little with which to take issue. But one curious point should be noted. There seems to be a deliberate ambiguity maintained by continually using the phrase "day care and early childhood services." Expansion of day care programs and expansion of early education programs are not the same thing. While all early childhood programs inherently involve care and education, one can take different positions on the need to expand day care programs and other early education programs. The ambiguity allows the task force to use the inadequacy of present *day care* services, excluding Head Start and nursery schools, as a rationale for all early *education* programs receiving public funds to be funded through the schools, presumably including Head Start and publicly-supported nursery schools. Similarly, the ambiguity allows the task force to offer the schools' ability to provide early education as proof of a capacity to provide child care services.

The task force also neglects to make an important point about expanding services. Expansion itself is not the end, the good desired. The goal is better child care and support of families, and there are various means to that end. Expansion proposals have to be evaluated in terms of the resulting benefits and costs to the kind of society that we value.

The Logic of Public School Sponsorship

The complexity and poor quality of existing services and the contrasting benefits of the public school system are the basic premises of the AFT position statement.

The Present System. The task force thoroughly details the chaotic, fragmented, child care delivery "system." The existing state of day care reflects its marginal position as a social institution. Most day care homes and centers are barely adequate or worse in terms of care and education. Standards of quality vary widely and official standards are usually minimal. Licensing procedures are often inadequate and standards go unmonitored. Coordination is lacking at all levels.

The task force makes a strong case against public dollars supporting profit-making centers and the need to develop alternatives to these centers which currently serve over fifty percent of the children who are in centers. They also argue that as long as day care support includes priorities based on income, day care will remain inadequately funded and largely custodial.

It is difficult to disagree with these statements. (The question of priority based on income is controversial and too complex to consider in this article.) However, it is curious that the AFT, unlike most critics, pays little attention to the actual low level of funding that the current delivery system has available. The clear implication is that while a great increase in funding is necessary, putting it into the present system is throwing good money after bad.

"School Systems Offer the Best Alternative." The AFT (1976) maintains that the public school system is a "single, democratically controlled structural entity" able to administer high quality comprehensive day care and early childhood services:

- School systems offer an existing coordinating system of quality regulations and standards, and an experienced administrative structure capable of developing and monitoring programs.

- School systems guarantee democratic control by taxpayers and have built-in provisions for parent involvement.

- School systems are in an ideal position to deliver comprehensive services because of their established relationships with related human service agencies.

- Public school coordination will have a beneficial effect on cost by the utilization of existing space and resources and the general efficiency of a single delivery system.

- Public schools are capable of providing variable and flexible programs and can incorporate existing homes and centers that can meet public school standards.

- Public schools offer the ideal framework for a free, universally available child care system.

"Public schools offer the best immediate guarantee of quality," but the task force, mindful of the suspicions of school critics and the early childhood education establishment's fear of a "downward extension of schooling," acknowledges there are "areas in need of development if the public schools are to assume responsibility for day care programs."

First mentioned is the need for a longer school day and year, and the task force quickly notes that this means a subsequent increase in compensation for teachers. Special arrangements may have to be made for parent involvement. Also, "without relaxing any standards," public schools will have to be flexible enough to admit existing programs. Schools will have to recognize the "variable developmental needs of preschool children" and avoid the schooling mold, but "most public school people really do understand this since they have been parents themselves" (a rather surprising and questionable argument). Certification of preschool personnel will have to be standardized and brought up to school standards. Thus, the AFT position is that schools are fully prepared with a viable delivery system and are aware of the necessary minor adjustments. Whether this is in fact the case is the critical issue.

Day Care and Schooling: Some Differences

Before examining the merits of the AFT position, it is important to pin down some of the differences between what is involved in day care and in schooling. We are accustomed to hearing day care and early education combined under the rubric "early childhood programs," and this tends to obscure the fact that there are basic differences. The distinctions tend to be elusive because they are largely a matter of priority and degree in two areas. One area involves who has primary responsibility and control over childrearing and socialization of the child: the family, or the state? The second concerns the development differences between infants and older children. That the distinctions are difficult to make does not alter their importance.

Differences in Orientation

Day care programs are designed to supplement a family's childrearing capability. The best day care has the home as its analogue. The concern is total development, physical, social, emotional, and cognitive, but not divisible into neat slots. Ideally the individual family's needs and desires would be in complete harmony with the goals and practices of the program. The parents' values and goals would provide the basis for the daily experience of the child. Like the family, day care should be idiographic: The care is a particular response to individual children rather than directed toward children in general. This does not imply an impossible task. Children are alike in many ways and families share many similar goals and values. Rather, program planners must recognize, appreciate, plan for, and act on the basis of how children differ as well as what they have in common. Further, they must understand that children are not only starting at different points and moving at different speeds but are also each on different roads with different destinations as well.

Also like the home, a day care program's first priority is the daily quality of life that the children experience. "Work," or training for future development, is an essential aspect of the program, but the first evaluative criteria is whether the center is a good place for the child to spend the day.

Public schooling's basic priorities are centered not on the individual family but on the broader goals of the community. Schools are designed to educate children in a certain manner, whether individual parents approve or not. Parents and children are expected to accommodate the schools. The primary focus of schools is not to enhance the specific development of an individual child, but to attempt to ensure that each child attain a certain level of knowledge and skills. The emphasis is nomothetic on the ways in which we want our children to be alike. Returning to the road metaphor, the children are all on the same road with the same destination. Individualization in school terms usually refers to children's need to travel at different speeds and with different aids. The school's concern is also narrower than day care, more focused on particular cognitive skills. And it is not the quality of life that the child experiences that is of primary importance, but his or her progression to a future state of knowledge and expertise. School is clearly the child's work.

Preschool education programs vary on the idiographic-nomothetic continuum. Traditional nursery programs tend to fall on the idiographic end while some more recent "compensatory" programs have a nomothetic emphasis.

It may seem unfair to compare day care as it ought to be and school as it is. Schools perhaps should have an idiographic focus. Many of the attempts at school reform have been directed at the need to pay more attention to the process, the quality of life that children experience, and to recognize individual and cultural differences. And certainly, most day care centers in many respects disregard individual differences and expect the children and their families to accommodate the center rather than the reverse. Yet the comparison is necessary because like it or not, schools have become primarily institutions of the state, and the individual's relationship to them is little different than to other state institutions. Childrearing has yet to be turned over to the state and if this separation is to continue, maintaining the home, not the school, as analogue is critical. Supplementing, not supplanting, the family is the function of day care.

Differences in Working with Younger Children

Important program implications stem from the nature of children under five years old. The younger the child, the more a program must accommodate the children to achieve desired goals. The young child is less able to accommodate the role demands, time schedules, and pace of others. Separating teaching and care is difficult because the child determines when his or her emotional or expressive needs require attention, and because the value of direct instruction is greatly reduced. It is important to recognize that the entire day is the day care curriculum—breakfast, small groups, naps, playground, and transition times.

Consistency of care and constancy of caregivers is important for young children. In day care with ten-hour days, it is even more important that children experience a reliable environment and a small number of adults with whom they can relate. This is administratively difficult, however, and usually requires administrative flexibility.

Organizational Requirements

In contrast to both public schooling and nursery schools, the scheduling of day care programs is determined by the needs of the parents. The long day and year are not based on administrative nicety or child development factors. Enrolling infants, having children arrive and leave at different times of the day or year, or having a twelve-hour day may not be sound from the basis of the best way to run an educational program. But this may be the best or only way to supplement the child care needs of the community.

Organization of day care programs is complicated and unfortunately has not always been given the careful thought that its complexity requires. To staff a ten- to twelve-hour day for twenty three-year-olds requires a minimum of four classroom staff. Infants and toddlers require more staff hours, four- and five-year-olds less. A day care classroom does not involve the solitary endeavor of one adult but a group effort. And to produce consistent care and quality education by a group process requires a sophisticated communication process.

Role Differences. The AFT position recognizes the need not to force programs for young children into a "schooling mold," but this recognition does not extend much further than the need to avoid didactic instruction. The "schooling mold" not only involves patterns of staff/child interaction but patterns (or the absence of patterns) of staff/parent and intrastaff interaction and communication.

Parent-staff relationships are necessarily different in day care than in public schools. Not only is more communication required, but there are shifts in power relationships. Parents are the only ones in a position to say "this is the kind of child that we are trying to raise"—independent or interdependent, aggressive, reflecting traditional sex roles, or manifesting certain cultural values. This is a right that parents in our society have always had. This is not to say that day care staff abdicate their professional judgment. However, professionals recognize that they cannot assist parents in raising children without knowing the expectations that the parents have. Parents need the benefit of staff knowledge and expertise and need expanded alternatives to their childrearing practices. They need support and, in turn, need to understand what the staff is doing and why. In good day care, parents have the opportunity to work with staff in nearly all stages of planning, implementation, and evaluation. Conflict and continual delicate negotiation are not inevitable since parents and staff usually agree and share similar values and goals. If there is disagreement, then parental rights and professional limitations must be clearly understood.

Day care classrooms usually involve a teacher and some combination of assistant teachers and aides. There has been little study of how these groups operate. Accustomed to a single teacher/classroom paradigm, we assume it without thought. But in day care the child's experience is the result of the actions of several adults. In a specific classroom, are we to implicitly assume that the outcomes are due to the expertise of the professional (teacher), assisted by additional arms, legs, and warm laps? Or do we use an additive model and assume the total collective knowledge and experience of all classroom staff generates the outcomes? Specifying division of responsibility and authority in job descriptions does not ensure that the division will prove workable and will be carried out in practice.

A study of Head Start teachers and aides found that most teachers and aides expressed a co-teacher ideology, dividing nearly all responsibility equally and disavowing the hierarchical authority relationship (Jacobson 1973). This is a common pattern in day care and may be due to:

- The work itself is difficult to divide on an instructional—noninstructional basis, the usual dividing line between teacher and aide.

- There are few definitive shared assumptions on what programs should entail and the necessary qualifications to carry out such a program.

- Class, race, and cultural differences are often overlaid with the above and may result in difficulties if the "nonprofessionals" are assigned to most or all of the menial tasks, as job descriptions often assume. But if they are not, then the claim to a professional—nonprofessional division is weakened.

- Even with authority granted by recognized expertise, or rank, most people would have difficulty with a hierarchical division of labor in a close working relationship.

We need to explore different alternatives in how to best organize day care programs. Why should a teacher and assistants model be accepted as standard as opposed to a collective work group of equals? Or a head caregiver with assistants, one of whom is an education specialist? One thing is relatively certain: A center classroom will involve a work group, and this means that the outcomes will be generated by the group process, whether we acknowledge this or not. This sets day care staff apart

from the elementary classroom teacher who works largely alone developing and implementing his or her program. The day care teacher may have to function simultaneously as supervisor and subordinate, team member, or manager of a group process, roles most American teachers are rarely called upon to play.

In summary, quality day care is different from schooling in some primary ways. Day care supplements the childrearing capacity of a family and is in concert with the values and goals of the families being served. Day care is idiographic, emphasizing the individual child's developmental continuum as opposed to the nomothetic orientation emphasizing certain things children need to have in common at a certain age. Parental control over childrearing is an American tradition, and day care assumes parental involvement in planning and evaluating the program. The age of the children and the hour of operation ensure a group teaching/caring process—more than one adult with responsibility for a single child. Teachers are cast in some different roles than school teachers are accustomed to, with different relationships to children, parents, and co-workers. In light of these differences, let us return to the AFT argument and the support that the task force advances for its position.

The AFT and Quality Day Care

"The Need for a Single Structure Delivery System"

The task force criticism of the present delivery system is difficult to fault. But do the failings of the present system necessarily point to the need for a "single structural entity"? The AFT does not consider that financing, not lack of coordination, may be the key variable determining quality. Further, they do not discuss the drawbacks inherent in a centralized system.

The issue is how to develop a rational, efficient system that is responsive to specific demand, providing the variety of child care necessary in a multicultural society.

The present system has one critical virtue: It is not overcentralized. A range of existing programs offers a choice of child care styles and ideologies. Child care occurs in homes, centers, schools, and churches. Care is provided by people of different classes and cultures who hold different beliefs and values. However, because of inadequate supply and lack of coordination, many families in reality have few choices and must take what they can find.

Yet increased coordination, like increased supply, is not an end in itself. Moving to a single structure delivery system is by no means a certain improvement. The central question becomes: What is the quality of care it can deliver and at what cost?

The Suitability of Public Schools

Clearly the public schools are best suited to coordinate and manage early childhood programs. Not only do they exist in every type of community, but they also have an established administrative structure and experience in managing large scale programs. Of equally important significance is the school's demonstrated ability to provide flexibility in curriculum, methodology, and delivery mechanisms. Anyone who argues differently has little knowledge of what is going on in schools today. (AFT 1976, p. 90)

Here is the heart of the issue, what the AFT must prove to skeptics. "Presumed prime sponsorship" assumes *all* public school districts are appropriate unless the school system itself chooses to opt out. Therefore we have to look at the general characteristics of schools and school systems, recognizing that there is a continuum of differences.

"The Best Immediate Guarantor of Quality." The AFT maintains that the school systems have the people, the sites, the standards, and the necessary relationships to parents and the community. A number of considerations calls this claim into question.

Throughout the report there is a complete insensitivity to the distinctions between day care and education. Making the case for day care in the schools is different than showing that the schools are capable of providing some early education programs. The task force does the latter and considers that sufficient. For example, in discussing how "early education programs will vary greatly in philosophy, methodology, and emphasis from one school system to another, and *possibly* from one school or classroom to another based on local needs and preferences," the program

variation mentioned is only in terms of educational curriculum models. Offering variety primarily from one school district to another is hardly sufficient.

The same insensitivity is evident in what the task force sees as "questions for the school board to consider" and what by implication are givens: Whether to extend child care beyond school hours, to lengthen the school year, to allow day care homes or nonschool-based programs, to allow infants or toddlers? All day care elements are *questions*, in spite of the fact that the argument for expansion centered on the need to meet the demand for day care. The givens for the AFT that need not be submitted to the school board are the need for certified school teachers and whether to have programs in the school setting. The AFT has reversed the priorities so that the beginning point is not day care but school-based early education. The difference in starting points is critical when it comes down to what is jettisoned in tight money situations or power disputes. Infant and toddler care may be granted lowest priority not because of demand, but because it is least compatible with "education" by teachers' definitions (a prime factor for its disappearance from day nurseries in the past). Program hours may be reduced for budgetary reasons negating the fact that day care serves working families. The AFT task force clearly has little understanding of the complexities involved in meeting the needs for day care.

"Democratic Control" and Parent Involvement. The democratic control discussed by the AFT is at the district level. The task force believes existing mechanisms, the school board, and competing pressure groups are adequate to ensuring democratic control, an arena where the AFT has been particularly successful. But school boards, like other boards, have been weakest in providing for programs that need some differentiation and in meeting the needs of minorities and small special interest groups that lack power. Day care by nature requires differentiation and sensitivity to community groups because it is a response to varied needs.

The AFT recognizes that parent involvement may need to be quantitatively increased: "Many school boards may want to have special advisory councils of early childhood and day care parents that will keep the parents closely informed of the needs and operations of the programs. School-parent linkages in the form of parent education are another possibility which many school systems may choose to explore" (p. 14). The AFT sees parent involvement as a process of influencing, educating, and informing parents. This is important, of course, but of equal importance is parental influence; parents having a direct influence on program goals and outcomes. Parent control of schools may be controversial, but parent control of childrearing is an American tradition. If day care is more closely aligned to the latter, then parent or parent/staff control should not be so controversial.

"Flexible Programming." Public school flexibility can either refer to: (1) whether schools are flexible enough to extend their operations to include younger children and extended hours, or, (2) whether the schools can offer a variety of programming for young children that is responsive to demand. The AFT maintains the schools are flexible in both respects. As evidence of the first point, they cite the broadening of schools to include kindergarten, special classes, adult education, and curriculum changes over the years. Examples of a Montessori classroom in Cincinnati, Philadelphia's and California's school-based child care programs, the Brookline Early Education Project, and the existence of home-based nutrition programs are heralded as examples of how "in one place or another, the public school system has already demonstrated its ability to provide a variety of forms of comprehensive early childhood services" (AFT 1976, p. 83). Also, the task force maintains that there is no obstacle to incorporating day care homes or existing variable day care programs into the public school network **if**, and this is a crucial if, they meet school standards. Standards which must not be relaxed, the task force adds.

The question is not whether a school district can administer some early childhood programs, but whether schools are the natural overseers of child care and that all federal dollars should be entrusted to them. The AFT arguments in favor of the school's suitability are woefully inadequate. True,

kindergarten has been assimilated into some schools, but not in a manner that has required much accommodation by the schools. Citing examples of where a few school systems have offered program variations simply leaves the impression that these are carefully chosen exceptions. We are also not provided with any indication whether these programs are successful. California children's centers run the gamut from abysmal to excellent.

Schooling in this country has largely been marked by its continuity and uniformity, not by flexibility and change. Schools today are alike in nearly all important respects. The self-contained, teacher directed, age graded classroom is the rule. Goodlad et al. (1970) discovered in a survey of schools that despite the beliefs of many teachers and administrators that they were engaged in new and innovative practices, this was rarely the case. Regardless of community, children and teachers are likely to be engaged in nearly identical activities in similar surroundings. For good or ill, most changes introduced in the schools continue to be eventually incorporated into the schooling mold. The following passage gives an indication of the thinking that makes this inevitable:

> Language and cultural differences are particularly delicate issues when dealing with very young children and school systems will have to make sure that they have the necessary *specialists* to handle the language training of preschool children and to deal with the sense of separateness which children of particular cultures or races may experience. In large cities, to be sure, the heavy use of paraprofessionals, many of whom tend to be from the community being served and therefore members of ethnic groups of the children they work with, will help fill these particular needs. (AFT 1976, p. 16)

Differences, like the language of young children, are handled by specialists or by adding special classes. If the population changes, then paraprofessionals from the "native" community can be brought in. Change is envisioned as adding on to the basic mold. Additional basic accommodation is not considered.

The task force qualifies all statements about allowing nonschool-based programs by insisting on the need to meet school standards. These standards are equated with quality. If programs cannot meet them then it is no loss because they are of insufficient quality. The AFT makes clear that teacher credentials are the key to standards, thus to quality. But credentialing involves not only educational issues, but socioeconomic and political ones as well. What education, training, and experience required will affect who will have access to credentials. The AFT adopts the traditional school approach and proposes that only teachers with at least a B.A. in education and some early childhood training can guarantee quality, a reasonable starting point perhaps. But an equally reasonable starting point would be a requirement that individuals responsible for child care programs must demonstrate an ability and willingness to understand, relate to, and utilize the culture of the community being served. One can argue either point but neither is really a guarantee of quality.

At every point in its report the AFT makes clear that there is no compromise on its position that "qualified" teachers must be used and existing teachers given priority. The first priority is jobs for teachers. There is no effort to try and deal with the complicated issues around credentialing. No attempts to explore what are some of the variables in quality day care. There is no concern to have minorities responsible for programs—minority paraprofessionals or specialists will serve that need. Flexibility in staffing is not an alternative to the AFT.

There is an additional probable obstacle to the "flexible" programming envisioned by the AFT. An original selling point was the existence of empty classrooms and available staff, attractive from a cost-efficiency standpoint. All the program variations mentioned either do not use these classrooms or people, or they require some changes and thus additional costs (retraining personnel or redesigning classrooms, for example). It is reasonable to assume that all cost-increasing accommodations to day care programs, given the current state of school funding, would not be implemented. Similarly, there is no guarantee that a requirement that teachers of young children have early childhood or day care training (or even have a desire to work with young children) will not fall before the imperatives of the seniority systems and teacher/school board politics.

Schools and the Potential for Change

Perhaps it may be argued that while schools have not shown much flexibility in the past, this does not mean that they cannot change and given the chance offer decent child care that is reasonably responsive to communities. This seems unlikely. If day care demands an idiographic orientation, a marked change from schooling, then a school system would have to begin its accommodation from that starting point. Special classes, an academic credential, or bureaucratic standards, may or may not be appropriate but we cannot start with them as givens. The new learning required by day care providers and the need to adopt new relationships to parents, children, and other school personnel will not happen in the midst of a large system where traditional attitudes and practices continue, ingrained by tradition and the resistance to institutional change. The point to consider schools as a viable alternative is when school stakeholders are offering evidence of their own flexibility: Unions discussing a more open credentialing process or parent rights; administrators considering decentralization and teacher-parent control over materials. It is when we are discussing alternatives to our present comfortable and valued ways of behaving to adjust to new demands that the potential for flexibility and change becomes realizable.

Day Care—Where

The schools cannot guarantee quality, only the provision of some services. They can offer no safeguard against the possibility that child care services, like schooling, will become uniform and the first step in a thoroughly institutionalized life.

What alternatives are there? There has been no serious national commitment to provide quality child care services. If a national family policy were developed and adequate resources committed, a variety of child care programs could be generated and monitored at the neighborhood level. Programs failing to meet *community* standards can be closed once alternatives are available. Child care funding can be removed from welfare programs and be used to subsidize supply as well as demand. We do not need a new bureaucracy; we need a new commitment of support and resources that can maintain quality and generate flexible responses to changing community needs.

Through a Glass Darkly:

Television and the Perception of Reality

DOROTHY H. COHEN

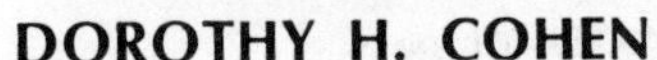

Dorothy H. Cohen is senior faculty member of the Graduate Programs for Bank Street College of Education in New York City, where she teaches Child Development.

TELEVISION is a remarkable invention that is clearly changing everybody's world, if for no other reason than the obvious one that all parts of the world— and outer space, too—can become visible to any individual anywhere. But this beautiful invention is at present only minimally devoted to extending our understanding of other people and cultures, to stretching our minds, and to expanding our spirits. Because of its commercial sponsorship, however, it is changing us, to an unfortunate extent, more toward accepting as reality a mindless, spiritless, distorted perception of life than it is toward deepening our understanding of what is truly real. Analyses of the negative aspects of the programming we are exposed to are only just beginning to be pieced together, and they form a frightening picture.

The connection between commercial sponsorship and the effect of television on our perception of the world was most recently explored by George Gerbner and Larry Gross of the University of Pennsylvania's Annenberg School of Communication. From their research into how and what viewers perceive, they concluded: "In the process of serving corporate needs, television has also become the mainstream of the symbolic environment cultivating common conceptions of life, society, and the world." [1]

How true to reality is that perception of life? What are its effects on people? The Gerbner-Gross study points out that "television realism makes it more difficult for viewers to distinguish between what they see on TV and real life." As one example, the authors quote the complaint of a district attorney that television makes it difficult to obtain convictions because juries expect a dramatic confession or revelation as evidence of guilt. The district attor-

"Through a Glass Darkley: Television and the Perception of Reality," *National Elementary Principal*, Vol. 56, No. 3, January/February 1977, pp. 22-29. ©1977 The National Elementary Principal.

ney's complaint stems from the fact that the judicial process as we see it on television rarely shows plea bargaining or the process through which judges do most of the judging. TV's image of juries and suspenseful drama in every courtroom seems to create unconscious resistance among jurors to engage in the struggle of sifting evidence and thinking their way through to a judgment about the guilt or inno- as full of police and detectives?

Research shows that children with a tendency to aggressive behavior increase their destructiveness after exposure to violent shows on television.[9] A study done over a ten-year period by Leonard Eron found that boys who preferred programs of violence at age eight were more aggressive at eighteen (regardless of the kinds of programs they watched) than other eighteen-year-olds. While the tendency to aggressive behavior could come from home and family, Eron suggests that there might be a "central developmental period in a boy's life when he is very susceptible to the influence of violent TV."[10] The whole question of critical periods for certain kinds of experience has not yet been assessed in relation to television's impact, nor in the planning of programs that children see.

Eron is also finding, in his more recent research, that nine-year-old girls are showing a taste for violence far greater

---

"Four times as many men as women appear on television and . . . most of the women shown are without jobs."

---

than was true when he started his study ten years earlier. Perhaps the influence of the women's liberation movement is inadvertently opening up this hitherto masculine status symbol to girls, which is, if true, a distortion of the meaning of liberation.

We also have empirical evidence that children who see a great deal of violence become satiated and apathetic about violence, lose their sensitivity to it, and cease

to react to it with revulsion. Some experienced early childhood teachers speak with concern about the failure of many children to even notice, much less react to, the aggressive behavior they see in others. This observation disturbs them more than the aggressive behavior itself. "It's as though they don't know the difference," the teachers say, "as though aggression is the norm." This blasé reaction becomes completely logical when we realize that the sense of reality in children of three, four, and five years of age is still hardly firm. For example, early childhood teachers know from children's conversations that they have difficulty distinguishing between program content and commercials; nor do children understand why the characters on the screen do not respond when they talk to them.

Two pieces of research on young children's viewing help explain why they are particularly vulnerable. The first, by Friedlander, Whetstone, and Scott, shows that young children have difficulty distinguishing relevant from irrelevant detail and figuring out the central informational themes of a program, which is completely consistent with Piaget's description of the preoperational child.[11]

The second, by Aimee Leifer, found that when young children watch shows of crime and violence, they fail to get the message that crime does not pay; instead, they take literally the message that violence is a primary method of solving all kinds of problems.[12]

It is a fact that television viewing starts early in babyhood and goes on forever after. Is it too much to suggest that television's projection of violence as the major strategy in problem solving, whether for good or bad purposes, is at least one important contributing factor to an American phenomenon that was described in a recent news report, carrying the headline: "Violence in Schools Now Seen as the Norm Across the Nation"?[13] The article stated that school officials themselves are anesthetized to the problem of violence and that many of them consider a certain number of incidents inevitable.

TV is obviously not responsible for the desperation that drives people to crime. But it is responsible for making violence appear to be an everyday fact of life, thereby dulling the senses of children and adults to brutality. It is TV that has established violence as a norm instead of the unusual occurrence that it is among most people—moreover, that it is something to be abhorred or understood when it does happen, not glorified. How can children develop a sense of balance about human behavior, much less a moral conviction about violence of people toward each other, when 71 percent of the Saturday morning children's programs regularly involve at least one violent action?

To the violence and prejudicial views of women that are prevalent on television, we can unhappily add the distortion of the life-style of minority groups. Although programs have been forced to change their attitudes toward nonwhite groups as a result of the civil rights movement, minority groups are still not being treated with total respect. In television shows as late as 1969, "foreigners and those not identifiable as Americans were increasingly more likely to become involved in violence and pay a higher price for it than were Americans." [14] And although blacks are now being given recognition in our television shows, their role is strongly as supporters of the status quo. Their television behavior is unbelievably conventional. The most undeveloped, the gross, and the ridiculous are other common aspects of black characterizations. [15]

Another norm of life developed for children through TV viewing is the attractiveness of being a consumer. A four-and-a-half-year-old child turned on his mother in a store recently when she refused to buy a military toy advertised on TV and forcefully stated his view of parenthood for all to hear. "You're not a good mother," he said. "You don't buy me everything I want." A little girl of the same age, interviewed by a student at the Harvard Graduate School of Education, said she loved "Captain Kangaroo" because of the commercials. "On 'Captain Kangaroo,'" this child said, "you see all of those things you want to buy, and you ask your mother if you can have them and she says, 'Put them on your Christmas list.'" When the mother was asked by the interviewer if this was so, she groaned and shook her head affirmatively.

A particularly disgraceful aspect of the early seduction into the consumer role by television is the indifference to children's health in appeals that violate known principles of nutrition. Despite the research by dentists and nutritionists about the harmful effects of sugar, the number of commercials on children's programs for sugared cereals over a nine-month period in 1975 was 3,832, in contrast to 2 commercials for meat and poultry; for candy and gum it was 1,627, in contrast to 1 for cheese and none for milk or eggs. Of the cereals in the top 20 advertised for children, only 3 had as little as 2.2 to 10.6 percent sugar in them. The rest were made up of from 29 to 68 percent sugar. [16] The advertising industry admits that this exploitation of children is deliberate. [17] The industry spares no expense and employs the most sophisticated research psychologists to find out what children are like— the better to seduce them with appealing commercials. [18] The young child's difficulty with self-denial is institutionalized to become a harrowing element of parent-child interaction. Unfortunately, five years of protest by parents through Action for Children's Television has thus far not made much of a dent.

Still other problems develop as children grow older. An unexpected by-product of the emphasis on consumerism is the appearance of cynicism in children long before any human being should, if indeed anyone ever should, become cynical.

A study by Bever and Smith, a psychologist and an advertising agent, revealed the following about children's responses to commercials: children of five and six tend to believe that everything on television, including the commercials, is entertainment, but children between seven and ten grow increasingly confused and upset as

"TV is obviously not responsible for the desperation that drives people to crime. But it is responsible for making violence appear to be an everyday fact of life..."

"they feel forced to accept practices they believe are immoral." In an article in the *Harvard Business Review,* the authors wrote, "The ten-year-old's anger appears to reflect the first realization that society allows for institutional hypocrisy, a fact that violates moral precepts he/she has been taught as a young child." This example is much like the letdown adolescents feel when they first encounter the contradictions between the idealized image and the reality of social practice. It is difficult enough for adolescents, who must develop their own value system and mode of functioning by first resolving the contradictions between the ideal and the social reality that upsets them. But this crisis is coming at a time when children are too young to cope with it, and they grow cynical, another way of saying they turn sour on life. As the researchers describe it, eleven- and twelve-year-olds in the study were no longer seriously affected by the commercials because "they had made certain accommodations to the adult world and its values." [19]

Familiarity with this state of development makes it likely that accommodation to value contradictions at age twelve does not involve the evolution of a personal code of ethics and a philosophical view of self and the world, but, instead, becomes the cynicism I am talking about. Children may indeed not be taken in by the commercials forever, but the premature adjustment to institutionalized hypocrisy may, in the words of the researchers, "lead to permanent distortion of their views of morality, society, and business."

∽

In assessing the total impact of television, many people point positively to the amount of new information that it is possible to acquire despite the medium's obvious shortcomings. This viewpoint is potentially, and even at times actually, true. Yet the management of information for young children has, for the most part, been less than adequate. More typically, children become quite knowledgeable in matters that are not too important or that are much beyond them; they become verbal, but not knowing. Their pseudo-sophistication raises a nagging question of whether *real* learning occurs from

"The young child's difficulty with self-denial is institutionalized to become a harrowing element of parent-child interaction."

watching much of what is presently offered. Terry Barton, writing about dual audio TV, a procedure that he hoped would aid comprehension in children, says:

TV has exposed the modern child to a greater variety of cultures than the best traveled and most highly educated man of fifty years ago and provided a bombardment of language unequaled in the experience of any previous generation. And yet many children come to school speaking few of the words they have heard—able to recite commercials and program titles, but knowing little information from TV that would be useful to them in school or later life. . . . How can a child watch TV for an average of seven hours a day, observing life, and listening to language, and yet learn so little? [20]

For the youngest children, there is not only the question of nonlearning, but the more serious question of whether television viewing—at least at the rate of many hours a day, which is presently popular in the United States—does not interfere with the learning process. There is evidence of such a possibility, although it is possible, of course, that certain children are more vulnerable than others to such interference for reasons we do not yet understand. According to Werner Halpern, director of the Children and Youth Division of the Rochester, New York, Mental Health Center and clinical assistant professor of psychiatry at the University of Rochester, "In 1972, there was a sudden upsurge of patients in the age-group [of] two to three from among all socioeconomic classes. Among fourteen out of sixteen cases, the principal symptoms were the children's driven restlessness at nap or bedtime, inattentiveness to parental guidance, and preference for manipulating articles rather than negotiating with people." The parents all thought the children were very bright. But Halpern saw toddlers who "compulsively recited serial numbers and letters, and who inspected their inanimate surroundings like restless, wound-up robots." [21]

The increase in two- and three-year-old applicants to a mental health clinic could not be explained by agency growth or new agency programs. But broadcasting time for "Sesame Street" had increased in Rochester in 1972, and since several children were reported to be habitually stimulated by that program (many showed learning from it), Halpern pursued that clue and analyzed the teaching method of "Sesame Street." He found the program to be dependent on repetition and rapid manipulation of object attributes, a style deliberately drawn from the commercials. Halpern describes the techniques of "Sesame Street" as ". . . the application of shock to the sense barriers by intrusive signaling of kinetic symbols; avoiding a time lag between messages so as to delay reflection; and capturing attention by using dominating visual and auditory patterns." [22]

Halpern's analysis led him to hypothesize that sensory overload was the cause of the children's strange behavior. Evidence that sensory overload affects the psychological state of adults was already available, and experimentation with monkeys had shown that when they were overloaded with stimulation to the senses, they "became obtuse to further learning and exhibited a tendency to aimless play and diffuse destructiveness in a 'permanent impairment of their adaptive responses.' "

Were it not that early childhood teachers and also teachers of older children see similar behavior among a sizable minority of children, we might dismiss the symptoms of Halpern's toddlers as a rare phenomenon. But given the increase in frenetic aimlessness, high distractibility, and inability to focus among many more preschool and primary children than experienced teachers remember, it is not too farfetched to suggest that sensory overload may be a significant factor in the almost epidemic proportions of nonlearning among children of all ages and socioeconomic classes now prevalent in American schools.

The assumption that organic limits to sensory loading exists is certainly justified. Millions of children watch television for hours each day without letup, and we know nothing of the effect on them of too much speed, noise, incomprehensibility, or distortion of reality. We can only guess by making analogies with the known effects of too much of any of these; for example, the effect of excessive noise on hearing. It may or may not be coincidental that during the last ten to fifteen years in the United States, we have seen increasing publicity, testing, screening, and manufacturing of materials focused on remedial, perceptual training of kindergarten and first-grade children because a great many children who are failing to learn to read have some kind of perceptual difficulties. Perception is necessary for information processing. Can we make a tentative connection between sensory overload and perceptual problems?

An authoritative volume of research on the process of reading explains perceptual development in the following way:

Perception is the process of abstracting information from stimulation emanating from the objects, places, and events in the world around us. Perceptual learning is learning to extract the relevant information from the available stimulation. . . . Perceptual learning is not response learning, like response to stimulus; it is not problem solving or inference. In a word, perceptual learning is not adding on anything. It is extraction or pulling out rather than adding on.

Perception learning means that perceptions become progressively more differentiated; that attention is better focused as the irrelevant is ignored; and that information is processed more efficiently as children learn to detect order and structure in available information. [23]

Bruner tells us that although learning is helped by repetition and problem solving is based on recognizing patterns in the environment, if the repetition is too complicated for the observer to understand, or if there are so many interferences that the patterns cannot be recognized, it becomes more difficult for children to make sense out of the environment. [24] Thus Bruner's work supports Halpern's assessment that too much, even of a good thing,

"Millions of children watch television for hours each day without letup, and we know nothing of the effect on them of too much speed, noise, incomprehensibility, or distortion of reality."

can be destructive, and it allows us to speculate that sensory overload interferes with normal perceptual development.

If we turn back to Halpern's hypothesis about the toddlers, it is clear that he was concerned that the very young child, who is in the process of developing perceptions of all kinds in sensory-motor fashion, can be diverted from developing the skills of processing information from the environment when that environment is too fast, too rich, largely incomprehensible, noisy, and frenetic.

This matter is yet to be researched, but we do know that children begin to watch television as babies and watch throughout the years when they are learning how to use the feedback from their encounters with the environment. Educators know that distractibility, poor concentration, and inability to focus are widespread. It is not unreasonable to hypothesize that sensory overload contributes to inadequate perceptual readiness for reading by aborting normal growth—even if only in children with certain kinds of vulnerability. In this regard, it is worth mentioning that Halpern noticed that by the middle of 1974, "Sesame Street" had toned down its intensity and rapidity somewhat, and there was a simultaneous drop in the referrals of two-year-olds to his mental health clinic. This observation surely suggests that children indeed have limits of tolerance to sensory bombardment, and that, if we are to use television wisely, we must learn to know what these limits are for individual children, as well as for children in general, at different stages of their development.

The largely negative picture I have drawn need not leave us feeling helpless or trapped. Television is an extraordinary invention that can, and in many ways does, enrich our lives. It should not surprise us, however, that the special needs of children are not known to program sponsors or directors, since these special needs are not always clear in the minds of the general public. What is surprising is that a generation of children has by now grown to adulthood without ever having experienced a world without television. Yet teachers and parents have not joined forces to take a hand in shaping the content and style of children's exposure to a world that impinges insistently on them and that, in their inexperience and immaturity, they can neither fully grasp nor evaluate.

As educators, we will have to play a positive role in counteracting the negative potential of television and supporting its positive possibilities before any changes will be felt. For one thing, teachers should become familiar with all the programs their students watch and draw parents into a joint analysis of the programs' messages and implicit values.

Older children can be involved with their teachers in critical analyses of the programs' attitudes toward violence, buying, male/female relationships, minority peoples, and other aspects of content. They can also be encouraged to differentiate between fact and fiction, images and reality, opinion and evidence, prejudice and honest description. Teachers should familiarize themselves with the possible programs that can be assigned as homework or simply recommended for enjoyment, as well as those that can be the basis of class discussions.

For children younger than six, it is important to share with parents the necessity of curtailing their time before the set and encourage a return to sensory experience and learning.

Television is a resource of an unusual kind. Its value as an educational resource will not necessarily lie in the development of specifically "educational" programs. Children learn from everything around them, and television is now part of that total environment. If teachers and their allies, parents, do not sift the possibilities critically for use with children,

"Children learn from everything around them, and television is now part of that total environment."

they will be victimized by the sponsors of programs whose major concern is sales and whose interest in the growth and development of children is minimal.

Here is how one teacher expressed her feelings about the effects of television on her students:

Things are getting harder and harder in school—in my job that is. I'm really concerned about the kids. No matter what they say, I feel that TV is very destructive. They know a lot of facts but seem unable to put thoughts together and come up with anything from it all. They live in a world where everything is loud and brassy. No subtleties, no awe, and they show so little emotion. It's hard to find out how they feel about things. And sometimes I think the only thing that's funny to them is when somebody falls on his face. Everybody talks at about 100 decibels and nobody listens. God, how their motors are racing! Nobody wants to do anything extra, academically. Curiosity is very rare, with exceptions such as a second grader who said, "I want a book with pictures of big boobies." Another second grader had 12 photos of sexual intercourse in his pocket. Really sad to have to grow up so fast and miss the good things in childhood. First graders are asking for copies of "Jaws." (I haven't bought any at all and don't plan to.) Yet, they're afraid when I turn out the lights to show a film.

Our school tests above average, yet the caliber of work is to me pitiful. I used to say we had a "happy" school. This was one of the first things visitors noticed and commented on. That's not the impression one gets now. I don't think the school has changed—but the kids sure have. I'm sick to death of hearing the "experts," (usually those who taught a year or two, twenty years ago) blame us for everything. I've worked with children, as a profes-

sional and a volunteer, all my adult life. I've been very successful and loved it, but it has never been so exhausting and so unrewarding as now. Our teachers are very discouraged about giving so much and getting so little back and that has nothing to do with money.[25]

Hearing sentiments of this kind from many teachers, one is impelled, despite a personal fondness for television and despite the recognition that it is here to stay, to stress its negative impact on children as it now functions.

If the medium is to fulfill its potential for children, it is all too possible that it will do so only when all of us—teachers, parents, and anyone else in the community—who care about the health and well-being of children put pressure on those who control the airways to present the "literature" of television with some of the criteria we have learned to expect from good literature in print. Literature allows us to deepen our understanding of the human condition. Television has the responsibility to do the same.

NOTES

1. George Gerbner and Larry Gross, as reported in a news item headed, "TV Now Our Society's Cultural Mainstream, Study Concludes," *Chronicle of Higher Education*, 21 January 1974.

2. Aimee Dorr Leifer (Address to a symposium on "Institutionalized Technology and the Rights and Needs of Children," annual meeting of the American Association for the Advancement of Science, New York, 30 January 1975).

3. Gerbner and Gross, "Society's Cultural Mainstream."

4. Mary Ellen Verbeyden-Hilliard, National Coordinator of Education Task Forces of NOW, testimony before the Communications Subcommittee of the Senate Commerce Committee, 5 April 1974.

5. Gerbner and Gross, "Society's Cultural Mainstream."

6. Helen Streicher, "Girls in the Cartoons," *Journal of Communication*, Spring 1974.

7. Based on an analysis in 1973-74 of 16 popular programs and 216 commercials. In "Channeling Children: Sex Stereotyping on Prime Time TV" (Princeton, N.J.: Women on Words and Images).

8. George Gerbner et al., *Violence Profile #7: Trends in Network Television Drama and Viewer Conceptions of Social Reality, 1967-1975* (Philadelphia: Annenberg School of Communications, University of Pennsylvania, 1976).

9. *Television and Growing Up: The Impact of Televised Violence*, Report to the Surgeon General, U.S. Public Health Service, from the Surgeon General's Scientific Advisory Committee on Television and Social Behavior (Washington: U.S. Government Printing Office, 1972).

10. Leonard Eron, "Relationship of TV Viewing

Habits and Aggressive Behavior in Children," *Journal of Abnormal and Social Psychology* 67, no. 3 (1963): 193-96.

11. B. Friedlander, H. Whetstone, and C. Scott, "Suburban Preschool Children's Comprehension of an Age-Appropriate Informational Television Program," *Child Development* 45 (1974): 461-65.

12. Aimee Dorr Leifer, "Contexts for Behavior in Television Programs and Children's Subsequent Behavior" (Paper read at biennial meeting of the Society for Research in Child Development, Philadelphia, 30 March 1973).

13. *New York Times*, 14 June 1975.

14. George Gerbner, "Violence in Television Drama: Trends and Symbolic Functions," in *Television and Social Behavior*, vol. 1, *Content and Control*, ed. G. A. Comstock and E. A. Rubinstein (Washington: U.S. Government Printing Office, 1972), p. 58.

15. C. C. Clark, cited in R. M. Liebert, J. M. Neale, and E. S. Davidson, *The Early Window: Effects of Television on Children and Youth* (New York: Pergamon Press, 1973), p. 20.

16. Robert B. Choate, chairperson, Council of Children's Media and Advertising, statement before the Task Force on Food and Farm Policy, New York State Legislature, 12 February 1976.

17. William D. Wells, "Children as Consumers," in *Knowing the Consumer*, ed. Joseph W. Newman (New York: John Wiley and Sons, 1966).

18. William Melody, *Children's Television: The Economics of Exploitation* (New Haven: Yale University Press, 1973).

19. T. G. Bever et al., "Young Viewers' Troubling Responses to TV Ads," *Harvard Business Review* 53 (November-December 1975): 109-120.

20. Terry Barton, "Dual Audio Television," *Harvard Educational Review* 44 (February 1971): 64-78.

21. Werner Halpern, "Turned On Toddlers," *Journal of the Annenberg School of Communication*, Fall 1975.

22. Werner Halpern, "Are the Terrible Two's Becoming More Terrible?" *Bulletin of the Rochester Mental Health Center* 7, nos. 1 and 2 (1975): 2-8.

23. Eleanor Gibson and Harry Levin, *The Psychology of Reading* (Cambridge, Mass.: The M.I.T. Press, 1975).

24. Jerome S. Bruner, Michael A. Wallach, and Eugene Gallanter, "The Identification of Recurrent Regularity," *American Journal of Psychology* 72 (1959): pp. 200-209.

25. Communication to Eda LeShan, 16 October 1975, following a television program in which she raised questions of the possible negative aspects of television.

CHILD ABUSE AND NEGLECT IN THE AMERICAN SOCIETY

A report of a recent Center conference on family violence

JERRY ALEXANDER *(Founder, Citizens Committee for Children and Parents Under Stress, Chicago)*: Violence is as American as apple pie. It permeates all levels of our society. For millions, violence is the first response to stress. The battered wives in America can attest to that. As for children, violence is done to them because parents do not understand what to expect of their children at various ages or how to cope with behavior that they do not like. Historically we have said that the American people are committed to justice, equality, and fair play. But those words are a travesty as far as children are concerned. Let us see what happens to them.

One study indicates that fifty thousand children will die from child abuse alone in the nineteen-seventies. Three hundred thousand more will be permanently damaged. In addition, untold millions will suffer emotional abuse.

We do not value parenting in our country. We do not teach it in our schools, as most civilized countries do. As a result, parents can bring to their parenting only what they themselves have been given. Yet studies document the fact that, nine times out of ten, abuse can be stopped when there is an intervention by professionals or trained volunteers, because most abusers love their children.

The civilized world responds to abuse by intervening, by, for example, placing a trained homemaker in the family. The American response is to remove the child and place him in a foster-care home, which breaks the love relationship. The child, wandering from home to home, is eventually emotionally destroyed. Foster care — never intended to be more than a temporary shelter — has become permanent for most such children. The former president of the Illinois Foster Parents' Association has said that there are all kinds of foster homes, and that some of them should not be allowed to have foster children. Foster homes cost three to four thousand dollars a year; homemakers cost far less.

Poorly worded state laws on child neglect — which, by the way, is six times more extensive than abuse — result in the abrupt removal of additional thousands of children from their homes. In Chicago and most other areas, the parent is called in for an interview, during which our middle-class syndrome usually prevails. Horrendous home conditions are too much for judges and social workers to tolerate, and the child is taken from the family. The Northwestern Legal Assistance Clinic visited dozens of parents who had lost their children in this manner. The clinic did find horrible home conditions, but they reported that, in almost all cases, they also found love and concern for the child. A typical crying, hysterical response from parents was, "They stole my baby." Leaders of the American Indian community tell us categorically that forty per cent of Indian families will, within the first year after arriving in Chicago, lose their children in this manner.

After the precipitous removal of a child, the problem is compounded when, as often happens, judges, inexperienced in children's problems, return the child to the abusing parents, despite the fact that no remedial intervention of any kind has occurred. This is because parental rights predominate. In effect, parents "own" their children. Under those circumstances, the child's needs for a safe, secure, and loving environment are seldom considered.

What are the consequences of this? A leading investigative psychologist has found a high degree of correlation between juvenile delinquency and the delinquents' having experienced brutal beatings from their parents in the first ten years of their lives. Out of the great pool of our neglected and battered children come significant numbers who will be involved in violent crime.

Many of the children from these violent backgrounds, when they enter their teens, run away from home. When runaways are lumped with chronic truants — those whose parents can no longer control them — they are called status offenders. Two thousand such children are being jailed every day in the United States, even though they have committed no crime for which any adult could be incarcerated. What happens to these children almost defies description. But it is well-documented. After these teenagers get out of jail, how do they sustain themselves on the street? The answer, far too often, is by prostitution, selling drugs, and other crimes.

The schools are of little help. Thousands of unruly and hard-to-handle children are suspended. There are few really caring, dedicated teachers. Also, the truancy rate is not to be believed. A recent Parent-Teacher Association study in Chicago discovered that up to one-third of the children of 186 schools in the poor section are truant every day. Often the truant officers are political appointees, so little help can be expected there.

Some of these truant children are kept home to baby-sit for younger children. That reveals another scandal. Nationwide there are twenty-seven million children under the age of eighteen whose mothers are working. Six million of these children are less than five years old. Yet there are day-care facilities for less than one million of these children in the United States. Other countries do a far better job with day care than we do.

In America, we have "lock-and-key" babies and "latch-key" children. The lock-and-key baby is exemplified by the four-year-old boy, who, when discovered alone in a Chicago apartment, awaiting his mother's return from work, said, "I baby-sit my own self." Usually the mothers of such children are too proud to accept charity, but have no resources for sitters. In the Chicago area, the Department of Children and Family Services places 130 to 140 such youngsters each month in emergency foster homes. In addition, the department receives two to three hundred reports of children left alone while the mother is out for a variety of reasons.

All teachers know about the latch-key children. These are the ones who come to school with the house key dangling from a string around their neck. They leave school at the end of the day to return to an empty home and wait for their parents' return. There are millions of latch-key children.

Compounding all this is the fact that ten per cent of all teenage girls will get pregnant this year and that six per cent will give birth. One of the editors of the Chicago *Tribune* says that teenage girls seldom make good mothers. They aren't ready — physically, emotionally, educationally, or socially — for the adult responsibilities of motherhood. Most need mothering themselves. More than half of these mothers will be on welfare within two years. Still, there are no significant courses in parenting now being taught in our schools.

The recent Supreme Court ruling on abortions does not provide for the long-term consequences of its own actions. We will be deluged with additional thousands of unwanted children, children who will be shortchanged on tender loving care and programmed for failure.

These devastating conditions in America exist because there is no real advocacy for children. Kids do not vote. The New York State Legislature, after a two-year study, summed it up beautifully: "There is an urgent need for a group or an agency that can speak for or advocate the needs of children, and work toward the coordination and strengthening of child welfare programs. There is no one, and no one agency in government, to speak solely for the needs of children. From the highest to the lowest levels of government, no one speaks on behalf of the over-all needs of the child. The thousands of children who rely upon the child welfare complex for care, treatment, and protection are unrepresented in government planning circles. The planning and policy-making phases of child welfare are as fragmented and uncoordinated as are all its other phases. The state and local departments of social services — the primary source of child-protection services —are preoccupied with the problems of welfare administration and family assistance planning. The few interested staff are overwhelmed by the other responsibilities of these departments."

Then the New York statement gets more radical: "A bureaucracy is rarely self-corrective. By its ponderous nature and slow feedback mechanisms, it cannot locate, much less correct, dysfunctional elements within its own system. It must depend upon, and usually responds to, the planned pressures of stimuli outside its own hierarchy. The rate of change within a bureaucracy can be measured by the source and intensity of pressure, multiplied by the time over which the pressure is exerted. For example, a concerted citizens' group applying vigorous pressure for specific reform over an extended period of time, may obtain some concession to current operative or conceptual procedures."

A few examples may demonstrate this gross lack of advocacy. In Illinois, despite the increase of reported abuses — from 1,200 to six thousand in recent years — the budget for the Department of Children and Family Services has remained virtually unchanged. Yet the governor finds millions of new dollars to build additional prisons.

Again, when the Chicago City Council was debating ordinances to prevent teenage runaways from selling themselves for sex, Chicago-area legislators in Springfield were helping to defeat a bill which would have removed the legal repercussions when social service providers counsel the teenagers against becoming runaways and looking to these sexual "answers" for their financial problems.

A bill making it mandatory for doctors and hospitals to report venereally diseased children — another untouched scandal — did not even come out of the committee in the Illinois Legislature this year. Two years ago, when the then Senator Walter Mondale's bill to increase day-care facilities was proposed, it never came out of committee. Why? It was because suddenly eight thousand mimeographed, unsigned letters hit Washington every day, calling Mondale's bill a "Commie plot for the feds to steal your children."

Senator Birch Bayh's bill to prevent juvenile delinquency went grossly underfunded. Former Senator John Pastore has said that there was seemingly little public demand for funding Senator Bayh's bill.

There is literally no one to advocate for America's children. If we think of the American home as a factory and the children as its product, look what we do to them. One out of every ten children will end up spending time in a mental hospital. One out of fifteen will be an alcoholic. One out of nine will be in trouble with the law before the age of eighteen. We are in the midst of a national tragedy and disgrace.

SYLVIA COTTON (*President, Day-Care Crisis Council, Chicago*): I take issue with one statement. Lots of groups are advocating for the children. The problem, and the tragedy, is that those who call themselves advocates are so fragmented. We haven't been nearly as effective as the opponents of child-care and day-care programs, for example.

It is tragic when the Secretary of Health, Education and Welfare is instructed by the Carter Administration to reform the welfare system, and yet is told he can't spend a single additional dollar. There is no way you can reform the welfare system and not spend a lot more money, particularly for those people in the society who are so desperately in need— notably the children.

WILLIAM CORTELYOU (*Dean of the Graduate School, DePaul University*): One of the best forms of advocacy in governmental circles is when you can make a case for cost effectiveness. I think you are suggesting that more money spent on child care might result, as a matter of fact, in huge savings.

ALEXANDER: Exactly. It costs twelve thousand dollars to keep one of these teenage children in a jail or detention center for one year. Half-way houses cost half that amount. Homemaker service is far cheaper than foster care, and so on. It is cheaper to do it right than it is to do it wrong.

CORTELYOU: Before this day is over, I will be at another meeting. An enormous number of teachers will be coming into Chicago to discuss a bill on "teacher centers." They want to keep their jobs which are now threatened as the birthrate keeps going down. We think of teachers as people who only work in schools and teach children from the age of about five or six on. We don't have much in the way of preschool work for teachers. Instead of teachers trying to reduce the sizes of their classes in order to keep their jobs, they might be smarter if they advocated something along the lines you are discussing here — day care, child care, and the like.

RICHARD MANDEL (*Chicago attorney*): State legislators do not care at all about long-term costs. They don't care that prisons cost a lot more over a long period of time than decent child-care facilities and services. They are not going to be in office ten years from now. They want to cut the dollars now, before the next election, so they can say, "We've balanced the budget," or "We've cut money from the budget today."

CLEO ANDERSON (*Inter-Agency Liaison, Department of Children and Family Services, State of Illinois*): In 1966, the Department of Children and Family Services had 483 referrals for child abuse. In 1976, it had 6,748 referrals. This year, we expect more than eight thousand referrals on abuse and protective services. In the first nine months of this fiscal year, about two thousand cases of child beating were referred to the department. There were 2,400 cases in which there was serious neglect of the child by the parent. In the first nine months of the fiscal year 1976, there were 432 cases of sexual abuse.

JEAN E. BEDGER (*Director of Research, Council for Community Services, Chicago*): A recent study showed that abusive families need very intensive, in-depth, long-term treatment. But most of the agencies seem to be going away from treatment. We find that mothers themselves need lots of care. We find that fathers are primarily the abusers. We find that children are abused not just once or twice, but over and over again. The mothers are more interested in their involvement with the male in the family than in the protection of the child. So this is not a simple problem. And yet, many people think you can train competent service workers just by giving them a few in-service training sessions. It is difficult for professionals to master all the different ramifications in abusive and neglectful families. We find, incidentally, that there is not much difference between abuse and neglect. Children who are abused are also neglected, and vice versa. We also find that abusive and neglectful parents were neglected and abused when they were children.

GRACE HOLT (*Professor of Speech and Director of Black Studies, University of Illinois, Chicago Circle*): We are dealing here with a crucial, deep-seated, core problem. It concerns the kind of people we want in our society and the kinds of families that can produce those people. When we talk about fifty thousand children killed and another three hundred thousand injured, that raises a fundamental question about what kind of an ideal we have in our heads in this society as to what a family should be and what parental roles should be.

We hear children referred to as "property," and the phrase "control of the child." Such concepts are the fundamental notions of family as it was in the early days of our society. Now we have a different phenomenon. We have changed in what and how we think about the family. But I am not certain that we are aware of that fact. If we continue to use the term "control of the child," what do we mean by that? Does that have any bearing on the fact that a kid gets beaten and abused? What do we mean by children as "property"?

RUTH BORN (*Program Specialist, Children's Bureau, U.S. Department of Health, Education and Welfare, Chicago*): Does our society want good things for its children? If it doesn't, what are the consequences of that?

Somebody needs to say, straight out, what we all avoid saying: it is that the statistics on abuse and neglect mean that nobody cares. We must come at this problem from a great variety of directions, including education; and we must have some definition, and redefinition, of parenting.

The problems in Illinois are only a microcosm of what is found on the federal level. Providing services to children has to come from national leadership, national policy, national espousement of the family as a viable institution. This is the "year of the family," according to the Carter Administration. But where is the money to provide the professional services families require? In our twenty-five-state survey, we found one state that allows a seventh-grade education as an entry level for a so-called "child welfare specialist." This is the person who is supposed to have the great skills needed in order to work with these disorganized and dysfunctioning families.

We need money to get children out of placement, once they are there, so that we can begin putting some of the families back together again.

RON STUYVESANT (*Coordinator, Child Abuse Training Project, Day-Care Crisis Council, Chicago*): One must deal with this complex problem in terms of identification and diagnosis, treatment, and education. We could spend a day talking on each one of these. The need is for coordination of all three actions.

Over the last few years, there has been increased reporting of the cases of child abuse and neglect. But there has been no corresponding increase in the amount of services provided.

SHELDON SCHIFF (*President, Children's Center for Learning Capacities, Chicago*): A caveat with respect to the efficacy of legislation: in the early nineteen-sixties, we got federal mental health legislation. Great amounts of money were appropriated for mental health, but the children received very little of that in terms of mental health facilities. Something seems to go wrong when we direct our attention to providing care. The nineteen-sixties' law urged us to direct our attention to primary prevention — that is, to identify people at risk before they actually become ill — and to do something about that. But again, the monies were frittered away in the direction of secondary prevention (early identification) and tertiary prevention (treatment of already recognized ills), because those are more popular and more visible.

How do we go about "inoculating" parents and families and children at risk on this kind of a problem? Is this as difficult a problem as someone suggested earlier? My experience indicates it isn't. This is not to deny the complexity of the problems that families face. But their struggles for mastery and coping and potency are struggles that can be helped at other levels. The struggles that adults have in understanding their children — their children's candor, creativity, curiosity, "hyperactivity," great energies — are problems that adults are going to have to cope with in all these programs. I am not sure where adults — including professionals — are learning how to do this. I am afraid that professionals are burdened in their professional training by such things as psychogenetic determinism, and they tend to look at a child and predict what his future will be in the light of the great complexities he will face, rather than seeing the tremendous optimism and capacities that children have.

SHEILA C. RIBORDY (*Assistant Professor of Psychology, DePaul University*): As someone who has been involved in a treatment program — and I think a successful one — with child-abuse parents and children, I must say we are doing good things, but we are not getting anywhere. We may help twenty people during a year. We need to look at this problem on the societal level.

Child abuse occurs when a society condones unlimited parental power over children. It occurs when we do not support the one-parent family. It occurs when we do not legislate money and support for day-care centers. It occurs when we allow violence in the media. I have been down the road of treatment — and I will continue to go down that road — but that is not the answer.

BERNARD SCHWARTZ (*Teacher, Marie Curie High School, Chicago*): Child abuse and family problems stem from our culture. Ours is a nuclear kind of culture, one in which the family breaks down. Instead of the extended family as found in the Japanese and Chinese cultures, in which everyone lives in a home and concentrates on the family and the importance of the family, we Americans break up the family. We stress individual attainment. Other societies stress what the family achieves.

In Japan the jails are not overcrowded. Very little is spent on jails in Japan. Why? Because in Japan it is the family's responsibility to take care of its individual members. A family is disgraced if any member has done something to harm someone else. Perhaps it is our American way of looking at life that is at fault. Margaret Mead has said that we have to restructure the family, and that to do that we must restructure our society.

ANDERSON: The current system — and I could say society rather than system — contributes to child abuse and neglect. For one thing, you cannot get into the system unless you are a casualty. I recall a fifteen-year-old girl who was asking for mental health service. She was all tied up. She said, "I need help." The only way she could get help was to take an overdose of drugs. Immediately people were there trying to help with her problem.

BORN: I am not so sure that the solution lies in reinstituting a family structure as we have known it in the past. Things are changing, and we need to take a look at the implications of that for what we now call families or what we perceive as families. We need to provide — literally — education in family planning. The educational system has to be involved. The helping professions have to be involved. Agencies as well as individuals need to begin to tell it like it is. We are all kidding ourselves in this society when we say we are a child-centered society.

ALEXANDER: Recent figures indicate that the number of runaway wives is now almost greater than the number of runaway husbands. That suggests to me that we no longer value parenting in this country. Women who are nonprofessionals still say apologetically, "I'm only a mother," or, "I'm just a housewife." We thus demean the toughest job a woman will have. And the women are leaving it.

What does it take to get all the groups that have expressed concern for children to work together on the kind of legislation and services that are needed? I am a member of the Sierra Club, a conservation group. We have a pyramid setup. The last time people tried to build a dam in the Grand Canyon, eighty-seven thousand telegrams were sent to Washington within four days. The dam did not get built. What does it take to get this kind of militancy, not for a dam, but for children? Can groups and organizations concerned about children work together?

CAROL ZIENTEK (*Probation Office/Educational Advocacy, Juvenile Court of Cook County, Illinois*): The children I have worked with who have been successful have been able to come up with a purpose in their lives. When a child or an adult lacks a purpose, then you have problems. The youngsters we see at Juvenile Court or in any of the other social agencies are drifting. They are bored and restless. They are looking for something they can hold onto, identify with, something that will be important to them, something they will be able to work toward which will bring them self-esteem. Many people disagree with the philosophy of the Moonies, but what have they given young people but a purpose in life? Our traditional religions seem to have drifted away from that. Children are growing into adults with no purpose.

RALPH TYLER (*Vice-President, Center for the Study of Democratic Institutions*): Perhaps the problem is not our values, but rearranging the hierarchy of our values in a time when there are so many conflicting pressures. Historically the effort to achieve freedom for the individual in American society goes back two hundred years. Bit by bit, the effort has been to free the individual from the domination of a social group, or the government, or the family. But every person also needs social support and social encouragement.

It is not quite as simple as saying that the American people are violent, or that the American people don't care about children. I think the American people are confused in a society that is changing. Somehow we must come to terms with the society that is being created and preserve important values in that society.

SALLY BRUCKNER (*Acting Executive Director, Citizens Committee for Children and Parents Under Stress, Chicago*): Four hundred parents call our Parental Stress Hot Line each month and receive help from unpaid volunteers who have been trained by professionals. Help comes from parent to parent, from friend to friend, at the grass-roots level. It bypasses some of the bureaucratic problems. So many of these people are isolated. Putting them into a Parents Anonymous group immediately breaks that isolation. It begins to build the societal ties that have been disappearing.

COTTON: We all can agree, regardless of our perspective, that the family is the basic unit of our society, of almost any society. That is an acceptable cliché, whether it comes all the way from the Right or all the way from the Left, and whether it refers to a single-parent family or to a local commune. We need to address ourselves to the question of how we can develop a national family-support system to help strengthen the family. We can deal philosophically with the child-abuse problem, but we also need to deal with the concrete things that we, as representatives of different groups, can do independently, and to the variety of things that we can do together.

Part of the tragedy with which we are wrestling is the fact that there are some means available for us to do a much better job than we have yet succeeded in doing. We haven't used the funds that are available to us. In Illinois we have used only seventy per cent of the Title 20 funds available to us. There is money available for preventive services, but we haven't developed an adequate mechanism. There is money available for the school system to institute parenting courses in every high school. Why haven't we done that? There is money available to set up a day-care center in every single high school so that kids who become pregnant can learn how to be parents if they intend to keep their children. We have let the right wing browbeat us to death on sex education.

Part of the reason why we lost the Comprehensive Child Care Bill — and why we are losing the battle in Washington in terms of adequate funding for some of these programs — is because all of us tend to echo the saying, "Government shouldn't be doing it." Well, unless government gives us the means to do it, private agencies will not be able to survive. Many private agencies are surviving today only because there is some government funding available. We have to reject absolutely the fact that our government — which, in essence, is our society, which speaks for all of us, and to which we all contribute — has no responsibility for these programs and services. We need to demand more of our government. I want the government to spend more on human services and less on the B-1 bomber.

Unless we talk to that issue, we will let the right wing take over. Recently I attended a meeting in Normal, Illinois, in connection with the International Women's Year Conference. The right wing's venom and hostility to what it calls "government-operated child care" was appalling. There is no "government-operated" child care. There is government-funded child care, and that is very appropriate. There are also government standards, which are appropriate; that is why we have licensing, why we need licensing, why we need government standards — in this case to protect children.

Look at the number of children who have not been immunized, the number of birth defects, the number of handicapped children not being treated, the out-of-school population. I'd like the public schools to keep their doors open until six p.m. every day, and use those teachers who are losing their jobs, use them to staff an after-school program in every community. Only one per cent of the school-age children of this nation have a decently supervised after-school program. Millions of children are out on the streets. Those are the kids who are breaking the windows and becoming, in their turn, the neglectful and abusive parents.

RIBORDY: All of us are saying we have such a difficult time dealing with the legislature and getting our particular programs funded. I am wondering if there isn't something about the legislature itself that is the problem. Is there something about lawyers? Is there something about men?

ANDERSON: This country was built on violence. We ran the Indians all the way across the country and into the Pacific Ocean. We dealt with our community problems by taking people off the streets and putting them into almshouses. We continued to do that until it became too costly. Then we began to look for alternatives. We weren't concerned about what was best for the kids. We were concerned about the dollars being spent.

When I look at the people who are trying to deal with this problem, I wonder why they are there. I am beginning to think that more and more of them are there because of the dollars they can get. I am talking about all levels of government. Does society really want a well-coordinated, integrated program? What that will mean is less dollars for certain people

in the community. For one thing, it will mean less dollars for the health profession because all kinds of free health services will be provided. Yet, the State of Illinois is in the lowest quarter when it comes to infant mortality. Three-quarters of the states provide more for health services than Illinois does, and Illinois is supposed to rank in the upper third of the states as far as wealth is concerned.

MANDEL: Ralph Tyler has said that this is a country built on individual accomplishments. And Mr. Anderson has said we are a country built on violence. The American family certainly believes in corporal punishment, which, to me, is as obscene as pornography. But the Supreme Court has upheld corporal punishment in the schools as something we believe in. The parents believe they have that right over the child, and that people who take the place of the family — that is, the teachers — should have the same right.

HOLT: Ms. Cotton raised the primary question: How do we develop a national family-support system? We might begin by asking, what already exists in various kinds of communities in our society for coping with abused children? The frustrations of parenting and coping with children are not new. Outside pressures have changed, but I am certain that as long as you have had parents you have had parents who would become upset, at times, who couldn't deal with crying children, who might be tempted to hit the kids and tell them to shut up.

Have there been any self-help systems, or subsystems, developed by various community groups, to help parents with these sorts of questions? Probably there are. Let me give you an example. Traditionally in black urban communities, when a teenaged girl got pregnant, the grandmother would take the baby and raise it. Another option was to send the baby down South. That practice is still rather prevalent. If you couldn't cope, you could send the baby to a relative in the South and say, "Keep the child for me until things get better."

Also, a black child understood that if a parent became too abusive, he or she could go to certain neighbors. The child could just show up and say, "I want to stay with you for a little while." I can remember in my own community, Inglewood, seeing those kids sitting on neighbors' doorsteps in the late afternoon. I suspect that other ethnic groups have something similar to those kinds of arrangements. All of this needs to be examined if we are to develop some sort of national family support system in our society.

ALEXANDER: A privately published newsletter has just been started, called the *Child Protection Report*. It is the only way I have to keep informed about what is going on in community efforts around the country. It tells you what is working, what is effective. I'll give one example.

Rochester, New York, has a large black population and a lot of unwanted children. It has made a beautiful start by somehow getting the board of education and the welfare department together and taking black mothers who are on Aid to Dependent Children and getting them paid, instead of by the welfare department, by the board of education. Two, three, and four of these mothers are put into the pre-kindergarten, kindergarten, first and second grades. And their marvelous mothering, loving, and caring has made a dramatic difference to those children. The original group of children is now in the sixth or seventh grade, and no one can tell which children are the disadvantaged and which are not.

NEEDED: MORE STATE LEADERSHIP IN PRESCHOOL EDUCATION

KEVIN J. SWICK

ASSOCIATE PROFESSOR
COLLEGE OF EDUCATION
UNIVERSITY OF SOUTH CAROLINA

PRESCHOOL education in some form is here to stay. Nationwide, nursery school enrollment has tripled during the past 10 years, rising to the current level of 1.6 million.[1] The number of working mothers has grown tenfold.[2]

Any discussion of such developments, of course, requires some definitions because of the lack of agreement nationally regarding the meaning of "day care" and "nursery school." As the terms are used in this article, a nursery school is a school or center for children up to the age of two. A day-care center is a school or center for children between the ages of two and five. These definitions are in accord with those used by federal and state agencies.

In the United States, day-care services have expanded but not at a rate commensurate with the increasing needs of children and families in our society.[3] For example, the South Carolina Department of Social Services reported this year that of the 170,703 children in South Carolina who have working mothers, or who are receiving "aid to dependent children," only 33,764 are receiving any type of day care.[4] Nationwide, there are day-care facilities to care for only between 3 and 15 per cent of the children needing such services.[5]

A National Survey

Because state departments of education have a major responsibility in providing leadership in attaining quality education at all levels of schooling, the chief state school officer (state superintendent of education) of each state was requested to participate in a survey conducted by the writer in the spring of 1976. The officer or a qualified staff member was asked to complete an extensive questionnaire regarding preschool education. The questionnaire was designed to ascertain what state departments of education are doing to provide leadership in their states to obtain quality educational programs for preschool infants and young children. Forty of the 50 state departments of education participated.

A significant component of any leadership system is the organizational design used to attain the desired goals. The survey revealed a discouraging situation insofar as the organizational thrust of state departments of education is concerned. Only 14 of the 40 states reported that they had specific offices or divisions devoted solely to preschool education. Slightly more encouraging was the fact that 25 of the 40 states responding reported that they had some kind of statement clarifying their leadership role and position with regard to the development of preschool programs. Seventeen of the 25 reported also that they distributed their position statements to all public schools and all public and private preschools in their respective states.

Twenty-three of the 25 states that had developed a philosophy of preschool education indicated also that they had either specific state office guidelines or mandated legislative requirements with respect to how preschool programs are to be operated. Although the fact that 25 states do have a basic underlying philosophy of preschool education is encouraging, the discovery that at least 15 states do not have any guidelines or statements is disconcerting. Some persons, of course, might argue that in many states the social services departments handle preschool activities. Of the 40 states responding in this survey, however, only one reported such an arrangement. In that case, the state department of education had the social services department complete and return the questionnaire.

A major criticism of nursery schools and day-care centers has been that they lack curricula and are not given any assistance in continuously improving their programs. The findings of this survey would support such criticisms. Only 24 state departments of education reported having preschool curriculum specialists working with preschool educators to improve their programs. Furthermore, only 8 of the 24 departments that had such specialists indicated that they worked regularly with preschool educators at the local level.

Only 13 state departments of education reported that they conduct some type of nursery-school and day-care program evaluation. Even among them, wide variations exist with respect to how, when, and where such evaluations are conducted.

Twenty-six state departments of education reported that they have developed curriculum guides for preschool educators to use in designing and improving their programs. Only one state, however, reported that it has developed a model preschool program design for preschool personnel to use or adapt to local needs.

The teacher is the key to the quality of any educational endeavor. Nevertheless, the state departments of education participating in the survey did not report any really important consideration of the qualifications of teachers. In fact, only eight states said that they have minimum certification standards for teachers of preschool infants and children; and three of the eight admitted frankly that they are unable to implement the standards because of the critical need for day-care and nursery-school personnel. One chief state school officer said: "I would have to close 90 per cent of the day care centers in this state if I were ordered to implement our standards of teacher certification."

State funding of preschool education appears to be very limited. Although 11 states participating in the survey do allocate some state monies for such programs at the local level, a majority of the states indicated that they rely upon federal dollars channeled through some state governmental agency to the local level as the means of meeting the educational needs of preschool children. Only 14 state departments of education reported that they were conducting studies to determine the need for preschool education but, surprisingly, 32 departments said that they were working with state universities to develop adequate training programs for the education of future teachers of preschool infants and young children.

A Need for Leadership

As of 1976, what is the status of the leadership provided in preschool education by state departments of education? At best, it is static, confused, and in many states lacking in substance. Although Maya Pines said in 1966 that the problems of such education could not be hidden forever,[6] ten years later no more than 15 per cent of the nation's preschoolers needing child care are receiving it. Furthermore, there is great uncertainty as to the quality of the care that even this relatively small number is receiving.

The need for preschool education programs of sound quality continues to grow while too many educators and community leaders seem indifferent in their efforts to meet the needs of young children. For example, state departments of education should be major sources of leadership but, in the area of preschool education, most of them are following the federal dollar or responding only periodically to local demands for some assistance in developing preschool programs. For that reason, educators and other concerned citizens must assume roles of leadership in urging state leaders to develop viable bases for developing preschool learning centers.

1. "Preschoolers: Pawns in the Latest Education Battle," *U.S. News and World Report*, 52 (June 14, 1976) : 41-42.

2. John W. Hollomon, "Discontinuous Mothering—Expanding the Alternatives," *Understanding and Nurturing Infant Development*, Joe Frost, ed. (Washington: Association for Childhood Education International, 1976), p. 37.

3. Maya Pines, *Revolution in Learning: The Years from Birth to Six* (New York: Harper and Row, Publishers, 1966), p. 186.

4. Memorandum from Office of Child Development, Department of Social Services, Columbia, South Carolina, January 12, 1976.

5. Hollomon, "Discontinuous Mothering — Expanding the Alternatives," p. 37.

6. Pines, *Revolution in Learning: The Years from Birth to Six*, p. 187.

7. Shirley de Leon, "The Verdict on Nursery Schools," *Parents Magazine* 22 (May, 1975) : 34-35.

INDEX

STAFF

Publisher	John Quirk
Director of Design	Donald Burns
Typesetting	Carol Carr
Cover Design	Donald Burns